THE LANGUAGES OF THE SOVIET UNION

CAMBRIDGE LANGUAGE SURVEYS

General Editors, W. Sidney Allen, B. Comrie, C. J. Fillmore,
E. J. A. Henderson, F. W. Householder, R. Lass, J. Lyons,
R. B. Le Page, P. H. Matthews, F. R. Palmer, R. Posner,
J. L. M. Trim

This new series will offer general accounts of all the major language
families of the world. Some volumes will be organised on a purely genetic
basis, others on a geographical basis, whichever yields the most convenient
and intelligible grouping in each case. Sometimes, as with the Australian
volume, the two in any case coincide.

Each volume will compare and contrast the typological features of the
languages it deals with. It will also treat the relevant genetic relationships,
historical development, and sociolinguistic issues arising from their role and
use in the world today. The intended readership is the student of linguistics
or general linguist, but no special knowledge of the languages under
consideration is assumed. Some volumes will also have a wider appeal, like
those on Australia and North America, where the future of the languages
and their speakers raises important social and political issues.

Already published:
The languages of Australia *R. M. W. Dixon*

Forthcoming titles include:
Japanese/Korean *M. Shibatani and Ho-min Sohn*
Chinese *J. Norman and Mei Tsu-lin*
S. E. Asia *J. A. Matisoff*
Dravidian *R. E. Asher*
Austronesian *R. Blust*
Afro-Asiatic *R. Hetzron*
North American Indian *W. Chafe*
Mesoamerican Indian *J. A. Suarez*
Slavonic *R. Sussex*
Germanic *R. Lass*
Celtic *D. MacAulay et al.*
Indo-Aryan *C. P. Masica*
Balkans *J. Ellis*
Creole languages *I. F. Hancock*
Romance languages *R. Posner*

THE LANGUAGES
OF THE SOVIET UNION

BERNARD COMRIE

Associate Professor of Linguistics
University of Southern California

CAMBRIDGE UNIVERSITY PRESS

Cambridge

London   New York   New Rochelle   Melbourne   Sydney

Published by the Press Syndicate of the University of Cambridge
The Pitt Building, Trumpington Street, Cambridge CB2 1RP
32 East 57th Street, New York, NY 10022, USA
296 Beaconsfield Parade, Middle Park, Melbourne 3206, Australia

First published 1981

Printed in Great Britain at the University Press, Cambridge

British Library Cataloguing in Publication Data
Comrie, Bernard
The languages of the
Soviet Union.
1. Russia – Languages
I. Title II. Hewitt, B. G. III. Payne, John R.
409_.47   P381.R8   80-49861

ISBN 0 521 23230 9 hard covers
ISBN 0 521 29877 6 paperback

CONTENTS

TABLES

PREFACE

This book has two main aims: first, to introduce the reader to some of the salient linguistic features of the various languages and languages-families of the U.S.S.R.; secondly, to give some indication of how the various languages of the U.S.S.R. interact in a multilingual society, especially of how they interact with Russian. Chapter I and the early parts of subsequent chapters and sections deal primarily with sociolinguistic background, while the body of the book deals with structural features.

In the sociolinguistic discussion I have taken for granted the existence of the U.S.S.R. as a multinational and multilingual entity, and have discussed the language policies that have been adopted in the light of this situation, including actual or implied comparisons (on the whole, favourable) with policies of the Tsarist government and policies adopted in other multilingual countries. A different, though, in the current political situation, unrealistic perspective, would have been gained by comparing how the languages in question might have fared if their speakers had formed independent nation-states outside the U.S.S.R.

The selection of linguistic (phonological, morphological, and syntactic) topics has necessarily been very restricted by the nature of the volume. Rather than attempt to give a superficial survey of every aspect of language structure, I have preferred to concentrate on those aspects of individual languages and language-families that strike me as particularly interesting and important from a general linguistic viewpoint. For this reason considerable space is, for instance, devoted to phonetics in Chapter 5 (Caucasian languages), to vowel harmony in Chapter 2 (Altaic languages), and to case-marking and negation in Chapter 3 (Uralic languages).

Likewise, the list of references has been considerably more restricted than would have been the case in a strict introduction to the comparative philology of one or other of the language families discussed. In general, no reference has been given for statements about individual languages or language-families that are uncontroversial; likewise, straightforward illustrative examples have often been taken or adapted from standard handbooks listed in the references without explicit statement of the source. Apart from references cited in the text, other references (i.e. in the Further reading sections at the end of each chapter) are designed, primarily, to direct the reader to one or more comprehensive grammars of each of the languages concerned, preference being given to those written in more accessible languages. In addition, references have been given to general works dealing with languages and language policies in the U.S.S.R., and to handbooks dealing with the language families covered. But the list of references is explicitly not claimed to be comprehensive, in particular in not including lexicographical materials or monograph studies on specific aspects of individual languages.

At the end of each chapter there is a sample of texts in the languages discussed, to give a more global, functioning picture of these languages. The texts have been selected solely for their illustrative value, from a range of styles (traditional stories, Soviet fiction, scientific writing), and the views expressed as the content of these texts are not necessarily my own.

Substantial portions of the text were written by two of my colleagues: J. R. Payne (University of Birmingham) wrote section 4.3.2 (Iranian languages) and also prepared the Tadzhik text; B. G. Hewitt (St John's College, Cambridge) wrote Chapter 5 (Caucasian languages) and collaborated with me in the writing of section 4.4 (Armenian). All other chapters and sections were written by me, and I also took overall responsibility for editing the whole volume. The glossing and translation of texts, and the translation of citations from foreign languages, were done by the author of the respective section/chapter.

Examples from languages of the U.S.S.R. are presented in accordance with the transcription system discussed on pp. xvi–xvii. Where relevant, hyphens are used in examples to indicate morpheme boundaries, though not all morpheme boundaries are so indicated (e.g. where they are not relevant to the point at issue). A morpheme-by-morpheme gloss is provided into English (with glosses of bound morphemes, in block capitals, abbreviated according to the list on p. xv); where necessary, this is accompanied by a freer translation.

The transliteration into Latin script of names of people, places, and languages in the U.S.S.R. presents immense problems, and no one system devised has met with universal acceptance. In the present work the following practices have been adopted. Russian family names have been transliterated according to the International system (see p. 286), family names of other peoples of the U.S.S.R. according to the transliteration of the Russian form of their name; where this differs from the form actually given on the title page of a book or article, the actual form, or a transliteration thereof, is appended in square brackets. Where the only reference by an author uses the Latin script, then this spelling is retained. Russian book and article titles and common nouns are also cited in the International system.

Place-names in the U.S.S.R. have been given in the form used by the *Times atlas of the world*, though with the alternatives Moskva/Moscow I have preferred the latter. For names of administrative units, however, where this atlas simply transliterates the Russian name, I have preferred to translate, e.g. South-Ossete Autonomous Oblast rather than Yugo-Osetinskaya Avtonomnaya Oblast; Appendix 2 includes the appropriate name in the form found in the *Times atlas of the world* where this departs radically from the form used here.

For language (and ethnic) names, accepted English terms have been used for those few languages of the U.S.S.R. whose names are in frequent currency among English-speaking linguists, such as Georgian (Russian: *gruzinskij*), Lapp (Russian: *saamskij*). For all others, I have used the standard Soviet Russian name, shorn of Russian-specific suffixes, in the usual nontechnical transliteration (i.e. as used in the *Times atlas of the world*). In addition to removing Russian suffixes, I have tried not to add English-specific suffixes, to make the stem of the language name quite transparent, i.e. Vot (rather than Votic); wherever possible, even the plural suffix has been omitted. This policy has been dictated by the orientation of the book as a volume on the languages of the U.S.S.R. rather than as an introduction to the philologies of individual language-families. No-one will be happy with all the forms we have chosen, which often do not correspond to those used by non-Soviet specialists (most noticeably for Uralic languages), or fail to make phonetic distinctions that specialists prefer to maintain in language names (as with many Caucasian languages). As small consolation to anyone offended by any of the spellings adopted, I have had to sacrifice my own favourite spelling of Chukchee for Chukchi. The language index gives the Russian form (transliterated) for each of the languages of the U.S.S.R. in parentheses after the English form adopted in this work.

In citations from other authors, differences concerned solely with transliteration have been removed in favour of the principles above. In the list of references, original spellings are, of course, retained.

In preparing this volume, the latest detailed statistical materials available to me were from the census of 1970. These statistics are already somewhat dated, in that a further census was carried out in 1979, but as the detailed breakdown of the returns of this census are unlikely to be available for some years, I have continued to use the present tense to refer to the situation as mirrored in the 1970 returns.

My interest in writing this book arose largely from a project on the linguistic typology of the non-Slavonic languages of the U.S.S.R., supported during 1975–8 by the Social Science Research Council, London: B. G. Hewitt and J. R. Payne also participated in this project. Although the present volume is not directly part of that project, the material we worked on during that period has been of immense help in preparing this volume. The administrative and scientific staff of various institutes in the U.S.S.R. have helped us in gathering and analysing material on the languages of the U.S.S.R., and we would like to express our thanks to members of the following institutes: Academy of Sciences of the U.S.S.R. (Linguistics Institute, Leningrad Section of the Institute of Linguistics, Leningrad Section of the Oriental Institute), Tbilisi State University, Sukhumi University and Research Institute, Academy of Sciences of the Georgian S.S.R. (Linguistics Institute), Academy of Sciences of the Tadzhik S.S.R. (Language and Literature Institute). Our participation in exchange programmes with these institutes has been facilitated by the cooperation of the British Academy, the British Council, and the University of Birmingham (Centre for Russian and East European Studies). I am also grateful to R. Austerlitz and R. Hetzron for comments on the manuscript.

The editing of the final manuscript was carried out while I was a Visiting Fellow in the Department of Linguistics, Faculty of Arts, the Australian National University.

Bernard Comrie
September 1979

ABBREVIATIONS

ABESS Abessive ('without X')
ABL Ablative ('from X')
ABS Absolute, Absolutive
ACC Accusative
ACT Active
ADJ Adjective
ADV Adverb(ial)
AFF Affective
AFFIRM Affirmative
ALIEN Alienable possession
ALL Allative ('to(wards) X')
AOR Aorist
AUG Augmentative
CAUS Causative
COL Column
COMIT Comitative ('(together) with X')
COMPAR Comparative
COND Conditional
CONT Continuous
COP Copula
DAT Dative
DEF Definite
DIM Diminutive
DO Direct Object
DU Dual
DYN Dynamic (Nonstative)
ELAT Elative ('out of X')
EMPH Emphatic
ERG Ergative
ESS Essive ('as X')
EXCL Exclusive
FEM Female, Feminine
FIN Finite
FOC Focus

FREQ Frequentative
FUT Future
GEN Genitive
GER Gerund (Verbal adverb)
HABIT Habitual
HUM Human
ILL Illative ('into X')
IMPER Imperative
IMPERF Imperfect
INAN Inanimate
INCH Inchoative
INCL Inclusive
INDEF Indefinite
INESS Inessive ('in X')
INFER Inferential
INFIN Infinitive
INSTR Instrumental
ITER Iterative
LOC Locative
MASC Masculine
N Noun
NARR Narrative
NEG Negative
NEUT Neuter
NOM Nominative
OBJ Object
OBL Oblique
OPT Optative
PART Participle
PARTIT Partitive
PASS Passive
PERF Perfect
PL Plural
PLUP Pluperfect
POSS Possessive

POT Potential
PRES Present
PRESUP Presuppositional
PREV Preverb
PROG Progressive
PROHIB Prohibitive
PROL Prolative ('along X')
PROTR Protracted
PTCL Particle
PURP Purposive
Q Question
REC Recent
RECIP Reciprocal
REFL Reflexive
REL Relative
REM Remote
RESULT Resultative
SG Singular
SIMUL Simultaneous
SU Subject
SUBJ Subjunctive
SUPERL Superlative
THEM Thematic suffix
TRANSFORM Transformative ('made of X')
TRANSL Translative ('becoming X')
V Verb
VERS Version
VN Verbal noun
1 First person
2 Second person
3 Third person
X→Y Subject (agent) X acting on object (patient) Y

NOTES ON TRANSCRIPTION

Examples from languages of the U.S.S.R. that use the Latin alphabet (i.e. Estonian, Latvian, Lithuanian) are presented in the current orthography, for which see below. Russian examples are presented in accordance with the International system of transliteration (see p. 286). Unassimilated loans from Russian into other languages of the U.S.S.R. are also presented in accordance with the International system, and are set in block capitals to distinguish them from the general transcription system discussed below.

Although specialists in Turkic, Finno-Ugric, Iranian, etc., languages use their own transcription systems, we have opted here for a uniform system of broad transcription throughout the book. This system is based on that of the Association Phonétique Internationale (I.P.A.), but with some deviations for the following reasons: the I.P.A. system is not well adapted to transcribing affricates, some of which are extremely frequent in the languages of the U.S.S.R.; in some instances, absence of detailed phonetic information has led us to use a somewhat less specific transcription (e.g. in not distinguishing palatal from palatalised alveolar); we have used some symbols to bring the transliteration more into line with orthographies of the U.S.S.R. and specialist transcriptions of the language-families discussed. The following departures from I.P.A. should be noted.

More front values of vowels (i.e. front, or central relative to back) are indicated by a diaeresis (i.e. *ü* = I.P.A. [y], and likewise *ẅ* for [ɥ]). The I.P.A. central vowel symbols [ɨ], [ə] are used also for back-of-central unrounded vowels where the back/central opposition is nondistinctive. The symbol *å* represents a low back unrounded vowel, and *ů* a vowel between [o] and [u]. Vowel length is indicated by doubling the vowel-sign, stress by an acute accent on the stressed vowel. *V̆* indicates a reduced vowel. Pharyngalisation is indicated by a subscript, e.g. *ạ*. Vowels with retracted tongue root take a subscript point, e.g. *u̱*. Closing diphthongs have their second component represented as *j* or *w* rather than *i* or *u*.

For consonants, we use *š* for I.P.A. [ʃ] and *ž* for I.P.A. [ʒ]. Coronal affricates are indicated as follows: *c* for [ts], *ʒ* for [dz], *č* for [tʃ], *ǰ* for [dʒ]. Palatalisation is indicated by an acute accent over or to the right of the consonant symbol (e.g. *ń*, *ĺ*); the same notation is used to indicate palatal or alveolo-palatal articulation where the difference among these is nondistinctive (e.g. *ń* for I.P.A. [ɲ], *ś* for I.P.A. [ɕ], *ć* for I.P.A. [tɕ]). Labialisation is indicated by a superscript circle to the right of the consonant symbol (e.g. *t°*), and pharyngalisation by a subscript, as in *ṭ*. Retroflex consonants are shown by a subscript point under the corresponding alveolar (e.g. *ḷ* for I.P.A. [ɭ]). A macron over a consonant indicates an intensive (see p. 200), e.g. *s̄*. In Armenian and the Kurdish dialect spoken in Armenia, *ŕ* indicates a more intense rhotic (usually trilled) than *r* (usually continuant). Other specific conventions are discussed in the text where they occur.

The Latin orthographies of the languages of the U.S.S.R. differ from the above system in the following ways. In Lithuanian, *ė* is mid [e] while *e* is open [ä]; *y* and *ū* are the long equivalents of *i* and *u*; *y̨*, etymologically indicating nasalisation, now simply indicates a long vowel (thus *į* and *y* represent the same sound); closing diphthongs have *i*, *u* as their second component, *ie* and *uo* are opening diphthongs; for the representation of tone, see p. 148–51; the affricates [ʒ] and [ǯ] are represented as *dz*, *dž* respectively; consonants are automatically palatalised before front vowels, while before back vowels a nonpalatalised consonant is indicated as *CV*, a palatalised consonant *CiV*.

Latvian has a distinction between [e] and [ä], long and short, though the orthography underdifferentiates qualitatively with the one symbol *e*; *o* is an opening diphthong [uo], except in some loans; long vowels are marked by a macron (e.g. *ā*); closing diphthongs have *i*, *u* as their second component; for the representation of tone, see p. 151; *dz* and *dž* represent the affricates [ʒ] and [ǯ] respectively; palatal consonants are indicated by a cedilla, i.e. *ķ, ģ, ņ, ļ, ŗ* (the last not in the current Soviet orthography).

In Estonian, *õ* represents I.P.A. [ɤ]; closing diphthongs have their second component symbolised *i*, *u*; palatalisation is (rather marginally) phonemic for dentals/alveolars, though not represented in the orthography; the orthography also underdifferentiates between long and overlong segments (see pp. 115–16).

Kaliningrad
Oblast

Estonian
SSR

Karelian
ASSR

Lithuanian
SSR

Latvian
SSR

Belorussian
SSR

Nenets NO

Komi ASSR

Yamal-Nenet
NO

Ukrainian
SSR

Moldavian
SSR

Komi-Permyak
NO

Crimea

Chuvash
ASSR

Mari ASSR

Udmurt ASSR

Khanty-Mansi
NO

Black
Sea

Mordva
ASSR

Tatar
ASSR

Bashkir ASSR

F
E
D
C
GB
A

Georgian
SSR

Armenian
SSR

Khakas
AO

Mountai
Altay A

Azer-
baydzhan
SSR

Caspian Sea

Kara-
kalpak
ASSR

Kazakh SSR

A Dagestan ASSR
B Kabard-Balkar ASSR
C North-Ossete ASSR
D Karachay-Cherkes AO
E Abkhaz ASSR
F Adyge AO
G South-Ossete AO

Uzbek
SSR

Turkmen SSR

I R A N

Kirgiz SSR

Tadzhik SSR

AFGHANISTAN

C H I N A

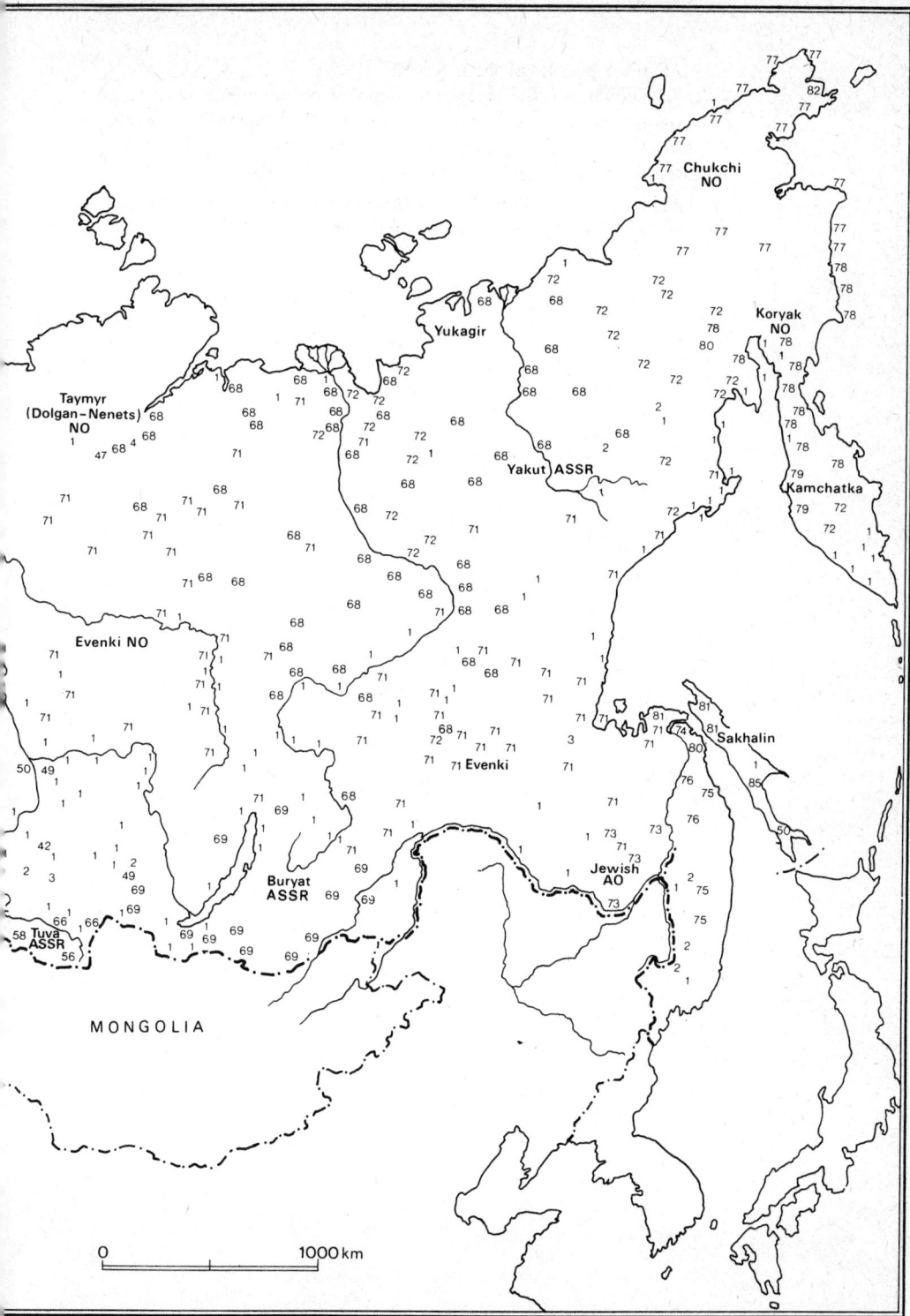

Taymyr
(Dolgan–Nenets)
NO

Yukagir

Chukchi
NO

Koryak
NO

Kamchatka

Yakut ASSR

Evenki NO

Sakhalin

Evenki

Jewish
AO

Buryat
ASSR

Tuva
ASSR

MONGOLIA

0   1000 km

Map of the peoples of the U.S.S.R.

(Not shown on this map are peoples occupying a very small geographical area, e.g. users of North-East Caucasian languages restricted to a single village or group of villages, or peoples with extensive geographical distribution as a minority, e.g. Gypsies.)

Adapted from E. Glyn Lewis, *Multilingualism in the Soviet Union: aspects of language policy and its implementation*, The Hague, 1972, map opposite page 1.

INDEX TO MAP

I

Introduction

To many educated people outside the Soviet Union, the concept U.S.S.R. is virtually synonymous with Russia, and the adjective Soviet with Russian. They might well be surprised to see a book entitled *The languages of the Soviet Union*, since they would imagine Russian to be the only language of this state other than, perhaps, a few peripheral languages spoken in border areas. But in fact, the U.S.S.R. is a multinational state, containing some 130 different ethnic groups, speaking some 130 different languages. According to the Soviet census carried out in 1970, Russians make up only 53.7% of the total population of the U.S.S.R. Even though this is a majority, it is a very small majority, although the numerical preponderance of Russian is enhanced by the fact that the remaining 46.3% is made up of a variety of other ethnic groups, of whom even the largest, the Ukrainians, comprise only 16.9% of the total, and the next largest, the Uzbek, only 3.8%. When one looks at the statistics for the number of speakers of individual languages of the U.S.S.R., Russian has a slightly larger majority, being spoken as a native language by some 58.6% of the total population. However, this still leaves 41.4% of the population of the U.S.S.R. with some other language as native language. And of the 46.3% of the population who are not ethnically Russian, slightly more than half (51.4%) claimed not to be able to speak Russian fluently either as a first or second language. Clearly, the view of the U.S.S.R. as being the same as Russia, or of Soviet citizens as being the same as Russians, is very misleading. By almost any criterion, the U.S.S.R. contains a number of often very different ethnic groups, speaking a number of languages that are often very different from one another. The purpose of this chapter is to summarise the details of this diversity, and to examine the relations between the various languages of the U.S.S.R. and Russian, the most widespread language. Later chapters will examine individual languages and language-groups in greater detail, primarily in terms of the structure of the languages concerned, though also in terms of their social function within the U.S.S.R.

1.1 Language and ethnic group: census statistics

At the beginning of this chapter, we cited certain statistics concerning the number of people belonging to various ethnic groups and speaking various languages. The statistics were from the most recent census of the U.S.S.R. carried out in 1970; except where otherwise stated, statistics cited in this book are from the published returns of this census (*IVPN* IV 1973). In the U.S.S.R. censuses are carried out at ten-yearly intervals, although this interval has been regularised in practice only very recently, since major upheavals (the Revolution of 1917, the Second World War) have impeded the realisation of this plan. The most complete pre-Revolutionary census was for 1897, and during the Soviet period we have census statistics for 1920, 1926, 1939, and 1959, in addition to 1970. Soviet census statistics are among the most detailed in the world giving information on the ethnic composition of the population and on the languages spoken. Although errors inevitably creep into any census breakdown through inefficiency, or even malevolence, whether on the part of the citizen giving the information or the census official recording it, the linguist interested in the linguistic composition of the U.S.S.R., and the correlations between ethnic and linguistic allegiance, is in possession of an unusually rich source of information.

Although the main interest in this book is the linguistic composition of the U.S.S.R., the published census statistics are arranged primarily in terms of ethnic groups. Ethnic group and language need not coincide: for instance, some 13 million Soviet citizens declared themselves in 1970 to be of non-Russian ethnic origin but to have Russian as their native language. At times the discrepancy can be even greater: only 12.8% of the Karaim, a Turkic-speaking group living for the most part in Lithuania, declared Karaim as their native language. In Russian, the relevant term for 'ethnic group' is *nacional 'nost'*, literally 'nationality', and this English term, in this sense, is found in many publications on the peoples and languages of the U.S.S.R., especially those published in the U.S.S.R. Unfortunately, this term is likely to lead to misunderstanding by an English-speaking audience, for whom the term 'nationality' may be taken to indicate citizenship. Nearly all people encompassed by Soviet censuses are citizens of the U.S.S.R., especially in view of the fact that the U.S.S.R. is not a major recipient of immigration population, so that the citizenship of the speakers of languages discussed in this book is unlikely to be at issue. What is at issue is their ethnic status, in the sense of the ethnic group to which they consider themselves to belong.

In the U.S.S.R. everyone has to have an ethnic status, and the moment when this is decided is when the citizen in question reaches the age of sixteen and has to be issued with a 'passport', i.e. an identity document for internal Soviet purposes. In principle, when a citizen applies for this identity document, he is free to choose the ethnic group to which he wants to belong. No doubt, if the registering official feels that a person's choice is facetious or obviously untrue, he would try to persuade the applicant to change his mind, but in principle this freedom of choice does exist. However, it may be presumed that virtually all applicants choose the ethnic group of their parents (if they are both of the same ethnic group), or of one of their parents in the case of mixed parenthood. Once the choice has been made and registered in the identity document, it cannot thereafter be changed. In giving information for a census, a Soviet citizen is not required to provide this documentation of his ethnic group, and so could in principle give a different ethnic group, although in practice we may again assume that the ethnic group given in the identity document will be declared. For children under the age of sixteen, census regulations allow the parents to choose the declared ethnic status of the child; if they cannot agree, the mother's ethnic status is automatically recorded.

For most of the ethnic groups in the U.S.S.R., it is reasonably clear whether or not someone belongs to the given ethnic group and where the delimiting line of that ethnic group is, but there are some exceptions. In particular, partly as a result of official policy, members of certain relatively small population groups have been or are being persuaded to declare themselves to be members of a larger group. For instance, the Mingrelians, who live in the Georgian S.S.R. and speak a language genetically related to Georgian, are not listed as a separate ethnic group in Soviet census statistics, and are said officially to have consolidated themselves with the Georgian ethnic group as a whole. Many of the smaller population groups in the Pamir mountain range in Tadzhikistan are being persuaded to consolidate themselves with the Tadzhik, and current census statistics do not list them separately. There are also a few instances of the reverse process: thus in 1970, the Negidal are listed as a separate ethnic group, whereas in 1959 they were not. In addition to such consolidation of whole population groups, there is also a certain amount of transfer between ethnic groups, whereby members of a given ethnic group gradually transfer their allegiance to some other ethnic group. One marked instance of this in the U.S.S.R. is with the Jewish ethnic group, which showed a decrease of some 5% between 1959 and 1970, although there is no reason to attribute this primarily to demographic, as opposed to cultural, factors. Some of the other ethnic groups registering a decline to be accounted for in this way are the Karelians, Mordva, and Ingrians, three Finno-Ugric-speaking peoples with a long history of interaction with Russians, by whom they are gradually being assimilated. However, in general, the constraint on not changing one's ethnic status after the age of sixteen, together with the tendency to declare the ethnic group of one of one's parents, militates against marked shifts in the ethnic distribution of the Soviet population.

The census questionnaire distributed in 1970 asks two main questions about language: each respondent is asked to name his native language, and is also asked which other language of the U.S.S.R. he speaks fluently. (A precise definition of the term 'language of the U.S.S.R.' is given below.) The questions are obviously open to a certain degree of misinterpretation, or at least freedom of interpretation, especially the second, and letters to various newspapers around the time of the census testify to the degree of confusion that surrounded these questions for many people. With respect to the question on native language, the census instruction booklet (*VPNVD* 1969) specifies that the respondent is free to declare whichever language he considers his native language, and that if he has difficulty in doing so the census official should write down the language which the respondent speaks best or uses in his own family. Problems with this question are obviously particularly acute in areas where several languages are in regular use, especially where individuals are in the process of shifting from one language to another. The booklet also makes explicit that the native language need not correspond to the person's ethnic status, this being one of the main sources of confusion.

In general in the U.S.S.R., for each ethnic group there is a corresponding language, and vice versa: thus there are Russians and a Russian language, there are Uzbek people and an Uzbek language, there are Ingrians and an Ingrian language (even though only 26.6% of Ingrians speak Ingrian), etc. This correlation is emphasised by the practice of using the same term for both ethnic group and language, even where other languages would prefer different terms, for instance *cyganskij*, the adjective for 'Gypsy' or 'Romany', and, most confusingly to outsiders, *evrejskij*, the adjective for 'Jewish' (as an ethnic appellation) and 'Yiddish' (the Germanic language which is the traditional language of Ashkenazic Jews).

However, as we have already seen, this is not an absolute one-to-one correlation, since members of a given ethnic group do not necessarily speak the corresponding language as their native language, or even speak it at all: the sense of belonging to a given ethnic group is dependent on a number of social and cultural features of which language is only one. Thus 13 million Soviet citizens speak Russian as their native language but do not consider themselves to be Russian. Conversely, of those who consider themselves ethnically to be Yukagir, a small people in the north-east of Siberia, only 46.8% speak Yukagir as a native language. In certain instances, the discrepancy between language and ethnic group applies to a whole population group rather than to individual members thereof. For instance, there are sometimes distinct ethnic groups which nonetheless speak the same language, or at least dialects of the same language. Thus the Soviet census statistics list the Kabard and the Cherkes as separate ethnic groups, although their language is considered one, Kabard-Cherkes; similarly the Karachay and Balkar speak one language, Karachay-Balkar. In yet other instances, even though a population speaks a language quite distinct from that of a certain ethnic group, for purposes of ethnic allegiance they consider themselves to be members of that ethnic group. A clear case of this is provided by the village of Khinalug, in northern Azerbaydzhan. The inhabitants of the village have Khinalug, a North-East Caucasian language, as their native language, although they are also bilingual in Azerbaydzhan, a Turkic language, genetically completely unrelated to Khinalug. Despite this, the inhabitants of Khinalug declare themselves to be of Azerbaydzhan ethnic status. Speakers of the various Pamir languages in Tadzhikistan are listed in census statistics as ethnically Tadzhik, even though many of them do not speak Tadzhik as their first language; both Tadzhik and the Pamir languages are genetically related, within the Iranian subgroup of Indo-European languages, which distinguishes this case from that of Khinalug, where Khinalug and Azerbaydzhan are completely unrelated. To a certain extent, the discrepancy between language and ethnic group in many instances in the U.S.S.R. could be compared to similar situations in other countries: in Wales, many people feel quite passionately that they are Welsh, not English, even though they may speak not a word of Welsh; and Englishmen and Americans differ on many cultural parameters even though they speak variants of the same language.

In addition to the traditionally recognised ethnic groups (peoples) who make up the U.S.S.R., recent Soviet official statements refer increasingly to the Soviet people (Russian: *sovetskij narod*) as a new kind of ethnic unit, resulting from the consolidation and interaction of the various peoples of the U.S.S.R. within the Soviet state. Since the concept of the Soviet people is rather different from that of ethnic group, it will not be further discussed here, except to note that, presumably, the only language that can be considered characteristic of the Soviet people as a whole is Russian (see section 1.4).

Soviet statistics are arranged primarily in terms of ethnic groups, rather than in terms of native language, as follows: for each ethnic group, we are given the total number of people claiming that ethnic allegiance, then the number of people claiming that ethnic allegiance who have the corresponding language as their native language. This means that for certain languages that have no corresponding ethnic group (such as Khinalug or the Pamir languages), no official language statistics are available. (These are for the most part languages with a small number of speakers, a few thousand or a few hundred, and so might in any event have been included under the rubric 'Others' reserved for small population groups not listed separately.) Moreover, for the most part the language statistics do not give the total number of people speaking the given language as their first language, but rather how many members of the given ethnic group have the given language as their first language. The only exception is for the languages of the Union Republics (for this term, see section 1.3.3), where the published statistics list the total number of speakers throughout the U.S.S.R. Apart from Russian, though, the discrepancy between 'total number of native speakers in the U.S.S.R.' and 'total number of native speakers in the U.S.S.R. among members of the corresponding ethnic group' is unlikely to be significant, since Russian is the only language where the number of native speakers who belong to different ethnic groups is statistically significant; for the languages of Union Republics, the relevant figures can be derived from Appendix 1. For those languages which are not listed separately in Soviet census publications, one can sometimes derive accurate or estimated numbers of native speakers from other publications, e.g. accounts of linguistic or ethnographic fieldwork, but these figures are, of course, for the most part approximate and unauthoritative.

Although native speakers of English, and of many European languages, tend to take for granted that one can identify clearly what constitutes a language, yet in many parts of the world this is not the case, for various linguistic and extralinguistic reasons; many parts of the U.S.S.R. fall into this latter category, so it is necessary for us briefly to consider this question. In terms of language structure, the main problem is differentiating between a situation where two speech varieties are different, though genetically related, languages, and one where they are two dialects of the same language. Linguists have tried to establish criteria for distinguishing between these two cases, the most widespread such criterion being mutual intelligibility, but there are problems with this criterion. First, mutual intelligibility is always a question of degree, i.e. all this criterion does is range speech forms on a scale from completely mutually intelligible to completely mutually unintelligible. Secondly, intelligibility of a different language variety can be enhanced by familiarity with this language variety: thus most English people now have little difficulty in following American English, although in the early days of talking films, marking the beginning of widespread contact between English and American language varieties, this was not necessarily so. Thirdly, the relation 'be mutually intelligible with' is not necessarily a transitive relation: very often one finds dialect chains where adjacent dialects are mutually intelligible, but nonadjacent dialects, especially the end points of the chain, are not. In such instances, the criterion of mutual intelligibility would suggest that in a dialect chain A–B–C, A and B are dialects of the same language, B and C are dialects of the same language, but A and C are different languages, which is of course inconsistent. The problem is further complicated by the inclusion of social and political considerations: thus, many dialects of German are structurally more similar to Dutch dialects than they are to many other dialects of German, yet German and Dutch are still considered distinct languages, with the language border roughly following the political frontier, because of the fact that Dutch and German serve different political entities with different cultural traditions. Conversely, the various 'dialects' of Chinese are considered dialects, rather than languages, because of the political-cultural unity they serve, despite the fact that they are not mutually intelligible. In the U.S.S.R. there are several similar situations, so that to a certain extent some of the language versus dialect boundaries are arbitrary, or motivated by cultural or political considerations rather than similarities and differences in linguistic structure.

A classic example here is that of the Turkic languages. Apart from two divergent languages, Chuvash and Yakut (the latter including Dolgan), the Turkic languages form a single dialect chain, or perhaps dialect cluster would be a more appropriate visual metaphor. It is extremely difficult to draw dividing lines between individual Turkic languages, and, as will be discussed in more detail in Chapter 2, it is often the case that a dialect is assigned to one language rather than another on the basis of cultural ties rather than structural similarity. However, if one takes extremely distant points in this continuum, then the level of mutual intelligibility is much lower, so that it would readily be accepted that one is dealing with two different languages rather than two different dialects of the same language. Moreover, the Turkic-speaking area of the U.S.S.R. as a whole has no single natural cultural centre, i.e. no one city whose language could be used as a standard language for speakers of all Turkic languages/dialects. The result of this has been the recognition of a number of distinct Turkic languages, most of them extremely similar to one another in all aspects of grammatical structure and vocabulary.

At the other extreme, we find languages recognised as a single language, on the basis of a cultural unity of speakers, even though the individual dialects are so divergent from one another that mutual intelligibility is low or nonexistent. One such example is the Uralic language Khanty, where dialect diversity is so great that up to five distinct written languages have been used to cater to different branches of Khanty (with 14,562 native speakers). In addition, there are some instances where Soviet official policy has not yet decided whether to consider two speech varieties different languages or dialects of the same language. The Uralic language Mari currently exists in two written forms, Meadow-Eastern Mari and Hill Mari, although it remains unclear whether they are to be considered distinct languages or simply different written dialects of one and the same language. A somewhat similar situation is presented by the unwritten language or dialect of the Dolgan: ethnically, they are distinct from the Yakut, but their speech has often been regarded as a divergent dialect of Yakut. The series *JaNSSR* (1966–8) does not include Dolgan as a separate language, although the degree of divergence between Dolgan and other dialects of Yakut is sufficient to prevent mutual comprehension.

The Soviet authorities have sometimes been criticised in the West for establishing ethnic and linguistic boundaries in such a way as to further malevolent political intent, in particular to divide potentially troublesome population groups into a number of different ethnic groups, each with its own written language. While it is in most instances impossible to verify the motives lying behind ethnic and linguistic policies of the Soviet authorities, given the widely different interpretations advanced by these authorities and their critics, it should always be borne in mind that the solution to the problem of 'same language' versus 'different language' is rarely an easy one, and that in many parts of the world, including much of western Europe, the decisions that have been made have been taken as much on social and political grounds as on linguistic ones.

In discussing the second language question in the 1970 census, the term 'language of the U.S.S.R.' was introduced, since the census questionnaire only asks which languages of the U.S.S.R. are spoken as second languages. Basically, a language of the U.S.S.R. is a language which can be considered to be autochthonous to the territory of the U.S.S.R., i.e. in particular to be spoken by a population group all or most of whose members were born in the U.S.S.R. (or territory which is now part of the U.S.S.R.) – this would thus exclude the languages of transient groups, such as foreign students and businessmen, and also of recent immigrants; secondly, the language in question must not be the official language of a foreign state – this excludes such languages as German (with over a million native speakers in the U.S.S.R.), Polish, Bulgarian, Korean, Hungarian, Greek (each with over 100,000 native speakers in the U.S.S.R.), as well as a number of other smaller population groups, members of ethnic groups whose main centre is outside the U.S.S.R. In many instances, the fact that these non-Soviet languages are included within the borders of the U.S.S.R. is a result of the fluctuating frontiers that have characterised much of Russian history.

However, the term 'language of the U.S.S.R.' does include some languages and ethnic groups which are represented predominantly outside the U.S.S.R. but are not official languages of the corresponding ethnic group anywhere outside the U.S.S.R. e.g. Yiddish, Romany, Kurdish, Aramaic (Assyrian). The characterisation is in large measure reasonable – even though it does exclude some large populations (e.g. the Soviet Germans) from consideration as peoples of the U.S.S.R. speaking a language of the U.S.S.R. – in that it delimits those languages that can clearly be regarded as integral parts of the linguistic composition of the U.S.S.R. from those that are spoken by people who just happen to live in the U.S.S.R. In a few instances, the speech form spoken by a sizable population group within the U.S.S.R. is very close to the official language of some foreign state, but despite this the Soviet authorities have preferred to consider the language as spoken in the U.S.S.R. as a language of the U.S.S.R.; in practical terms, this has been achieved by declaring the language variety spoken within the U.S.S.R. to be a different language from that spoken outside, as with the declaration of Moldavian to be a language distinct from Romanian, or of

Tadzhik to be distinct from Persian. In such instances, the political separation can, however, be expected to lead with time to increased linguistic differentiation, so that Tadzhik and Persian are already rather different from one another in abstract and technical vocabulary, with Tadzhik borrowing heavily from Russian, and Persian from Arabic.

As indicated above, respondents to the census were also asked to declare which other language of the U.S.S.R. they speak fluently; as a result of this question, we have detailed data not only on the first languages spoken in the U.S.S.R. but also on the level and kind of bilingualism. The census instructions do, incidentally, specify that only one language can be declared as the reply to this question. Several areas of the U.S.S.R. have widespread trilingualism, e.g. Abkhaz, Mingrelian, and Russian in some parts of the Abkhaz A.S.S.R. (with Georgian sometimes added as a fourth component); the census statistics give no information on such multilingual situations, since only the nonnative language (if any) that the respondent speaks best is included. The only gloss on 'fluently' given in the census instructions is that the respondent must be able to converse in the second language, so considerable leeway is left for individual interpretation. The language of the U.S.S.R. most widespread as a second language is, of course, Russian, which is claimed as a second language by almost half of those declaring some other language as their first language. For certain individual ethnic groups, however, bilingualism in some second language other than Russian is more dominant or almost as dominant as bilingualism in Russian, but such kinds of bilingualism are restricted to certain specific regions where there is either a mixed population (as with Uzbek and Tadzhik in much of Uzbekistan and Tadzhikistan) or a traditional lingua franca that predates Russian influence in the area (as with Avar in much of Dagestan, Tadzhik in the Pamir, or Georgian in South Ossetia). Bilingualism is often, though not invariably, one stage in the replacement of one language by another, as is happening with Yiddish and Mordva. There are, however, also instances of stable bilingualism extending over long periods of time, for instance that between Tadzhik and Uzbek.

1.2 **Classification of the languages of the U.S.S.R.**

There are several criteria according to which one could classify the languages of the U.S.S.R. and by almost any of these criteria the U.S.S.R. emerges as a very heterogeneous country indeed. For the linguist, an obvious way of classifying languages is in terms of genetic language-families, though more recently the possibility of comparing languages in terms of shared structural similarities (typological classification) has again become popular, irrespective of whether or not these structural similarities are due to genetic relatedness. Someone more interested in the sociolinguistic composition of the U.S.S.R. might prefer other criteria, such as the number of speakers, the social function of the language in the U.S.S.R., the traditional technological level of the society speaking the language, or other aspects of their traditional culture such as religion. In the following sections, we shall examine these various classificatory criteria.

1.2.1 *Genetic classification*

As can be seen from the body of this book, the languages of the U.S.S.R. fall into five main groups from the viewpoint of genetic classification (with reservations to be elaborated below), in addition to a few languages that are isolated genetically within the U.S.S.R. but have genetically related languages outside, such as the Semitic language Aramaic or the Sino-Tibetan language Dungan. These five main groups are: Indo-European, Uralic, Altaic, Caucasian, and Paleosiberian (Paleoasiatic). The genetic unity of the Indo-European family and of the Uralic family can scarcely be in doubt; indeed Indo-European is the paradigm case of a genetic family. The same cannot be said of the other three groups. Paleosiberian is the least cohesive of these three, since it has probably never been intended to refer to a single genetic family: rather, Paleosiberian refers to those languages spoken in Siberia that do not belong to any of the major language-families spoken in the area, such as Altaic (or any of its branches), Uralic, Indo-European, Sino-Tibetan. Paleosiberian includes one small language-family, Chukotko-Kamchatkan, as well as three languages that are, to the best of current knowledge, isolates, with no demonstrable genetic relation to any other established family: Yukagir, Nivkh, and Ket. Chukotko-Kamchatkan, Yukagir, Nivkh and Ket are, incidentally, very different one from another. Another small language-family, Eskimo-Aleut, is sometimes included within Paleosiberian.

The view that the Turkic, Mongolian, and Tungusic languages together form a single genetic family, Altaic, is widespread both among specialists in these languages and as common lore among linguists, and considerable popularity has been gained recently by the idea that Korean and Japanese can also be included in this family. However, for reasons some of which are discussed in Chapter 2, the genetic unity of even the three groupings Turkic, Mongolian, Tungusic should not be taken for granted, and there are certainly reasons for questioning the arguments that have been advanced to date for their genetic unity. It is, incidentally, clear that each of these three groupings is internally a genetic unit. The inclusion of a single chapter on Altaic is thus to some extent a concession to tradition, rather than acceptance of Altaic as a single language-family. The same is true to an even greater extent of Caucasian, which consists of at least three, and possibly four, groupings, whose genetic relations to one another are far from reliably established. The three groupings are South Caucasian (or Kartvelian), North-West Caucasian, and North-

East Caucasian; the unity of the last of these has even been questioned, which would mean replacing North-East Caucasian by Nakh and Dagestanian, as is discussed in Chapter 5. Although the view that North-West and North-East Caucasian are related genetically as North Caucasian is quite widespread among Caucasianists, especially in the U.S.S.R., there are also many sceptics, and even if this North Caucasian grouping were to be accepted, its genetic relationship with South Caucasian would remain very questionable indeed.

The account of genetic classification outlined above, and followed in the body of this book, is extremely cautious in proposing genetic affiliations, and readers should note that this is the author's bias on this point. At the opposite extreme, some linguists would advocate considering all languages of the world as being genetically related, or, a slightly less extreme position, all the languages of Europe and northern Eurasia (which would thus include all or most of the languages of the U.S.S.R.). One version of this last-mentioned approach is associated with V. M. Illič-Svitič, who used H. Pedersen's term Nostratic for a language-family that would include Indo-European, Semitic, South Caucasian, Uralic, Altaic, Dravidian, and Chukotko-Kamchatkan. There are indeed some indications in favour of such a family, for instance in the personal pronouns, where a first person singular with *m* or *b* and a second person singular with *s* or *t* are widespread across these languages (e.g. Latin accusative *me*, Georgian *me*, Komi *me*, Azerbaydzhan *män*, Chukchi *yəm* 'I'; Latin accusative *te*, Komi *te*, Chukchee *yət* 'you (singular)'). Intermediate positions would be the recognition of a genetic relation between Uralic and Altaic, as Uralo-Altaic, or between Yukagir and Uralic. In this book, relatively little attention will be paid to controversies of genetic affiliation, largely because these for the most part require detailed consideration of aspects of the individual languages that go beyond the presentation possible here. Moreover, even if all the languages discussed in this book should turn out to be related genetically, it will still be the case that any individual Turkic language is more closely related genetically to any other Turkic language than to any Tungusic or Indo-European language, so that the hierarchical relations established by the classification would remain essentially the same.

1.2.2 *Typological classification*

When one starts asking about the typological classification of the languages of the U.S.S.R., then certain groupings emerge that transcend the above-mentioned genetic boundaries, though there still remain some languages that stand out both genetically and typologically against the background of their neighbours (e.g. Ket), and it must be emphasised that typological similarities are no evidence for genetic affiliation. As has been seen again and again, close proximity of two languages can lead to so great a degree of mutual influence that the languages come with time to resemble one another more than they did originally: the classical example of this is the Balkan *sprachbund*, where a number of features have diffused among Bulgarian, Modern Greek, Albanian, and Romanian, to make them more similar in some respects to one another than to other languages that are more closely related to them genetically (see further section 4.6). In this section, we shall list some typological features that are widespread across the languages of the U.S.S.R.; more detailed discussion of these features can be found in the individual chapters to follow.

One feature that is common to many of the language-families of the U.S.S.R. is verb-final word order, often as part of a general word-order pattern whereby adjuncts always precede their head (adjectives, genitives, and relative clauses precede their head nouns; nouns precede their postpositions): this phenomenon is found most consistently in the Altaic languages (whether or not one considers Altaic a single language-family); to a lesser extent it is also found in Uralic languages, especially the more easterly languages (those spoken further west have word order patterns much more similar to those of Germanic or Slavonic languages). In certain languages and language-families, the word order varies between verb-final and verb-medial, and there may be other deviations from the strict order adjunct–head, as in many Caucasian languages and the Chukotko-Kamchatkan languages. The question of whether Proto-Indo-European was verb-final, with adjunct–head as its basic word order, remains controversial (Lehmann 1974; Friedrich 1975; Watkins 1976), and the verb-final order that is found frequently in some of the modern Indo-European languages of the U.S.S.R. (e.g. Armenian, Iranian languages) can be attributed to influence from neighbouring Turkic languages. At any rate, one can say that the languages of the U.S.S.R. overall show a tendency towards verb-final order, more so than that shown by the rest of Eurasia, though perhaps not more than is shown by the languages of the world as a whole.

One phenomenon that seems to co-occur with verb-final word order in a large number of languages is the use of nonfinite verbal forms – participles, nominalisations, verbal adverbs (gerunds) – rather than finite subordinate clauses, the latter being the norm in most European languages, including Russian. In Tatar, a Turkic language, for instance, the usual way of saying 'the man who went' is *bar-gan keše*, literally '(the) having-gone man', where *bar-gan* is the past participle of the verb *bar* 'go'; 'when he left, I stayed' is *ul kit-käč, min kaldəm*, where *kit-käč* is the past verbal adverb of the verb *kit* 'leave', and the only finite verb is *kaldəm*, first person singular (*-m*) of the past tense (*-də*) of *kal* 'stay'. Widespread use of such nonfinite forms correlates highly with verb-final word order, being the basic means of expressing subordination in the Altaic languages, also in several Uralic languages (with many remnants even in the more westerly languages) and Caucasian languages. Indeed, the occurrence of conjunctions marking subordinate clauses is

Table 1.1. *Morphological typology of Lithuanian and Tatar*

| | Lithuanian 'friend' | | Tatar 'apple' | |
	SG	PL	SG	PL
NOM	draũg-as	draug-aĩ	alma	alma-lar
GEN	draũg-o	draug-ų̃	alma-nəŋ	alma-lar-nəŋ
DAT	draũg-ui	draug-áms	alma-ga	alma-lar-ga
LOC	draug-ė̃	draug-uosè	alma-da	alma-lar-da

something of a rarity among the languages of the U.S.S.R., though, as will be shown in section 1.4, under the influence of Russian, and also the earlier influence of certain other languages (e.g. Arabic on many Turkic languages, German and Scandinavian languages on some Balto-Finnic languages within the Uralic family), many languages of the U.S.S.R. have recently developed or are in the process of developing subordinating conjunctions, either borrowing them directly from Russian or calquing them on the structure of Russian conjunctions.

One morphological feature that is widespread across languages of the U.S.S.R. is agglutination, i.e. the inflection of words by means of a sequence of morphemes each of which carries a single piece of meaning. This contrasts both with isolating languages (such as Vietnamese) where there is no inflection at all, and with fusional (flectional) languages, where several grammatical categories are normally fused together into a single morpheme. This can be seen by comparing partial paradigms for noun declension in Tatar, an agglutinative language of the Turkic family, and in Lithuanian, a fusional language of the Baltic branch of Indo-European (Table 1.1). In Tatar, the grammatical category of plural number is indicated consistently by the morpheme -*lar*; likewise, each of the cases has its own marker (genetive -*nəŋ*, dative -*ga*, locative -*da*). In Lithuanian, on the other hand, the indications of number and case are so inextricably bound together that it is impossible to segment the one from the other: all one can say is that -*as* is nominative singular, -*ui* dative singular, -*aĩ* nominative plural, and -*ams* dative plural, without the possibility of identifying any constant formal marker of plural number or of nominative or dative case. The Indo-European languages, including those spoken in the U.S.S.R., are typically fusional, although many branches of Indo-European, including Armenian and Iranian, have developed a significant degree of agglutination over their recent history, this being perhaps an areal feature, resulting from their contact with Turkic languages. All of the Altaic languages are agglutinative. In the Uralic family, many languages are agglutinative, and all show signs of having been until quite recently largely agglutinative, but several Uralic languages, especially the Balto-Finnic languages, Lapp, and the Samoyedic languages, have undergone complex sound changes leading to such widespread analogical formations, that they have moved considerably in the direction of fusion. Of the Caucasian languages, the North Caucasian languages are basically agglutinative, while the South Caucasian languages are much more mixed, with a high degree of fusion especially in the structure of the verb.

On many other parameters, the languages of the U.S.S.R., especially those of different genetic families, differ from one another as much as any two languages anywhere in the world do. Thus we find languages with gender/class systems (many Indo-European and North Caucasian languages, also the language-isolate Ket) and languages without such systems (other Indo-European languages, Altaic and Uralic languages); languages with ergative morphology (many Iranian languages, Georgian), languages with both morphological ergativity and some syntactic ergativity (some North Caucasian languages, some Chukotko-Kamchatkan languages). and languages which have no more ergativity than does English (most Indo-European languages outside the Iranian branch, and also Tadzhik within the Iranian branch, Uralic and Altaic languages). In terms of phonological typology, the languages of the U.S.S.R. are also very different from one another. Although vowel harmony is found in nearly all Altaic languages, the phonetic feature that conditions the vowel harmony is different in Tungusic languages from that in Turkic and Mongolian languages; otherwise vowel harmony is found in some, but not all, Uralic languages, and in some, but not all, of the Chukotko-Kamchatkan languages. The U.S.S.R. contains languages which approach the world record for the number of distinct consonant phonemes: the Caucasian language Adyge has 68 in its Bzhedug dialect; and while it does not have languages as poor in consonants as many Polynesian languages, Chukchi is relatively poor with only fourteen consonant phonemes.

Until recently, one might have ventured to say that the U.S.S.R. is basically lacking in languages with phonemic tone, the only exceptions being Dungan (which is structurally a dialect of Mandarin Chinese) and the Baltic languages Lithuanian and Latvian. However, recent detailed phonetic work has uncovered tonal oppositions in the language-isolate Ket (Dul'zon 1969; Feer 1976) and also in several North-East Caucasian languages (Kibrik et al. 1978); moreover pitch seems to play a more important role than was thought hitherto in the series of length distinctions made in such Balto-Finnic languages as Estonian and Liv, so that the investigation of prosodic features in many languages of the U.S.S.R. is only in its infancy, and it is difficult to foresee what typological generalisations will finally emerge. The various points mentioned in this paragraph are discussed in more detail in appropriate sections of the following chapters.

1.2.3   *Sociological classification*

Perhaps the most obvious sociological classificatory feature, from even a cursory examination of Soviet language statistics, is the great discrepancy in the number of speakers. As already mentioned, Russian is spoken by over 58% of the population; indeed, the three genetically closely related East Slavonic languages (Russian, Ukrainian and Belorussian – in terms of number of speakers the first, second, and fourth largest languages of the U.S.S.R. respectively) account for over 76% of the total population. At the other extreme, there is a long list of languages with only a few thousand or a few hundred speakers, and even some with fewer than a hundred speakers, of which Aleut (96 speakers in 1970) is listed separately in the census statistics. In fact, the language with the smallest number of speakers in 1970 was Kamas, a Uralic language (Samoyedic branch), which had just one speaker; it had been thought that this language was long since extinct, until this one speaker was discovered, who had kept her language alive in her prayers, and who was brought to attend the Third International Congress of Finno-Ugrists in Tallinn (Estonia) in 1970. Previously, Kamas had presumably gone unnoticed among the 'Others' figure in the census statistics. In determining the viability of a language, however, the number of speakers is not the only factor to consider, although it is an important consideration; there are languages with very few speakers, for instance in isolated parts of the Caucasus, which seem quite viable, with no tendency to replacement by other languages.

On the other hand, languages with a large number of speakers scattered across a wide area, especially if they are a minority in most or all of that area, show low figures for language retention in the U.S.S.R. A clear example is Yiddish, with 381,078 speakers, but everywhere a minority language greatly outnumbered by the local language. A good pair of languages to compare here are Estonian and Mordva, both Uralic languages. Mordva actually has slightly more speakers than Estonian, although the difference is very slight, both having just under a million. However, Estonian is spoken by a compact population group which is a decisive majority on its own territory (almost 70% of the population of Estonia is Estonian), whereas the Mordva are scattered across a vast area to the south of Kazan', and even in the area of their greatest concentration, the Mordva A.S.S.R., they constitute only 35.4% of the population (58.9% is made up of Russians). In the light of this, the significant difference in the rates of language retention are not surprising: in 1970, 95.5% of Estonians declared Estonian as their native language, a slight increase on the 95.2% figure for 1959, whereas only 77.8% of the Mordva declared Mordva as their native language, a slight decrease on the 1959 figure of 78.1%.

In addition to shifts in relative numbers of speakers due to different levels of language loyalty among the languages of the U.S.S.R., there have also been marked shifts due to differences in the rate of natural increase of population among different ethnic groups. The highest birth-rates are among the traditionally Islamic peoples of Central Asia and the Caucasus, with, for instance, increases between 1959 and 1970 of 52.9% for the Tadzhik and 46.5% for the Avar, compared with an average for the U.S.S.R. of 15.7%. Very low birth-rates were noted for the Baltic republics, and more generally for European urban areas, despite official encouragement of large families. Between 1959 and 1970, the number of ethnic Uzbek outstripped that of Belorussians, the Moldavians outstripped the Lithuanians and the Jews, the Turkmen and Kirgiz outstripped the Latvians, while the Tadzhik outstripped the Germans, Chuvash, and Latvians.

Probably the most significant sociological parameter necessary to a discussion of the pre-Soviet status of the various ethnic groups, and still relevant to a certain extent in the Soviet period, is the extent to which different ethnic groups had been integrated into the mainstream development of European technology and its associated philosophical and cultural ideas. As stated, this is a very ethnocentric characterisation, implying that nonwestern cultures should be integrated into western culture, the only question being the extent to which they have achieved this. However, in relation to the U.S.S.R., it is difficult not to adopt this position as one's expository stand, irrespective of whether or not one accepts it ideologically, since it lies at the heart of much of Soviet thinking on the question of ethnic relations. At the time of the Revolution, the Russian Empire was one of the most backward countries in Europe, but was also characterised by an extreme internal diversity of cultural level. One of the main aims of the new revolutionary government was to correct this backlog, by bringing Russia up to the level of western Europe in industrialisation, education, etc., and by bringing the whole of the new Soviet state up to this same level. At the time of the Revolution, the Russian upper classes, at least, had in large measure assimilated to western European technology and culture – indeed, Russian literature and music in the nineteenth century made a considerable contribution to the development of European culture. A few parts of the Russian Empire were even more advanced than Russia proper in this respect, in particular Poland and Finland in the west, which gained their permanent independence from Russia at the time of the Revolution, but also the Baltic provinces, especially Estonia.

One measure of the stage of development is the figure for literacy in various parts of the Empire according to the 1897 census: for the Russian Empire as a whole the percentage of people aged between 9 and 49 and able to read (though not necessarily to write) was 28.4%, with a marked discrepancy between town (57%) and country (23.8%). The literacy figure for the population in what is now the R.S.F.S.R. was only slightly higher (29.6%), reaching 61.1% in urban areas of what is now the R.S.F.S.R. The only Union Republics on whose territory in 1897 the majority of the population between these ages was able to read were Estonia (an astounding 96.2%), Latvia (79.7%), and Lithuania (54.2%), i.e. the three Baltic republics. (In the case of Estonia, and to a lesser extent Latvia, one important factor may have been the Protestant religion, with its greater emphasis on the ability to read the Bible.) In the U.S.S.R. today, the literacy percentage is 99.7%. In 1897, however, in the territories of many Union Republics the literacy percentage was well under 10% (Armenia, Kazakhstan, Moldavia, and all the Central Asia republics, the lowest being Tadzhikistan with 2.3%). For many of the peoples of the Russian Empire, the question of literacy simply did not arise, since their own language had no written form, and they were often not familiar with Russian. While literacy gives one useful statistical measure, several other, less readily quantifiable, measures, would give essentially the same result: industrialisation was most developed in the west of the Empire, while much of Siberia was so isolated that its inhabitants had only just begun to engage in contacts with Russians and other Europeans.

One useful way of classifying the peoples of the U.S.S.R. sociologically is to inquire about their traditional culture, and to divide the territory into zones on this basis. The frontiers of individual zones are necessarily rather fluid, since in many areas there was mixed Russian and non-Russian population, or other mixed population situations, but overall the following division gives a reasonable picture of traditional cultural areas. First, we may consider the Baltic area, i.e. what is now the republics of Estonia, Latvia, and Lithuania, characterised by a more Western outlook, reflected in the predominance of western European religions (Catholicism in Lithuania and most of Latvia, Lutheranism in Estonia and part of Latvia), and the strong influence of Poland, Germany, and Scandinavia. These were, and to a large extent remain, the most advanced parts of the Russian Empire/U.S.S.R. Secondly, we may look at what is perhaps the least well-defined area, namely European Russia (in the pre-Revolutionary sense of Russia, i.e. including the Ukraine and Belorussia); this area shades off fairly indefinitely into the east and south, where many non-Russian peoples had been largely assimilated in culture, though not in language, to the Russians, e.g. the Komi and the Chuvash.

A third area is the Caucasus (including Transcaucasia), which, though small in area, is an important cultural area in view of its bridging position between Europe and Asia. Within the Caucasus, a major division must be made between the predominantly Christian peoples (Armenians, Georgians), and the predominantly Muslim peoples (most of the other Caucasus inhabitants), although a few groups, e.g. the Ossete, fall outside this classification. Although languages of several different genetic families are represented in the Caucasus (Turkic and Iranian, in addition to Caucasian), the Islamic peoples of the area in particular form a cultural unity that cuts across linguistic boundaries. The main centre of Islam however is Central Asia, which as a cultural area can be taken to include Kazakhstan, except for its northern perimeter, which is essentially an extension of the Ural industrial belt. Indeed, apart from Russian, Islam can probably be considered the main single force that shaped the traditional culture of large parts of the present-day U.S.S.R., in so far as it covered the whole of Central Asia and also extended further afield, for instance to the Volga khanate of Kazan', which at one time controlled much of Siberia. Culturally, this area did not differ significantly from other feudal Islamic states. Although most of the Turkic peoples of the U.S.S.R. live within this Central Asian extended cultural zone, as one moves further east one comes to a relatively small cultural area, inhabited mainly by speakers of Turkic and Mongolian languages, where the predominant religious influence was Buddhism, emanating from (Outer) Mongolia, and earlier still from Tibet. Most of the remaining territory of the U.S.S.R. forms the sixth and last cultural area, Siberia and the Far North, extending from the Lapps in the west right across northern Eurasia to include most of Siberia, to meet the traditionally ill-defined line where Russian interests met those of China, Japan, and the United States. The religious beliefs of this area were predominantly animist, more particularly often shamanist, and the economy was essentially a subsistence economy based on hunting and fishing.

As was mentioned above, very few languages of the Russian Empire had their own written forms, and we may profitably conclude our discussion of the sociological classification of the languages of the U.S.S.R. by considering briefly those that did. We have already discussed the languages of the Baltic states, which developed as written languages relatively late by European standards, but with considerable success, as can be seen from the 1897 census statistics on literacy. Russian itself, of course, had a well-established literary tradition, even though the literacy rate was rather low. Two languages of the Caucasus, Armenian and Georgian, had written forms going back to the middle of the first millennium, although the literacy rates for speakers of these languages, especially Armenian, were very low. Arabic was used as a written language by some Islamic peoples, or rather by very small numbers of individuals, while for other languages of Islamic peoples there existed writing systems based on the Arabic alphabet: these writing systems, were, however, controlled by only a minute fraction of the population, so that one cannot speak of a popular literary language in these cases. A somewhat similar position was occupied by Classical Mongolian for some of the Buddhist peoples. Over most of the Russian Empire, however, the peoples inhabiting the Empire had no writing system, and there are very few areas indeed of the Russian Empire where we can speak of a democratic written language, in the sense of a written language available to or being made available to the population at large.

1.2.4 Historical background

The heterogeneity of the Russian Empire at the beginning of the twentieth century, which has continued in some measure to the present day, can be understood by viewing it against the historical development of the present-day boundaries of the Russian Empire/U.S.S.R. – the frontiers of the Empire in 1917 are actually very close to those of the U.S.S.R. today. Around the beginning of our millennium, the East Slavs, not yet differentiated into (Great) Russians, Ukrainians, and Belorussians, had established a number of political entities in eastern Europe, the most important being Kiyev in the south and Novgorod in the north. Even at this early period, there was some assimilation of non-East Slav peoples. Toponymic evidence suggests that much of what is now northern Russian was originally inhabited by Baltic and Finno-Ugric tribes, who were assimilated in the prehistoric or early historical period: the early Russian chronicles mention several Finno-Ugric tribes which no longer survive as separate ethnic entities, and the present-day assimilation of the Karelians, Ingrians, and Mordva by the Russians can be viewed as a natural continuation of this process. One problem that plagued the East Slav states of that period, and has continued to plague the rulers of Russia ever since, is the absence of any well defined natural boundaries to their territory: basically, frontiers are determined by the ability to hold them. These early East Slav states proved unable to hold their frontiers, largely as a result of internal squabbling, with the result that large parts of their western territory were taken over by Poland and Lithuania, while more easterly territories were taken over by the then powerful Islamic states to the east, in particular the Tatar, with their centre in Kazan': traditionally, the period of Tatar suzerainty over Russia is dated from 1240 to 1480.

This position changed radically from the fifteenth century on, with the consolidation of their hold over Russia proper by the grand dukes of Muscovy (Moscow), who played a leading role in the struggle for national independence against the Tatar. A key event in the internal consolidation of power was the capture of Novgorod in 1478. Even more important, however, was the capture of the Tatar stronghold of Kazan' in 1552 by Ivan the Terrible, to be followed four years later by the capture of their other stronghold, Astrakhan'. On the one hand, this broke the back of the Tatar threat. Even more importantly, it effectively opened the door to Russian colonisation of Siberia: much of western Siberia had also been under Tatar suzerainty, so that the Russian expansion into northern Asia now met no real obstacles until it came face to face with the then effete Chinese Empire, and perhaps more significantly, at least in the short term, with Japan and the United States. The frontier with the United States was settled in 1868, when the Russian Empire formally ceded Alaska to the U.S.A., thus establishing the Bering Strait as the frontier. Relations with Japan have been more complex, with a series of military engagements, the most decisive being the Russian defeat in the Russo-Japanese War of 1905, when Russia ceded southern Sakhalin to Japan, and the Russian recapture of this area, plus the Kuriles, after the Second World War.

In addition to the eastward expansion, Russia was also able to undertake expansion in other directions. In the Caucasus, a series of military campaigns and treaties led to the incorporation of the Caucasus range and the present-day Transcaucasian republics, although the border with Turkey and Iran was decided militarily shortly after the Revolution. In the west and north-west, parts of the Ukraine were regained from Poland in the seventeenth century, and around 1700 Peter the Great's campaigns against Sweden established Russia as a major power on the Baltic. The westward expansion reached its greatest extent at the time of the partitions of Poland (1772, 1793, 1795), when large tracts of Polish territory, including Warsaw, were incorporated into the Empire. Finally, expansion took place to the south-east, into Central Asia, although the precise relation between local rulers and the Tsar in Saint Petersburg remained unclear. At best, this expansion led to the drawing of a line dividing Russian and British (Indian) spheres of influence.

These brief remarks should serve to indicate how the present frontiers of the U.S.S.R. and the assembly of ethnic groups which live within these frontiers, are in large measure the result of accidental impediments to expansion, with the result that the U.S.S.R. still does not have a clear set of natural frontiers. Even during the history of the U.S.S.R., these frontiers have changed considerably: after the Revolution, the Baltic states gained their independence, and Poland acquired much of the territory which is now western Ukraine and Belorussia. The Transcaucasian states (Armenia, Azerbaydzhan, and Georgia) had brief periods of independence, and the establishment of Soviet power in many of the more peripheral areas, such as Central Asia and the Far East, was delayed for several years after the Revolution. The success of the U.S.S.R. in the Second World War led to a considerable territorial gain, in particular the Baltic states and Bessarabia (Moldavia) (nominally occupied in 1940, but not effectively integrated until the cessation of hostilities), and large areas with mixed Polish–Ukrainian or Polish–Belorussian populations, in addition to a small part of the former German province of East Prussia. The present boundaries of the U.S.S.R. run very close to those of the Russian Empire in 1905, so that in a real sense one can speak of a continuity of the ethnic and linguistic problems faced by administrations having responsibility for this territory, even where the solutions adopted in the light of these problems have differed considerably.

1.3 **Language policy**

1.3.1 *Pre-Revolutionary policy*

In the period before the Revolution, Russian was the official language for almost the whole of the Russian Empire. The only areas where a limited amount of local autonomy permitted the use of other languages were the Russian parts of Poland, Finland, and the Baltic provinces. In Finland, which had been ceded to Russia by Sweden in 1809, the Swedish minority occupied a dominant political and economic position, and Swedish was used as the official language in the nineteenth century. In the Baltic provinces, a similar position was held by German, the language of the land-owners. But for most of the Russian Empire, languages other than Russian had no rights whatsoever. In some instances, languages were actively discouraged or even forbidden, as happened with Ukrainian between 1876 and 1905 as part of the government's policy to discourage Ukrainian separatism. And even where the use of languages other than Russian was not actively discouraged, the languages were treated with official neglect: they were not admissible for official purposes, and any encouragement given to their use was the work of private individuals. Several private individuals were interested in these languages, and devised written forms for some of them (e.g. Chuvash, Abkhaz), but these were essentially private efforts with, usually, very limited effect; often, they were linked to missionary activity, such as that of the Translation Commission of the Orthodox Missionary Society in Kazan', which translated parts of the Bible into several languages of non-Orthodox peoples. For some of the languages with a literary tradition, such as Armenian, Georgian, the Turkic languages of Central Asia, and Tadzhik (Persian), the traditional written languages continued in use, but by only a minute fraction of the population, usually in connection with religious education.

The treatment of the non-Russian peoples of the Russian Empire was similar to that of their languages, or in a few cases even worse, as with the Jews. Ukrainians were encouraged to think of themselves as a subdivision of the Russians, whence their name 'Little Russians' during the Tsarist period, as opposed to the 'Great Russians' (Russians proper). If any member of one of the non-Russian ethnic groups wanted to advance himself, then effectively the only way to do this was by assimilating to the Russian population. Though there are examples of this having been accomplished successfully – for instance, many Muslim nobles converted to Orthodoxy after the fall of Kazan' and took on important positions in the Tsarist administration – there was no explicit plan envisaged or executed to enable non-Russians to learn Russian and assimilate, and of course no possibility was provided for them to develop within their own culture, in their own language. To the extent that there was any choice, it was between assimilating to the Russian population –

and this could only be done by one's own efforts, since there was no widespread educational programme of instruction in Russian for non-Russians, etc. – or remaining within one's own ethnic community and stagnating for lack of opportunity.

1.3.2 *Soviet policy*

The policy of the Bolshevik party and of the Soviet government was radically different from this, both in conception and in execution. Part of the general new social policy was a commitment to the equality of all peoples and of all languages, and the drafting of guidelines to implement this principle was one of the tasks occupying much of the time of Lenin and his associates before and after the October Revolution. In terms of ethnic relations, the new programme declared the equality of all the peoples of the new state, and one of the most obvious aspects of this declaration was its linguistic side. First, the new state was to have no official language, and this still remains true *de jure* for the U.S.S.R. and its constituent parts: Russian is not *the* or one of the official languages, nor are any of the languages of Union Republics or lower levels of autonomy. Secondly, everyone was to have the right to use his own language, both in private and for public matters, such as addressing meetings, correspondence with officials, giving testimony in courts. Thirdly, everyone was to have the right to education and availability of cultural materials in his own language. As often with an idealistic policy statement of this kind, there were immense practical difficulties in implementing this goal, leading in certain instances to partial abandonment of the goal, and it is with the successes and partial failures of this policy that the following discussion will be concerned.

One of the main practical problems facing the new regime was the need to unify the country, so that all of its peoples would feel part of the new development, contributing to it and drawing benefit from it. Obviously, one requirement dictated by this, especially in view of the extreme centralisation of the Soviet state, is the existence of a common language to facilitate communication among members of different ethnic groups, and the obvious choice for this language was Russian, for reasons we shall discuss in more detail in section 1.4.

Since few of the languages of the new Soviet state had written forms, or at least written forms controlled by any but a tiny minority of those speaking the language, one of the first priorities was the creation of a writing system and the development of literacy programmes. In some instances, even further preparatory work was required, because some of the languages, in particular languages of the Far North, had not even been analysed linguistically to an extent sufficient to make possible the creation of a serviceable orthography. For those languages which already had writing systems, attempts were made, and in most instances carried through, to make the writing system easier to learn, and thus more accessible to the mass of the population. Even Russian orthography was simplified slightly in 1918, by the removal from the alphabet of certain orthographic distinctions that had no phonetic counterpart (Comrie and Stone 1978: 200–20). A few of the orthographies of the country, such as Armenian and Georgian, and also some of those created during the nineteenth century (e.g. Chuvash), were phonemic or close to phonemic, and thus required no modification. The writing systems that caused most problems were those of the Islamic peoples of the U.S.S.R., which used the Arabic alphabet, in general poorly adapted to indicate the range of phonemic differences that are found in such languages as Turkic languages (with a large number of vowel quality distinctions), or North-East Caucasian languages (with many consonant and vowel distinctions that are not found in Arabic). The first attempt here was to devise a simplified form of the Arabic script. However, this idea was soon abandoned, and it was decided to introduce writing systems based on the Latin alphabet for all languages of the U.S.S.R. other than those with other traditional alphabetical writing systems (i.e., effectively, the East Slavonic languages, Armenian, Georgian, and a very few others).

The choice of the Latin alphabet might, at first sight, seem rather surprising, given that the majority of the population, the Russians, as well as large minorities such as the Ukrainians and Belorussians, use the Cyrillic alphabet. One of the main reasons given for the choice of the Latin alphabet at this period was the need to avoid the impression, especially among traditionally Islamic peoples, that the replacement of their traditional script, with its religious connotations, was part of a policy of linguistic, cultural, and religious Russification. The Latin alphabet was thus a compromise neutral between the conflicts of the Arabic and Cyrillic scripts. At this time, there was also some talk of converting Russian to the Latin alphabet, so this can also be seen as part of a plan to generalise the Latin alphabet for all languages of the U.S.S.R., although no plan to replace Cyrillic by Latin for Russian has ever in fact made any headway.

During the early post-Revolutionary years, writing systems were devised, either anew or by modification and Latinisation of existing scripts, for over half of the languages of the U.S.S.R., including all of those with substantial numbers of speakers. Written forms were also created for several languages with very small numbers of speakers, such as the Finno-Ugric languages Karelian, Veps and Lapp. However, as will be indicated below, many of the writing systems devised for very small population groups had only a very short life, and in at least one case, Itelmen, were apparently never put into practical use. Many languages with small numbers of speakers, however, received writing systems during the 1920s and early 1930s and have retained their writing systems, in modified form, to the present day, for instance

Nanay, Nivkh, Koryak, and Chukchi in the Far East, and Khanty and Mansi in western Siberia. The development and implementation of these writing systems, even where flaws can be detected in the details of individual writing systems, must be seen as one of the most impressive achievements of Soviet language policy, given that this policy was not dictated by short-term economic or political gain. Only in very recent years have other countries with similar multilingual problems started attempting to implement similar policies.

One of the problems facing the development of writing systems in many parts of the U.S.S.R. was the fact that many of the languages are so varied dialectally; indeed, as was noted in section 1.1, it is often difficult to draw the dividing line between different dialects of the same language and different languages. In general, this dividing line is drawn in the U.S.S.R., often by criteria of mutual intelligibility, but also taking into account social and political factors. Once the division into distinct languages is effected, the problem remains of deciding on the particular dialect that is to serve as the basis for the standard language, in the first instance for the written language. In a very few cases, this may already be decided in that one dialect has already achieved recognition as the dialect par excellence for communication among speakers of different dialects (e.g. the Khunzakh dialect of Avar) but for most of the languages of the U.S.S.R. that required new writing systems this was not the case, so that this particular sociological criterion could not be used. In the absence of this criterion, the decision is to some extent arbitrary, and the kinds of criterion used were of the following types.

First, it is preferable to choose a dialect spoken by a large number of people rather than one spoken by only a few: thus the Ossete written language is based on the Iron dialect rather than on the Digor dialect, which latter is spoken by only a minority of Ossete. Secondly, the dialect should be one that is maximally comprehensible to speakers of other dialects, which usually means selecting a dialect from the centre of a language area rather than from the periphery. This may, however, mean that the new written language is unsuitable for use by speakers of some peripheral dialects, if the level of mutual intelligibility is low: this was found, for instance, with the Dolgan dialect of Yakut (assuming that Dolgan is a dialect, rather than a separate language), which is so different from the main body of Yakut dialects that standard Yakut is understood only with difficulty by the Dolgan. In some instances the problem of dialect base for the standard language could not be solved because of dialect disparity, and several written languages were developed for different dialects: an extreme case of this is Khanty, where up to five different dialects have been used in publication; probably the only reason for considering Khanty a single language is the sense of ethnic unity among its speakers. Finally, in certain instances the standard was chosen on the basis that one dialect, to be the standard, is more easily acquired by speakers of another than vice versa. This last criterion is why standard Abkhaz is based on the Abzhuy dialect, which has a somewhat poorer consonantal system than the Bzyp dialect, which was used to a limited extent before the Revolution: it is easier for Bzyp speakers to learn not to make certain phonemic consonantal contrasts than for Abzhuy speakers to acquire them.

When a language has been given a written standard and is used in publication, that variety of the language is called, in the U.S.S.R., the literary language, and the language as a whole is said to have attained the status of a literary language. The former use is close to the more usual western term 'standard language', the latter to 'written language'. The term 'literary language' (Russian: *literaturnyj jazyk*) does not imply any restriction to artistic literature (belles lettres), nor imply any comment on the literary value of works composed in the literary language.

These criteria for establishing the dialect base of the literary language are not watertight, and in certain instances can conflict: partly as a result of this there have been instances where the dialect base of a language has been shifted during its brief history as a written language of the U.S.S.R. Perhaps the clearest case of this is in the development of written Uzbek. The first post-Revolutionary standard was based on the dialect of Turkestan, in the north of the Uzbek speaking area (the town is actually administratively in Kazakhstan); unlike many other dialects of Uzbek, in particular that of the capital Tashkent, this dialect has undergone relatively little Iranian influence. Subsequently, however, it was decided to shift the base of the written language to that of Tashkent, as the main population centre of Uzbekistan, i.e. by applying the criterion of number of speakers of each dialect. Current standard Uzbek is thus based largely (though with some modifications) on the dialect of Tashkent, and differs considerably from the earlier standard. Of the many other languages which have undergone similar shifts, we may mention Belorussian, which underwent a number of changes in the reform of 1957. While the reasons for these changes are often to serve better a greater number of speakers of the language in question, they inevitably hinder the development of written languages and can even lead, especially in conjunction with changes in alphabet (see section 1.4), to generation gaps, where older and younger people are unable to write to one another in their own language.

For some languages spoken by small population groups, written languages were not created, so that speakers of these languages have been dependent, for their education and other reading, on some other language. In most instances, this phenomenon simply continues a traditional situation where speakers of one of the smaller languages used a language with more speakers as their second language, for all communication outside their own narrow circle. For example, many of the smaller Caucasian peoples use one of the larger languages – in many instances, Avar

– as their lingua franca and as their first medium of literacy. In the Pamir region of Tadzhikistan, Tadzhik plays a similar role. In these cases, it is probable that the failure to create a written language actually responded to the desire of the speakers of the language in question: they were accustomed to using a different language for all but their most private and local transactions, and felt it natural that this other language should play the major role in their new awareness of the world of literacy.

Especially from the 1930s onward, however, there was a certain amount of retrenchment in the development and maintenance of literacy programmes in various languages, with the discontinuation of publication in certain languages having a small number of speakers, or restriction of the range of social functions exercised by certain languages. Four examples of this are the discontinuation of the Finno-Ugric languages Ingrian, Karelian, Veps, and Lapp as written languages within the U.S.S.R. (Lapp is used as a written language in Finland, Norway, and Sweden, though the extent of dialect differences is sufficient to make Soviet materials unusable in these countries and vice versa). Written Veps existed from 1932 to 1936/7. At this time there were around 34–35,000 Veps. Their number since then has declined dramatically, mainly as a result of assimilation to the surrounding Russian population: in 1959 they numbered 16,374, in 1970 only 8,281, of whom only 34.3% spoke Veps as their native language. Schooling in Veps was introduced in 1932, along with the printing of the first Veps book, but was discontinued at the beginning of 1938 (Mullonen 1967). Lapps in the U.S.S.R. number 1,884, with a language retention rate in 1970 of 56.2%. The first Soviet Lapp primer was published in 1933; schooling in Lapp was discontinued in 1937 (Kert 1967). Ingrian also existed as a written language from 1933 to 1937, during which time some twenty-five different titles were published in Ingrian (Selickaja 1969); in 1970, only 208 of the 781 ethnic Ingrians declared Ingrian as their native language.

In all these instances, and in similar instances in other parts of the U.S.S.R. the reasons given for the cessation of written languages are that the written languages were not viable because of the small number of speakers and because the people in question were for the most part bilingual in one of the larger languages of the U.S.S.R. and preferred to use this as their written language. As always with official Soviet statements about the desires of population groups, it is impossible to test the reliability of these claims, but in many instances they seem not unreasonable.

Whatever the actual desires of smaller ethnic groups and speakers of smaller languages, it is clear that official Soviet policy is to encourage their consolidation with larger groups, so that in the near future the U.S.S.R. will contain fewer, but larger, ethnic groups and operate with fewer languages, especially written languages. This is stated explicitly, for instance, by Isaev (1977: 200–1), an author who mirrors very closely official thinking on language policy: 'The mother tongues of the small ethnic groups and communities continue to function as a means of communication in everyday life. In cases of this type bilingualism should be viewed as a transitional stage to monolingualism which will be reached by the small ethnic groups when their assimilation into the corresponding nations is complete.'

In addition to phasing out languages with a small number of speakers, there was one period in Soviet history when certain written languages were forcibly discouraged: as discussed on p. 30, at the beginning of the Second World War, certain ethnic groups were accused of collaboration with the enemy, and in addition to being deported they had their written languages banned. Subsequently, the written languages were reinstated, with the apparently continued exception of Crimean Tatar.

We may now turn to the social functions of various languages within the U.S.S.R., in particular contrasting their present status with that outlined above for Tsarist times. At one end of the scale, we have languages that are spoken by very small population groups, that have no written form, and are normally spoken by people who are bilingual in one of the larger languages, such as Aleut and Khinalug. Secondly, there are languages that have a written form and are used to a very limited extent in publication, but are not used as media of education. In many instances, this must be viewed as a transitional stage in the phasing out of a written language, since clearly a written language will soon cease to have an audience if its speakers are not taught how to read it. One such language is Yiddish in the U.S.S.R. Other examples are Koryak (Koryak was used in education into the 1950s, but then discontinued), and Kurdish. In some instances, even where a language is discontinued as a medium of education, it is still taught as a school subject to its speakers: this is the case with Kurdish in Armenia.

The third class in this functional classification is where a language is used quite extensively in publication (for instance, children's books, basic political literature, often also newspapers, short stories, even novels), and is also used as the medium of instruction in the first few grades of school, after which instruction shifts to another language (though the native language may still be taught as a school subject): an example is Chukchi. Fourthly, there are languages which are used in a wide range of publications, including some technical subjects, and are used as media of education throughout the school system (though often not in further education); into this group fall most of the languages of A.S.S.R.s, such as Abkhaz, Tatar, Komi. Fifthly, there are languages which, in addition to having the above functions, are also used as educational media in universities (often alongside Russian), and are effectively used as co-government languages with Russian in the internal administration of the corresponding administrative area: these are the languages of the fourteen Union Republics other than the R.S.F.S.R. Finally, only Russian in the U.S.S.R. has the additional function of being the lingua franca between speakers of a sizeable number of different languages, and of being used in relations with countries other than the U.S.S.R.

The basic feature of the Soviet educational system in relation to language policy is that parents have the choice, wherever educational systems in different languages are provided, of sending their children either to a school where the basic language of instruction is the native language, or to one where this language is Russian. In addition to the languages of the U.S.S.R. (except those with very small numbers of speakers), this same choice is also offered for certain other languages which are spoken by large population groups in the U.S.S.R., e.g. German (especially in Kazakhstan) and Polish (in Lithuania). As will be shown in section 1.4, in schools where Russian is not the medium of instruction it is in effect a compulsory subject. In Russian-medium schools outside the R.S.F.S.R. and in autonomous administrative areas within the R.S.F.S.R., the local language is often available as a school subject for speakers of that language, and in some Union Republics at least the local language is available as a school subject for speakers of other languages, including Russian. It must be noted, however, that bilingualism among ethnic Russians is very low in the U.S.S.R.: on average, 21.5% of the population of the U.S.S.R. is bilingual; for non-Russians the figure is 42.6%, for Russians only 3.1%.

To sum up the discussion of this section, one can observe that the U.S.S.R. has expended considerable time and effort on the development of the languages spoken within its frontiers, on the provision and development of literacy in these languages, and on the provision of educational and other cultural facilities in a wide range of these languages. One outward sign of this is the rapid rise in the literacy rate: whereas only 28.4% of the population of the Russian Empire between the ages of 9 and 49 was able to read in 1897, this figure advanced as follows in succeeding censuses: 44.1% (1920), 56.6% (1926), 87.4% (1939), 98.5% (1959), 99.7% (1970); this figure includes numerous people who are literate in their own language and not in Russian. Practical concerns have seen a certain amount of retrenchment in this policy with respect to languages with small numbers of speakers, and the general line of current policy is probably to be seen as consolidation of the most viable written languages, certainly with no resuscitation of written languages that have been abandoned or creation of new written languages. In comparison with almost any other country, until very recent times, the language policy of the U.S.S.R. has been one of the most enlightened. Only in very recent years have other multilingual countries, such as Great Britain, the United States, or Australia, made any significant steps towards even halfhearted programmes of bilingual education comparable to those of the U.S.S.R. However, the development of some of these programmes outside the U.S.S.R. does sometimes mean that even very small communities are being given written languages and educational programmes, whereas in the U.S.S.R. practical considerations, coupled perhaps with relatively weak desire for a written language on the part of native speakers, have militated against this development.

1.3.3   *Autonomous administrative units*

As the final part of the discussion of ethnic relations among the non-Russian peoples of the U.S.S.R., before turning to the influence of Russian on their languages, brief consideration may be given to the way in which the ethnic and linguistic composition of the U.S.S.R. is mirrored in its internal administrative divisions. Although the details of the composition of the U.S.S.R. in a political sense have varied considerably, the basic principle has remained the same since the creation of the U.S.S.R. in 1922. The present system is laid down in the constitution of 1977, though in the relevant respects this differs but little from the constitution of 1936, which has governed the U.S.S.R. for most of its history.

The U.S.S.R. is in principle a federal state, consisting at present of fifteen Union Republics (Soviet Socialist Republics, abbreviated S.S.R.). The U.S.S.R. was in fact formed as a federal state in 1922, by the federation of the Russian Federation (Russian Soviet Federated Socialist Republic, abbreviated R.S.F.S.R.), the Ukraine, Belorussia, and the Transcaucasian Federation (Armenia, Azerbaydzhan, and Georgia). With the establishment of Soviet power in Central Asia, Turkmenia and Uzbekistan were added to the list of Union Republics. During the late 1920s and early 1930s certain territories were advanced in status to Union Republics to give the republics of Armenia, Azerbaydzhan, Georgia, Kazakhstan, Kirgizia, and Tadzhikistan. Finally, territorial expansion in 1940 introduced Estonia, Latvia, Lithuania, and Moldavia. As indicated above, the R.S.F.S.R. is itself in name a federal republic, although in practice its administration is not federal in structure.

The next lowest level of autonomy is provided by the Autonomous Soviet Socialist Republics (A.S.S.R.s), of which there are sixteen in the R.S.F.S.R., one in Azerbaydzhan, two in Georgia, and one in Uzbekistan. Next come the Autonomous Regions (A.O.s, Russian: *avtonomnye oblasti*) (five in the R.S.F.S.R., one each in Azerbaydzhan, Georgia, and Tadzhikistan), and finally the National Areas (N.O.s, Russian: *nacional'nye okruga*) (ten, all in the R.S.F.S.R.). In general, each such unit is named after the ethnic group for which it was created, sometimes with additional nomenclature where there is more than one unit serving the same ethnic group. The following exceptions to this principle should be noted: the Dagestan A.S.S.R. is named after its geographical area (Dagestan), in view of the multiplicity of peoples who live there, the most numerous being the Avar, Lezgi, Dargva, Kumyk, and Lak; the Nakhichevan A.S.S.R. is apparently not an ethnic unit at all, since the overwhelming majority of its population is Azerbaydzhan, but it is geographically separated from the mass of Azerbaydzhan; although the Adzhar are a distinct subgroup ethnically within the Georgian people overall, they are not now considered a separate ethnic group, but still have their own Adzhar A.S.S.R.; the Mountain-Karabakh A.O. in Azerbaydzhan has a majority of Armenian population, and is thus probably to be regarded as an Armenian ethnic group unit; the main native groups within the Mountain-Badakhshan A.O. of Tadzhikistan are the various Pamir peoples, but officially they are not considered separate in ethnic status from the Tadzhiks.

The basic criteria for the establishment of an autonomous administrative unit are that the people in question should be a substantial proportion of the population of the area, and that they should be sufficiently compact to make creation of a geographically defined autonomous unit feasible: the criteria are applied with greater stringency the higher the level of autonomy. In each of the Union Republics, the ethnic group after which the republic is named forms a majority, except in Kirgizia, where the Kirgiz are, however, the largest single ethnic group, and Kazakhstan, where the Kazakhs are actually outnumbered by the Russians: this is largely because northern Kazakhstan is an extension of the Ural industrial belt, with overwhelming Russian population. At lower levels of autonomy the percentages may be much smaller. Ethnic groups which have large populations in the U.S.S.R. in absolute terms but do not have their own Union Republic are those which are scattered across large areas, interspersed with other ethnic groups. Thus the Tatar, who rank fifth in number of population, have only an A.S.S.R.

In certain instances, the degree of autonomy may seem arbitrary, as with the Jewish A.O., which is not a traditional area of Jewish settlement and where Jews form only a small minority of the population, or the Karelo-Finnish S.S.R., where the population was overwhelmingly Russian, and which was absorbed into the R.S.F.S.R. in 1956. Over the history of the U.S.S.R. there have also been substantial changes in the degree of autonomy of certain units. Perhaps the most noticeable such change, and also one of the blackest spots in the history of ethnic relations in the U.S.S.R., was the abolition of several autonomous units at the beginning of the Second World War, when their inhabitants were accused of actual or potential collaboration with the Nazis: the units affected were the Crimea, the Volga-German A.S.S.R., the Chechen-Ingush A.S.S.R., the Kabard-Balkar A.S.S.R., and the Kalmyk A.S.S.R. The populations of these areas were transported into Siberia and Kazakhstan, with considerable loss of life. Only in 1957 were most of them allowed to return to their homes, the corresponding autonomous units reestablished, and the written languages revived. The Crimean Tatars and Volga Germans, though officially rehabilitated, have not been allowed to return.

The degree of political independence that is afforded by these various degrees of autonomy would be considered very small indeed by students of federal systems elsewhere in the world, and since each of these units has a Soviet government it is unlikely that this government would want to advocate seceding from the overall protection of the Soviet system (although the Union Republics do, in principle, have the right to secede). However, this system does provide an administrative framework for the realisation of cultural and linguistic autonomy, in that the language of an autonomous unit has greater *de facto* use in that autonomous unit. In the case of several languages of the U.S.S.R., this has meant an immense increase in the range of their functions, for instance the use of Union Republic languages throughout the educational system and at all levels of government and administration within the Union Republic. Thus the administrative division of the U.S.S.R. is an important reflection of the cultural and linguistic distinctiveness of its peoples.

1.4 The influence of Russian

In this section, two aspects of the interaction of Russian and the other languages of the U.S.S.R. will be considered: first, the influence of Russian on those languages as individual languages; secondly, the extent to which Russian is replacing these languages in some of their functions. It should also be noted that there is hardly any influence of other languages of the U.S.S.R. on Russian, except in the pronunciation of Russian by members of other ethnic groups. One has to search very hard to find even lexical items borrowed into Russian from other languages of the U.S.S.R. in recent times: the example usually cited is the loan from Georgian, *tamada*, referring to the toast-master at a banquet. Most other loans are concerned with realia specific to the area where they were borrowed, e.g. *samostijnyj* 'independent, separatist' from Ukrainian is used particularly with reference to the Ukraine, and *aryk* 'irrigation ditch', a nineteenth-century loan from one of the Turkic languages of Central Asia, refers to something specifically Central Asian (Comrie and Stone 1978: 157–8).

As we noted above, in order to carry out the practical programme of modernising the new Soviet state, especially in view of the degree of centralisation implied by the policies of the new government, it was necessary to have a working language that would be common to all the peoples of the U.S.S.R., even if this was not to be declared the *de jure* official language. This choice inevitably fell on Russian: Russian was the native language of the majority of Soviet citizens (indeed of a greater percentage then than now, given the subsequent inclusion of territories populated by non-Russians, and the low birth-rate of the Russian population relative to the Central Asian and Caucasian peoples); Russian had already assimilated much of western technology and culture, and so did not have the problem, faced by many other languages of the U.S.S.R., of first coming to terms with these phenomena;

finally, Russian had already, partly by force and partly by choice, become the lingua franca of most parts of the Russian Empire, and no other language came near to satisfying this criterion.

Thus one of the main educational aims of the Soviet government, alongside the fostering of local languages, was the development of a sound command of Russian: even though there was no explicit attempt to replace local languages by Russian, it was envisaged at the least that non-Russians should become bilingual in their local language, for local affairs, and in Russian for communication with representatives of other ethnic groups. With very few exceptions, there was and is no widespread bilingualism between languages of the U.S.S.R. other than between a local language and Russian. The implementation of this policy was the effective introduction of Russian as a compulsory subject in all schools. Official policy views this as the implementation of the wishes of the population concerned to master Russian as the key to a full life as a Soviet citizen, although it is impossible to check the validity of this claim in general or in individual cases. Despite the length of time that this policy has been in effect, it is still the case that in 1970 over half the non-Russian population of the U.S.S.R. considered itself not to be fluent in Russian, and often fluency in Russian comes not from the educational system, but rather from contact with Russians in areas where there is a large Russian population. The problem of spreading knowledge of Russian is still a major priority of the Soviet educational system.

When one turns to the influence of Russian on individual languages of the U.S.S.R., no doubt the most superficial such influence is the fact that nearly all languages of the U.S.S.R. use the Cyrillic alphabet, essentially in its Russian form, though sometimes with diacritics or special letters to indicate sounds that do not occur in Russian. The only languages not to use the Cyrillic alphabet are the languages of the Baltic republics (Latvian, Lithuanian, Estonian) with their traditional Latin-based orthographies, Armenian and Georgian with their own alphabets, and Yiddish, which continues to be written in the Hebrew alphabet. The use of the Cyrillic alphabet represents a major shift in Soviet language policy which was conceived and for the most part carried out during the 1930s. Previously, nearly all languages of the U.S.S.R. had used the Latin alphabet. However, certain practical problems had arisen with literacy projects, especially where students – including adults – were being taught literacy in both the local language and Russian: acquiring literacy was a big problem in itself, made only worse by the need to acquire two different alphabets, especially given that many letters of the two alphabets are similar in form but have different phonetic values (e.g. the Cyrillic letter c is pronounced [s], p is pronounced [r], в is pronounced [v]). In addition to this educational reason, there was probably also a more political reason: at this time, the U.S.S.R. was becoming increasingly inward-looking, with the realisation that world revolution was not imminent and that the U.S.S.R. would for a long time be virtually the sole Soviet-style state, surrounded by hostile political systems. This led to a consolidation of internal unity, and demarcation from outside forces, both of which functions were served by the Cyrillic alphabet. At the time, some linguistic arguments were also advocated, in particular that the Cyrillic alphabet has more letters than the Latin alphabet and is therefore better suited to representing languages with a large number of phonemes. However, the special Cyrillic letters used to represent either a sequence of *j* plus vowel or a vowel after a palatalised consonant are rarely needed (though often used) in other languages of the U.S.S.R., and some distinctions that can be made with the Latin alphabet are not possible with the Cyrillic alphabet except by using diacritics (e.g. *k/q*, *x/h*, *v/w*).

Many of the adaptations of the Cyrillic alphabet to other languages of the Soviet Union are essentially arbitrary, so that one often finds the same sound being represented in different ways in different languages, e.g. front rounded vowels by means of a diaeresis, by means of postposed ь, or by modification of the typographical symbols for back rounded vowels; conversely, the same symbol is often used for different purposes in different languages, as when кь represents [k̄] in Abaza but [tɬʼ] in Avar. Some of the idiosyncrasies of Russian orthography are usually taken over into the orthography of the local language, e.g. the use of the special letters я [ja], e [je], ё [jo], ю [ju] to represent sequences of *j* and a vowel; since Russian does not have the sequence [ji], there is no special Russian letter for this, and the letter sequence йи must be used. The disadvantage of this can be seen in Chukchi orthography, especially since Chukchi has alternation between *i* and *e*: the stem of the word 'language' is *jil-*, cf. nominative plural *jil-ət*; by vowel harmony, this can become *jel-*, as in the allative singular *jel-etə*; in Cyrillic these two forms come out looking quite different: йилыт and елеты. The problems of adapting Cyrillic to other languages have been felt by users of these spelling systems, and some of the languages of the U.S.S.R. have undergone intermittent spelling reforms designed to iron out some of the worst problems. Unfortunately, the effect of such frequent reforms is often to confuse people, as nonspecialists rarely keep track of changes in the spelling rules of their language. An extreme example of orthographic and alphabet changes is provided by Abkhaz, which had a Cyrillic-based orthography before the Revolution, then switched to the Latin alphabet, then to the Georgian alphabet (the Abkhaz A.S.S.R. is part of Georgia), then back again to a modified Cyrillic (with several letters that are not found in any other Cyrillic or modified Cyrillic alphabet).

The second most obvious instance of Russian influence is in vocabulary, especially technical vocabulary. At the time of the Revolution, few languages of the U.S.S.R.

were in the position of having assimilated western technology and culture and the corresponding vocabulary to the same extent as Russian, therefore part of the problem of developing these other languages was to provide them with the requisite vocabulary. There were two possible solutions to this problem: one, to create new lexical items from the language's own stock of morphemes, the other to borrow the corresponding words from some other language, i.e. from Russian. In the early post-Revolutionary years, many languages indulged extensively in creation of new words from their own resources. To this period belong such Chukchi neologisms as *kaletkoran* 'school' (literally 'house of writing') and *riŋeneŋ* 'aeroplane' (literally 'flying-thing'). As part of the internal consolidation of the U.S.S.R., however, this policy was soon discouraged, and emphasis placed on borrowing from Russian as the main source of new terms. The policy is basically that such words should be taken into the local language in their Russian orthographic form (even, in general, where this conflicts with the orthographic norms of the local language), and should be pronounced in the Russian way, or at least as close thereto as is possible for speakers of the language in question. In this way, many phonetic features of Russian find their way into other languages, such as palatalised consonants, and free stress, though for the most part they remain restricted to these loanwords. Especially for languages which had previously had minimal contact with western technology and culture, the mass of such loans was very great indeed, so that often in looking at a page of modern Chukchi, for instance, unless it deals with traditional life, the impression given to the reader is of basically Russian vocabulary with a few strange words and a number of strange inflectional affixes.

Since much of the literature in languages of the U.S.S.R. is translated from Russian, there has also been Russian influence on the syntax of many languages, especially those whose basic syntactic structure differs most from Russian. Here we may mention in particular those languages where the basic means of expressing subordination is not by means of subordinating conjunctions, but rather by means of special verbal forms, usually verbal adverbs (gerunds), verbal adjectives (participles) or case-forms of verbal nouns (nominalisations). As will be seen in later chapters, this is particularly characteristic of Altaic languages, North Caucasian languages, and the more easterly Uralic languages. Under Russian influence, subordinating constructions have come to play a much more important role in such languages. In most instances it is not a case of actually borrowing a conjunction from Russian in its Russian form, but rather of calquing a conjunction in the language in question on the basis of the morpheme structure of the Russian conjunction, as with Adyge *sǝda p'ome* 'because'. Sometimes even the Russian form is borrowed, as with the coordinating conjunction *a* 'and, but', in Tuva:

(1)   *oon*   *čogum ad*   *-i*   *sendi, a*   *šola*   *-zi* *odaar*
         he-GEN real   name 3SG Sendi but nickname 3SG Odaar
         'his real name is Sendi, and his nickname is Odaar'

(This example is cited by Monguš and Sat (1969: 200).)

Finally, we may turn to the extent to which various languages of the U.S.S.R. are receding in the face of Russian. At the one extreme, we have already noted that there are certain areas of the U.S.S.R. where the assimilation of non-Russians to the Russian ethnic group has been going on for a considerable period, the present situation being just the last phase of that process: this is true with many of the smaller Finno-Ugric peoples, such as the Ingrians, Veps, and Vot, though also with some larger groups, such as the Mordva. There are also instances of smaller groups being assimilated by larger groups other than Russian, e.g. the Liv by the Latvians, the Pamir peoples by the Tadzhik. At the other extreme, there are languages which seem to be fully viable, which are spoken by nearly all members of the corresponding ethnic group, and whose speakers may even have relatively low proficiency in Russian: this is the case, for instance, with the languages of the Baltic republics, the major languages of Central Asia, and also many of the Caucasian languages. In between, various different stages of assimilation are found. Many of the languages of Siberia are in a process of rapid assimilation to Russian. These languages always had small numbers of speakers, since the climate together with their traditional economy was incapable of supporting larger numbers. However, technological developments enabled outsiders, in particular Russians, to colonise the area in large numbers, so that these people soon found themselves a small minority in what had previously been their exclusive territory. As soon as this situation arises, in the context of the U.S.S.R. (for reasons to be discussed below) a fairly rapid switch-over to Russian seems inevitable.

First, one can see linguistic reasons for this change-over. As we mentioned above, most of the languages of the U.S.S.R. had no technological vocabulary of their own referring to elements of western technology or culture, but borrowed such words from Russian. Since this accounts for a large part of the vocabulary used by anyone in an urban environment, and, given the increasing extent of urbanisation in the U.S.S.R., even if the speaker of such a language wants to maintain his native language he will find it increasingly permeated by Russian vocabulary items, and perhaps even Russian syntactic constructions, so that there comes a time when it is as easy to switch over completely to Russian as to maintain a hybrid language.

The main reasons for the change to Russian, however, are social. Wherever people of different ethnic backgrounds meet together in the U.S.S.R., in particular if this is in order to work together (including military service, compulsory for all male citizens), then it is almost certain that the only language they will have in common will be Russian. This is true even if none of the members of the group is a native speaker of Russian. So, in any mixed group of this kind, Russian inevitably becomes the lingua franca. Children growing up in this group will hear Russian at least as much as they hear the language of their parents. Indeed if, as is increasingly the case, their parents have different native languages, then Russian will probably be the only language that the child hears, and certainly the only language that he will grow up speaking. Even for children from a more homogeneous background, there are practical pressures on parents to send their children to Russian-medium schools. Unless someone wants to be restricted to working in his local area, knowledge of Russian is essential, especially if that person's career is to be at all technically oriented: in very few areas of the U.S.S.R., for instance the Baltic republics, would it be feasible to engage in a technical career without a good command of Russian. Given the advantages that accrue to someone with a good knowledge of Russian, parents anxious about their children's future are often persuaded to overcome feelings of local loyalty and give their children an education with emphasis on sound acquisition of Russian, i.e. in a Russian-medium school.

Russian is also making inroads into existing patterns of bilingualism involving other languages. Interesting data are provided here by the 1970 census statistics for Georgian. Georgia has a large Armenian minority, settled in the confines of Georgia long before the incorporation into the Russian Empire. Most of these Armenians have Armenian as their native language, but of the others rather more have Russian (36,410) than Georgian (32,246). The number of Armenians in Georgia declaring Russian as their second language is more than three times that declaring Georgian (160,435 to 51,477). The statistical differences are even more marked for the Abkhaz minority in Georgia: of those who are not native speakers of Abkhaz, twice as many are Russian-speakers as are Georgian-speakers (1,492 to 749); only 1,584 declare themselves to have Georgian as a second language, compared to 47,090 for Russian. Even allowing for some misreporting, and the exclusion of statistics on trilingualism, it is clear that within an area like Georgia bilingualism involving Russian is taking over from bilingualism involving Georgian.

The official view of the role of Russian within the U.S.S.R. is reflected in the following quotation from Isaev (1977: 300–1):

> Because of the specific historical circumstances within which the Soviet Union is developing many other nations and ethnic groups of the U.S.S.R. have also long since acquired a knowledge of Russian. Because it is the language of the Union's most developed nation, which guided the country through its revolutionary transformations and has

won itself the love and respect of all other peoples, the Russian language is naturally being transformed into the language of communication and cooperation of all the peoples of the socialist state. This has been produced by growing economic and production ties among nations, by a rapid process of internationalisation of the population, and a replacement of previous psychological barriers by bonds of brotherly friendship, mutual trust, and mutual help.

The U.S.S.R. has no official policy of replacement of the non-Russian languages by Russian. To the extent that there is any long-term ethnic policy, this is phrased in terms of the accepted Marxist principle that at some time in the future all ethnic groups will fuse into one, but this is a very long-term goal, and certainly not the aim of any current policies. Linguistically, the fact that Russian influences other languages of the U.S.S.R., but is not influenced by them, would seem to preclude the possibility of an amalgam language distinct from Russian finally developing. For the foreseeable future, current policies and trends will no doubt continue. The basis of this policy is fostering of local languages to the extent that this is consonant with the wishes of speakers of those languages (however these wishes are assessed), together with fostering of bilingualism in Russian. Current trends suggest that all but the largest, most consolidated speech-communities will probably eventually go over to Russian (or one of the other large speech-communities): with some small speech-communities this process is almost complete, but in many other instances it seems that we are in the middle of a very long process of gradual linguistic assimilation. It is unlikely that this trend will be reversed by discouraging the transference of linguistic allegiance from local languages to Russian where this is already taking place as a natural process.

FURTHER READING

The only general work in English on the languages of the U.S.S.R., incorporating information on the structure, genetic affiliation, and historical–geographical background of these languages, is Matthews (1951); unfortunately, the statistics in this book are very out of date (from censuses in the 1920s and 1930s), in addition to a number of inaccuracies elsewhere. A good introduction in French is Creissels (1977), which includes grammatical sketches of some representative languages from a typological perspective. Among works dealing more exclusively with the sociolinguistic perspective, one may cite Lewis (1972), which is concerned primarily with educational aspects of bilingualism, and Isaev (1977), which essentially echoes the official assessment of language-planning policies in the U.S.S.R. A critical bibliography covering most languages of the U.S.S.R. is provided by *CTL* 1 (1968).

Most literature on languages of the U.S.S.R., either as a whole or on individual languages, is available only in Russian. The most comprehensive work is *JaNSSSR* (1966–68), which includes a grammatical sketch of each of the languages of the U.S.S.R.; some parts of these sketches are, necessarily, rather brief, especially in their treatment of syntax. This detailed information on the structure of the languages of the U.S.S.R. can be supplemented by two popular-scientific books dealing more with sociolinguistic aspects: Isaev (1970; 1978); some of the material from these books is incorporated into Isaev (1977).

More detailed accounts of the sociolinguistic interaction of languages in the U.S.S.R. are provided by the series *ZRLJa* (1969–76), which deals with linguistic changes in the various languages treated during the Soviet period, including those that result from Russian influence; and *VVJaNSSSR* (1969), a collection of short articles on individual topics within this general area.

General accounts of languages and language families of the U.S.S.R. can also be obtained from some encyclopedias, such as *EBM* (1974–) and *BSÈ*, especially the second (1950–58) and third (1970–) editions of the latter; the third edition of *BSÈ* is also appearing in an English-language edition.

Two recent collections of articles on the languages of the U.S.S.R. in English are *LLNRPSU* (1977) and *SLUSSR* (1980). See also *PCNSLUSSR* (1979).

2

Altaic languages

The term 'Altaic' is used in a number of different senses, differing in the precise range of languages that are claimed to be included in this genetic family. At its narrowest (Micro-Altaic), Altaic includes three branches: Turkic, Mongolian, and Tungusic (Manchu-Tungusic); each of these three branches is a well-defined genetic unity, although, as will be shown below, the genetic relations among the three groups are not so clear as is often made out. Many linguists would argue for the inclusion of at least Korean as genetically related to Altaic in the narrower sense, thus giving rise to a wider sense of Altaic, which one might call Macro-Altaic. Since claims have also been made about the genetic relation of Japanese to Korean, one could include Japanese (together with the genetically clearly closely related Ryukyuan) as yet another branch of Macro-Altaic, thus giving five branches in all. In addition, it has been suggested that the Uralic languages are genetically related to Micro-Altaic (the Uralo-Altaic hypothesis), which would include yet another branch within Macro-Altaic. Since Japanese and Korean are not languages of the U.S.S.R. – although there are 357,507 Koreans in the U.S.S.R., mainly in Central Asia, where most of them arrived as refugees from the Japanese occupation of Korea – we need not consider them further, especially as we shall cast some doubt even on the validity of Micro-Altaic as an established genetic unit.

It is clear that there are many similarities among the three groups within Micro-Altaic. Many of these, however, are typological, for instance the agglutinative morphological structure using exclusively suffixation, the strict verb-final word order, with adjuncts always preceding their head, the use of numerous nonfinite verb constructions, and such similarities could be found in many other languages of the world, e.g. Quechua in South America, the Dravidian languages in southern India. Many other common features are the result of recent contact, often limited to only certain languages within each of the groups: for instance, a long period of recent contact between the Turkic language Yakut and the Tungusic language Evenki has resulted in considerable areal diffusion between these two languages. The question that arises is the following: once one excludes those features that can reasonably be attributed to general typological principles or to areal diffusion, is there a sufficient body of remaining reliable correspondence to justify the recognition of (Micro-)Altaic as a single genetic family?

One of the problems that has always been faced by proponents of the Altaic hypothesis is that there are relatively few features that are common to all three of Turkic, Mongolian, and Tungusic, and only to these three language groups. For instance, in terms of vocabulary, and also to a certain extent morphology, there are many close parallels between Turkic and Mongolian languages, and also between Mongolian and Tungusic languages, but hardly any between Turkic and Tungusic languages. If the three groups of languages were genetically related, one would expect to find residual similarities whichever pair of language groups one took, but the fact remains that there is no direct evidence for such a link between Turkic and Tungusic. For instance, several colour terms are almost identical in Turkic and Mongolian, as can be seen from the following, using Turkish and (Khalkha) Mongolian as representative languages: Turkish *kara*, Mongolian *xar* 'black'; Turkish *gök*, Mongolian *xöx* 'blue'; Turkish *boz*, Mongolian *bor* 'grey'; however, these terms have no close correspondents in Tungusic languages. The same applies to such Turkic–Mongolian parallels as the locative in -*da* and allative in -*a*. This situation is actually more consistent with the diffusion hypothesis than with the genetic unity hypothesis; it is known that there have been close historical ties between Turkic and Mongolian peoples, and between Mongolian and Tungusic peoples, but not between Turkic and Tungusic peoples (except for very recent contact, such as that between the Yakut and the Evenki). This would account for the existence of Turkic–Mongolian and Mongolian–Tungusic parallels and the absence of Turkic–Tungusic parallels, while the genetic relation hypothesis cannot explain the Turkic–Mongolian parallels and Mongolian–Tungusic parallels without at the same time positing a genetic relation between Turkic and Tungusic.

There are, however, some similarities between all three groups that would make up Micro-Altaic. For instance, the forms of the singular personal pronouns are very similar, as can be seen from Table 2.1. However, if one takes these similarities to be evidence of genetic relatedness, they do not constitute evidence specifically for Altaic as a genetic unit, since, as can be seen from the various non-Altaic forms given in the same table, similar forms are found in a variety of other languages in northern Eurasia. Given that the first person singular pronoun appears with either *b* or *m* in different Turkic languages, and that the reconstructed Proto-Mongolian form for the second person singular pronoun has initial **t*, the basic characterisation of the putative Proto-Altaic forms would have to be that the first person pronoun has a characteristic bilabial consonant, while the second person pronoun has a characteristic dental-alveolar consonant. Precisely this same distribution is found in

Table 2.1. *Singular personal pronouns in Altaic, Uralic, Indo-European and*
Chukotko-Kamchatkan

	Turkish	Azerbaydzhan	Mongolian	Manchu	Latin	Komi	Chukchi
'I'	ben	män	bi	bi	me	me	yəm
'you'	sen	sän	či (‹*ti)	si	te	te	yet

Indo-European, cf. the Latin forms given in Table 2.1, in Uralic, and in the
Chukotko-Kamchatkan languages; in the Chukchi forms, *yə* can be abstracted to
give the characteristic consonants *m* and *t*, which reappear in the plural pronouns
muri 'we' and *turi* 'you'. Thus if the similarities among all three groups of languages
within 'Altaic' are evidence of anything, they are evidence of a genetic family much
larger than Micro-Altaic (or, for that matter, Macro-Altaic), and so do not argue for
any particularly close relation between Turkic, Mongolian, and Tungusic languages,
other than what has come about by contact.

The fact that there are any morphological similarities at all among Altaic
languages, and more specifically between Turkic and Mongolian languages, might at
first seem strong evidence for their genetic relatedness, given that morphology is
usually much less amenable to borrowing than vocabulary. However, the
agglutinative nature of morphology in all three groups of languages in question
means that the morphology is readily segmentable, and morphological affixes which
are readily segmentable are much more easily borrowed than more complex
morphological patterns: thus the Turkish plural suffix *-lar* was readily borrowed into
Albanian, a genetically completely unrelated language of the Indo-European family.
The recent discussion of Turkic morphology by Ščerbak (1977: 9–14) throws
interesting light on the possible historical background to morphological similarities
between Turkic and Mongolian by comparing these similarities to those that are
found in areas of intense contact between Uzbek and Tadzhik. Uzbek and Tadzhik
are genetically unrelated, being Turkic and Iranian (Indo-European) respectively,
and are quite different from one another in basic structure, vocabulary, and
morphological affixes. Nonetheless, several Uzbek suffixes have been borrowed into
Northern Tadzhik dialects, giving rise to a situation reminiscent of the similarities
noted between Turkic and Mongolian, but without any possible genetic affiliation to
explain the similarity. Significantly, one of the suffixes cited often as evidence of
Turkic–Mongolian genetic relatedness, the agentive suffix *-či*, e.g. Uzbek *etik-či*
'shoemaker' (cf. *etik* 'boot'), Kalmyk *xöö-če* 'shepherd' (cf. *xö-n* 'sheep'), has been
borrowed from Uzbek into Tadzhik, where it has spread into all dialects.

Since the main emphasis of this presentation is on the synchronic state of the
languages in question, it will not be necessary to go into further details of the

2. Altaic languages

controversies concerning relations among the various groups within 'Altaic', whether in its broader or narrower sense. In sections 2.2–2.4 below dealing with structural features of Turkic, Mongolian, and Tungusic languages, the arrangement is by topic, and for each topic all three language-groups are taken together. This should not be taken as implying a belief in their close genetic relation, but follows rather from the close typological similarities among the three language groups, which make it feasible to treat their structural properties in this way.

2.1 The individual languages

2.1.1 *Turkic languages*

The majority of the Turkic languages are languages of the U.S.S.R., indeed most Turkic languages have all or most of their speakers within the U.S.S.R., where Turkic-speaking ethnic groups compose five of the fifteen Union Republics, as well as several A.S.S.R.s and A.O.s. The major exception is of course Turkish, spoken by over 24 million people, mainly in Turkey, though also in Cyprus, Bulgaria, and adjacent countries. (Note that 'Turkish' (Russian *tureckij*) refers to this specific language, sometimes called more explicitly Osmanli Turkish, while 'Turkic' (Russian *tjurkskij*) refers to the whole family.) Other languages which are spoken outside the U.S.S.R. are Balkan Gagauz (Balkan Turkic) (Balkan countries, excluding Turkey), Khaladzh (Iran), Khoton (Mongolia), Yellow Uygur (China, some 4,000 speakers), and Salar (China, some 30,000 speakers); although Uygur is spoken in the U.S.S.R. most of its speakers are in China. Incidentally, the term Yellow Uygur (Sari Uygur) can be misleading, since it is the ethnonym of a people in China who are divided linguistically into four subgroups: those (mentioned above) who speak a Turkic language, those who speak a Mongolian language (also called Yellow Uygur), those who speak Chinese, and those who speak Tibetan. Moreover, several of the Turkic languages of the U.S.S.R. also have a sizable number of speakers in adjacent countries, especially Iran and Afghanistan.

The internal classification of Turkic, and the decision as to where to draw language boundaries as distinct from dialect boundaries, is extremely complex, for reasons discussed in greater detail below. The various Turkic languages are in general very close to each other, forming a dialect complex where speech forms are very often mutually intelligible at considerable distances, with intelligibility decreasing the greater the distance. Only two Turkic languages fall outside this general dialect complex: Chuvash, clearly the most divergent of the Turkic languages, and Yakut (including Dolgan, which is sometimes considered a separate language), which has been separated for some time from the main body of Turkic and has undergone considerable Tungusic influence. A further complication is that the population within the area covered by speakers of Turkic languages has always been extremely mobile, especially as many of the main paths of invading armies in Eurasia (Huns, Mongols, Tatars) have passed through this territory: even where these armies were nominally led by non-Turkic peoples, as with the Mongols, their composition was largely Turkic. One brief example of a recent move will suffice to give some indication of the complications this mobility can introduce into genetic classification of languages. Trukhmen is historically a dialect of Turkmen, and is indeed often still considered so. However, the Trukhmen migrated from Turkmenia to the northern Caucasus (around Stavropol'), where they came into contact with Nogay, another Turkic language from a different subgroup of Turkic. As a result of this contact, Trukhmen has lost many of the characteristics of Turkmen (e.g. systematic retention of phonemic vowel length, pronunciation of *s and *z as [θ] and [ð]) and gained some of the features of Nogay (e.g. the formation of the present tense as in *baradur/baradir*, where Turkmen has *barar*). Such dialect mixture is responsible for many of the problems to be noted below with detailed classifications of Turkic languages.

Another result of population mobility among the Turkic peoples, and the resulting break-up and regrouping of speech-communities, is that one often finds relatively newly formed speech-communities, in the sense of converging groups of dialects, where the individual dialects belong to different groups within Turkic according to the usual classificatory criteria. Thus Uzbek belongs basically to group IV in the classification given below, but some of its dialects belong more closely to group III (the so-called Kipchak dialects of Uzbek). Crimean Tatar consists of two main dialects, northern and southern: the northern dialects are closer to group IIIa, while the southern dialects are closer to group II. Yellow Uygur and Salar combine features of groups IV and V, as does Khoton. Although all dialects of Altay belong to group V, the dialect diversity, especially of Northern Altay dialects relative to the main body of Southern dialects, is so great that different dialects of Altay would belong to different subgroups of V, as noted below.

An added problem is presented by the nomenclature of Turkic peoples, since often an ethnonym is transferred from one people to another, from speakers of one branch of Turkic to another, or survives as an ethnonym among Turkic peoples whose languages clearly belong to different groups. This phenomenon is, of course, not unknown elsewhere, e.g. in Slavonic, where we have the South Slavonic Slovenes, the West Slavonic Slovaks and Slovincians, and in tribal times the East Slavonic tribe of the Slověne, all using ethnonyms derived from the same stem as Slavonic, while the South Slavonic Serbs and the West Slavonic Sorbs share another common ethnonym, without this implying any particularly close ethnic or linguistic relation within Slavonic. The most notorious such term within Turkic is Tatar, which was once used as a very general term for nearly all Turkic peoples other than those clearly recognizable as Ottoman Turks. In recent times, however, with the development of individual names for various Turkic subgroups, the term Tatar has been gradually restricted in usage, so that now Tatar, without any accompanying adjective, is restricted to what was formerly called Volga Tatar, i.e. the ethnic group with its traditional centre at Kazan'. In addition, some other ethnic groups, not having been given distinct ethnonyms of their own, retain the term Tatar together with some distinctive attribute, e.g. Crimean Tatar, Chulym (Melet) Tatar. The (Volga) Tatar, Crimean Tatar, and Chulym Tatar, despite the common name Tatar, are not particularly closely related to one another ethnically or linguistically within Turkic. In certain instances, it is not clear whether a people using the name Tatar should be considered a subgroup of Tatar speaking a dialect of Tatar, or as a distinct people with a distinct language; thus Baskakov (1969) considers Baraba Tatar a dialect of Tatar, while *JaNSSSR* II (1966) treats it as a separate language.

Another ethnonym which has undergone similar transformations is Uygur, since languages called Uygur have at different periods belonged to groups IV and V of the classification given below – even though in Baskakov's classification the division between these two groups is the main bifurcation within the Turkic family tree – with modern Uygur being in group IV, and Yellow Uygur and Salar on the borderline between groups IV and V (probably group V with considerable more recent influence from group IV); as already noted, the ethnonym Yellow Uygur is retained by population groups who do not now even speak a Turkic language. The terminological confusion can be seen from the fact that in Baskakov's classification there are two groupings within Turkic that contain the name Uygur, namely Karluk-Uygur and Uygur-Oguz; the language Uygur belongs to neither of these. The terms Kazakh and Kirgiz have even undergone a confusing transformation in official Soviet nomenclature. The people and language who are now called Kazakh were originally called Kirgiz, while those now called Kirgiz were then called Kara-Kirgiz.

When we turn to the details of the classification, and to the various conflicting classifications that have been proposed, we see that there is a level of classification at which there is considerable agreement, even though the placement of individual languages may differ (largely because different investigators place different weight on different features in languages on the borderline between groups): this gives the grouping into five major classes, as shown in Table 2.2. The problem was felt to be so acute by the compilers of *PhTF* I (1959) that they included not one, but two genetic classifications of Turkic languages in this standard reference work. The groups that require further subgrouping in Table 2.2. are II and V. Baskakov (1969) subdivides II into three subgroups: Oguz-Seldzhuk (Turkish, Azerbaydzhan), Oguz-Bulgar (Gagauz, Balkan Gagauz), and Oguz-Turkmen (Turkmen, Trukhmen). Group V is divided into two, Kirgiz-Kipchak (Kirgiz and Altay, though not the Northern dialects of Altay which would be Uygur-Oguz) and Uygur-Oguz; the latter is then further divided into Uygur-Tuküy (Tuva, Tofa), Yakut (Yakut), and Khakas (Khakas, Shor and Chulym Tatar). Baskakov also subdivides IV into two subgroups, Karluk-Uygur and Karluk-Khorezm, but all the living Karluk languages are in the Karluk-Khorezm subgroup.

One problem in grouping these five major groups into larger groupings is the position of Chuvash, which, as we have already noted, is synchronically the most divergent of the Turkic languages. The question is whether this divergence reflects a deep-rooted genetic split within Turkic, between Chuvash and Common Turkic (as is usually supposed by non-Soviet scholars), or whether the divergence of Chuvash is the result of its geographic and cultural isolation from the main body of Turkic: this latter factor is, for instance, clearly responsible for the (somewhat less) divergent nature of Yakut. The position of Chuvash is also intimately connected with the controversy over the Altaic hypothesis: on the basis of some of the isoglosses that separate Turkic from Mongolian (whether one considers these isoglosses to apply to inherited vocabulary from Proto-Altaic or to borrowed vocabulary), Chuvash falls on the Mongolian side of the line, for instance in having *r* where other Turkic languages have *z*, e.g. Turkish *buzağı* [buzai], Chuvash *păru*, Buryat *buruu* (Classical Mongolian *birayu*) 'calf'. In the classification adopted by Baskakov, Chuvash is not given so isolated a position, and groups I–IV are all taken together as Western Hunnic, versus group V alone, which is named Eastern Hunnic. Thus the main features of these two classifications are as follows: the first classification distinguishes Chuvash from Common Turkic, which is then subdivided into the four groups II–V of Table 2.2; the second classification first separates group V from groups I–IV, these last four being coordinate members of Western Hunnic.

In addition to the living Turkic languages, which are classified in Table 2.2, there are also several attested extinct Turkish languages, which may be briefly mentioned here. Old Turkic, attested from the eighth century A.D., comprises two main traditions: Runic Turkic (Yenisey-Orkhon inscriptions from around 700 A.D.) and Old Uygur, including in particular Manichean and Buddhist texts written in the Uygur script, a derivative of Sogdian; this script subsequently gave rise to the Classical Mongolian and Manchu scripts. Old Oguz (more specifically, Oguz-Turkmen) is attested in the tenth–eleventh-century dictionary of Mahmud al-Kashgari, while Seldzhuk and Ottoman Turkish are older forms of Turkish, within Oguz-Seldzhuk. The oldest texts from group III, more specifically IIIa, are in Cuman (Polovets, the latter being the usual Russian designation), the main text being the *Codex Cumanicus*, a Latin–Persian–Cuman dictionary from the end of the thirteenth century. Group IV is represented by Uygur texts of the Karakhanid and

Table 2.2. *Genetic classification of modern Turkic languages*

I	Chuvash
II	(Southern Turkic, South-western Turkic, Oguz)
	Turkish (Osmanli)
	Azerbaydzhan (Azeri Turkic)
	Khaladzh
	Gagauz
	Balkan Gagauz (Balkan Turkic)
	Turkmen (including Trukhmen)
III	(Kipchak)
IIIa	(Ponto-Caspian, Kipchak-Cuman)
	Karaim
	Kumyk
	Karachay-Balkar
	Crimean Tatar (also assigned to II)
IIIb	(Uralian, Kipchak-Bulgar)
	Tatar
	Bashkir
IIIc	(Central Turkic, Kipchak-Nogay)
	Nogay
	Karakalpak
	Kazakh
IV	(Eastern Turkic, Karluk)
	Uzbek
	Uygur
	Khoton (has also some features of V)
V	(Northern Turkic, Eastern Hunnic)
	Tuva (Uryankhay)
	Tofa (Tofalar, Karagas)
	Yellow Uygur (Sari Uygur) (also assigned to IV)
	Salar (also assigned to IV)
	Yakut (Sakha) (including Dolgan)
	Khakas (Abakan Tatar, Yenisey Tatar) (including Kamas)
	Shor
	Chulym (Melet) Tatar
	Kirgiz
	Altay (Oyrot) (Northern dialects are very divergent)

post-Karakhanid periods, i.e. from the eleventh century – Baskakov (1969) assigns this language to a special, Karluk-Uygur, subgroup of IV – and by Chagatay (Old Uzbek), the literary language of Uzbekistan and surrounding areas into the twentieth century. The languages of many other older Turkic peoples, such as the Bulgars, and the Pechenegs, are known only from isolated words or brief inscriptions, so that virtually nothing is known of their languages.

In looking at individual Turkic languages, it is important to bear in mind some of the cultural influences that have shaped these languages, of which the main one is undoubtedly the spread of Islam: Islam is the traditional religion of the majority of speakers of Turkic languages, excluding some in the far west (the Gagauz and Chuvash are for the most part at least nominally Christian), and those east of the traditional dividing line between Islam and non-Islam in Siberia, the River Irtysh. In geographical terms, this means that all Turkic peoples from the Turks in the west to the Kazakh and Kirgiz in the east are Muslim, with only a very few exceptions, such as the Karaim, who are by religion (though not ethnically) Jews, a unique survival of the adoption of Judaism as the official religion of the Khazar empire. East of this dividing line, some of the Turkic peoples accepted Buddhism from the Mongols, who in turn accepted this religion from Tibet: this applies to the Altay, Khakas and, especially, Tuva. Other Turkic peoples of Siberia were unaffected by the main religious innovations of Eurasia, usually retaining their shamanistic beliefs.

These different religious divisions of Turkic are reflected by different foreign linguistic influences in the pre-Soviet period. The Islamic peoples underwent strong Arabic and Persian influence on their languages, especially in terms of vocabulary, but also on phonology (assimilation of sounds and sound sequences not previously found in Turkic languages) and syntax: examples of this influence will be discussed below. More widespread Persian influence is found in those Turkic languages and dialects that coexist with Iranian languages and dialects, for instance in Uzbek (widespread bilingualism with Tadzhik especially around Tashkent and the Fergana Basin) and in Iranian dialects of Azerbaydzhan. The languages of Buddhist peoples have undergone some lexical influence from Mongolian, including Tibetan, Sanskrit, and in at least one instance Greek, transmitted through Mongolian: the Tuva word *nom* 'book' derives ultimately from Greek *nomos* 'law'. As noted above, Chuvash has remained isolated from the trends affecting the main body of Turkic languages, and the close interaction of Chuvash with Uralic languages, in particular Mari, has led to considerable Uralic influence on Chuvash, and vice versa.

The most significant of these influences from the viewpoint of Turkic as a whole has been the influx of Arabic and Persian features through Islam. In Kazakh, for instance, we find such loans not only with religious terms (e.g. *namaz* 'prayer', *künä* 'sin'), but also for many other abstract terms (e.g. *yilim* 'science', *tarix* 'history'. *waqit* 'time'), words connected with learning (e.g. *kitap* 'book'), and even very ordinary words such as *xabar* 'news' (from Arabic) and *baqša* 'garden' (from Persian). In many instances, these are now perfectly ordinary lexical items in the Turkic language concerned, no more strange than Latin or French loans into English like *certain* or *very*. In the section on phonology below, we shall see how the assimilation of Arabic loans into Turkic languages has modified their phonology quite considerably in certain respects, with this modification again not being felt as abnormal by speakers of the language concerned, often irrespective of their educational level. In syntax, one of the most noticeable features has been the borrowing of Arabic coordinating conjunctions (e.g. Arabic *wa* 'and') and Persian subordinating conjunctions (e.g. Persian *ke* 'that', borrowed into many Turkic languages as *ki*), where Turkic languages would otherwise normally use either parataxis or nonfinite verbal forms, respectively.

In the period since the Revolution, there has been a tendency to reduce the amount of Arabic and Persian influence on the Turkic languages of the U.S.S.R., especially such influence as was characteristic primarily of the older written languages and had no counterpart in the corresponding spoken languages. Thus in Uzbek, the Persian subordinating conjunctions have been largely lost. New lexical items are borrowed from Russian, rather than from Arabic. It should be borne in mind that some of the written languages of the Islamic period were often more Arabic and Persian than Turkic, and largely incomprehensible to speakers of Turkic languages who had not also studied Arabic and/or Persian. A similar purge of excessive Arabisms and Persianisms was undertaken in Turkey after the revolution of 1919–1923, one of the outward signs of the change being, as in the U.S.S.R., the replacement of the Arabic script by the Latin script, in 1929.

We may now look briefly at the individual Turkic languages of the U.S.S.R., noting salient structural features of each and also commenting on its sociological status within the U.S.S.R. Some of the specific structural features will be taken up again in the sections dealing with phonology, morphology, and syntax. The order of presentation will follow that of Table 2.2.

The Chuvash form the dominant population of the Chuvash A.S.S.R. (70%), although large numbers of Chuvash also live in areas adjoining this republic (49.5% of the total number of Chuvash). 86.9% of the 1,694,351 Chuvash have Chuvash as their native language. In the Chuvash A.S.S.R., Chuvash is used throughout the education system, and is also widely used in publishing. As indicated above, Chuvash is the most divergent of the Turkic languages, having been isolated from other Turkic languages geographically and culturally for many centuries, and has also had closer contacts with Uralic languages and, more recently, Russian – the influence of Russian can be seen in the widespread adoption of the Orthodox religion, and related to this the early development of a written language, starting in the eighteenth century, though not really developing until the late nineteenth century (the work of I. Ja. Jakovlev from the 1870s) and especially after the Revolution. One noticeable item of Uralic influence is the formation of the negative imperative with the preposed particle *an* (borrowed from a Permic language, probably Udmurt), where all other Turkic languages have a negative suffix in the imperative as in other verb forms (in which Chuvash retains the Turkic suffix).

Azerbaydzhan, in addition to being the language of the Azerbaydzhan S.S.R., where 86.2% of the 4,379,937 Soviet Azerbaydzhan live, constituting 73.8% of the total population, is also widely spoken in north-western Iran (over 3 million speakers), where it is widely used as a lingua franca even among speakers of Iranian languages other than Persian. In Iran it has no official status, unlike the U.S.S.R., where it is used alongside Russian for all functions within the Azerbaydzhan S.S.R. The dialects of Azerbaydzhan spoken in Iran have been less thoroughly studied than those of the U.S.S.R., and it is conceivable that some of the putative Azerbaydzhan dialects will have to be considered separate languages, in view of the divergence from the main body of dialects, as happened with Khaladzh. Of the total Azerbaydzhan population in the U.S.S.R., 98.2% have Azerbaydzhan as their native language.

In the U.S.S.R., the Gagauz (156,606) live in Moldavia and adjacent parts of the Ukraine, with a remarkably high language-retention rate of 93.6%. In addition, around 5,000 Gagauz live in Bulgaria and Romania. One of the main structural characteristics of Gagauz (in common with some Karaim dialects) is the tendency for vowel harmony to be replaced by consonant harmony (palatalised versus nonpalatalised consonants rather than front versus back vowels). During the early twentieth century, when the main areas inhabited by the Gagauz were part of Romania, there was a certain amount of religious publication (the Gagauz are Christian), but the initiation of Gagauz as a fully-fledged written language did not come about until the late 1950s, and Gagauz is now used for a certain amount of publication and primary education in the Moldavian S.S.R.

92.9% of the 1,525,284 Soviet Turkmen live in the Turkmen S.S.R. where they constitute 65.6% of the total population. In addition to the Turkmen in the U.S.S.R., 98.9% of whom have Turkmen as their native language, there are some 800,000 Turkmen scattered about other countries of the Middle East: Iraq, Afghanistan, Iran, Turkey, Syria and Jordan.

The Karaim are being rapidly assimilated, ethnically and especially linguistically, to the surrounding Russian population: in absolute terms their number has shrunk from 5,727 in 1959 to 4,571 in 1970, of whom only 12.8% gave Karaim as their native language. There are three main dialects of Karaim: Crimean, Southern (in the south-western Ukraine), and Northern (in Lithuania, as the result of recent migration). One of the characteristics of the Northern dialect is the partial replacement of vowel harmony by consonant harmony. The traditional religion of the Karaim is Judaism (although the Karaites – the religious designation corresponding to the ethnolinguistic term Karaim – are not considered Jews by orthodox Jews), and they developed a written language using the Hebrew alphabet; their language also has a large number of religious and nonreligious terms from Hebrew, e.g. *adonaj* 'God', *sem* 'name', *guf* 'body'. At present this written language is used only for liturgical purposes.

Kumyk is one of the written languages of Dagestan, where 89.5% of the Kumyk live, forming the fourth largest ethnic group of the A.S.S.R. 98.4% of the 188,792 Kumyk have Kumyk as their native language. Kumyk is used throughout the school system (though not beyond secondary school), as well as in publishing.

Karachay-Balkar is the single language of two ethnic groups, the Karachay and the Balkar. 98.1% of the 112,741 Karachay and 97.2% of the 59,501 Balkar have Karachay-Balkar as their native language. As the two ethnic groups live separated from one another geographically, they live predominantly in different autonomous units: the Karachay together with the less numerous Cherkes (who speak a North-West Caucasian language) in the Karachay-Cherkes A.O., the Balkar together with the more numerous Kabard (also North-West Caucasian) in the Kabard-Balkar A.S.S.R. Karachay-Balkar is used in schooling and publication.

The original home of the Crimean Tatars, as their name suggests, was the Crimea, but at the start of the Second World War they were accused of complicity with the Nazi invaders and deported en masse to Uzbekistan. Since then, they have not figured in any detailed Soviet statistics, and unlike other peoples deported for similar reasons have not been permitted to return to their original homeland. A written language was in use until the deportation, but not since.

Tatar (formerly Volga Tatar) is the fifth largest language of the U.S.S.R., in terms of number of native speakers, but as the Tatar are spread across huge areas of the U.S.S.R., including not only the Tatar A.S.S.R. but also surrounding areas and well across Siberia, much of which was formerly under Tatar suzerainty, their autonomous status is only that of an A.S.S.R., within which the Tatar constitute 49.1% of the population (the largest ethnic group within the republic), but where only 25.9% of them live; a further 15.9% live in the Bashkir A.S.S.R., where they slightly outnumber the Bashkir. 89.2% of the 5,930,670 Tatar have Tatar as their native language. In view of the close genetic and cultural relations between Tatar and Bashkir, we may treat the two languages together here. Some 72% of the Bashkir live in the Bashkir A.S.S.R., but form only 23.4% of the total population, being slightly outnumbered by Tatar and heavily outnumbered by Russians. Language retention among the Bashkir (total population: 1,239,681) is low: 66.2%. Both Tatar and Bashkir are written languages, but Tatar has much wider currency, being used at all levels of education in the Tatar A.S.S.R. and also in schooling in the Bashkir A.S.S.R., as well as in publishing. Bashkir is used in publication, but at present it is used either little or not at all in the educational system, which in the Bashkir A.S.S.R. is in either Russian or Tatar, with Tatar schools being attended by many Bashkir speakers. The two languages are very close to one another, and share a unique common innovation in the raising of Proto-Turkic mid vowels (*e, *o, *$ö$) to high vowels (i, u, $ü$), and the lowering of Proto-Turkic high vowels to close-mid vowels (*i, *u, *i, *$ü$, to e, o, $ə$, $ö$).

Nogay is spoken by 89.8% of the 51,784 ethnic Nogay who live in the northern Caucasus area, about half of them in the Dagestan A.S.S.R. and half in the Stavropol' kray, where their language is used as a written language for some publication and in schooling.

Karakalpak is the native language of 96.6% of the 236,009 ethnic Karakalpak, 92.2% of whom live in the Karakalpak A.S.S.R. in Uzbekistan, where Karakalpak is used as a written language. They constitute only 31% of the total population of their A.S.S.R., but are the largest single ethnic group there, slightly outnumbering the Uzbeks.

Although the Kazakh are the name-bearing ethnic group of the Kazakh S.S.R., they are now outnumbered by the Russians and constitute only 32.6% of the total population of the republic; however, this statistic is slightly misleading, since there is a marked tendency for the Russian population to be concentrated in the northern part of the republic, which is economically an extension of the industrial belt that extends the length of the southern Urals: in some of the southern regions of the republic, the Kazakh are a substantial majority. 79.9% of the Kazakh live in the Kazakh S.S.R. and the language-retention rate for the Kazakh is very high, at 98%, i.e. of the same order as other Turkic peoples giving their name to Union Republics. In addition to the 5,298,818 Kazakh in the U.S.S.R., there are over 600,000 in China and Mongolia. Kazakh is used, alongside Russian, for all purposes within the Kazakh S.S.R.

Uzbek is the second largest Turkic language, after Turkish, and the third largest language of the U.S.S.R., in addition to having over a million speakers in Afghanistan, and some 15,000 in China. In the U.S.S.R. 98.6% of the 9,195,093 Uzbek have Uzbek as their native language. 84% of them live in Uzbekistan, where they constitute 65.5% of the population. Uzbekistan has a substantial Russian population, but this is mainly concentrated in the cities: the capital, Tashkent, for instance, has a slightly larger Russian than Uzbek population. Another large area of Uzbek settlement is Tadzhikistan, and indeed the close historical ties between the Uzbek and the Tadzhik, especially in terms of mixed marriages, means that it is often somewhat arbitrary which ethnic status a bilingual of mixed parentage chooses. Uzbek has undergone strong influence from Tadzhik, especially the Uzbek dialects of Tashkent and the Fergana Basin, on which the current standard language is (with small deviations) based. One of the main areas where this influence is felt is the tendency for the vowel system to shift from the typical 8/9-vowel quality system of most Turkic languages to a 6-vowel system, with loss of distinct front rounded and back unrounded phonemes, to give a phoneme system that is almost identical down to phonetic detail to that of Tadzhik (*i, e, a, o, ů, u*). However, although Uzbek is often described as having a 6-vowel system, this hides a somewhat more complex system, at least in the standard language, which is at best intermediate between an 8/9-vowel and a 6-vowel system, with partial retention of rounding as a phonemic distinctive feature. This will be discussed further in section 2.2 in the treatment of vowel harmony. Uzbek is used, alongside Russian, for all purposes within the Uzbek S.S.R.

Although Uygur is technically a language of the U.S.S.R., since it is not the official language of any other country, most Uygur live in China, where they number over 4 million. Of the 173,276 Uygur in the U.S.S.R., 88.5% have Uygur as their native language. They live in various parts of Central Asia, including Kazakhstan, and have their own written language used for some publication. As a result of various sound changes, the neat general Turkic vowel harmony system has been disturbed considerably in Uygur, so that Uygur, like Uzbek, is considered typologically one of those Turkic languages to be in the process of losing vowel harmony. Another characteristic of Uygur is the large volume of loans from Chinese, reflecting intense contact with Chinese speakers.

Tuva is the native language of 98% of the 139,388 ethnic Tuva, 97.1% of whom live in the Tuva A.S.S.R., where they constitute 58.6% of the total population. Some 18,000 Tuva live in Mongolia. In the inter-War years, Tuva was an independent state with a Soviet-style government. In 1944 this government negotiated with the U.S.S.R. for admission into the U.S.S.R., entering first as an A.O., advancing in 1961 to A.S.S.R. status. Prior to around 1930, Tuva was not used as a written language, and the official written language in the country was Classical Mongolian, reflecting the traditional cultural orientation of the Tuva. At present, Tuva is used in publication and schooling in the Tuva A.S.S.R. Tuva stands out among the general run of Turkic languages by virtue of the large number of Mongolian lexical loans, and also because of some unusual phonetic features: where most Turkic languages have an opposition between weak consonants which are usually voiced and strong consonants which are usually somewhat aspirated, in Tuva aspiration is the main distinctive feature keeping the two series apart, with voicing only intermittent for the unaspirated series; in addition to an opposition between long and short vowels, found in several Turkic languages, Tuva also has a distinctive series of pharyngalized vowels, as in *ạt* 'horse' versus *at* 'name'.

Tofa (also called Tofalar, actually the plural of Tofa, and Karagas) is very close to Tuva, but because of the ethnic distinctness of the Tofa it is usually considered a separate language, spoken by only 56.3% of the 620 ethnic Tofa, a dramatic drop from 89.1% in 1959, demonstrating how rapidly a small ethnic group can be assimilated linguistically, in this instance to Russian. As might be expected from the small number of speakers, the language is not written.

96.3% of the 296,244 Yakut have Yakut as their native language and 96.5% live in the Yakut A.S.S.R., where they constitute 43% of the total population, being slightly outnumbered by the Russians. In addition, Dolgan is usually considered an aberrant dialect of Yakut, and is spoken by 89.8% of the 4,877 ethnic Dolgan, living primarily in the Taymyr' (Dolgan-Nenets) N.O.; ethnically, the Dolgan are distinct from the Yakut, and probably represent a Tungusic people who have adopted the Yakut language with strong Tungusic substratum influence. Yakut is very divergent from other Turkic languages – though less so than Chuvash – as a result of long separation from the body of Turkic speakers, and influence from the neighbouring Tungusic languages (even stronger in Dolgan) and Mongolian languages. One of the marked phonetic characteristics of Yakut is the diphthongization of long mid vowels, to give *ia*, *uo*, *ie*, *üö*. Although some books came out in Yakut during the nineteenth century, as the result of missionary activity, it was only in the post-Revolutionary period that Yakut was substantially developed as a literary language, being used also in the school system. Dolgan has never been used as a written language, and is sufficiently different from the main body of Yakut dialects to make standard written Yakut unsuitable as a written and educational medium for the Dolgan. Yakut is not the Yakut name for themselves, which is *saxa* (a reflex of the same Proto-Turkic form as *Yaku(t)*); Yakut is thus one of the few languages of the U.S.S.R. where a traditional Russian name has been retained rather than the name used by the ethnic group concerned.

Khakas, also known as Abakan Turkic and Yenisey Turkic after the geographical location of the Khakas, is spoken by 83.7% of the 66,725 Khakas, over 80% of whom live in the Khakas A.O., where they are heavily outnumbered by Russians. The dialect diversity within Khakas is rather marked, but currently the standard language is being spread through publications and the school system. One dialect of Khakas is spoken by a small ethnic group distinct from the Khakas: this is Kamas, and the Kamas were originally speakers of a Samoyedic language assimilated linguistically by the Khakas; in 1970, there was one speaker of the Samoyedic language Kamas, and about 200 Kamas altogether, most of whom use Russian as their written language.

Shor is an unwritten Turkic language spoken by 73.5% of the 16,494 ethnic Shor (Shorts, also known by various other names in earlier literature, such as Mras Tatar, Kondoma Tatar, Kuznetzk Tatar, Tom'-Kuznetsk Tatar, after the area where they live in the Altay mountains). It is close to Khakas, and the Shor use Khakas or Russian as their written language.

Chulym Tatar, the language of a number of Turkic peoples in the Chulym river basin (Chulym Tatar, Ketsik (Kezik), Küerik), is another unwritten Turkic language of Siberia. Statistics on the number of speakers have not been available, and Russian is used as the main medium of writing.

The last of the Turkic languages of Union Republics to be considered is Kirgiz, spoken by 98.8% of the 1,452,222 Kirgiz in the U.S.S.R., plus some 80,000 in China and 25,000 in Afghanistan. Most of the Soviet Kirgiz, 88.5%, live in the Kirgiz S.S.R., where they constitute 43.8% of the population, the largest single ethnic group in the republic; in addition to Russians, the republic also has a sizable Uzbek population (11.3%), and the Southern dialects of Kirgiz have been influenced by Uzbek. Like the languages of other Union Republics, Kirgiz is used alongside Russian in publications and education at all levels in Kirgizia. Kirgizia shows an especially marked discrepancy between the ethnic composition of the rural and urban populations: in the cities, Russians outnumber Kirgiz by three to one, and in Frunze, the republic's capital, by over five to one.

Finally, we may consider Altay, formerly also known as Oyrat, after the Oyrat tribe that once lived in this area, though the Oyrat are in fact Mongolian (the Kalmyk are one branch of the Oyrat). 87.2% of the 55,812 Altay have Altay as their native language. Over 90% of the Altay live in the Altay kray, most of them in the Mountain-Altay A.O. Altay did exist before the Revolution in a limited way as a written language, as a result of activity by Orthodox missionaries, though some secular works were also published. At present Altay is used widely in publication and education up to secondary level. There is marked divergence between the Northern dialects and the Southern dialects, which latter have most speakers, indeed genetically the Northern dialects actually belong closer to the Khakas group of languages; the formation of the Altay as a single people is thus evidence of the way in which Turkic languages and dialects, as a result of the small degree of divergence between them overall, can be reconstituted as the result of reconstitution of ethnic groups.

2.1.2   *Mongolian languages*

The internal classification of the Mongolian languages is, if anything, even more complicated than that of the Turkic languages. As with Turkic, different members of the Mongolian family are very close to one another genetically, though not always mutually intelligible – this applies in particular to those languages that first broke off from the mass of Mongolian speakers. Part of the problem is that, during the population expansion that accompanied the military expeditions of the Mongol Khans, various branches of Mongolian split off from the central mass of Mongolian, which means that Mongolian proper is almost defined negatively as the language of those that remained behind: moreover, the process of splitting off continued almost up to the present day, so that there are some instances where it is difficult to say whether a given speech variety still belongs to Mongolian proper or is already a distinct language. The problem of dialect versus language is relevant not only for Mongolian proper, but also for some of the Mongolian languages that have split off from the main stem, so that lists of Mongolian languages (as opposed to dialects) often vary considerably.

A further complication is presented by the nomenclature: whereas we have different terms for Turkish, the language, and Turkic, the language-family, there is no suitable pair of terms for Mongolian, which thus ranges ambiguously between the name of the whole family and the name of the largest single language within that family; sometimes the language itself is called Khalkha, after its principal dialect and the basis of the standard language, but this can be equally confusing, because there are also dialects of the Mongolian language other than Khalkha, and it is incorrect to use Khalkha to cover them. Finally, many of the Mongolian languages, with the exception of those that split off early from the main stem, have developed under the strong influence of Classical Mongolian, the only Mongolian written language from the thirteenth to the twentieth century: thus all literate speakers of Mongolian languages (and this meant, primarily, members of the lamaseries) read and wrote the same language, written in a vertical script derived from the Uygur alphabet, even though they would pronounce in accordance with the sound changes that had taken place in their own language or dialect. The vertical script is still used for writing Mongolian in China, and apparently is still quite widely used for private purposes in Mongolia (i.e. the Mongolian People's Republic), although the official script there is Cyrillic, with a few additions to the Russian alphabet for specifically Mongolian sounds, e.g. the front (actually, central) rounded vowels *ö*, *ü*.

The easiest way to approach the problem is first of all to divide off those Mongolian languages that have long been out of contact with the mass of Mongolian languages and dialects, including Classical Mongolian. These are: Moghol (Mongul, Monguor – but not to be confused with the other Monguor below), spoken in north-western Afghanistan; Monguor, Dagur, and Pao-an, spoken in China, with Santa, Tung-hsiang, and Yellow Uygur (i.e. the language of those Yellow Uygur who speak a Mongolian language) sometimes also considered separate languages. The remaining languages fall into three sets, reasonably clearly differentiated from one another but all having developed until recently under the influence of Classical Mongolian: Buryat, Oyrat, and Mongolian (proper). Buryat is the easiest of these to deal with, since it is relatively homogeneous, and is also a language of the U.S.S.R.: 92.6% of the 314,671 ethnic Buryat in the U.S.S.R. have Buryat as their native language; 56.8% of them live in the Buryat A.S.S.R., where they constitute 22% of the total population (nearly three quarters are Russian); most of the remainder live in the Irkutsk and Chita oblasts in the Ust'-Ordynskiy Buryat N.O. and the Aginskiy-Buryat N.O., in which latter the Buryat constitute just over half the population. In addition, some 24,000 Buryat live in China. In the U.S.S.R., Buryat is used as a written language, with Cyrillic script, for publication and schooling.

The Oyrat are scattered widely across the Chinese–Soviet border area, and also in Mongolia, and exact statistics, as well as dialect descriptions, are not available. One group within the Oyrat, the Kalmyk, separated from the mass of the Oyrat in the seventeenth century and migrated westwards, entering the Russian Empire and finally settling to the west of the lower Volga, on land which, like that settled by the Volga Germans further north, had become empty following the collapse of power of the Golden Horde, with its centre at Astrakhan'. Since this area is technically in Europe, the Kalmyk became the only Mongolian and Buddhist people with their home in Europe. Until the 1920s, the Kalmyk used a modified version of the Classical Mongolian vertical script. Since then, they have switched from Cyrillic to Latin and back again. At present Kalmyk is spoken by 91.7% of the 137,194 ethnic Kalmyk in the U.S.S.R.: they constitute 41.1% of the population of the Kalmyk A.S.S.R. (slightly less than the Russians), and 80.4% of the Kalmyk live in their own A.S.S.R. During the Second World War, the Kalmyk were accused of collaboration with the Nazis, and deported from their home, being allowed to return only in the late 1950s; in the intervening period, there was no publishing in Kalmyk, but the language is now used again in publication and schooling. Comparison of the Kalmyk population in 1959 (106,066) with that of 1926 (129,000), taking into account expected natural increase, gives some idea of the harshness with which the deportation was carried out.

We may now briefly survey the rest of Mongolian, although we are no longer dealing with languages of the U.S.S.R. Essentially, what remains is the language Mongolian, although some dialects of Mongolian proper are sometimes separated off as distinct languages, e.g. Ordos and Khorchin; however, speakers of all these dialects use Mongolian as their written language. As mentioned above, Mongolian is written in the Cyrillic script in the Mongolian People's Republic, where the overwhelming majority of the nearly 700,000 speakers of Mongolian speak the Khalkha dialect. In China, especially Inner Mongolia and Manchuria, Mongolian is still written in the vertical Uygur script, and is the native language of over a million Mongolians. Precise statistics for most Mongolian languages and dialects are difficult to ascertain, and estimates for the total for all languages and dialects in the family range from $2\frac{1}{2}$ to 5 million.

Since most Mongolian languages are not languages of the U.S.S.R., in the detailed discussion in sections 2.2–2.4 we shall be concentrating on Turkic and Tungusic languages, most of which are languages of the U.S.S.R., drawing on Mongolian data, especially from Buryat and Kalmyk, for purposes of comparison and contrast.

2.1.3 *Tungusic languages*

The Tungusic languages are spoken in the border areas of China and the U.S.S.R., in the Far East, and also well into the U.S.S.R. in eastern Siberia; in addition, there are some Evenki in Mongolia. The classification of Tungusic languages is reasonably straightforward, though not without controversy, and the main problem is ascertaining just how many Tungusic languages there are: for the U.S.S.R. there are descriptions of the languages and many of their dialects, but the Tungusic languages of China are much less well studied, and several ethnonyms appear in earlier literature for which we have no subsequent mentions – most probably they refer to dialects of one of the larger languages. In the U.S.S.R., it is usual to refer to this group of languages as Tungus-Manchu, and divide it into two main branches, Tungusic (proper) and Manchu. The latter consists of the almost extinct Manchu and Juchen, the extinct forerunner of Manchu. The main reasons for this grouping seem to be the great typological differences between Manchu and Juchen on the one hand and the other languages, but this typological difference is not evidence of genetic difference, and with Manchu one must always bear in mind the strong influence exerted by Chinese (nearly all Manchu texts are translations from Chinese); although Manchu has also influenced the other Southern Tungusic languages. The alternative grouping, adopted here, is into a Northern group versus a Southern group, which latter includes Manchu as one of its subbranches. The overall grouping is shown in Table 2.3, which includes all the Tungusic languages of the U.S.S.R., in accordance with the usual differentiation thereof into separate languages, and those non-Soviet languages for which evidence is clear, i.e. Solon, Manchu and Juchen.

All of the Tungusic languages that survive are spoken by small population groups, numbering at most in the tens of thousands. For most of these ethnic groups, this simply reflects the inability of their habitat to support large populations in the pre-technological period. An exception must be made for Manchu, since the Manchu were once a major political force in the area, having conquered China in the seventeenth century. However, like all foreign conquerors of China, they were ultimately absorbed by the greater power of Chinese civilisation, so that even though the Manchu exist as a distinct ethnic group, and controlled the Chinese Empire until 1911, their language has been almost completely replaced by Chinese. The most reliable data on Manchu speakers today concerns the Sibe (Sibo) dialect, spoken by some 20,000 people; whether more central dialects of Manchu are still spoken at all remains debatable. Manchu is, incidentally, written in the vertical Uygur script, borrowed from Mongolian.

Of the three Northern Tungusic languages spoken in the U.S.S.R., Evenki and Even have written forms, used for publication and in primary schooling, while

Table 2.3. *Genetic classification of the Tungusic languages*

Northern (North-Western, Siberian, Evenki) Tungusic
   Evenki (also called simply Tungus; includes Orochon)
   Even (Lamut)
   Negidal
   Solon
Southern (Amur) Tungusic
   South-Western Tungusic
      Manchu (including the Sibo dialect)
      Juchen
   South-Eastern Tungusic
      Nanay (Gold) ⎫
      Ulcha (Olcha) ⎬ Nanay subgroup
      Orok (Ulta) ⎭
      Udege ⎫
      Oroch ⎬ Udege subgroup

Negidal is unwritten. These three languages, like all the Tungusic languages of the U.S.S.R., have relatively low language retention rates, with marked falls between 1959 and 1970, a result of the fact that the Tungusic peoples are now usually small minorities among Russians in their traditional homes. Evenki is spoken as a native language by 51.3% of the 25,149 ethnic Evenki. Despite their small numbers, the Evenki are spread across a huge area in central Siberia, so that the Evenki N.O., notwithstanding its area of 767,600 square kilometres, contains just over 12.8% of the total number of Evenki. In earlier literature, the Evenki are often simply referred to as Tungus, sometimes also by names of subdivisions of the Evenki, e.g. Orochon, Manegir. Even is spoken by 56% (in 1959: 81.4%) of the 12,029 Even scattered across north-eastern Siberia; nowhere is there a concentration of Even population sufficient to have justified setting up an autonomous unit for them. Negidal, in many ways a bridge between Evenki and the Southern Tungusic languages, is spoken by 53.3% of the 537 Negidal, most of whom live in the lower Amur.

Of the South-Eastern Tungusic languages, spoken along the lower Amur and Ussuri and their tributaries, and also on Sakhalin island (in the case of Orok), only Nanay has a written language, used in primary schooling and some publications. (Udege had a brief and very restricted currency as a written language in the early 1930s.) The terminology of the names for the South-Eastern Tungusic peoples is very confusing, because the term Nanay has been used by various of them (Nanay, Ulcha, Oroch) – it means 'people of the land/locality' – and some of the other names are no less confusing: the term Oroch, which replaced the earlier term Nani, is Evenki for 'reindeer-breeder', although the Oroch do not in fact breed reindeer. In current official terminology, the term Nanay is restricted as indicated in Table 2.3 to the ethnic group formerly referred to as Gold, while the other languages, which differ sufficiently from Nanay to make written Nanay unsuitable as their written medium, are given the names listed in Table 2.3. Nanay is spoken by 69.1% of 10,005 ethnic Nanay; Ulcha by 60.8% of the 2,448 Ulcha; Udege by 55.1% of the 1,469 Udege; and Oroch by 46.8% of the 1,089 Oroch. The 1970 census statistics do not include figures for the Orok, though previous estimates are around 400 ethnic Orok.

2.2 **Phonology**

The main aspect of the phonology of the Altaic languages that has attracted the interest of general linguists is vowel harmony, whereby all the vowels of a work have to have certain features in common, and it is with a detailed consideration of vowel harmony that we shall be primarily concerned in this section. Although the details of vowel harmony differ somewhat from language to language, there is a single general system that is common to nearly all of the Turkic languages, and a very similar system common to the Mongolian languages. Even though the phonetic nature of vowel harmony is rather different in Tungusic languages, on a more abstract level the kind of system that operates (as opposed to its phonetic realisation) is of essentially the same kind. Vowel harmony also has certain repercussions on the pronunciation of consonants, mainly of an assimilatory kind; otherwise, the consonantal systems of Altaic languages are relatively straightforward.

We may start our discussion of vowel harmony by looking at the system in Kirgiz, a Turkic language, and one of the most consistent and symmetrical vowel harmony systems. Kirgiz has what might be regarded as a canonical Turkic vowel system, with eight vowel phonemes distinguished by quality (in addition, Kirgiz, like many other Turkic languages, has phonemic vowel length), the logical possibilities using binary oppositions of front versus back, rounded versus unrounded, and high versus nonhigh (the nonhigh vowel *a* is low, the others mid). This is represented diagrammatically in Table 2.4. (The system can, of course, be represented more revealingly in three dimensions, one for each of the parameters height, frontness, and rounding). In a given word (with the exception of compound words, and loans from other languages, to which we return later), all the vowels must share the same feature for front–back and the same feature for rounded–unrounded. This means that the value for these two parameters is determined once and for all for a word, and all vowels in that word must show the same feature values. Vowel harmony does not affect the height dimension in Turkic languages, so that high and nonhigh vowels freely combine with one another in words. The easiest way to see the operation of vowel harmony is not by examining long lists of words to check that this principle is

Table 2.4. *Kirgiz vowel quality system*

	Unrounded		Rounded	
	Front	Back	Front	Back
High	i	ɨ	ü	u
Nonhigh	e	a	ö	o

observed, although this could of course be done, but rather to look at what happens when suffixes combine with stems to give longer words.

The same restriction on co-occurrence of vowels applies to all morphemes within a given word, with the result that in Kirgiz each suffix has four forms, one for use with front unrounded stems and containing only the vowels *i* and *e*; one for use with back unrounded stems and containing only the vowels *ɨ* and *a*; one for use with front rounded stems and containing only the vowels *ü* and *ö*; and one for use with back rounded stems, and containing only the vowels *u* and *o*. Since the only vowel contrasts that can be found in a suffix are thus high versus nonhigh, it is convenient to use the symbol *I* as a cover symbol for any high vowel (the precise quality being determined by the frontness and roundness of the stem), and *A* as a cover symbol for any nonhigh vowel. We may then see how suffixes combine with stems of the various classes. For this purpose, we shall examine two suffixes: the suffix *-InčI* (*-nčI* after vowels) forms ordinals from cardinal numerals, and the suffix *-dAn* (*-tAn* after voiceless consonants) forms the ablative case of nouns. Table 2.5 illustrates the possibilities. If a series of suffixes is added, then vowel harmony operates through the whole sequence, so that by adding the third person possessive suffix *-(s)I(n)* and the locative suffix *-dA* (*-tA* after a voiceless consonant), we get such forms as *ata-sin-da* 'at his father', *ene-sin-de* 'at his mother', *köz-ün-dö* 'in his eye', *tuz-un-do* 'in his salt'.

The regularity of the Kirgiz system is actually rather untypical of Turkic languages as a whole, in particular the consistency with which vowel rounding is maintained throughout a word (so-called labial harmony, as opposed to palatal harmony, concerning the front–back dimension). Before looking at some of these deviations, however, it is necessary to emphasize two aspects of vowel harmony. First, vowel harmony involves neutralisation: although Kirgiz has eight distinct vowel qualities, in suffixes there are effectively only two possibilities, high or nonhigh, or more generally: once the frontness and roundedness of a word are determined by the first vowel of the stem (we shall see below why this vowel is determining), the front–back and rounded–unrounded oppositions are neutralised for all following vowels. Secondly, vowel harmony involves assimilation: not only is the quality of vowels of succeeding syllables determined by that of the first syllable, but the vowels

Table 2.5. *Illustrations of Kirgiz vowel harmony*

CARDINAL	ORDINAL	
bir	bir-inči	'one'
beš	beš-inči	'five'
alti	alti-nči	'six'
ǯijirma	ǯijirma-nči	'twenty'
üč	üč-ünčü	'three'
tört	tört-ünčü	'four'
toguz	toguz-unču	'nine'
on	on-unču	'ten'

NOMINATIVE	ABLATIVE	
iš	iš-ten	'work'
et	et-ten	'meat'
ǯil	ǯil-dan	'year'
alma	alma-dan	'apple'
üj	üj-dön	'house'
köl	köl-dön	'lake'
tuz	tuz-don	'salt'
tokoj	tokoj-don	'forest'

of those successive syllables share the same parameter value for frontness and backness. One could easily imagine a system that would have neutralisation without assimilation, e.g. in which all noninitial vowels would be back unrounded, irrespective of the value of the initial vowel; we shall see below that something approaching this does in fact characterise many Turkic languages.

One way in which many Turkic languages differ from Kirgiz is in having not eight, but nine vowel qualities, with distinction of *e* from *ä* in the front unrounded nonhigh box of Table 2.4. Maintenance of this distinction is scattered across the Turkic languages, and shows only weak correlation with subgroup and even language boundaries: for instance, Azerbaydzhan has the distinction, whereas standard Turkish does not, although many dialects of Turkish do, as in *äl* 'hand' versus *el* 'people'. For purposes of vowel harmony, *ä* and *e* behave alike, and most languages that have both phonemes allow only one of them in suffixes (thus Azerbaydzhan has only *ä* in suffixes).

The main deviation that is found in many Turkic languages concerns labial harmony, in particular with the nonhigh vowels. In many Turkic languages the rounded–unrounded parameter is simply neutralised to unrounded for noninitial nonhigh vowels, i.e. we have neutralisation without assimilation. In Table 2.6 we give a number of Azerbaydzhan words with the suffixes *-In* of the genitive case and

Table 2.6. *Illustrations of Azerbaydzhan vowel harmony*

NOMINATIVE	GENITIVE	LOCATIVE	
jarpag	jarpaɣ-in	jarpag-da	'leaf'
küläk	küläj-in	küläk-dä	'wind'
ox	ox-un	ox-da	'arrow'
söz	söz-ün	söz-dä	'word'

-*dA* of the locative case; the stem-final consonant alternations that are to be observed in these examples are quite regular; the alternation between -*dA* and -*tA* (the latter after voiceless consonants) is not reflected in Azerbaydzhan orthography, and we have retained the more morphophonemic transcription here. It will be seen from these examples that, whereas the high vowel behaves precisely as in Kirgiz, the nonhigh vowel in suffixes shows palatal harmony, but only neutralisation with respect to roundedness. This can be seen not only in suffixes, but also in stems: for instance, we have the word *küläk*, not * *külök* 'wind', just as we have *söz-dä* and not * *söz-dö*. Other similar violations of labial harmony, right up to complete absence of labial harmony, are found in many Turkic languages. For instance, Turkish has a system much like that of Azerbaydzhan, except that within stems the high vowels are automatically rounded after a labial consonant, so that rounded high vowels can occur in words where the preceding vowels are not rounded, e.g. *tavuk* 'hen'.

Above, we indicated in passing that vowel harmony in Turkic languages is determined by the first vowel of the stem. One argument for this claim can be deduced from the existence of neutralisation of rounding rather than harmony, in noninitial syllables in languages like Azerbaydzhan: the initial syllable always has the full range of potential vowel qualities, while two vowel qualities, *o* and *ö* are excluded from noninitial syllables. While one can predict the lack of rounding in the second syllable in *küläk*, there is no way of predicting that of the first vowel, even knowing the second. Actually, the generalisation that the first vowel is determining is part of a more general principle, namely that vowel harmony in Turkic (and more generally Altaic) languages operates from left to right, with each vowel affecting the quality of the succeeding vowel. Another manifestation of this principle can be seen when we combine high-vowel and nonhigh-vowel suffixes in a language like Azerbaydzhan with inconsistent labial harmony. We shall take the noun *söz* 'word', and the suffixes -*Im* 'my' and -*lAr*, indicating plurality. If we add -*Im* directly to *söz* we get *söz-üm*, the frontness and rounding of *ö* carrying over into the high vowel of the suffix. If we add -*lAr* to *söz*, the result is *söz-lär*, with the frontness of the *ö* carrying over, but the neutralisation of rounding to unrounded for the nonhigh vowel. If we add both suffixes, in which case the possessive suffix must follow the plural suffix, then the result is *söz-lär-im* 'my words', and not * *söz-lär-üm*. Thus the quality of each vowel is determined (except for height) by that of the preceding vowel; only the initial vowel, which of course has no preceding vowel, is independent in this respect.

An interesting variation on neutralisation rather than complete labial harmony is provided by Tatar, with respect to the close-mid vowels, which, it will be recalled from the general discussion of Tatar in section 2.1, derive from Proto-Turkic high vowels. The distinction between *o* and *ə*, and the distinction between *ö* and *e* are lost in noninitial syllables, with unrounded vowels after unrounded vowels; after rounded vowels, one finds progressive delabialisation from left to right in the word, so that in a word like *öterge* 'chisel' the first vowel is fully rounded, the second less so, the third even less so, and so on for longer words; the current orthography writes unrounded vowels in noninitial syllables.

Although we have spoken so far about harmony only in relation to vowels, in fact phonetically the assimilatory part of vowel harmony also affects consonants, with consonants being palatalised (or having a more forward articulation for consonants, like velars, where the soft palate is the primary place of articulation) in front-vowel words, and velarised (or having a more retracted articulation where the soft palate is the primary place of articulation, e.g. uvular articulation rather than velar) in back-vowel words; in addition, consonants in words with rounded vowels are allophonically rounded, although it is the palatalisation versus velarisation that is most relevant. The phonetic difference is most marked with the velars (prevelar in front vowel words, uvular in back vowel words) and *l*. Thus, a narrower transcription of the Kirgiz word *köl* 'lake', which we introduced above, would be *köl'*; a narrower transcription of the word *tokoj* 'forest' would be *toqoj*. Since this distinction is, with certain exceptions to be noted below, allophonic, we have not in general noted it in transcriptions. In some languages, instead of uvular plosives we find uvular fricatives: thus Azerbaydzhan *ox* 'arrow' corresponds to Turkish *ok* (phonetically *oq*); continuant values are also sometimes found for the voiced prevelar in certain positions, especially intervocalically, as *j*; thus the Azerbaydzhan form *küläjin* 'wind (GEN)' contains a *j* representing a prevelar intervocalically.

Although the distinction palatalised versus velarised consonants is in general less salient phonetically than that between front and back vowels, and can therefore be considered purely allophonic, there are some Turkic languages and dialects where the phonetic onus of maintaining the distinction has been shifted from the vowels to the consonants, so that one has a tendency towards consonant harmony rather than vowel harmony. In both Gagauz and Karaim, front vowels are backed after a palatalised consonant, so that in Karaim we have *ќoźuḿḋa* for expected *közümde* 'in my eye', and *öźań* for expected *özen* 'stream'; in Gagauz, we have *ƀań* 'I' rather than *ben*, and *aač üśťuńa* 'on the tree' rather than *aač üstüne*. It will be seen from these examples that the front–back opposition is not carried completely by the consonants: words with an initial vowel still retain initial front, including front rounded, vowels, since the backing takes place as a historical process only after consonants. Most descriptions of Uzbek imply that Uzbek has undergone a similar historical process, losing the oppositions *u/ü*, *o/ö*, and *i/i*, leading to phonologisation of the oppositions between *k* and *q*, *g* and *G*, *l* and *ł*, so that Uzbek would have *kůl* 'lake' versus *qůł* 'arm', cf. Turkish *köl* versus *kol*. However, as will be shown below, this analysis of Uzbek fails to take account of certain oppositions between vowels that are clearly phonemic.

The main complications introduced into the vowel harmony rules of Turkic languages have been through the introduction of large numbers of loanwords, in particular of Arabic and Persian words into the languages of Muslim peoples, and more recently of Russian words into the Turkic languages of the U.S.S.R. (and of Western European loans into Turkish, Chinese loans into Turkic languages of China), since words in these languages are not subject to vowel harmony. While these loans are sometimes assimilated to the native vowel harmony pattern, as when Turkish derives *mümkün* from *mümkin* from *mumkin* 'possible', with successive diachronic processes of regressive and progressive vowel assimilation, the vast mass of such words remain as exceptions to vowel harmony, and are now fully assimilated as such into the languages in question. Examples of such words in Azerbaydzhan are *maddä* 'substance' from Arabic, *dilavär* 'bold' from Persian, and *revolusija* 'revolution' from Russian. Although these stems violate the general rules of vowel harmony, the regular vowel harmony rules still apply when suffixes are added, and since, as indicated above, vowel harmony always operates from left to right, it is the last vowel of the stem which determines the vowel qualities of the suffixes. Thus the plurals of the nouns given above are *maddä-lär* and *revolusija-lar*.

A similar phenomenon is found with some native words, in particular those that derive etymologically from a series of separate words, e.g. compound words, and certain complex verb forms. An example of a compound noun would be Azerbaydzhan *suiti* 'seal', literally *su-it-i* 'water dog-its', with the two roots *su* 'water' and *it* 'dog'; its plural is, of course, *suitilär*, the quality of the suffix being determined by the preceding vowel. Several dialects of Turkmen form the present tense with the suffix *-jor/-joor*, which is not subject to vowel harmony and derives etymologically from a separate auxiliary verb, e.g. *al-jor-un* 'I take', *gel-jor-un* 'I come', the vowel of the suffix being determined by the preceding vowel *o*. In standard Turkmen and other dialects, this suffix has been assimilated to the regular vowel harmony rules, as *-jAr* (i.e. *-jar* or *-jär*, since Turkmen regularly does not have nonhigh rounded vowels in noninitial syllables).

Loanwords from Arabic, in addition to leading to massive violation of vowel harmony in roots, also lead to complications with some of the consonants, especially in their relation to adjacent vowels: Arabic has a number of phonemic distinctions in its consonant system which are purely allophonic in Turkic. Thus Arabic has separate phonemes *k*, *q*, *x*, and *γ* (the last two phonetically uvular), whereas in Turkic languages *k*, *q*, and *x* are usually all allophones of *k*, while *γ* is an allophone of *g*; conversely, Arabic lacks front rounded and back unrounded vowel phonemes. Arabic also has phonemic oppositions between so-called plain and emphatic consonants, the latter being velarised and/or pharyngalised. In most Turkic languages, in the process of adapting Arabic words into the given language attempts were and are made to retain the range of phonemic distinctions that Arabic has. With respect to the velar versus uvular oppositions, this meant having many instances of uvular consonants adjacent to front vowels, and prevelar consonants adjacent to back vowels, and most Turkic languages now have a fairly large number of words with this structure. Thus Tatar has such loans from Arabic as *diqqät* 'attention', *mäynä* 'meaning', while Azerbaydzhan has such loans (from Persian) as *ğul* 'rose'.

While one way in which vowel harmony can be disrupted is externally because of loans from other languages, vowel harmony can also be disrupted internally, if sound changes occur to change the original quality of one of the vowels concerned. A relatively minor instance of this is to be found in Azerbaydzhan, where the opposition between *i* and *ı* is lost word-initially, both being merged to *i*, in the dialects on which the standard language is based. Thus the standard language has *isig* 'light', where many other dialects have *ısıg*. In general, this does not affect the vowels of subsequent syllables, so that exceptions to vowel harmony arise. With monosyllabic stems, however, the loss of any phonetic indication that the word is a back-vowel word leads to its reinterpretation as a front-vowel word, so that, for instance, the plural of *il* 'year' (cf. Turkish *yıl* [jil]) is *il-lär* (cf. Turkish *yıl-lar* [jillar]). A more thoroughgoing breakdown of vowel harmony as a result of diachronic change is to be found in Uygur, where Proto-Turkic **i* and **ı* merge as *i* everywhere, giving rise to such forms as *ani-si* 'his mother', cf. *ana* 'mother'. In monosyllables, vowel harmony is reintroduced by fronting the vowel *a*, so that from *mal* 'cattle' we form *mel-i* 'his cattle', although there are exceptions to this rule among loanwords, e.g. *kar* 'deed' (from Persian), *kar-i* 'his deed'. The end-product of these processes in Uygur is words with vowels from different vowel harmony series, and also the shift of roots from one series to another as certain suffixes are added, e.g. back vowel *mal* to front vowel *mel*.

Finally, in our discussion of vowel harmony in Turkic languages, we may consider those languages which are considered, or at least certain of the dialects of which are considered, to have lost vowel harmony, usually leading to phonologisation of at least the oppositions between *k* and *q*, *g* and *G* (or the corresponding fricative), often also *l* and *ł*. It does seem to be the case that certain Turkic languages on the periphery of the Turkic-speaking area, in particular Uzbek and Uygur, are moving in this direction through loss of the phonemic oppositions i/i, $u/ü$, and $o/ö$; in Uzbek, this would lead to a vowel system like that of the neighbouring Iranian language Tadzhik, i.e. i, e, a, o, $ŭ$ and u, and most published accounts of Uzbek do in fact assign to Uzbek a vowel phoneme system of precisely this kind. Such analyses claim that the occurrence of phonetic front rounded $ü$ and $ŭ$ in Uzbek is the result of assimilation to adjacent fronted consonants, i.e. the phonemes /u/ and /ŭ/ have allophones [ü] and [ŭ] when adjacent, in particular, to k and g as opposed to q and G. The problem that arises with this analysis concerns such minimal pairs as the following, given in fairly narrow phonetic transcription: *tur* 'stop', *tür* 'sort', *uč* 'end', *üč* 'three', which are minimal pairs for many speakers of Uzbek, and in the standard language. In the traditional analysis, of which Kononov (1960: 19, 32) may serve as an example, u and $ü$ are said to be allophones of a single phoneme; however $č$ and $č̓$ are not set up as distinct phonemes. In other words, the quality of the vowel is determined by the adjacent consonants, but the quality of the consonants is in turn determined by the adjacent vowel, leading to a classic violation of biuniqueness in phonemic analysis (moreover, one that cannot be saved by a more abstract analysis). While it may be doubtful whether to assign the phonemic distinctiveness quality to the vowel or to one or other of the consonants, or to assign it to the root as a whole rather than to any specific segment thereof, still the distinction must be made somewhere. Incidentally, Uzbek orthography does not distinguish between such pairs as those given above, although in the case of words containing velar/uvular consonants different symbols are used for the consonants; while Uzbek is probably moving in the direction indicated by the orthography, it is clear that the standard language, at least, has not yet reached there.

Before turning to vowel harmony in the other branches of Altaic, we may briefly mention some of the other salient characteristics of Turkic phonology. The opposition between voiced and voiceless consonants, especially plosives, is very restricted in Turkic languages, being widespread only in intervocalic position, with relatively few minimal pairs even there. Word-finally, the distinction is usually neutralised in favour of the voiceless member, though the distinction may resurface when suffixes are added to make the consonant intervocalic again, especially in loanwords, e.g. Tatar *kitap* 'book', *kitab-əm* 'my book'. Word-initially, the prevalence of voiced or voiceless plosives is one of the main criteria for subgrouping Turkic languages, so that, for instance Chuvash, and Khakas and Shor, have almost exclusively initial *p* whereas most Turkic languages have almost exclusively initial *b*. Whether this represents the loss of a voicing contrast that existed in Proto-Turkic, or creation of a new opposition, remains unclear.

Many Turkic languages have an opposition between short and long vowels that seems to continue a Proto-Turkic length distinction: Altay, Kirgiz, Tofa, Tuva, Turkmen, Khakas, Shor, and Yakut; in Gagauz, some words retain Proto-Turkic long vowels, but the distinction has largely been neutralised. Most Turkic languages have also developed secondary long vowels, either through the loss of syllable-final consonants with compensatory lengthening, e.g. Gagauz *iinä* 'needle' from **ignä*, or through vowel contraction after the loss of intervocalic consonants, as in Gagauz *ii* 'well' from *iji*, or in retention of long vowels in loans from other languages, especially Arabic, e.g. Azerbaydzhan *aalim* 'scholar'.

The syllable structure of Turkic languages is generally very simple, with at most one initial consonant and two final consonants. Earlier loans from foreign languages simplify or break up clusters of consonants that violate this rule, but at present such loans, especially from Russian, are taken over in unmodified form. Since high vowels, especially *i*, have a tendency to be reduced or even lost between certain consonants, phonetic initial consonant clusters can arise in this way even in native words, especially in rapid speech, as in Uzbek *birinči* or *brinči* 'first'. Many Turkic languages have stress on the final syllable of words, including words with several suffixes attached, as in Tatar *balá* 'child', plural *balalár*, third person singular possessive *balalaró*, genitive *balalaranóŋ* 'of his children'. Certain suffixes, however, fail to take the stress, for instance the negative suffix *-mA*, giving rise to phonemic stress distinctions in a few instances, such as Uzbek *olmá* 'apple' versus *ólma* 'don't take'. There are also individual native words, and large numbers of foreign words (especially of Russian origin) that do not fall under this rule for final stress.

The general principles of vowel harmony in Mongolian languages, and in particular in Buryat and Kalmyk, are very similar to those of Turkic languages, so here we shall concentrate on the differences. For Proto-Mongolian, we can reconstruct a vowel system exactly like that given in Table 2.4 for Kirgiz. The modern Mongolian languages also have phonemic vowel length, though this is always secondary, through loss of intervocalic consonants that were present in Classical Mongolian. In many modern languages, including Buryat, the so-called 'front rounded' vowels are actually central rounded vowels ([ʉ] and [ө]). One major departure from the system of Table 2.4, however, that is found even in Classical Mongolian, is the neutralisation of the *i/i* opposition, so that only the one vowel *i* occurs phonetically, in both front and back vowel words; subsequently, this vowel palatalised preceding consonants. Otherwise, palatal harmony is as strict in Classical Mongolian as in most Turkic languages, and this strictness is retained, with specific exceptions to be noted below, in the modern languages. In addition to general exceptions to be noted below, there are also individual exceptions in Mongolian languages resulting from compounding and loans from other languages; as in Turkic languages, it is the last vowel of such words that is decisive in determining the vowel of suffixes. The alternation of front and back vowels in suffixes can be seen from such Buryat examples as *xeb* 'form', plural *xebüüd*, *nom* 'book', plural *nomuud*, or, using the separate plural suffix *-nAr* for humans, *axa* 'elder brother', plural *axanar*, *düü* 'younger brother', plural *düüner*. The vowel *i*, neutral with respect to vowel harmony, can be seen in suffixes in *mal* 'cattle', *mal-ni* 'my cattle', *ger* 'house', *ger-ni* 'my house', and in front and back vowel stems such as *limbe* 'limba' (a kind of musical instrument) and *ilalta* 'victory'.

Diachronically, the main way in which this system has been disrupted has been in the monophthongisation of the older diphthongs *aj, oj, uj*, and *ej*, especially the first three, since phonetically the result of these monophthongisations is a long front vowel, e.g. in Buryat for the first three [ää], [öö], [üü] (distinct from [өө], [ʉʉ]). In the more westerly Mongolian languages, including Kalmyk, the end result of this is the transference of words which had these diphthongs into the front vowel class. In Buryat, however, they remain as back vowel words, so that the classification into front versus back words is no longer purely phonetic, since the phonetically front vowels [ää], [öö], and [üü] behave morphophonemically as back vowels, as in *ajl* [ääl] 'village', locative *ajlta* [äälta], not [äältä]. Since none of the back diphthongs actually merges phonetically with any of the front diphthongs in Buryat (in particular, *üj* is usually retained as a diphthong, thus avoiding merger with *uj*), these new long vowels behave consistently as back vowels.

It will already have been noted from some of the examples above that labial harmony does not work in the same way in Mongolian languages as in the most typical Turkic languages, given such forms as Buryat *xebüüd* 'forms', with rounded *ü* following unrounded *e*. With respect to the high vowels, Mongolian languages have neither labial harmony nor labial neutralisation, so that *i* can occur after any vowel, *u* after any back vowel, and *ü* after any nonback vowel. With nonhigh vowels, Mongolian languages have at least neutralisation of the labial feature. In the more westerly languages, including Kalmyk, there is consistent neutralisation to the unrounded vowels *a, e* in noninitial syllables, whether the initial syllable has a rounded or an unrounded vowel, as in *xöker* 'merry'. In the more easterly languages, including Buryat and Khalkha Mongolian, the quality of the preceding vowel is determining provided that that vowel is also nonhigh. In effect, this means that in noninitial syllables, *o* only occurs following *o* and *ö* only occurs following *ö*, with the additional proviso that the two nonhigh rounded vowels may be separated from one another by the neutral vowel *i*. Thus the instrumental suffix in Buryat has the variants *-(g)aar/-(g)eer/-(g)oor/-(g)öör* (i.e. *-(g)AAr*), as in *mal* 'cattle', *malaar*; *deŋ* 'candle', *deŋgeer*; *bulag* 'source', *bulagaar*; *soxoj* 'chalk', *soxojgoor*; compare also the locative suffix *-d/tA*, as in *xońin* 'sheep', locative *xońindo*.

In the dialects of Buryat on which the standard language is based, one further refinement has been added: the short vowel *ŏ* has been unrounded to *e* (although the long vowel *ŏŏ* remains), so that the locative of *dürŏŏ* 'stirrup' is *dürŏŏde*. Labial assimilation can, however, still carry across such instances of *e*, as in *xŏŏreldŏŏn* 'conversation'. Since the long vowel *ee* and the earlier diphthong *ej* are often pronounced alike as [ee], and since unrounding affected the vowel of original *öj*, one can also have phonetic [ee], deriving from *öj*, after *ŏŏ, as in tŏŏdej* [təədee] 'grandmother'. Thus, although the current vowel harmony system of Buryat is easily explicable on the basis of an original phonetic system to which various sound changes have applied, synchronically it is no longer a purely phonetically based vowel harmony system.

In general in Mongolian languages, short vowels are pronounced indistinctly (tending towards schwa for the nonhigh vowels) in noninitial syllables, so that an alternative analysis of Mongolian vowel harmony would be to say that in noninitial syllables with short vowels there is simply neutralisation of vowel quality other than the high–nonhigh opposition, with slight assimilation in quality to preceding vowels; this is, for instance, the analysis of Khalkha Mongolian adopted by Poppe (1970). Other than in notation, this does not differ significantly from the analysis presented above. However, it should be noted that standard Kalmyk orthography adopts an extreme version of this analysis, simply omitting all noninitial short vowels (and writing noninitial long vowels with a single vowel symbol, whereas those in initial syllables are written with two). This gives rise to such orthographic curiosities as *nojrxlhn* '(political) state', pronounced *nojarxalhan*, where *a* represents a schwa-like vowel. Since the position of the vowel is not absolutely determinable from the consonant sequence, this is a departure from phonemic orthography. In Mongolian languages in general, not more than one consonant is permitted in both syllable-initial and syllable-final positions.

Within the Tungusic languages, there is much more variation from language to language in the type of vowel harmony system, but it seems that a single type can be reconstructed for Proto-Tungusic, utilising a phonetic basis for the division of vowels into vowel harmony classes, then explaining some of the idiosyncrasies of individual languages in terms of sound changes that applied to that original system. One of the most consistent systems is found in Even, and we may start from this, especially as Even is in many respects a very conservative Tungusic language. In Even, the vowels are divided into two classes, traditionally referred to as hard (indicated by a subscript dot, except for *a*) and soft (no subscript; hard *a* corresponds to soft *e*). Each of the hard vowels is slightly lower and further back than its soft counterpart. The vowel phonemes of Even are illustrated in Table 2.7; vowel length is phonemic, except for *ə*, and there are in addition two rising diphthongs, soft *ie* and hard *ịa*. The phonetic basis of the system might seem to be vowel height, with

Table 2.7. *Even vowel system*

Soft vowels		Hard vowels	
i	u	i̯	u̯
	ə		ə̇
e	o	a	o̯

each hard vowel lower than its corresponding soft vowel, but in fact this would have to be relative height (since hard *i̯* for instance, is in absolute terms higher than soft *e*), whereas the front–back dimension in Turkic vowel harmony refers to absolute front versus absolute back. It has recently been argued (Ard 1980) that the basic phonetic feature that conditions vowel harmony in the Tungusic languages, or at least in Proto-Tungusic and still in some Tungusic languages, such as Even, is advancement versus retraction of the tongue-root, a kind of vowel harmony that is otherwise well-attested in West African languages. We may now give some examples to illustrate vowel harmony in Even, using the stems *berken* 'crossbow' and *ʒuu* 'dwelling'; in the dative, they are *berken-du*, *ʒuu-du̯;* in the allative, *berken-təki*, *ʒuu-tki̯*; in the allative-locative *berke-kle*, *ʒuu-kla*; in the allative-prolative *berke-klə*, *ʒuu-klə̇*. The harmony, incidentally, also affects certain consonants: in particular, *k* has an allophone [q] in hard vowel words, and *g* a fricative allophone (probably [ʁ]) in hard vowel words, conditioned by the retraction of the tongue.

Nanay shows essentially the same phonetic basis to its vowel harmony system, although it has far fewer phonemic vowel qualities, having the soft vowels *i*, *u*, *ə*, and the hard vowels *i̯*, *u̯* (orthographically *o*), and *a*, in addition to numerous diphthongs. Evenki shows modification of a system of this kind, as shown in Table 2.8. The vowels *i(i̯)* and *u(u̯)* are neutral with respect to vowel harmony, since they represent the merger of **i* and **i̯*, **u* and **u̯*. The vowel *ee* is also neutral, and represents the merger of soft and hard diphthongs *ie*, *i̯a*. The only soft vowel is *ə*; the only hard vowels are *a* and *o*, which contrast only in the initial syllable, their occurrence being otherwise determined by labial harmony: *o* occurs only if the preceding vowel is *o*. This means that suffixes containing *i*, *u*, or *e* do not have vowel harmony variants, whereas those containing the other vowels have three variants, *ə* in soft vowel words, and *a* or *o* in hard vowel words, depending on whether the preceding vowel is *o* or not. Thus the accusative suffix *-v/p/mA* occurs in *bira-va* 'river', *dət-və* or *dət-pə* 'tundra', and *oron-mo* 'reindeer'. Labial harmony is attested in a number of Tungusic languages, not always with absolute consistency. Thus Oroch, for instance, has two vowels neutral with respect to vowel harmony, *i* and *ä*; an alternation between soft *u* and hard *u̯*; and an alternation between soft *ə*

Table 2.8. *Evenki vowel system*

i, ii		u, uu
ee	ə, əə	o, oo
a, aa		

and hard *a*, except that after *o* one finds hard *o*, as in the following forms: *ụgda-va-ńi* 'his boat (ACC)' (literally 'boat-ACC-3SG'), *ụgda-dụ-ńi-da* 'also in his boat' (literally 'boat-LOC-3SG-AND'); *xuŋkə-və-ńi* 'his (sea-going) boat (ACC)', *xuŋkə-du-ńi-də* 'also in his (sea-going) boat'; *otoŋgo-vo-ńi* 'his (one-person) boat (ACC)' *otoŋgo-dụ-ńi-da*; the last example shows that labial harmony does not operate across intermediate vowels that are not subject to this process.

The orthographic systems that have been devised for Evenki, Even, and Nanay fail to indicate some of the phonemic vowel differences discussed above, in addition to not marking vowel length. Syllable structure is simple in the Tungusic languages, as in other branches of Altaic, being at most one syllable-initial and one syllable-final consonant. The possibilities for syllable-final consonants tend to decrease as one moves southwards in the family: in Nanay, even word-final *n* is lost, though it does leave nasalization in the preceding vowel, as in *ịxụ̃* 'settlement' (cf. locative *ịxụn-dụ*).

2.3 Morphological structure and categories

In section 1.2.2, it was noted in passing that the characteristic trait of the morphological structure of the Altaic languages is agglutination, whereby there is, corresponding to each category, a separate affix (in Altaic languages, invariably a suffix) encoding the appropriate value for that category, such as singular/plural number, etc. Since we have already used Turkic illustrational material, we may now take some examples from the Tungusic language Evenki. Some of the noun suffixes of Evenki are: plural *-l*, accusative *-wa*, dative-locative *-duu*, ablative *-git*. Since it is possible to combine number and case separately, one has combinations such as those in Table 2.9 for *bira* 'river'; the case suffix always follows the number suffix. The same agglutinative structure can be seen in the conjugation of verbs: in Evenki, the suffix *-ćaa* marks past tense and *-ǯaŋaa* one of the future tenses; the person-and-number endings are: singular: first person *-v*, second person *-s*, third person *-n*; plural: first person exclusive *-wun*, inclusive *-t* or *-p*, second person *-sun*, third person *-tin*. These endings are combined in Table 2.10 with the tense suffix always preceding the person and number suffix, for the verb *baka-* 'find'.

Since the Altaic languages, perhaps especially the Turkic languages, have a large number of categories that can be expressed by means of suffixes, it is possible to build

Table 2.9. *Illustration of Evenki declension*

	SG	PL
	SG	PL
NOM	bira	bira-l
ACC	bira-wa	bira-l-wa
DAT-LOC	bira-duu	bira-l-duu
ABL	bira-git	bira-l-git

Table 2.10. *Illustrations of Evenki conjugation*

	PAST	FUTURE
SG1	baka-ćaa-v	baka-ʒaŋaa-v
2	baka-ćaa-s	baka-ʒaŋaa-s
3	baka-ćaa-n	baka-ʒaŋaa-n
PL1 EXCL	baka-ćaa-wun	baka-ʒaŋaa-wun
INCL	baka-ćaa-t (or -p)	baka-ʒaŋaa-t (or -p)
2	baka-ćaa-sun	baka-ʒaŋaa-sun
3	baka-ćaa-tin	baka-ʒaŋaa-tin

very long words by utilising a number of such categories, and many such words are perfectly natural in ordinary discourse, e.g. Uzbek *sŭzla-s-gan-imiz-da*, literally 'talk-RECIP-PASTPART-1PL-LOC', i.e. 'in our having talked to each other', i.e. 'when we were talking to each other'. With nouns, one can form such complexes as Uzbek *kitob-lar-im-da*, literally 'book-PL-1SG-LOC', i.e. 'in my books'. As we shall see below, the order of suffixes within a word is fixed.

Before looking at some individual categories of nouns and verbs in Altaic languages, it will be necessary to expand in somewhat more detail the nature of agglutination in its purest form, and as it appears in Altaic languages, since in all Altaic languages there are certain deviations from strict agglutination. In a sense, there is a deviation from strict agglutination in the existence of vowel harmony, and also other assimilatory processes at morpheme boundaries, since they mean that a given category value does not always have the same morphemic representation; so that, for instance, the ablative in Kirgiz can appear as either -*dan*, -*dän*, -*don*, -*dön*, -*tan*, -*ten*, -*ton*, or -*tön*, or even (with a less regular alternation) as -*an*, -*en*, -*on*, -*ön* after the third person possessive suffix, as in *at-in-an* 'from his horse'. However, as a general rule one can say that such alternations are determined by general principles of the phonological structure of words in the Altaic languages, the alternations effectively serving to prevent violations of these general principles, so that the mere fact of regular alternations does not detract from the strict interpretation of agglutination.

However, in Altaic languages one does find, albeit much less frequently than in typically fusional languages like the older Indo-European languages, some instances where segmentation into separate morphemes is unclear or impossible, and instances where the expression of a given category value has different forms depending on other morphemes with which it is associated. We shall illustrate these deviations in turn. First, an example of problematic segmentation has already been introduced, namely the third person possessive ending in Turkic languages, where we may use Kirgiz as a typical example. In isolation, when added to a consonant-final root, the third person ending is usually *-I* in Turkic languages, and this is the form we find in Kirgiz; if, however, case suffixes are added to this form, then an *n* must be inserted between the possessive and case suffixes, as in *at-i-n-da* 'in his horse'. By setting the *n* up as a separate morpheme here, we have left open the question of whether the *n* should be assigned to the possessive ending (allomorph *-in* before a case ending) or to the case suffix (allomorph *-nda* after the third person possessive ending), and in some sense the choice is arbitrary. The segmentation is even more complicated in the accusative singular: after a vowel, one would expect the accusative ending *-nI*, as in *töö* 'camel', accusative *töö-nü*, but the accusative of *at-i* 'his horse' is *ati-n*, although *-n* does not otherwise function as an accusative suffix, and seems rather to parallel the *n* inserted between possessive and case endings. Further, the accusative ending *-I* in Turkic languages is itself somewhat problematical as an exponent of a single category, because it actually combines expression of case and definiteness, being used only for definite direct objects (see pp. 80–1).

Use of different suffixes in combination with other suffixes is found in certain instances in Turkic and other Altaic languages, so that in Kirgiz, for example, the first person plural suffix is *-k* in the past tense, e.g. *kal-di̇-k* 'we remained', but *-biz* in one of the future tenses, e.g. *kal-ar-biz* 'we will remain'. Similar phenomena are to be found in other branches of Altaic: in Evenki, one of the other future tenses has a set of suffixes rather different from those given above: *baka-da-m*, *-ńńi*, *-n*, *-ra-w*, *-p* (or *-t*), *-s*, *-ra*, where the first person plural exclusive form makes it clear that first person exclusive means speaker (first person singular, *-w*, which alternates with *-m* in Evenki) plus third person (*-ra*).

Another feature that distinguishes Turkic languages from such fusional languages as the older Indo-European languages is the absence of morphological classes of major parts of speech (e.g. nouns, verbs), such that different nouns would belong to different morphological classes and require, at least in certain instances, different suffixes. For Indo-European, we can illustrate this by contrasting Russian *ruka* 'hand', plural *ruki*, with *selo* 'village', plural *sela*, where in the second declension *-a* indicates nominative singular and *-i* nominative plural, while with declension 1b (first declension neuter) the nominative singular ending is *-o*, and *-a* functions as nominative plural. In general in Turkic and other Altaic languages, all nouns decline alike and all verbs conjugate alike: there is no division into classes, and there are no irregular items.

To this overall generalization, a small number of provisos must be made. Thus pronouns in Altaic languages, as in many others, show morphological idiosyncrasies, as when Azerbaydzhan has genitive *män-im* 'of me' for expected **män-in*, or Turkish has nominative *ben* 'I' but dative *ban-a*, with back vowels, for expected **ben-e*. There are also a few other morphological irregularities, such as, often, the verb 'to be', which as in many languages may show suppletion. In the Mongolian languages the distinction between human and nonhuman classes of noun is relevant in forming plurals: in Buryat, for instance, only human nouns can form a collective plural in *-nar*, e.g. *axa-nar* 'elder brothers'. No Altaic language, however, has a grammaticalised gender distinction, although Tungusic languages have some male–female lexical pairs differing only in vowel harmony class, e.g. Manchu *haha* 'man', *həhə* 'woman', and even *huwaśan* 'monk' (a loan from Chinese) *huwəśən* 'nun'. In some Tungusic languages, verbs are divided into a small number of conjugation types, depending largely on their phonetic structure, though also with some idiosyncrasies. In Nanay, for instance, there are four classes, and the different present tense formations can be seen from the following examples: *ʒubu-am-bi* 'I work', *ba-ra-mbi* 'I find', *agbin-da-mbi* 'I appear', *ga-da-mbi* 'I gather berries'; classes 3 and 4 differ in the past tense, e.g. *agbin-ka* 'he appeared', *ga-ća* 'he gathered berries'. But despite these deviations from strict agglutination, the morphology of Altaic languages does approach very close to the canonical agglutinative type.

In a brief survey of this kind, it is obviously impossible to describe adequately all the morphological categories across the range of Altaic languages, and so in the remainder of this section we shall concentrate on some of the major categories of nouns and verbs, pointing out in particular differences among different branches of Altaic or among individual languages.

All Altaic languages have the categories of number and case. The number distinction is singular versus plural (no separate dual), with a suffix marking the plural. The number of distinct cases in Altaic is usually fairly small, certainly in comparison to some of the systems in Uralic and Caucasian languages, the basic system being nominative, accusative, genitive (not Tungusic, except Manchu), locative, dative (more accurately: allative), and ablative, with instrumental often present too; loss of the genitive is rare, but is exemplified in Yakut. The locational cases simply distinguish place at versus motion towards versus motion away from, without specifying whether the location is more specifically 'in', 'on' or 'at', e.g. Kirgiz *at-ta* 'in, on, by the horse'. More accurate locational specifications require the use of postpositions or genitive expressions, as in Evenki *moo doo-duki-n* 'out of the tree', literally 'tree inside-ABL-3SG', i.e. 'from the tree's inside'. Postpositions are also used for relations where no separate case exists, as with the instrumental in most

Turkic languages, e.g. Azerbaydzhan *taxta ilä* 'with a board', where *ilä* is the instrumental postposition. Actually, this particular postposition in Azerbaydzhan has almost been transformed, at least optionally, into a new case suffix, since it can also occur suffixed to its noun, as *-la/-lä*, i.e. with vowel harmony variants. Where a noun has both the plural suffix and a case suffix, all Altaic languages agree in having the order case suffix after the number suffix.

Possessive suffixes on nouns are found in all Turkic languages, in most Tungusic languages (though not in Manchu), and in many Mongolian languages (including Buryat and Kalmyk; in Mongolian (Khalkha), the system of possessive suffixes is still in the process of developing). In the Tungusic and Mongolian languages, the possessive suffixes are of very recent origin, and are transparently reduced forms of the genitive of personal pronouns. Although the Turkic possessive suffixes probably derive from pronouns, this etymology is no longer transparent. One of the major morphological differences between Turkic on the one hand and Tungusic and Mongolian on the other is that in Turkic languages, the possessive suffixes precede the case suffixes, whereas in Tungusic and Mongolian we have the opposite order, reflecting the recent development of possessive suffixes in Tungusic and Mongolian from postposed unstressed pronouns. Thus in contrast to Kirgiz *at-im-da* 'horse-1SG-LOC', i.e. 'by my horse', we find in Buryat *gal-da-m(ni)* 'fire-LOC-1SG', i.e. 'by my fire', and in Even *ʒuu-dụ-n* 'boat-LOC-3SG', i.e. 'in his boat'.

From the suffix orderings given so far, the reader can deduce that in Tungusic and Mongolian languages the order where plural is included is Number–Case–Possessive. Within Turkic, nearly all languages have the order Number–Possessive–Case, as in Uzbek *kitob-lar-im-da* 'book-PL-1SG-LOC', i.e. 'in my books'. The only exception is Chuvash, which has lost the Common Turkic plural suffix *-lar*, replacing it by *-sem*, probably a recent innovation, since it does not undergo vowel harmony; this plural suffix follows the possessive suffixes, as in *tus-ăm-sem-e* 'friend-1SG-PL-DAT', i.e. 'to my friends'. The phenomenon of innovating a plural morpheme, though not the form itself, is shared by Chuvash with the Permic languages and Mari, with which it is in close contact. In the possessive suffixes, as in the pronominal system generally, the distinction made is between the three persons in the singular and plural; the distinction between first person inclusive and exclusive is found in some Mongolian and Tungusic languages. Common to the Mongolian and Tungusic languages is a special series of reflexive possessive suffixes, contrasting with the other person-and-number combinations, and used when the possessor is coreferential with the subject of the sentence, as in Nanay *buə məənə ụgda-ći-ari ənə-j-pu* 'we go to our own boat', literally 'we own boat-ALL-REFL go-PRES-1PL'; these reflexive forms must be used irrespective of the person and number of the subject.

Very similar to possessive suffixes on nouns are subject-agreement suffixes on verbs, with almost exactly the same distribution between the two across languages; no Altaic language, incidentally, has agreement with nonsubjects. Subject agreement is found in all Turkic languages, is widespread though clearly innovatory in Mongolian languages (and found in both Buryat and Kalmyk), and is found in nearly all Tungusic languages, though not in Manchu. Although a fully-developed system of verb agreement is clearly an innovation in the Mongolian languages, the suffixes developing from unstressed postposed subject pronouns, some of the verb forms found in Mongolian languages have subject person reference built into their meaning. In Buryat, for instance, there are several modal suffixes which can only be used when the subject is either first, or second, or third person, even though there is no separate indication of the person of the subject. Thus the form in *-ja* indicates a first person inclusive plural invitation, e.g. *jaba-ja* 'let's go'; the bare verbal stem is a second person singular imperative, e.g. *bü xele* 'don't cry'; the suffix *-g* gives a third person command, e.g. *jaba-g* 'let him/them go'. In Pao-an and Monguor, verbal forms have been discovered where the difference between final *-i* and final *-a* or *-o* distinguishes first person from second and third, e.g. *be varǯi* 'I finish', *če teerǯo* 'you hold', *nǯaŋ xaaǯo* 'he closes'. Since these forms have no obvious etymology, they are probably archaisms, and thus indicative of an earlier period when Mongolian languages had a very different system of person and number agreement.

In Turkic and Mongolian languages, subject suffixes are also regularly added to predicative nouns, adjectives, and other non-verbs, as in Azerbaydzhan *siz ham-iniz gatil-siniz* 'you all 2PL murderer-2PL', i.e. 'you are all murderers', *siz öz-ünüz ga ǯavan-siniz* 'you self-2PL also young-2PL', i.e. 'you yourselves are also young', or Buryat *ende-b* 'here-1SG', i.e. 'I am here'. While some Tungusic languages make frequent use of this construction, e.g Nanay *sii alu̠uṣimdi̠-ṣi̠* 'you teacher-2SG', i.e. 'you are a teacher', others use an overt copula, e.g. Evenki *ənii-m kolkosnisa bi-si-n* 'mother-1SG collective-farmer be-PRES-3SG', i.e. 'my mother is a collective-farmer'.

Altaic languages have a wide range of inflectional and derivational suffixes that can be added to verbs, the former expressing differences of tense, aspect, and mood, the latter primarily serving to indicate differences of voice or valency (e.g. passive, causative, reciprocal), and also certain aspectual and other values, such as inchoative, direction, etc. As an example of the kind of complexes that can be built up, one may cite Uzbek *juv-in-tir-il-moq* 'to be forced to wash oneself', literally 'wash-REFL-CAUS-PASS-INFIN'. In addition, aspectual values are often expressed by means of auxiliary verbs: thus, in the last sentence of the Tatar text on p. 86, the auxiliary verb *tor* ('stand' as a lexical verb) with the present gerund expresses progressive aspect, i.e. *selk-ep tor-də* 'shake-PRES-GER stand-PAST-3SG', i.e. '(it) was shaking'. In this general survey, it is impossible to do justice to this range of phenomena, and reference should be made to grammars of individual languages; the texts and example sentences also contain examples of different verb forms. In the following section on syntax we will, however, be looking in some detail at the interrelation of finite and nonfinite verb forms.

One characteristic verb category that is found widely in Turkic languages is that of inferentiality, whereby the speaker indicates that he cannot vouch from personal experience for the truth of the situation described (or the circumstances leading up to it). Thus in Uzbek we have, in addition to *xato qili-di-m* 'I made a mistake' (past tense in -*di*) and *xato qili-gan-man* 'I have made a mistake' (perfect based on the participle in -*gan*), a further form *xato qili-b-man* 'I have, it seems, made a mistake', based on the gerund in -*b*.

2.4 **Syntax**

The Altaic languages show overall a very consistent syntactic typology, although there are deviations in individual languages and language-groups. Basically, this typology can be summarized by saying that an adjunct always precedes its head, i.e. adjectives and genitives always precede the head noun, noun phrase arguments always precede their verb. In addition, the position before the verb is reserved for the focus of the sentence, that is for the essential new information carried by the sentence – although the general validity of this last statement has hitherto only been tested in detail against certain Turkic languages. Finally, conjunctions, whether coordinating or subordinating, tend to be absent, and either one finds finite clauses strung one after the other paratactically, or longer periods are built up in which all subordinate verbs are nonfinite, and only the last verb in the whole period is a finite form. We shall examine these various phenomena in order. In general, of the three branches of Altaic, Turkic languages adhere to this strict typology most closely, with more divergence in Mongolian and especially Tungusic.

Within noun phrase syntax, the main realisation of the rule that the adjunct must precede its head is that adjectives and genitives precede their head nouns. Examples with adjectives are: Tatar *kizil alma* 'red apple', Buryat *sesen xün* 'clever person', Evenki *aja bəjə* 'good person'. In general in the Altaic languages, adjectives do not agree with their head nouns in any morphological category, and in Turkic languages this is an absolute rule. In Mongolian one does, however, find deviations, to the extent that in some languages (including Classical Mongolian, albeit rarely) adjectives can agree in number with their head noun, or even take the number suffix instead of the noun, e.g. Buryat *exe ger-nüüd*, *exe-nüüd ger*, or *exe-nüüd ger-nüüd* 'big houses'; the former is the more traditional form, and the most usual in speech. There is, however, no case agreement, e.g. *sesen xün-höö* 'from the clever person'. In Tungusic languages, adjectives do not agree with their head noun, except to a limited extent in Even and more fully in Evenki. Indeed, Evenki takes adjective agreement so far that one can find adjectives agreeing in number, case, and possession, as in *aja-l-ʒi-tin awi-l-ʒi-tin* 'with their good boats', where plural *-l*, instrumental *-ʒi*, and third person plural possessive *-tin* appear on both adjective and noun.

The same principle manifests itself in the ordering of genitive and noun. In Turkic languages, the basic construction is for the expression referring to the possessor to appear in the genitive case, while the head noun takes a possessive suffix agreeing with the expression referring to the possessor. Thus we have Tatar *kamilä-neŋ ul-ə* 'Kamilä's son', literally 'Kamilä-GEN son-3SG', i.e. 'Kamilä's his-son', in a pseudo-English rendering that comes close to the Tatar original. The same construction is used with first and second person possessors, when it is desired to lay emphasis on the possessor e.g. *min-em kitab-əm* 'my book', literally 'I-GEN book-1SG'. Of course, if there is no stress on the expression referring to the possessor, then the suffix alone will suffice, i.e. *kitab-əm*. In addition to this basic construction, traditionally called the izafet, there are three further constructions that are found in Turkic languages. The construction closest to English, with the genitive case of the possessor and no possessive suffix on the head, is rare, and apparently restricted to first and second person possessors, as in colloquial Tatar *min-em kitap* 'my book'. The second additional possibility, no marking on either noun, is again very restricted, occurring especially with nouns as adjuncts which refer to the material of which something is (or seems to be) made, e.g. *altən kəlgan* 'golden feather-grass'. The final possibility is rather common, and the precise distinction between this type and the basic type is one of the main practical problems in describing genitive constructions in Turkic languages. In this construction, the adjunct takes no suffix, but the head noun has the appropriate possessive suffix. In Yakut, which has lost its genitive, except in set expressions, this serves as the basic way of expressing possession: *ial-lar buruo-lar-a* 'house-PL smoke-PL-3', i.e. 'the smoke of the houses' (the combination *-lar-a* functions as third person plural possessive suffix, though this combination, across Turkic languages, is ambiguous: it may refer to a single object possessed by several possessors, several objects possessed by one possessor, or several objects possessed by several possessors). In other Turkic languages, it expresses a more intimate connection between possessor and possessed (though without being identical to inalienable possession), e.g. Tatar *tukaj sigər-lär-e* 'Tukaj poem-PL-3', i.e. 'Tukaj's poems'. Very often, it corresponds to an adjective in English, e.g. Tatar *rus ukučə-sə* 'Russia scientist-3', i.e. 'the Russian scientist'.

In Mongolian languages, where the possessive suffixes are in any event less integrated into the language as a whole, one finds most frequently the English construction with the possessor in the genitive and no suffix on the head: *ax-iin nom* 'brother-GEN book', i.e. 'brother's book'. In Tungusic languages, on the other hand, even though the possessive suffixes seem to be of recent origin compared to those of Turkic, the basic construction requires the presence of a possessive suffix. Indeed, in the absence of a separate genitive case, this is the sole outward mark of the possessive construction, as in Evenki *purta suwərəkəə-n* 'knife tip-3SG', i.e. 'the tip of the knife'. However, the most interesting aspect of the grammar of possession in Tungusic languages is the distinction made here, but not elsewhere in Altaic, between alienable (indirect) and inalienable (direct) possession (Boldyrev 1976). The distinction may be illustrated from Nanay, which, like the other Tungusic languages, inserts a suffix before the possessive suffix to indicate alienable possession. In Nanay, *naj dịlị-nị* 'person head-3SG', i.e. 'the person's head' refers to the person's own head, the one that sits on his shoulders. On the other hand *naj dịlị-ŋu-nị* 'person head-ALIEN-3SG' would refer to the head of, for instance, some animal which the person in question happens to own, for instance a trophy.

When we turn to sentence syntax and word order phenomena, the most consistent verb-final patterns are found in the Turkic and Mongolian languages, while in Tungusic languages in general freer order is found, although there is still a strong tendency for the finite verb to come sentence-finally; see, for instance, the Orok text on page 89. Verb-final order may be illustrated by means of a Tatar sentence, in what is a reasonably neutral word order:

(2) *KOLXOZčə   -lar uzgan jel   bu TRAKTOR-nə*
     collective-farmer PL last   year this tractor   ACC
     satəp al-gan   -nar i -de
     buy   PAST-PART PL be PAST

     'The collective farmers bought this tractor last year'

The subject occurs at the beginning of the sentence; the verbal complex occurs at the end, with the finite verb *ide* in absolute final position; the direct object immediately precedes the verb, and other constituents are arranged between the subject and the direct object. Although this is the normal word order, it is certainly not the only word order. First, it is possible to permute the individual noun phrases ('the collective farmers', 'last year', 'this tractor'), to give sentences with the same cognitive meaning, but different emphases. Thus the noun phrase in sentence-initial position will normally be interpreted as topic of the sentence, and the constituent immediately before the verbal complex as focus, so that, for instance, *bu TRAKTORnə uzgan jel KOLXOZčəlar satəp algannar ide* would mean something like 'as for this tractor, the ones who bought it last year were the collective farmers', although this rendering is much less natural than the original Tatar. The fact that the focus occurs immediately preverbally is also reflected in the fact that special question words (such as 'who', 'what'), requesting an essential new piece of information, also occupy this position, as in the following Kirgiz questions: *kerege-de emne bar*? 'frame-LOC what be', i.e. 'what is in the frame?', *KARTA kajda asil-ip tur-at* 'map where hang-GER be-PRES', i.e. 'where does the map hang?'. If the answer to a special question is a whole sentence, then the new information immediately precedes the verbal complex, e.g. in answer to the first question: *kerege-de kat bar* 'in the frame there is a letter (*kat*)'; in answer to the second: *KARTA keregede asilip turat* 'the map hangs in the frame (*keregede*)'.

However, even in Turkic languages, deviations from verb-final word order are found, especially in the spoken languages: with the written languages, the rule of verb-final order has become part of prescriptive grammar, so that published texts often give a much greater impression of verb-finality than is true of other styles. Indeed, those Altaic and, especially, Turkic languages that are said not to have verb-final order are all languages with an exclusively oral tradition, and it is conceivable that the absence of any rule of rigid verb-final order for such languages is as much a reflection of this difference in stylistic functions as anything structural. For instance, Gagauz is described as having a basic word order with the verb following the subject (SVO), or in descriptive prose with the verb initial and the subject final. There are two reasons how this could have come about: first, due to the influence of neighbouring non-Turkic languages, such as Slavonic languages and Romanian; second, due to the stylistic function noted above, which was not then countered when Gagauz was elevated to the status of a written language in the 1950s. Only further detailed work on spontaneous speech in various Turkic and other Altaic languages will be able to resolve this problem.

One interesting word order phenomenon in Classical Mongolian, and some modern Mongolian languages (e.g. (Khalkha) Mongolian), is the postposition of an unstressed subject after the verb, thus breaking the usual verb-final word order. Such postposed subjects, when pronominal, are the origin of the subject-agreement suffixes that are found in such Mongolian languages as Buryat and Kalmyk.

As far as syntactic properties are concerned, Altaic languages in general make a sharp distinction between subject and direct object, for instance in that verbs agree only with their subject, and that in the passive only an original direct object can appear as subject of a passive verb (verbs without direct objects may, however, be passivisable as impersonal passives). However, this syntactic distinction is not reflected by any clearcut morphological distinction: while the subject, at least of a finite clause, nearly always appears in the nominative, there is no single morphological case in which all and only direct objects stand. In Turkic languages, the general principle is that indefinite direct objects are in the nominative, while definite direct objects are in the accusative, as in Tatar *bala-lar kitap uk-ij-lar* 'the children read a book' versus *bala-lar kitap-nə uk-ij-lar* 'the children read the book'. This special definite accusative is usually distinct from all other case forms; only in Chuvash is it identical to the dative. Although the distinction between the two direct object forms is often stated as being in terms of definiteness, thus presumably correlating with the presence versus absence of the definite article in languages like English, the definite accusative in fact has a somewhat wider use than this (Comrie 1978): it is also used if the direct object is part of a definite set (e.g. 'one of the books'), and where the referent of the noun phrase is important for the discourse as a whole (e.g. 'a certain book'). Mongolian languages have a similar distinction between marked and unmarked direct objects, though here animacy is also important, in addition to definiteness, so that even indefinite human direct objects tend to take the accusative ending. In Classical Mongolian, and more literary varieties of (Khalkha) Mongolian, subjects of finite clauses sometimes stand in the ablative case, if they refer to a person; this usage is apparently not characteristic of Buryat or Kalmyk.

Traditionally, in the Altaic languages, there seem to have been no finite subordinate clauses of the Indo-European type, various nonfinite constructions being used instead, with verbal adverbs (often called gerunds, especially in Soviet works, or con-verbs), verbal adjectives (participles), and verbal nouns (nominalisations). To introduce this discussion, we may examine some examples from the Turkic language Tatar. In Tatar, as in most Turkic languages, there is a reasonably clearcut distinction between verbal adverbs and verbal adjectives/nouns, although the internal division within the last class is difficult to draw. Certain nonfinite forms can be used as predicates, just as can adjectives and nouns, which tends to blur, but not remove, the distinction between finite and nonfinite forms.

English relative clauses are normally translated into Tatar by using a participle in place of the verb of the relative clause. This construction can be used to form a relative clause where the head noun has one of a wide range of functions within the relative clause, such as subject as in 'the man who went', direct object in 'the letter that you are sending', comitative in 'the man with whom we conversed'. These three expressions translate as follows into Tatar:

(3)   *bar-gan   keše*
        go PAST-PART man

(4)   *sez žirli -j   tor   gan   žir*
        you send PRES-PART PROG PAST-PART letter

(5)   *bez söjlä-š-   kän   keše*
        we talk RECIP PAST-PART person

In some Turkic languages, e.g. Turkish, there is a formal distinction between verbal adjectives and verbal nouns, corresponding roughly to the difference between relativising on subjects and relativising on other constituents (Underhill 1972). In most Turkic languages that have a system like that of Tatar, for relativising on nonsubjects the subject of the participle stands in the genitive, and the head noun takes the corresponding possessive suffix, as in the following example from Uzbek:

(6) *men-iŋ   joz -gan   xat -im*
     I   GEN write PAST-PART letter 1SG

This means 'the letter that I wrote', literally 'my having-written letter'.

The same verbal noun forms are used to replace nominal clauses, for instance the direct object clause in a sentence like 'he found out that I had seen', which would come out in Tatar as (7) or (8), since Tatar here has optional use of the genitive and possessive suffix:

(7) *min kür-gän   -ne   bel -de*
     I   see PAST-PART ACC know PAST

(8) *min-em   kür-gän   -em -ne bel -de*
     I   GEN see PAST-PART 1SG ACC know PAST

In this construction, it will be noted that the verbal noun declines just like any other noun, occurring here in the accusative case. In the locative, this same form can be used to indicate time when, as in:

(9) *min üze-m -neŋ ete -m   belän bergä   sokər bujlap*
     I   self 1SG GEN dog 1SG with together ravine along
     kütärel-gän   -dä
     ascend PAST-PART LOC
     'when I was climbing along the ravine together with my dog'

Verbal adverbs take no suffixes to indicate the subject of their own clause; usually, this is the same as that of the main clause, though it is possible for a different subject to be overtly expressed. In English, they can often be translated by verb forms in *-ing*, although they are used much more frequently than in English, and often the most natural English translation is just a coordinate construction, i.e. 'Zäjnäp read the letter and rejoiced greatly', 'the rain stopped and the children went out onto the street'; gerunds are also the most natural way of translating such coordinate sentences into Turkic languages, e.g. Tatar:

(10) *xat -nə ukə -gač, zäjnäp bik satlan-də*
       letter ACC read GER Zäjnäp much rejoice PAST

(11) *jaŋgər tukta-gač, bala -lar uram-ga   čək -tə   -lar*
       rain   stop   GER child PL street ALL go-out PAST PL

In Mongolian languages, essentially the same possibilities obtain, except that the distinction between finite and nonfinite verb forms is even less clear: since subject–verb agreement is a relatively recent phenomenon, many finite verb forms are simply nonfinite forms with the appropriate person and number suffixes. The main additional complication in Mongolian languages is the expression of the subject of nonfinite verb forms, which may be in the genitive, the accusative, the nominative, or even the ablative. Much work remains to be done in isolating and explaining the criteria which condition the selection of case.

From the above Turkic examples, it will be noted that the usual rules of Turkic word order are obeyed even when a constituent is a complex deverbal construction rather than just a noun or an adjective, in particular that attributes precede their head, and that the verb follows its object. The Tungusic languages have nonfinite constructions very similar to those of Turkic languages, but the word order rules are much less strict, with more complex expressions being placed after their head, as in the following Evenki examples:

(12) *bi PIS'MO-wa ga -ća   bi -si   -m,*
       I letter   ACC receive PAST-PART be PRES 1SG
       akii   -m   min-duləə uŋʒə-rii -wəə -n
       brother 1SG I   LOC send PART ACC 3SG
       'I have received the letter which my brother sent to me'

(13) *ənii -m   əə -ćəə -n saa -rə si*
       mother 1SG NEG PAST 3SG know   you
       tənəwə   əmə -nəə   -wəə -s
       yesterday come RESULT-PART ACC 2SG
       'my mother doesn't know that you arrived yesterday'

(14) *urə   ojo-loo -n oo -rii -duu   -w,*
       mountain top LOC 3SG be-at PART DAT-LOC 1SG
       umnəət xaktiral-la   -n, agdi -la   -n
       suddenly darken INDEF 3SG thunder INDEF 3SG
       'when I reached the mountain top, it suddenly grew dark and thundered'

Evenki also has verbal adverbs, but with these it is not possible to give separate expression to the subject of the verbal adverb, which must be the same as that of the main verb; this is therefore an example of a 'same-reference' construction, with the same-subject constraint, as opposed to a switch-reference construction (which would require distinct subjects) or a neutral construction, like the Tatar verbal adverb or the Evenki participle, which may or may not have the same subject. The following example is of an Evenki verbal adverb:

(15)   *taduu ʒuja-wii   oo -kaim,*
        there   tent REFL-POSS put NON-SIMUL-GER
        aanŋet   -ćee   -m
        spend-night PAST 1SG
        'having pitched my tent there, I spent the night'

Many Tungusic gerunds have distinct singular and plural forms (see the Orok text on p. 89).

Although such nonfinite forms are the basic and traditional way of expressing subordination (and also sentence coordination, when not by simple juxtaposition) in the Altaic languages, under the influence of other languages constructions more similar to those of English have been introduced. The most striking influence here, at least until very recent times, was that of Arabic and Persian on the Islamic languages, which borrowed from Arabic the coordinating conjunction *wa* 'and' (e.g. Azerbaydzhan *va*), and from Persian the subordinating conjunction *ke* (e.g. Azerbaydzhan, Turkish, Uzbek *ki*). The stylistic evaluation of these loans, and the extent to which they are used, varies considerably from language to language. In Uzbek they were apparently never part of ordinary speech, and have been more or less banished from current writing in the U.S.S.R. In Azerbaydzhan, on the other hand, which has a long history of close contact with Persian, subordinating *ki* and other conjunctions based on this (e.g. *čünki* 'because') are very frequent, and have been so, apparently, since the thirteenth century. The following examples are therefore taken from Azerbaydzhan:

(16)   *känd   -in   xäräbä-lär-in -dän määlum i -di   ki,*
        settlement GEN ruin   PL 3SG ABL clear   be PAST that
        buraan dusmän keč -miš   -dir
        here   enemy PASS INFER 3SG
        'from the ruins of the settlement, it was clear that the enemy had come by here'

(17)   *oγul lazim   -dir ki, bu čätinlik -lär-dän*
            son necessary 3SG that this difficulty PL ABL
            bas cixar-sin
            cope   COND
            'one needs a son who would cope with these difficulties'

This construction type differs in several ways from the original Turkic equivalents. First, its verb is finite. Second, the subordinate clause follows the main clause, in particular following the verb of that clause; in the case of relative clauses, the relative clause also follows its head, and may be separated from that head. However, there is one interesting respect in which the construction borrowed by the Turkic languages has been transformed in the borrowing process: in Turkic languages, the conjunction *ki* is pronounced as part of the preceding clause, and not as part of the subordinate clause, as in Indo-European languages or Arabic; thus *ki* is strictly a main clause-final marker indicating that there is a subordinate clause to follow.

Especially in the less widely spoken Altaic languages of the U.S.S.R., and in particular the Tungusic languages, which have developed as written languages under strong Russian influence, there has been a marked tendency to calque subordinate clause types on Russian models, for instance by using interrogative pronouns to introduce relative clauses, or to introduce time clauses, like Russian *kogda* 'when', which, like English *when*, can introduce both questions and time clauses.

TEXTS IN ALTAIC LANGUAGES

TATAR TEXT

ASFAL'T jul -dan bar-gan   AVTOMAŠINA, kinät
asphalt   way ABL go PAST-PART motor-vehicle   suddenly
borəl-əp,   urman-ga   ker -de.   ul altən
turn PRES-GER forest ALL enter PAST-3SG it gold
börk -el   -gän   kebek bul-əp   sargaj   -a
splash PASS PAST-PART as-if   be PRES-GER turn-yellow SIMUL-GER
bašla-gan   agač-lar ara   -sən -nan, tar   jul -dan
begin PAST-PART tree PL middle-space 3SG ABL narrow way ABL
bar-u -nən   dävam   it -te.   MAŠINA-da bar-učə
go VN 3SG-ACC continuation do PAST-3SG vehicle   LOC go PRES-PART
jäs   -lär-neŋ ǯər -ə, urman eč   -en-ä   ker -gäč,
young PL GEN song 3 forest inside 3 ALL enter PAST-GER
tagən da köčle -räk   bul-əp   jaŋgəra-də.
again also strong COMPAR be PRES-GER sound PAST-3SG

jele　　　　-gez!　　　　-di -p　　　　　kəčkər-də　　　　　kemder.

bend-down IMPER-2PL say PRES-GER shout　PAST-3SG someone

jul kərəj-ən -da,　MAŠINA-da　kil-üče　　　　-lär-ne,

way edge 3SG LOC vehicle　　LOC go PRES-PART PL ACC

kočag　-ən -a　　al -ərga　telä -gän　　　　　-däj　botak - lar-ən

embrace 3SG ALL take PURP wish PAST-PART ADV branch PL ACC

ǯäj　　　　-ep,　　　　kart imän utər-a　　　　　i -de.

spread-out PRES-GER old　oak　sit　　SIMUL-GER be PAST-3SG

üt -ep　　　　barəšlə beräv anəŋ　berničä jafrag-ən

pass PRES-GER en-route one　it-GEN some　　leaf　ACC

öz　　-ep　　　　al -də.　　　　imän, xäjerle jul!

tear-off PRES-GER take PAST-3SG oak　　happy way

di -gän　　　　kebek, julčə　-lar küz-dän jugal　-gančə,

say PAST-PART as-if　　traveller PL eye ABL disappear FUT-GER

botag -ən　selk -ep　　　　tor -də.

branch ACC shake PRES-GER stand PAST-3SG

(Adapted from a text by M. Xäsänov, reprinted in S. Ramazanov and X. Xismätullin, *Tatar tele GRAMMATIKAsə: FONETIKA häm MORFOLOGIJA*. Kazan', 1954.)

Notes

Phonetic: The symbols *e*, *ə*, *o*, *ö* represent close–mid vowels (corresponding to Proto-Turkic *i, *i, *u, *ü). The symbols *č*, *ǯ* represent, in standard Tatar, fricatives rather than affricates; *č* is more palatalised than *š*.

di-p kəčkər-də: literally 'saying, (he) shouted'; in Tatar, as generally in Turkic languages, only the verb *di* 'say' can introduce direct speech, and if necessary this must be used in the gerund form together with any other verb of linguistic communication (e.g. 'shout').

öz-ep al-də: literally 'tearing-off, (he) took'; the combination of the present gerund with the auxiliary verb *al* 'take' indicates a complete action.

jugal-gančə: future gerund of *jugal* 'disappear'; this form means 'before V-ing'.

selk-ep tor-də: literally 'shaking, (it) stood'; the combination of the present gerund with the auxiliary verb *tor* 'stand' indicates progressive aspect.

FREE TRANSLATION

Turning suddenly, the vehicle which had been going along the asphalt road went into the forest. It continued its journey along the narrow path in between the trees, which had begun to turn yellow, as if splashed with gold. Having entered the interior of the forest, the song of the young people travelling in the vehicle sounded again more strongly.

'Duck down!' someone shouted. By the edge of the path stood an old oak, spreading out its branches as if wishing to take those travelling in the vehicle into its embrace. In passing by, one person tore off some of its leaves. The oak, as if saying, 'Bon voyage!', went on shaking its branches until the travellers disappeared from sight.

BURYAT TEXT

xelen   tuxaj jürenxii medeen   -üüd.
language about general information PL

   xelen   geeše oloñiitiin üzegdel   jüm.   'xelen   bolbol
   language SU   social   phenomenon COP-PRES language SU-COP

xün   -üüd-ej   beje beje -tejee   xarilsa   -xa, hanal
person PL GEN body body COMIT-REFL be-in-relation VN opinion

bodol -nuud-aa   andalda -lsa   -xa, beje beje -e
thought PL   ACC-REFL exchange RECIP VN body body ACC-REFL

ojlgo   -lso   -xo arga zebseg   mün.'
understand RECIP VN means instrument COP-AFFIRM

   xelen   geeše uxaan bodol -toj   sexe xolboo-toj
   language SU   mind thought COMIT direct link   ADJ

baj-dag   tuladaa   hanal   bodol andalda -xa arga
be FREQ on-account-of opinion thought exchange VN means

bolo   -žo   šada   -na.   xün   -üüd xamtiin - gaa
becomes PRES-GER be-able PRES person PL common ABL

xüs -öör   ažabajdal-aa   baj-guul -ža,   ažal
effort INSTR life   ACC-REFL be CAUS PRES-GER work

xüdelmeri xe -že   jaba-xa -daa,   mede-že,
work   do PRES-GER go   VN DAT-LOC-REFL know PRES-GER

ojlgo   -žo   aba -han   bügede-jee
understand PRES-GER take PERF-PART all   ACC-REFL

xel   -eeree,   todorxojl-on   xele -bel,
language INSTR-REFL explain   SIMUL-GER speak COND

üge - nüüd-iije   medüülel bolgon xolbo-žo
word PL   ACC sentence as   link PRES-GER

bexi -ž -üül   -deg.   xün   - üüd hanal   bodol -oo
strong V CAUS FREQ person PL opinion thought ACC-REFL

xododoo üge - *nüüd-eer*   *ba medüülel dotor ünen- üüd-ej*
always   word PL   INSTR and sentence within truth PL   GEN
taaral   - *nuud-aar*   *garga* - *n*   *xar-uul* - *dag,*
correspondence PL   INSTR produce SIMUL-GER see CAUS FREQ
t'iig - *ee* - *güj* *haa, hanal* *bodol* *bolo* - *žo*
do-thus PAST NEG if   opinion thought become PRES-GER
šada - *xa* - *güj* *jüm.*
be-able FUT NEG COP-PRES

(Excerpted from D. D. Dugar-Žabon, *Buŕat xelen, negedeẋi xuƃi: LEKSIKe, FONETIKe ba MORFOLOGI.* Ulan-Ude, 1958.)

Notes

Phonetic: *ö* and *ü* represent central vowels; *aj, ej, oj, uj* are phonetically long front vowels; see pp. 68–9.

geeše, bolbol: these are subject markers, although their precise function (perhaps in terms of topic–comment structure) is not understood.

jüm, mün: these are some of the invariable copular particles found in Buryat and other Mongolian languages.

beje beje-: literally 'body body'; the use of *beje* twice indicates reciprocity, i.e. 'one another'.

ojlgo-žo aba-han: literally 'understanding, having taken'; this gerund with the auxiliary verb *aba-* 'take' indicates doing something for oneself, i.e. 'having understood for oneself'.

Note the frequent stylistic device of adjoining near synonyms, e.g. *arga zebseg* 'means instrument', *hanal bodol* 'opinion thought'.

FREE TRANSLATION

General information about language.

Language is a social phenomenon. 'Language is an instrument so that people can be in relation with one another, exchange thoughts, and understand one another.'

Language is able to be a means for exchanging thought because it is directly linked with thought. People, in building their life by common effort and performing labour, know and understand everything with their language, more accurately speaking, they consolidate the words by linking them as a sentence. People always express their opinion with words and with reflections of truths in a sentence, otherwise thought would not be able to arise.

OROK TEXT

ȝarguli amba   -nne
wolf   evil-power 3SG

   xalaanda bolo   puttabee -la -ni   new   -munə -səl getta
   once   autumn snare month LOC 3SG younger-brother COMIT PL Getta

putta- tći- nda-ma   -ri ŋənə -yə   -ći.   noo -ći   ugda-ȝi   geeda
snare V   GO SIMUL-GER PL go-off PAST 3PL they 3PL boat INSTR one

unnee   solo   -yo   -ći.   ća   uni -ki   noo -ći   bolon -bolon
river-ACC go-upriver PAST 3PL that river PROL they 3PL autumn autumn

putta- tću-uki   -li bi -tći   [-ći].   ŋənə -mȝe   geeda
snare V   HABIT-PART PL be PAST   3PL go-off SIMUL-PROTR-GER one

muŋgə   -du   xak -kotćee   -ri. ćai-va   umi -ya   -ći. ćai-va
river-bend LOC land NON-SIMUL-GER PL tea ACC drink PAST 3PL tea ACC

umi -ma   -ri xodi -ya   -ći. agduma   -ni   ȝisei
drink SIMUL-GER PL finish PAST 3PL elder-brother 3SG from-shore-to-forest

kapa -xa   -ni   itə-ndə-mi   xaida pokto-ni   [bi-wə -ni].
go-up PAST 3SG see GO PURP what track 3SG be ACC 3SG

   noo-ni   ća   kapa -yatći   itə -xə   -ni   geeda kadara poktoo   -ni.
   he   3SG thither go-up PAST-GER see PAST 3SG one   bear   track-ACC 3SG

tar kadara-ŋu   -ni unnee   solo   -i   pukći-xə   -ni
that bear   ALIEN 3SG river-ACC go-upriver PRES-PART run   PAST 3SG

pokto-ni. kadara xamara-kke -ni xasa -ma   -ri ȝiŋ bara ȝarguli
track 3SG bear   behind PROL 3SG pursue SIMUL-GER PL very many wolf

ŋənə -yə   -ći. tamatću noo-ni ugda-taki əw   -du   -xə   -ni.
go-off PAST 3PL then   he 3SG boat ALL go-down RETURN PAST 3SG

(Adapted from T. I. Petrova, *Jazyk orokov (ul'ta)*. Leningrad, 1967.)

Notes

Phonetic: Consonants are palatalised before *i*, *e*. The source indicates that the oppositions *i/į* and *u/ų* are being lost in Orok, and does not indicate them. Certain inconsistencies of the original have been retained, in the absence of independent checks on the data.

   noo-ći 'they', *noo-ni* 'he': in Orok, the third person pronoun stem *noo-* requires the corresponding possessive suffix to distinguish these two forms.

   bolon-bolon: reduplication can indicate distributivity, i.e. 'each autumn'.

   putta-tću-uki-li: for *putta-tći-wki-li.

FREE TRANSLATION

The evil power of wolves.

Once, in autumn, in the month of snare-setting, Getta and his younger brother went off, setting snares. They went up one river by boat. Along that river they used to set snares every autumn. When they were going, after they had landed at a certain river-bend, they drank tea. They finished drinking tea. The elder brother went up from the shore to the forest to go and see whose tracks were there.

Having gone up there, he saw the tracks of one bear. The tracks of this bear of his ran upriver. Very many wolves went chasing along behind the bear. Then he went back down to the boat.

FURTHER READING

General introductions to the field of Altaic linguistics, presupposing at least the genetic unity of Micro-Altaic, are Poppe (1965), Ramstedt (1957–52), and Benzing (1953), the last concentrating on Turkic languages. Possible syntactic typological arguments for the unity of Uralo-Altaic are discussed in Fokos-Fuchs (1962). *HdO* 1, 5.1–3 (1963–8) is a handbook on Altaic linguistics dealing separately with Turkic, Mongolian, and Tungusic languages.

The standard Soviet introduction to Turkic linguistics is Baskakov (1969). Of works available in English, Menges (1968) provides information both on comparative grammar and on individual languages, while Wurm (1954) examines the sociolinguistics of the Turkic languages of the U.S.S.R., adopting a very critical view of Soviet policies in this area. The first two volumes of a controversial new comparative grammar of Turkic languages are Ščerbak (1970; 1977). Outline sketches of individual Turkic languages from a comparative-historical perspective, written in English, French, or German, are given in *PhTF* I (1959), while sketches of the Turkic languages of the U.S.S.R. constitute *JaNSSSR* II (1966). Gadžieva (1973) is a recent Soviet work on syntactic typology of Turkic languages. Although Turkish is not a language of the U.S.S.R., it remains the most fully described Turkic language: an excellent reference grammar in English is Lewis (1967).

The following reference grammars for individual Turkic languages of the U.S.S.R. follow the order of languages in Table 2.2.

For Chuvash, there is a description in English by Krueger (1961).

For Azerbaydzhan, in addition to a comprehensive grammar in Russian, *GAzJa* (1971), there is a more basic treatment in English by Simpson (1957) as well as a pedagogical grammar, concentrating on the dialects of Iran (Householder and Lofti 1955). A comprehensive account of Gagauz, including syntax, is now available in Pokrovskaja (1964; 1978). For Turkmen, in addition to the first volume of a grammar in Russian by Baskakov (1970), there is a more basic treatment in English (Dulling 1960).

Musaev (1964) is the standard work on Karaim, while Dmitriev (1940) remains the standard comprehensive account of Kumyk. For Karachay-Balkar, Aliev (1972) deals with syntax only. There is no recent literature on Crimean Tatar.

For Tatar there is a comprehensive grammar in Russian, *STLJa* (1969–71), and a more basic treatment in English, Poppe (1963). For dialects of Siberia, see Tumaševa (1977). For Bashkir, the most recent Soviet treatment is Dmitriev (1948), while in English there is Poppe (1964).

The most recent monograph account of Nogay is Baskakov (1940), though there is a more recent sketch of Nogay grammar by Baskakov in *NogRS* (1962). For Karakalpak, the standard work is Baskakov (1951–2); in addition, there is a discussion of Karakalpak phonology in English by Menges (1947). For Kazakh, standard works in Russian are *SKazJa* (1962) on phonetics and morphology, and Balakaev (1959) on syntax.

The standard Russian grammar of Uzbek is Kononov (1960), while in English there is the briefer treatment by Sjoberg (1963), as well as a pedagogical grammar by Raun (1969). Von Gabain (1945), in German, deals with Uzbek as written before the switch to the Cyrillic alphabet. For Uygur, reference should be made to Nadžip (1960), also available in an English translation.

The standard grammar of Tuva in Russian is Isxakov and Pal'mbax (1961). Of the very limited material on Tofa, Rassadin (1978) deals with morphology only. The Russian literature on Yakut is particularly extensive, with Xaritonov (1947) on morphology and Ubrjatova (1950–76) on syntax, the latter making Yakut one of the most fully discussed Turkic languages of the U.S.S.R. from a syntactic viewpoint. In English there is Krueger (1963), while a classic description, still of value, is that in German by Böhtlingk (1851).

GXakJa (1975) is the standard account of Khakas in Russian, while for Shor reference must be made back to Dyrenkova (1941). There is no comprehensive description of Chulym Tatar. An older reference in Russian for Kirgiz is Batmanov (1939–40), while Batmanov (1963) is the first volume of a new series: in English, there is Herbert and Poppe (1963). For Altay, Baskakov (1958) should be consulted.

For Mongolian languages, Poppe (1955) provides an introduction in English. Sanžeev (1953; 1963) is a standard comparative grammar in Russian. Sketches of Buryat and Kalmyk are included in *JaNSSSR* V (1968). Poppe (1970), though devoted primarily to (Khalkha) Mongolian, also includes some general information on the other Mongolian languages. Given the interplay between the modern languages and the classical language, a reference to the latter is in order: Poppe (1954) (in English). The most fully described Mongolian language is (Khalkha) Mongolian, for which see Street (1963); Bertagaev (1964), on syntax; also the transformational syntax approach adopted in Binnick (1979).

Buryat is described in English in Poppe (1960), and in more detail in Russian in *GBurJa* (1962), on phonetics and morphology, and Bertagaev and Cydendambaev (1962) on syntax. For Kalmyk, see Sanžeev (1940).

The only comprehensive comparative grammar of the Tungusic languages is Benzing (1956), but more specific problems are treated in the following: phonology in Cincius (1949); verbal morphology in Sunik (1962); and syntax in Sunik (1947). Sketches of the individual languages of the U.S.S.R. are to be found in *JaNSSSR* V (1968), and for most of the smaller languages these are the only comprehensive recent accounts. For Evenki, comprehensive accounts of phonetics and morphology are provided by Konstantinova (1964) and of syntax by Kolesnikova (1966). Even is described in German by Benzing (1955), and in Russian by Cincius (1947). For Nanay, there is the detailed description by Avrorin (1959–61). For the smaller languages, one may cite the brief description of Ulcha by Petrova (1935), and the same author's account of Orok (Petrova 1967).

3

Uralic languages

In looking at the various branches of Altaic, in particular the Turkic languages, we were faced with immense problems in the internal classification of languages into genetic subgroups, but with a very consistent typology across all the languages concerned. In the case of Uralic languages, we have precisely the opposite problem: the internal classification of Uralic into subgroups presents few problems (though there are more complicated situations when one comes to the subclassification of individual branches), but typologically the Uralic languages vary immensely from one to the other, especially in phonology (including morphophonemics) and syntax. The straightforward genetic classification of the Uralic languages is in large part a reflection of the historical circumstances that gave rise to the current distribution of Uralic languages: various groups of speakers of Uralic dialects/languages gradually split off from the main branch of Uralic, in the order: Samoyedic, Ugric, Permic, the remainder then splitting into Volgaic and Balto-Finnic; only Lapp stands somewhat outside this classification, since it is considered a separate branch of Uralic, despite its close affinities to Balto-Finnic. In addition, the various branches of Uralic developed in relative isolation from one another, often geographically separated from one another as a result of immigration of other peoples (especially Turkic and Russian) into intervening areas, and also as a result of their own migrations, most spectacularly in the case of the Hungarians.

In typological perspective, it is in general the case that the more easterly Uralic languages adhere more closely to the canonical subject–object–verb (SOV) typology, i.e. like Turkic languages, whereas the more westerly languages are close to the general European type, in particular with subject–verb–object (SVO) as their basic word order. There are, however, individual exceptions to this, especially in morphophonemics, where Balto-Finnic and Samoyedic share a number of complications. The usual explanation given for this situation is that Proto-Uralic was typologically similar to Turkic languages, and that the more westerly languages have come under strong Indo-European influence, leading to areal diffusion of SVO features. However, it must also be noted that many of the more easterly languages, as well as some of the centrally placed languages, have been under strong Turkic influence, which could have originated, or more likely reinforced, those aspects of their structure that are characteristic of canonical SOV languages. There is really no evidence that Proto-Uralic was consistently SOV in typology, although it was probably more so than the Uralic languages currently spoken in the west of the area occupied by Uralic-speaking peoples, in particular the Balto-Finnic languages.

Most of the Uralic languages are languages of the U.S.S.R., but, just as with the Turkic and Mongolian languages, the best-known and most widely spoken Uralic languages are not, namely Finnish and Hungarian (although, as we shall see, there are substantial numbers of Finns and Hungarians in the U.S.S.R.). One further language, Lapp, is technically a language of the U.S.S.R., being spoken by an autochthonous population without being the official language of any foreign state, but in fact most Lapps live in northern Scandinavia (including, here, Norway, Sweden, and Finland), so Lapp is rather marginally a language of the U.S.S.R. All the other Uralic languages are spoken almost exclusively within the U.S.S.R.

In cultural terms, the various Uralic peoples are very different from one another, indeed it is misleading to speak of an ethnic, as opposed to a linguistic, unity of the speakers of Uralic languages. In general, speakers of Uralic languages do not differ markedly in appearance and customs from their neighbours, at least not more so than do any adjacent speech-communities. Thus, the Hungarians present their own admittedly distinct brand of central European culture, but it is still more recognisably central European than related to that of their nearest linguistic relatives, the Khanty and Mansi in western Siberia. Likewise, the Finns fit into the general pattern of Scandinavian culture, as to a large extent do the Estonians. Most of the other Uralic peoples in European Russia differ little in appearance and customs from the surrounding Russian population, and in the case of the smaller population groups in particular (e.g. the smaller Balto-Finnic languages) are often undergoing the last stages of a process of ethnic and linguistic assimilation that began before the earliest Russian chronicles from the beginning of the present millennium. The Uralic peoples of Siberia and the Far North, e.g. Ob'-Ugric and Samoyedic peoples, fit traditionally into the same kind of subsistence economy, with primary emphasis on hunting, fishing, and reindeer-breeding, as do the non-Uralic peoples of the same area.

Table 3.1 presents the customary genetic classification of the Uralic languages, reflecting the way in which the various branches of Uralic have in turn split off from the main branch; the somewhat anomalous position of Lapp in this diagram will be discussed below. Before going on to the detailed discussion below, some preliminary points relative to Table 3.1 need to be discussed. First, the initial division of Uralic into Samoyedic and Finno-Ugric is a major division, and in many ways the modern

Table 3.1. *Genetic classification of the Uralic languages*

Samoyedic
  Northern Samoyedic: Nenets (Yurak Samoyedic)
                             Enets (Yenisey Samoyedic)
                             Nganasan (Tavgi Samoyedic)
  Southern Samoyedic: Selkup (Ostyak Samoyedic)
                             Kamas (Sayan Samoyedic)
Finno-Ugric
  Ugric: Hungarian (native ethnonym: Magyar)
    Ob'-Ugric: Khanty (Ostyak)
            Mansi (Vogul)
    Finno-Permic: Permic: Komi (Zyryan): Komi(-Zyryan)
                                 Komi-Permyak
                  Udmurt (Votyak)
        Finno-Volgaic: Volgaic: Mordva: Erzya-Mordva
                                   Moksha-Mordva
                          Mari (Cheremis): Meadow-Eastern Mari
                                         Hill Mari
                Lapp
                Balto-Finnic: Finnish (Suomi)
                             Karelian
                             Ingrian (Izhora)
                             Veps
                             Vot
                             Estonian
                             Liv

Samoyedic and Finno-Ugric languages are very different from one another. However, their genetic relationship is not really in doubt. Since the Finno-Ugric languages are much better known, and have been much more thoroughly studied than the Samoyedic languages, and also since there are more Finno-Ugric than Samoyedic languages with far more speakers, the term Finno-Ugric is often used loosely to include the Samoyedic languages. In the present work, we shall distinguish the terms, with Finno-Ugric being one of the two main branches of Uralic.

The genetic unity of Finno-Ugric was, incidentally, established slightly earlier than was that of Indo-European: in 1770 János Sajnovics published his *Demonstratio idioma Ungarorum et Lapponum idem esse (Demonstration that the language of the Hungarians and Lapps is the same),* while in 1799 Sámuel Gyarmathi published his *Affinitas linguae Hungaricae cum linguis fennicae originis (Affinity of the Hungarian language with the languages of Finnish origin);* many of the specific parallels noted by these scholars have withstood the test of time, and given that the similarity of Hungarian to Finnish or Lapp is much less obvious than that of Latin, Greek, or Sanskrit to one another, their work stands as a remarkable achievement.

In Table 3.1, it will be noted further that most of the Uralic peoples have at least two ethnonyms which are current in the literature: usually, one of these is the name given to themselves by speakers of the language concerned (or a large subgroup thereof, where no uniform name is used by all members of the group), and the other was originally that given to them by one of their neighbours and subsequently adopted by the scientific community. Since outsiders usually learn about a given people in the first instance from that people's neighbours, this situation is not uncommon in ethnography. In pre-Revolutionary Russia many of these nonnative ethnonyms took on pejorative connotations, so after the Revolution a policy was adopted here, as elsewhere in the U.S.S.R., of using primarily the native name, and this policy has now been extended to all Uralic peoples of the U.S.S.R. (though not to the non-Soviet peoples, the Hungarians and Finns, where the native ethnonyms, Magyar and Suomi respectively, are not used by the international community). In the present work, we adhere basically to this Soviet policy, given the orientation of our book as a treatise on the languages of the U.S.S.R. In most non-Soviet specialist literature on Uralic languages, the traditional nonnative terms are used, so reference will have to be made to the comparative nomenclature as given in Table 3.1. The only departures we have made from this policy are to use Ingrian (which is used by one subgroup of the Ingrians) rather than Izhora (Russian *ižorskij*), since the two are basically just phonetic variants of the same etymon, and to use Lapp rather than the native name Saame (Russian *saamskij*, which has replaced the earlier term *loparskij*), our motivation here being that the term Lapp is so well-known to the English-speaking community that it would be pedantic to insist on Saame.

3.1 The individual languages

In this section, we shall look at each of the languages in turn, concentrating on languages of the U.S.S.R., following the reverse order of branches from that given in Table 3.1, i.e. essentially working from west to east.

3.1.1 *Balto-Finnic languages*

The Balto-Finnic languages form a very closely-knit genetic group, and internal classification within this group is extremely difficult, indeed even the question of how many distinct languages are to be recognised has been the subject of considerable controversy, especially in so far as it served during the first half of this century to motivate and exacerbate territorial disputes between Finland and the

U.S.S.R. Within Balto-Finnic, two extremes of divergence can be recognised, represented by Finnish and Estonian. Most of the other customarily recognised languages are closer to Finnish than they are to Estonian (e.g. Karelian, Ingrian, Veps), while Vot stands between the more Finnish-like and the more Estonian-like languages, probably the result of Finnicisation of an originally more Estonian speech-variety. Liv stands somewhat apart from this classification, because of a number of idiosyncratic features, though it is clearly closer to Estonian than it is to Finnish. One of the main distinguishing criteria between Finnish and languages closer to it on the one hand and Estonian and languages closer to it on the other is the extent to which final vowels and consonants are retained (as in Finnish) or lost (as in Estonian). The application of this criterion is complicated by the fact that neither Finnish dialects nor Estonian dialects are consistent in this respect, with South-Western Finnish dialects having a more Estonian appearance than the general mass of Finnish dialects, and North-Eastern Estonian dialects having a more Finnish appearance. Probably the best internal classification of Balto-Finnic is as a dialect chain, though one where several intermediate links are missing, largely as a result of their assimilation to Russian, but partly as a result of the consolidation of remaining Balto-Finnic languages, with peripheral dialects assimilating to the more central dialects.

Finnish is the native language of almost all Finns, the majority of whom live in Finland, although there are also Finnish minorities in Sweden and the U.S.S.R., as well as elsewhere; the total number of speakers is over 4 million. In Finland itself, over 90% of the population is ethnically Finnish, speaking Finnish as a native language. However, the Swedish minority occupies a special position because of the particular historical development of Finland, and Swedish is an official language of Finland alongside Finnish, although the percentage of Swedish speakers has declined noticeably over the last hundred years, from over 14% in 1880.

At least until the declaration of Finnish independence in 1917, Finland and territories to the east were the subject of competing territorial claims by Sweden and Russia. From the Middle Ages Finland was under Swedish rule, but Sweden, after being forced to cede territories to the east and south of present-day Finland to Russia in various treaties during the eighteenth century, finally ceded Finland to the Russian Empire in 1809. However, Tsarist policy in Finland was very different from that in other non-Russian parts of the Empire: Finland retained a large measure of internal autonomy, in particular much of the control of the Grand Duchy was left in the hands of the Swedish aristocracy. Until almost the end of the nineteenth century, the sole official language of Finland was Swedish. In the second half of the nineteenth century, Finnish-speakers won a number of concessions, leading finally in the Constitution of 1919 to the declaration of Finnish and Swedish as coequal official languages of the newly formed republic, a situation which continues to the present day.

The differences among Finnish dialects is quite marked, and there are even instances where differences among dialects of Finnish (defined as a language in ethnic and political terms) are greater than those between some dialects of Finnish and some other Balto-Finnic languages: this applies in particular to Karelian. The current standard is not based specifically on any single dialect, and developed in the mid-nineteenth century as a compromise between competing claims of several individual dialect areas. In vocabulary, Finnish is one of the most puristic of European languages, but the development of Finnish syntax shows considerable foreign influence, especially of Swedish.

In the U.S.S.R. there are 84,750 Finns, a decline from the 1959 figure of 92,717, and the rate of language retention in 1970 is given as only 51%. Although the Finns in the U.S.S.R. had, in a sense, their own autonomous unit during the existence of the Karelo-Finnish S.S.R., the abolition of this Union Republic in 1956 and its replacement by the Karelian A.S.S.R. means that the Karelians, but not the Finns, have regional autonomy; however, as we shall see below, Finnish, in the Latin alphabet, is used as a language in education and publication in the Karelian A.S.S.R.

The descendants of the Balto-Finnic tribe of the Karelians do not form a unit, culturally or linguistically. The more westerly Karelians joined together with their neighbours to the west in the formation of the present-day Finnish people, and there is no more reason to distinguish them from Finns in general than to do so for any of the other tribes that joined with the name-giving tribe, the Suomi, in this process. The more easterly Karelians, however, had much closer contacts with Russians, and adopted basically Russian customs, including the Orthodox religion. When part of their territory was annexed by Sweden in the seventeenth century, some of these Karelians were so aggravated by the religious and other interference from the Swedes that they migrated well into Russian territory, to Tver' (now Kalinin), where their descendants still live. The term Karelian should be understood here, in its reference to a separate Balto-Finnic people and language, to refer to the eastern Karelians. Karelian falls into three main dialects: Karelian proper, Olonets (in Soviet work, especially, often called *livvikovskij*), and Lud. Of these, Karelian proper is closest to Finnish. In 1970, there were 146,081 ethnic Karelians, of whom 63% had Karelian as their native language, a noticeable drop from 71.3% of 167,278 in 1959. 57.6% of Karelians live in the Karelian A.S.S.R., where they form, however, only 11.8% of the total population (as against Russians with 68.1%); a further 26.1% live in the Kalinin oblast – these are the descendants of those who moved here to avoid Swedish control.

Karelian was used to a very limited extent before the Revolution as a written language, primarily for religious works. In the 1930s, a written language was used in the U.S.S.R. for some educational and publishing purposes, but its duration was very short-lived. Despite the large number of Karelian speakers, certainly relative to many of the other languages of the U.S.S.R., most Soviet Karelians are bilingual in Russian, as a result of living in areas where the population is increasingly Russian, and use Russian as their written language: even in the early post-Revolutionary years, substantially more Karelians were literate in Russian than in Finnish. However, standard Finnish is so close to Karelian that most Karelians can, with very little effort, become literate in standard Finnish. At present, both Russian and Finnish are used as written languages, in education and publishing, by the Karelians, with Russian playing the dominant role, especially in view of the ethnic and linguistic assimilation of the Karelians to the Russians.

Ingrian has often been considered as a dialect of Finnish and/or Karelian, and arose from the language of Finnish and Karelian settlers who migrated to this region, to the west of present-day Leningrad. Currently, the Ingrians are being rapidly assimilated to the Russians: in 1959 there were 1,062 ethnic Ingrians, in 1970 only 781; in 1959, 34.7% of Ingrians gave Ingrian as their native language, in 1970 only 26.6%. An Ingrian written language was used for very basic purposes in the 1930s, but was then discontinued.

Veps is another language at present in the process of rapid assimilation to Russian, a process which has been going on since the earliest written mention of the Veps a thousand years ago. The number of ethnic Veps fell dramatically from 16,374 in 1959 to 8,281 in 1970, the language-retention rate falling from 46.1% to 34.3%. They inhabit the triangle formed by the lakes Ladozhskoye, Onezhskoye and Beloye Ozero. In the 1930s, Veps, like several of the smaller Balto-Finnic languages, was used as a written language, but its status as a written language was soon discontinued.

Vot is spoken further west from Ingrian, between Leningrad and the Estonian border; it is very close to some Estonian dialects, indeed Vot and North-Eastern Littoral dialects of Estonian are mutually comprehensible, making these speech-varieties closer to one another than are extreme dialects of Estonian itself. The number of Vot speakers is very small, indeed so small that they are not listed separately in official Soviet statistics in recent years. In the 1940s there were around 500 Vot, but they suffered badly in the Nazi occupation and retreat from this part of the U.S.S.R. Ariste (1968) estimates that the number of Vot speakers is probably under 100. Vot has never been used as a written language.

With the Estonians we come to the second most numerous of the Balto-Finnic peoples, and the only Balto-Finnic language other than Finnish to have a written form at present. Most Estonians live in the U.S.S.R.: 1,007,356 (the smallest of any ethnic group having a Union Republic), of whom 95.5% speak Estonian as their native language. 91.8% of Soviet Estonians live in the Estonian S.S.R., where they constitute 68.2% of the total population. The Estonians thus form a compact population group and this, together with their own well-developed culture, developed largely in isolation from Russian, has kept them very independent linguistically: Estonians have something of a reputation in the U.S.S.R. for not speaking Russian well.

Although part of Estonian was under Russian (Kiyevan) rule in the eleventh century, their territory was for most of the intervening period the subject of struggles between German, Polish, and Danish invaders (the name of the capital city, Tallin (Estonian: Tallinn), meant originally 'Danish fortress'), with the Germans finally gaining control. Even when Estonia became part of the Russian Empire in the eighteenth century, the economic and political power of the German landowners remained paramount. After the Revolution, Estonia became independent, like Latvia and Lithuania, only to be reoccupied by the U.S.S.R. in 1940 as part of the nonaggression pact with Germany. Estonia was subsequently occupied by the Germans, and its effective incorporation into the U.S.S.R. started after the Second World War. Estonia is generally regarded as the technologically most advanced republic in the U.S.S.R., with continued maintenance of some of its cultural ties towards Scandinavia, especially Finland. Large numbers of Estonians also live abroad, mainly refugees from the incorporation of Estonia into the U.S.S.R., the greatest concentrations being in Sweden and North America.

Largely as a result of the long period of foreign rule during which Estonian culture was completely subordinated to that of the rulers, Estonian developed relatively recently as a unified standard language. Indeed, even the ethnonym Estonian gained wide acceptance among Estonians only during the nineteenth century. Another retarding factor in the development of a standard language was the great disparity between different dialects of Estonian. Indeed, on purely structural grounds, one could argue that there are actually two Estonian languages, North Estonian (or Estonian proper) and South Estonian, with the former being closer to Finnish than it is to the South Estonian. Once again, however, cultural and political factors have won out over structural similarity in defining language boundaries, so that Estonians as a whole have a feeling of unity among themselves and of distinctness from speakers of other Balto-Finnic languages. Within North Estonian there is also a cleavage between the mass of North Estonian and the North-Eastern dialect, which is closer to Finnish. In the early development of written Estonian, the Southern dialect played a major role, mainly because it was the language spoken around Tartu (then called Dorpat), Estonia's only university city. However, the numerical preponderance of speakers of Northern Estonian, and the fact that the capital city Tallin (formerly Revel) is in the Northern dialect area, determined the eventual adoption of a standard based on the Northern dialect, and the Southern dialect is no longer used as the basis of a written language.

Estonian has a number of features distinguishing it from the mass of Balto-Finnic languages. Lexically, it has a large number of loans from German (including Low German), e.g. *preester* 'priest' (German *Priester*), *piht* 'confession' (German *Beichte*), *kriit* 'chalk' (German *Kreide*), *kleit* 'dress' (German *Kleid*). In addition, during the development of standard Estonian in the late nineteenth century and early twentieth centuries several neologisms were created on an essentially arbitrary basis, many of which have been surprisingly successful, e.g. *relv* 'weapon', *reetma* 'to betray'. From a structural viewpoint, however, the most characteristic feature of Estonian (all dialects except the North-Eastern) is the three-way phonemic length opposition in consonants and vowels, as in *lina* 'flax', *linna* 'town-GEN', *linna* [linnna] 'town-PARTIT'. We shall examine this phenomenon more closely, as well as some of its implications for Estonian morphological structure, in sections 3.2 and 3.3.

The last of the Balto-Finnic languages to be considered is Liv, at present spoken by perhaps 300 people on the Kurland (Courland) peninsula in Latvia; all are bilingual in Latvian, and indeed their inevitable absorption soon into the Latvians ethnically and linguistically can be viewed as the final stage in the merging of Baltic (Indo-European) and Balto-Finnic substratum to give rise to Latvian (cf. p. 147). In the Middle Ages the area where Liv was spoken was a much larger area along the Gulf of Riga, and on the eastern side of the gulf Liv became extinct only during the nineteenth century. Liv is markedly divergent from the other Balto-Finnic languages, though with some similarities to Estonian, especially the dialect of Sarema (Estonian: Saaremaa) island, with which the Liv probably maintained close contact. Like Estonian, and unlike most Balto-Finnic languages (other than South-Western dialects of Finnish), Liv has many words ending in a wide variety of consonants, diachronically the result of loss of final vowels; however, it does not have the complex quantitative distinctions of Estonian. Unique to Liv among the Balto-Finnic languages is a phonemically distinct broken intonation (glottal constriction and devoicing in the second part of a vowel), clearly due to Latvian influence (see p. 151), although its occurrence in Liv follows from regular sound changes (e.g. from loss of *h*, and before certain newly geminated consonants); in addition, Liv has rising and (rarely) falling tones. In Estonian, incidentally, the quantitative distinctions also have pitch correlates, so that in a wider perspective these prosodic systems can be grouped together as characteristic of Estonian and Liv as opposed to other Balto-Finnic languages.

Liv was used in a limited way as a written language during the period of Latvian independence, the last publication being in 1939. At present it is not used as a written language, and Latvian serves the function of written language for the Liv. Liv is under strong Latvian influence, most noticeably in the lexicon, but also typologically, for instance in the development of the broken tone, perhaps also in the recent unrounding of front rounded vowels, and perhaps also in the development of a dative case separate from the allative, although the morphological material used for this distinction is Balto-Finnic (thus Liv distinguishes dative *jaalgan* from allative *jalgəl*, whereas Estonian has *jalale*, from *jalg* 'foot', in both functions).

3.1.2 *Lapp*

The position of Lapp within the family-tree of Uralic is one of the few points of unclarity in the relations among the major branches of this language-family, and this applies in particular to the relation between Lapp and Balto-Finnic. Ethnically, the Lapps are clearly distinct from the Balto-Finnic peoples, and their language is much more different from any Balto-Finnic language than any one Balto-Finnic language is from any other. However, there is no evidence for one traditional view, that the Lapps were originally a non-Uralic-speaking people who adopted a Uralic language from their neighbours, and in particular the retention of reconstructed Proto-Uralic vocabulary in Lapp is not noticeably lower than that in many other Uralic languages. Lapp does have a number of clear similarities to Balto-Finnic, including individual morphological affixes, in addition to typological similarities which may be the result of common origin or of contact (for instance, consonant gradation in morphology, discussed in section 3.2 below). The presently available evidence suggests that Lapp is a branch separate from Balto-Finnic, but more closely related to Balto-Finnic than to any other branch of Uralic, so that the family-tree of Uralic can be modified by inserting a Finno-Lappic group above Lapp and Balto-Finnic: Finno-Lappic would thus be coordinate with Volgaic within Finno-Volgaic, and it would in turn consist of two coordinate branches, Lapp and Balto-Finnic.

The differentiation within Lapp is very great, and it is thus misleading to think of Lapp as a single language, despite the clear ethnic unity of the Lapps. In fact, in recent work, around eight distinct Lappish languages have been recognised. Dialect differences do not correspond to the political frontiers of the area in which the Lapps live, so that the terms Norwegian, Swedish, Finnish, Soviet (Russian) Lapp are even more misleading. The three main dialect areas are Western (Northern), Southern, and Eastern, of which only the third is represented in the U.S.S.R. Subdivisions of Western Lapp are Ruija (the most widely spoken Lapp language/dialect), Lule, and Pite. Southern Lapp proper is spoken south of the river Ume, while Ume Lapp is transitional between Western and Southern Lapp. Eastern Lapp consists of the Inari, Skolt (Koltta), and Kola dialects, most Soviet Lapps being speakers of one of the subdialects of the last named.

The 1970 census recorded 1,884 Lapps in the U.S.S.R., of whom 56.2% have Lapp as their native language. In absolute terms, the number of Lapps continues to rise, i.e. ethnic assimilation seems not to be marked, in contrast to the smaller Balto-Finnic peoples, but linguistic assimilation is clearly on the increase. Outside the U.S.S.R., there are some 19,000 Lapps in Norway, 8,000 in Sweden, and 2,000 in Finland. Lapp is used as a written language in Scandinavia, though because of the marked differences between different varieties of Lapp several written languages are in fact in use. Lapp is everywhere strongly influenced by the dominant language of the country in which it is spoken (Norwegian, Swedish, Finnish, Russian).

3.1.3 *Volgaic languages*

The Volgaic branch of Uralic is rather less homogeneous than most of the other branches; in particular the two main subbranches within Volgaic, Mordva and Mari, are very different from one another, with Mordva having more similarities to Balto-Finnic than Mari does. However, the grouping together of Mordva and Mari, on the basis of shared innovations not shared with other Uralic languages, is beyond question. Both subbranches of Volgaic have been subject to considerable Turkic influence, as they are spoken in areas where various Turkic languages are also represented (Chuvash, Tatar), and this Turkic influence is most noticeable in Mari, which is quite similar typologically to a Turkic language, with verb-final word order and widespread use of nonfinite verb forms; as noted on pp. 92–3, it is unclear to what extent this can be regarded as a survival of the Proto-Uralic state as opposed to Turkic influence, but at the least Turkic influence must be attributed with having reinforced these features of Mari.

The Mordva fall into two major groups, differing from one another ethnically and linguistically, although the basic unity of the Mordva ethnic group is not compromised thereby: these two groups are the Erzya and the Moksha, the Erzya outnumbering the Moksha by about two to one, although detailed statistical data on the population numbers for Erzya and Moksha individually are not available. Linguistically, the differences between Erzya and Moksha are so great that speakers of the one are often unable to understand the other, and at present two written languages are in use. Indeed, in Soviet linguistic, as opposed to ethnographic, literature, it is usual to consider Moksha and Erzya separately, as different languages within the Mordva subbranch of Volgaic.

The Mordva are the most numerous Uralic people in the U.S.S.R., slightly outnumbering the Estonians both in absolute numbers and in number of speakers of the corresponding language (assuming Erzya and Moksha are counted together). Of 1,262,670 Mordva, 77.8% have Mordva as their native language. However, despite the large absolute numbers, the Mordva live scattered across a huge territory, where they are almost everywhere a minority among a Russian majority (and often mixed with other ethnic groups, e.g. Tatar). This reflects in part the history of the Mordva, and their attempts to evade first Tatar, then Russian domination by migrating frequently, until they were finally forced to adopt Orthodox Christianity in the eighteenth century. Only 35.4% of the population of the Mordva A.S.S.R. is Mordva (the majority is Russian), and only 28.9% of Mordva live in their A.S.S.R., the remainder being scattered across adjacent administrative oblasts.

Mordva was used in a very limited way before the Revolution for religious publications, but it was only after the Revolution that the two literary languages, Erzya and Moksha, were finally developed as media of education and publishing. While the phonemic system of Erzya does not depart significantly from the range represented in the majority of Uralic languages, Moksha has a number of unusual phonemic oppositions, in particular between voiced and voiceless nasals and liquids, e.g. *kalnä* 'fish-DIM', *kaḷnä* 'fish-NOM-PL', *kaĺ̥* 'willow-DEF-GEN', *kaʄ̥* 'willow-NOM-PL'; the voiceless phonemes occur, in general, only at certain morpheme boundaries.

The Mari are rather more compactly settled than the Mordva, although they too have been split up by Russian colonisation along the Volga, and this is reflected in the much higher language-retention rate: 91.2% of 598,628 ethnic Mari, even though the drop from 95.1% in 1959 is noticeable. The Mari constitute 43.7% of the population of their A.S.S.R., though there are also compact areas of Mari settlement in neighbouring administrative areas, especially the Bashkir A.S.S.R., where 18.3% of all Mari live. The question of whether Mari is a single language, or rather two languages, namely, Meadow-Eastern Mari and Hill Mari, remains undecided in official Soviet publications, although it is clear that the Mari constitute a single ethnic group, and equally clear that at present two written languages are in use, with the names as given above. If Mari is considered a single language, then these would be the two major dialects (in addition to a third, unwritten, Eastern dialect), each with its own written form. There are apparently no practical plans for the creation of a single Mari standard language. One phonetic characteristic of both forms of Mari is the existence of voiced fricatives, to the exclusion of voiced plosives (except as allophones of the former after nasals), in particular β, δ, and γ, in addition to z and $\check{z}$.

3.1.4 *Permic languages*

The present-day Permic languages are very close to one another, and indeed the earliest attested Permic language, Old Permic, cannot readily be described as the ancestor of any one individual modern Permic language, although it is closer to Komi than to Udmurt. The development of Old Permic as a written language is a unique phenomenon in the pre-Revolutionary language situation of Russia. At the end of the fourteenth century, actually before the final incorporation of the area inhabited by speakers of Permic languages into the Muscovite state, Stephen of Perm undertook missionary activity among the Permians, having himself learned their language, and devised a Permic written language, using an alphabet of his own creation. Written Old Permic was known to only a small proportion of the local population, and the use of this written language soon died out, but the surviving texts are of extreme importance for historical–comparative study of Uralic languages, because Old Permic is the oldest Uralic language attested by connected texts after Hungarian; and since Hungarian is strongly aberrant from the general Uralic pattern, the importance of Old Permic is thereby increased considerably.

At present, the Komi are considered, ethnically and linguistically, to form two separate groups, the Komi-Zyryans and the Komi-Permyak. However, in terms of linguistic structure, Komi-Zyryan and Komi-Permyak are very close to one another indeed, and if one were to divide the whole of the Komi area into major dialect groups, these would probably be Komi-Zyryan, Komi-Permyak, and Yaz'va, with the Yaz'va dialect actually being the most divergent of the three; speakers of the Yaz'va dialect are generally reckoned officially in with the Komi-Permyak. In non-Soviet literature, the term Komi tends not to be used, being replaced by Zyryan, which is thus a cover-term for all the Komi. In the U.S.S.R., Komi is often used without any qualification to refer specifically to Komi-Zyryan. The 1970 census figures give both combined statistics for all Komi, then separate statistics for Komi-Zyryan and Komi-Permyak. Komi-Zyryan was the native language of 82.7% of 321,894 ethnic Komi-Zyryan, 85.5% of whom live in their own A.S.S.R., where they constitute 28.6% of the population (the overwhelming majority is Russian). The Komi-Permyak constitute a majority in their own N.O. (58.2%), where 80.6% of them live; the language-retention rate is 85.8% among the 153,901 ethnic Komi-Permyak. It is interesting to note that, although the Komi-Zyryan are more numerous than the Komi-Permyak and have a greater level of local autonomy, language-retention is actually higher among the latter than among the former: the rate for Komi-Zyryan fell from 89.3% to 82.7% between the 1959 and 1970 censuses, that for Komi-Permyak from 87.6% to 85.8%.

After the rapid consignment of the Old Permic written language to oblivion, Komi was used to a very limited extent for religious and certain other purposes before the Revolution. At present, Komi is used for education and publication in the Komi A.S.S.R., while Komi-Permyak serves similar functions, to a slightly more limited extent, in the Komi-Permyak N.O.

The Udmurt are considerably more numerous than the Komi, though they have roughly the same percentage of language retention: in 1970, 82.6% of 704,328 Udmurt gave Udmurt as their native language; the Udmurt constitute 34.2% of the population of their A.S.S.R., which has a Russian majority population, and 68.7% of all Udmurt live in that republic. Apart from religious and a few other texts published in the nineteenth century, Udmurt was not used as a written language before the Revolution, whereas now it is used for schooling and publishing in the Udmurt A.S.S.R.

In concluding this section, we may note that representatives of the Volgaic and Permic peoples do not, in general, differ in appearance or general customs from the Russian population with whom they live, language being often the main distinguishing criterion. (Of course, assimilated speakers of Uralic languages have played a large part in determining the ethnic composition of the Russian people themselves.) Only in the north-east of the Komi-populated area, bordering on the areas inhabited by the Khanty and Mansi, do Komi speakers start presenting a more Siberian physiognomy, resulting from their closer connections with Siberian peoples, in particular the Ob'-Ugric peoples, to whom we now turn.

3.1.5 Ugric languages

The Ugric languages fall into two subbranches, Ob'-Ugric and Hungarian. The Ob'-Ugric languages are so-called because they are spoken on the river Ob' and its tributaries in western Siberia. The original home of the Ugrians was to the west of the Urals, from which the Ob'-Ugric peoples undertook a short migration to the east of this mountain range, while the Hungarians embarked on the most far-reaching migration of any of the Uralic peoples, bringing them eventually to present-day Hungary in the late ninth century A.D. Hungarian and the Ob'-Ugric languages are very different from one another in many respects, and it has been suggested that Ob'-Ugric and Hungarian should actually be regarded as distinct branches of Finno-Ugric rather than as subbranches of a single branch. The idiosyncrasies of Hungarian could, of course, equally be accounted for by the long period of separation between Hungarian and Ob'-Ugric (and indeed between Hungarian and all Uralic languages), leading to both different spontaneous innovations in either group of languages and strong foreign influence on Hungarian.

The two Ob'-Ugric languages are Khanty and Mansi. Khanty is spoken by 68.9% of the 21,138 ethnic Khanty, while Mansi is spoken by only 52.4% of the 7,710 ethnic Mansi. 57.8% of the Khanty and 86.7% of the Mansi live in the Khanty-Mansi N.O., but they constitute a total of only 7% of the population of this predominantly Russian-settled area. The Khanty and Mansi were incorporated into the Russian Empire at the time of the collapse of the Tatar khanate of Kazan', of which they had previously been vassals. They live scattered across vast areas in north-western Siberia, mainly along the river Ob' and its tributaries, engaging traditionally in hunting and fishing, with the reindeer as the main domesticated animal. The assimilation of speakers of Ob'-Ugric languages to Russian will probably increase dramatically in future years, as the reserves of oil and natural gas discovered in their N.O. are exploited.

The dialects of Khanty are extremely divergent, more so than for any other Uralic language, so that it is essentially the ethnic unity of the Khanty that leads to their language being considered a single language with several dialects rather than as a group of languages forming a subgroup within Ob'-Ugric. The major division is between Western and Eastern dialects. Within the Eastern dialects, there is a further bifurcation between the Surgut dialect and the Vakh-Vasyugan dialect: the latter of these is highly aberrant, both in phonetic structure (large number of vowel phonemes, including four reduced vowels, back rounded, back unrounded, front rounded, front unrounded, participating in a strict front–back vowel harmony system), and in syntax: Vakh Khanty is the only Uralic language to have a clearly defined ergative construction, as will be illustrated on pp. 130–1. Within Western Khanty, we have the relatively homogeneous dialect of the mouth of the Ob' (also known as the Obdorsk dialect), the virtually extinct Irtysh dialect, and finally the Ob' dialect, with three subdialects: Sharyshkary, Kazym, and Central Ob'. The divergences among all these dialects is so great that mutual intelligibility is excluded, and no attempt has been made to create a single written Khanty language that would serve speakers of all dialects. In practice, five dialects have been developed as written languages in the U.S.S.R., though they are used to varying extents: Surgut, Vakh-Vasyugan, Sharyshkary, Kazym, and Central Ob' (more specifically the Sherkaly variety of Central Ob'); the last named of these has been the most widely used. Written Khanty is used in basic education (first two grades), is taught as a school subject beyond this level, and is also used for a certain amount of publication. However, the lack of a unified standard language and the strong Russianisation of the area where the Khanty live will undoubtedly soon lead to the adoption of Russian as the basic medium of reading and writing, no doubt soon to be followed by the adoption of Russian as the spoken language too.

Though not to the same extent as Khanty, Mansi is also characterised by marked differences among the various dialects, of which four dialect groups are usually recognised, referred to geographically as Western, Eastern, Northern, and Southern. The area where the Southern dialect is spoken has been subject to most intense Russian influence, and this dialect is almost extinct. The highest language-retention rate is for the Northern dialect, and it is in this dialect that publishing is at present carried out, as well as instruction in the first two grades of primary school, after which Mansi remains as a school subject through further grades. As with Khanty, the low rate of language retention, the dialect diversity, and the influence of Russian, will probably soon lead to the extinction of Mansi.

Hungarian is not, of course, a language of the U.S.S.R., although there are some Hungarians in the U.S.S.R., predominantly in Transcarpathia, in areas ceded to the U.S.S.R. by Hungary after the Second World War. Hungarians in the U.S.S.R. number 166,451, of whom the remarkably high proportion of 96.6% have retained Hungarian as their native language, much higher than that for other ethnic groups, e.g. the Slovaks, who found themselves in the U.S.S.R. as a result of similar frontier shifts. Although the position of Hungarian in the family-tree of Uralic is relatively clear, and although Hungarian has the longest recorded history of any Uralic language–the first continuous text, the *Halotti Beszéd (Funeral Oration)* dates from the early thirteenth century – Hungarian is very divergent from the basic mass of Uralic languages and its role in the reconstruction of Proto-Uralic and in tracing the development of Uralic in general is correspondingly small. Hungarian vocabulary, for instance, reflects the chequered history of the Hungarians, with loans from the peoples with whom the Hungarians came into contact in their wanderings from the Urals (Chuvash, Ossete, various Turkic languages other than Chuvash), from the peoples with whom they came into contact in their new homeland in Europe (Slavonic languages), and from the peoples under whose rule they lived for many centuries (Turkish, German), as well as from Latin, for a long period the administrative language of Hungary. At present, Hungarians constitute almost the whole population of Hungary, but, as a result of the creation of other independent states after the First World War, in particular Romania, Yugoslavia, and Czechoslovakia, Hungarians form large national minorities in these countries. Some 12,700,000 Hungarians live in Hungary, over $1\frac{1}{2}$ million in Romania, and $\frac{1}{2}$ million each in Yugoslavia and Czechoslovakia.

Since Hungarian is not a language of the U.S.S.R., and since it is so divergent from the general run of Uralic languages, we shall refer to Hungarian relatively little in the ensuing discussion, except for certain specific points where Hungarian presents interesting parallels to the Ob'-Ugric languages or revealing contrasts with other Uralic languages.

3.1.6　*Samoyedic languages*

Although Samoyedic is coordinate with Finno-Ugric as a branch of Uralic, the speakers of Samoyedic languages number far fewer than do those of Finno-Ugric languages, and live scattered across vast areas of northern and central Siberia, extending into the far north of European Russia too. In current Soviet usage, the Russian term *samoedy* 'Samoyeds' has been replaced by *samodijcy* 'Samodi', mainly because the term Samoyed came to be felt as insulting in pre-Revolutionary Russian (because, in part, of association with the Russian prefix *samo-* 'self' and the root *-ed* 'eater', although the Russian for 'cannibal' is, in fact, not *samoed* but *ljudoed*, i.e. people-eater). Since this is essentially just a phonetic variant of *samoedy*, we have retained the customary English term Samoyed in this presentation.

The Samoyedic languages fall into two main branches, Northern Samoyedic and Southern Samoyedic. While the Northern Samoyedic languages are still reasonably viable, the Southern Samoyedic languages are witnessing the last stages of assimilation by other languages, in earlier periods by Turkic languages of central Siberia, more recently by Russian. The only Southern Samoyedic language with a sizable number of speakers is Selkup. The only other Southern Samoyedic language still spoken (or, at least, spoken in 1970) is Kamas, with just one speaker in 1970. Other Southern Samoyedic languages are known essentially by name only, having been assimilated before detailed recordings could be made of them, e.g. Karagas, Koybal, etc.

The most numerous of the surviving Samoyedic peoples are the Nenets, who live across a vast area stretching from the White Sea in European Russia to the Taymyr peninsula in Siberia. In 1970 there were 28,705 Nenets, making them the largest of the 'peoples of the North, Siberia, and the Far East'; 83.4% of them claimed Nenets as their native language. The Nenets have, in whole or in part, three N.O.s named after them: the Nenets N.O., where 20.4% of the Nenets live, constituting 15% of the population; the Yamal-Nenets N.O. (61.1% of all Nenets, constituting 21.9% of the population); and the Taymyr (Dolgan-Nenets) N.O. (7.5% of the Nenets, constituting 5.9% of the population). The majority population of each of these national areas is Russian. There are two main dialects of Nenets: Tundra and Forest Nenets, the latter with only about 1,000 speakers. Intelligibility between the two dialects is low. Internally, however, each dialect is remarkably homogeneous – in the case of Tundra Nenets this was fostered by close contacts between all groups of Nenets as the result of frequent meetings between different groups during their nomadic existence, as well as by relatively recent expansion over much of the area in which they live. Nenets (in the Tundra Nenets variety) is the only Samoyedic language to be used at all widely as a written language, including educational materials for the first five grades of primary school.

Enets is the closest of the Samoyedic languages to Nenets, in the south of the Taymyr peninsula. Precise statistics of the number of ethnic Enets and the percentage of Enets speaking Enets are not available, as the Enets usually classify themselves as Nenets or Nganasan in the census (depending on which group they live and work most closely with), and are in any case too few to be listed separately in the published census returns. They probably number around 200. Their language has never been used as a written language.

Finally, among the Northern Samoyedic peoples, the Nganasan inhabit the northern part of the Taymyr peninsula, making them the northernmost people in the U.S.S.R., in one of its climatically least hospitable parts. In 1970 they numbered 953, of whom 75.4% spoke Nganasan as a native language.

One of the phonetic characteristics of the Northern Samoyedic languages is at least one phonemic glottal stop. In Nenets and Nganasan there are two glottal stops, usually described as nasalised and nonnasalised respectively: most Soviet accounts list them as distinct phonetically and phonemically, and they are certainly distinct morphophonemically. Morphophonemically, the former alterates with *n* and *j*, the latter with *s* and *d* (these data are for Nenets; in Enets, the range of sounds with which they alternate is broader).

Of the Southern Samoyedic languages, only Selkup can really be said to survive, being spoken by 51.1% of 4,282 ethnic Selkup, a percentage that has remained more or less constant since the 50.6% registered in 1959. There are two main dialects of Selkup, the more southerly Narym dialect and the more northerly Taz dialect. The speakers of Narym Selkup have been almost completely assimilated by the Russians, so that Taz is the only dialect with a substantial number of speakers. There does exist a Selkup written language, but its use is very restricted, at present apparently to a single primer used in the first grade of primary school. Because of their close ties with the Khanty (formerly known as the Ostyak), to the south of whom they live, in earlier literature the Selkup (like the genetically completely unrelated Ket) are often confused with the Ostyak, or given the name Ostyak Samoyeds. Linguistically, however, there is no close genetic connection between Khanty and Selkup, and no genetic connection whatsoever between either of these and Ket.

3.2 Phonology

As soon as one starts looking at typological properties of Uralic languages, one finds, in contrast to Turkic languages, or even Altaic languages as a whole, a relatively wide range of diversity. Even though Uralic languages are clearly all related genetically, while this cannot be said of Altaic languages, they present a much wider range of structures in both phonology and syntax. For instance, there are Uralic languages with vowel harmony and Uralic languages without vowel harmony, the distinction not necessarily correlating with genetic subgroups within Uralic: thus Finnish and Hungarian have vowel harmony, whereas Estonian does not. There are Uralic languages with basic subject–object–verb word order, such as the Ob'-Ugric and Samoyedic languages, and Uralic languages with basic subject–verb–object word order, such as the Balto-Finnic languages.

Even more surprisingly, one often finds languages that share typological features in common as a result of historical accident, i.e. two Uralic languages which are not closely related genetically end up having some feature in common that was not directly inherited from the proto-language, and which may be absent from other languages more closely related to these languages than these languages are to one another. For instance, both Finnish and most Hungarian dialects have exactly the same system of short vowel phonemes: *i e ü ö ä u o a*. In both languages, with respect to vowel harmony *i* and *e* are neutral, the morphophonemic back–front opposition opposing only *u*, *o*, *a* to *ü*, *ö*, *ä*. Yet these systems developed in large measure independently in the two languages, the front rounded vowel *ö* of Hungarian, in particular, being a relatively recent innovation.

In this section on phonology, we shall be concerned with two main phenomena in various Uralic languages: vowel harmony, and consonant (and vowel) gradation. Before embarking on these topics, we should just mention a few other salient features of Uralic phonology, although it will be borne in mind that not all of these statements apply to all Uralic languages, and some individual Uralic languages have quite marked idiosyncratic properties, as was discussed in the introduction of individual languages in section 3.1.

Front rounded and, to a lesser extent, back or central unrounded vowels are characteristic of a wide range of Uralic languages, and are not restricted to languages that show vowel harmony. Unusual consonant segments, such as voiceless sonants in Moksha Mordva, the nasalised glottal stop in Nenets and Enets, are restricted to individual languages. The syllable structure of most Uralic languages, inherited from Proto-Uralic, is *CVCC* (consonant–vowel–consonant–consonant). Simpler syllable structures characterise many Balto-Finnic languages, with exclusion of word-final and word-medial sequences of syllable-final consonants through simplification of consonant clusters; in the southern Balto-Finnic languages, this pattern has since been reversed through loss of final vowels, so that Estonian, for instance, now has word-final sequences of consonants again, as in *jalg* 'leg' (cf. Finnish *jalka*). In the Mordva languages, exceptionally, consonant clusters are not infrequent in word-initial position, e.g. Erzya *ksna* 'belt', Moksha *traks* 'cow'. Vowel alternations other than those due to vowel harmony, assimilation, and vowel gradation are found in many Uralic languages, and are particularly widespread in the Northern Samoyedic languages, e.g. Nenets *sa* 'trace (of harness)', accusative plural *so*; *toś* 'to arrive', imperative *tu?*.

In Uralic languages that have vowel harmony, the determining vowel feature is front versus back; only very occasionally do other parameters also play a role, such as rounding. Consistent front versus back systems are rare in Uralic, as opposed to Turkic and Mongolian, but one such system is found in Vakh Khanty, in which a given word has either all front vowels (*i e ä ü ö ӟ ö*) or all back vowels (*i a u o ə ə*). Note that the front vowel *e* has no back counterpart, a situation which may be compared with Turkic languages like Azerbaydzhan, which have the two front vowels *e* and *ä* but only one corresponding back vowel *a*. The operation of the alternations that result from Vakh vowel harmony can be seen in the following examples. The imperative of the definite object conjugation (see pp. 125–6) ends in *-i/-i*, e.g. *pəni* 'put it', *vöri* 'do it'. The first person singular possessive suffix is *-am/-äm*, as in *olvam* 'my threshold', *semäm* 'my eye'. The dual number of nouns is indicated with the suffix *-yən/-yön*, e.g. *ontiwyən* 'two spears', *pösänyön* 'two tables'. The alternation *0/ö* is found in the ablative suffix *-oy/-öy*, e.g. *juy-oy* 'from the tree', *köy-öy* 'from stone'. Exceptions to vowel harmony in native words are almost unknown, being restricted to compound words, also the suffix *-uj* (passive), which does not have a variant *-üj*; in such instances, the last vowel determines the front/back quality of vowels in subsequent affixes, e.g. *versujəm* 'I was made'. In loans, especially from Russian, exceptions to vowel harmony are, of course, more frequent. Thus, in the text on p. 138, we have the Russian given name *MIRON*.

A more frequent kind of front/back vowel harmony in Uralic languages is where the vowels *i* and *e* are neutral, occurring in both front vowel and back vowel words, whereas the other vowels divide strictly according to phonetic criteria – this includes the front unrounded vowel *ä* as well as the front rounded vowels *ö* and *ü*, opposed to all the back vowels, rounded or not. This system is found, in particular, in the northern Balto-Finnic languages and in Hungarian. Examples may be given from Karelian, where the adessive (used in Karelian also in allative meaning) has the variants *-lla/-llä*, e.g. *pihalla* 'on the street', but *šeinällä* 'on the wall'. Suffixes containing only the vowels *i* and *e* do not, of course, show any alternation, as in the comitative *-nke*, e.g. *pihanke* 'with the street', *šeinänke* 'with the wall'. The words *piha* and *šeinä* also illustrate the neutral vowels *i* and *e* co-occurring with both front and back vowels in back vowel and front vowel roots respectively. Roots which consist solely of the neutral vowels may be either front vowel or, less commonly, back vowel words, so that in Hungarian, for instance, the word *cím* [ciim] 'address' is a front vowel word (dative *címnek* [ciimnek]), whereas the word *híd* [hiid] 'bridge' is a back vowel word (dative *hídnak* [hiidnak]). There are even minimal pairs of the type Hungarian *ír* [iir] (back vowel) 'write', *ír* [iir] (front vowel) 'Irish'. One even finds words with inconsistent assignment, such as Finnish *meri* 'sea', which is basically front vowel, e.g. inessive *mere-ssä*, but takes the back vowel alternant in the partitive singular: *mer-ta*.

Some Uralic languages that have basically the system outlined above have other deviations from the straightforward system, in particular a tendency for vowel harmony not to extend beyond the first few syllables of a word. In Veps, for instance, vowel harmony is usually restricted to the first two or three syllables, after which only back vowel alternants occur. In Estonian, this tendency has been carried to an extreme, so that the distinction between back vowel and front vowel alternants has been neutralised in noninitial syllables. What this means, in effect, is that Estonian has neutralisation of the front/back opposition, but without the assimilation to the preceding vowel that characterises vowel harmony proper. In Estonian, then, the nonneutral front vowels *ä ö ü* occur only in initial syllables, and there is no alternation left over from the vowel harmony that characterised Proto-Balto-Finnic.

Given the neutral nature of the vowels *i* and *e* in so many Uralic languages, and the fact that words containing only neutral vowels may be either front vowel or back vowel words morphophonemically, it is tempting to distinguish two vowels morphophonemically where only one is present phonetically, i.e. to distinguish the morphophonemically front vowels /i/ and /e/ from the morphophonemically back vowels /ɨ/ and /ə/, even though both series are always realised phonetically as *i* and *e*. There is no direct evidence in favour of this as a historical account of what took place, with merger of original front and back unrounded vowels. Although some of the Balto-Finnic languages, in particular Estonian, have back unrounded vowels (Estonian has [ɤ], written õ), this seems to be a secondary development, with retraction of certain original instances of *e* in back vowel words. Of course, equally, there is no evidence against this as a historical explanation – the question simply remains open. Synchronically, there would be certain problems for this abstract morphophonemic analysis, for instance words like *meri* 'sea' in Finnish, which behave sometimes as if they contained back vowels and sometimes as if they contained front vowels. This suggests that roots containing the vowels *i* and *e*, and no nonneutral vowels, but which behave like back vowel roots, are simply to be marked as exceptions to the general vowel harmony rule, and such exception marking can, of course, be subject to other idiosyncratic features, such as the opposition partitive singular versus all other case–number combinations in Finnish *meri* (partitive singular *merta*, but partitive plural *meriä*).

Labial harmony is much less common in Uralic languages. It is found, for instance, in Hungarian, which has, as already noted, been separated from the mass of Finno-Ugric languages for a very long period, during much of which it has been in contact with Turkic languages. In Hungarian, only the mid vowels are affected, so that there is alternation between *o* in back vowel words (no labial harmony, since Hungarian has no unrounded vowel corresponding to *o*) and *e* or *ö* in front vowel words depending on whether the preceding vowel is rounded or not. For instance, the first person singular indefinite-object conjugation ending is *-ok/-ek/-ök*, as in *állok* [aallok] 'I stand', *veszek* [vesek] 'I take', *ülök* 'I sit'. Although the high front rounded vowel *ü* can trigger labial harmony, as in *ülök*, it does not participate in this alternation, i.e. there are no alternation sets *-i/-u/-ü*. A restricted kind of labial harmony, or rather assimilation (since it is morphologically restricted and does not apply to all vowels of a given word) is found in Meadow-Eastern Mari: certain suffixes have three alternants -*e*/-*o*/-*ö*, the last two being used only if the initial (stressed) vowel is rounded, e.g. with locative -*šte*/-*što*/-*štö*: *kindište* 'in bread', *olikišto* 'in the meadow', *kürtništö* 'in iron'. What is unusual about this assimilation, in the general context of vowel harmony in Uralic and Altaic languages, is that it is not a characteristic of adjacent syllables, but involves rather conditioning of the vowel of the suffix by the initial vowel of the root, with intervening vowels perhaps belonging to differing phonetic series.

The second phonological feature of Uralic languages that we shall examine is consonant gradation, which is restricted effectively to the Balto-Finnic and Lapp branches of Uralic, at least as a systematic set of alternations; only a few languages within these branches of Uralic, e.g. Veps and Liv, do not have consonant gradation, and in these languages gradation has clearly been lost recently. Viewed diachronically, gradation consists in the weakening of the phonetic value of a consonant when it occurs at the beginning of a closed syllable, so that where one has a geminate voiceless plosive at the beginning of an open syllable in one form of a word, then in forms of that same word where the syllable is closed a single voiceless plosive appears. Where one has a single voiceless plosive at the beginning of an open syllable, then one has a voiced plosive, a fricative, or zero at the beginning of a closed syllable – the choice among these three depends on the individual language/dialect, on the individual consonant, and also on the environment in which that consonant appears. We may illustrate this phenomenon by taking some examples from Karelian, of nouns ending in a vowel (hence an open syllable) in the nominative singular, with the ending -*n* in the genitive singular, thus closing the syllable (Table 3.2).

The alternation of geminate voiceless plosives and single voiceless plosives is the same in all languages that have this alternation, but there are variations with other consonants and consonant clusters: for instance, standard Finnish does not have the alternation of *ts* (corresponding to Karelian *čč*) in *metsä* 'forest', genitive *metsän*, or alternation of plosives after another plosive, as in *matka* 'journey', genitive *matkan*. With consonants other than those described, there is no alternation, e.g. with sonants, as in *tuomi* 'bird-cherry tree', genitive *tuomen*. Incidentally, the fourth example in Table 3.2, which is a loan from Russian *pamjat'* 'memory', shows that the alternation can apply to loanwords, although it usually does not apply to more recent loans other than those containing a geminate voiceless plosive in the appropriate position.

As was indicated in introducing consonant gradation above, the alternation is the reflex of a regular sound change, whereby consonants were weakened in closed syllables. In all languages that have this alternation, however, the alternation has been morphologised, to a greater or lesser degree, by loss of some of the conditioning factors, so that there are now closed syllables that have the strong grade consonant at

Table 3.2. *Consonant gradation in Karelian*

NOM SG	GEN SG	
kukka	kukan	'flower'
ńäppi	ńäpin	'pinch'
ajtta	ajtan	'storeroom'
puametti	puametin	'memory'
mečcä	mečän	'forest'
soba	sovan	'shirt'
ruado	ruavon	'work'
peldo	pellon	'field'
matka	matan	'journey'

their beginning and, even more frequently, open syllables that have the weak grade. In the northern Balto-Finnic languages, there are relatively few such exceptions. In Karelian, for instance, the illative singular, though ending in *-h*, does not take the weak grade, so that the illative of *abu* 'help' is *abu-h*. At an earlier period, there was a following vowel, cf. Finnish (older and dialectal) *apu-hun* (standard Finnish has *apuun*, through loss of intervocalic *h*). Another example of strong grade in a closed syllable is *tuatto-š* 'your father', where again there was originally a final vowel i, cf. the Finnish second person singular possessive ending *-si* (although here it should be noted that the morpheme boundary between a noun and its possessive ending is strong enough to block gradation even where there is a closed syllable, as in Finnish *apu-nsa* 'his help').

The inverse phenomenon, weak grade in an open syllable, is found in Karelian *late* 'floor' (genetive *lattien*), and in the imperative *kuvo* of *kudu-o* 'weave-INFIN'; in these words, a final consonant has been lost: some Finnish dialects have a final glottal stop in such words. With such forms, the occurrence of the strong versus the weak grade is determined not by the phonological structure of the word, but by synchronically arbitrary morphological characterisation (e.g. the imperative takes the weak grade). Given the synchronic arbitrariness of the alternation in certain instances, one often finds grades that are not justifiable etymologically, and even doublets with different grades developing from the same etymon, as with Finnish *ikäinen* 'year old', *iäinen* 'eternal', both with the same derivational pattern applied to *ikä* (genitive *iän*) 'age'.

In most of the northern Balto-Finnic languages and dialects, deviations from the strict synchronic phonetic conditioning of consonant gradation are relatively rare. When one looks at the southern Balto-Finnic languages, however, and in particular Estonian, the situation is very different: Estonian has undergone so many historical processes of loss of final vowels and consonants and simplification of geminate clusters, while still in general retaining strong and weak grades in the same morphological categories, that there is now virtually no correlation between strong grade and open syllable, weak grade and closed syllable. We may illustrate this by looking at two Estonian nouns, *sõda* 'war' (weak grade *sõja*) and *jalg* 'foot' (stem *jalga-*, weak grade *jala-*). The nominative singulars are as given above, *sõda*, *jalg*. In the genitive singular, Balto-Finnic has the ending *-n*. In Estonian, however, word-final *n* is generally lost, so that in fact the bare stem appears as the genitive in Estonian. Since the syllable was originally closed by the final *n*, one finds the weak grade, even though synchronically the syllable is open, i.e. *sõja*, *jala*.

One result of this is that for certain nouns, such as *sõda* 'war', the difference in grade is the only distinction between the nominative and genitive singulars, a clear illustration of morphologisation of a phonological alternation. For words which happen to contain a nonalternating consonant, nominative and genitive singular are identical, e.g. *ema* 'mother'. In Estonian, the inessive has the ending *-s*, corresponding to Proto-Balto-Finnic **-ssa*; in both Proto-Balto-Finnic and Estonian the syllable is closed, so that here we do have weak grade correlating with a closed syllable: *sõja-s*, *jala-s*, cf. Finnish *soda-ssa* (weak grade of *sota*), *jala-ssa*. In the allative, however, Estonian has the suffix *-le*, which does not close the syllable, corresponding to Finnish *-lle*, which does close the syllable; thus Estonian again ends up with weak grade in an open syllable, e.g. *sõja-le*, *jala-le* (cf. Finnish *soda-lle*, *jala-lle*). Finally, we may note the example of the comitative case in *-ga*, where Estonian again has weak grade in an open syllable: *sõja-ga*, *jala-ga*; the comitative derives from the genitive plus a postposition, i.e. from an intermediate form of the type **-nka*, which closed the preceding syllable, again accounting diachronically for the weak grade in Estonian, although again synchronically one can only specify that this particular morphological ending requires the weak grade. Where Estonian open syllables continue Proto-Balto-Finnic open syllables, the strong grade is retained, e.g. genitive plural *sõda-de*, *jalga-de*, although morphological analogy has led to the introduction of weak grades in some such instances, e.g. essive *sõja-na*, *jala-na* – weak grade, as in most other singular oblique cases; cf. Finnish *sota-na*, *jalka-na* (strong grade).

In Estonian, these alternations have been carried one stage further, in that in many instances where the northern Balto-Finnic languages have alternation between open and closed syllables without any alternation in the stem, Estonian has introduced some alternation into the stem, even though the original distinction between open and closed syllable may have been lost. Thus the alternation between strong and weak grades is extended to give an alternation between long consonants or vowels (in an original closed syllable) and overlong vowels or consonants (in an original open syllable). For instance, the noun *kool* [koool] 'school' has its genitive *kooli* (phonetically [kooli]), and its illative *kooli* (phonetically [koooli]). The noun *laul* [lawwl] 'song' (Finnish *laulu*) has genitive *laulu* (phonetically [lawlu]) (Finnish *laulu-n*), and illative *laulu* (phonetically [lawwlu]) (Finnish *laulu-un*). The noun *linn* [linnn] 'town', cf. Finnish *linna* 'castle', has genitive *linna* (phonetically [linna]) (cf. Finnish *linna-n*), but illative *linna* (phonetically [linnna]) (cf. Finnish *linna-an*). From these examples, it will be seen that an originally long vowel (including a diphthong, which also has two moras) or long consonant becomes overlong (three moras) in an originally open syllable.

Since the conditioning factor of open versus closed syllable is frequently lost, and since there is already a two-way phonetic distinction of length, Estonian ends up with a three-way phonetic distinction of length, as in *koli* 'rubbish', *kooli* 'school-GEN', *kooli* [koooli] 'school-ILL', or *lina* 'flax', *linna* 'town-GEN', *linna* [linnna] 'town-ILL'. Estonian orthography, incidentally, does not usually distinguish between long and overlong segments, except in the case of the plosives, where the orthography writes short *b* (voiceless in Estonian), long *p*, overlong *pp*. Long and overlong contrast in many environments, but not all: for instance, in monosyllables there is no contrast, and phonetically the vowel of *kool*, the diphthong of *laul*, the final consonant of *linn* are all redundantly overlong. The long/overlong opposition is, incidentally, found in all Estonian dialects except the North-Eastern Littoral dialect.

In recent work (e.g. Remmel 1975), some evidence has emerged that, at least for certain speakers of Estonian, there is actually a four-way length opposition, although the distinction between overlong and doubly overlong is very restricted morphologically, but minimal triplets between long, overlong, and doubly overlong (Q2, Q3, Q4) can be found, as in the following inflectional forms of *õu* 'courtyard': genitive singular *õue* (Q2), partitive singular *õue* (Q3), illative singular *õue* (Q4). The length distinction between Q2, Q3, and Q4 is, incidentally, also accompanied by pitch differences, so that a combination of length and pitch provides the usual cue for distinguishing the three nonshort quantities; moreover, native speakers of Estonian who make the Q3/Q4 distinction consistently apparently have difficulties in perceiving it in minimal pair listening experiments.

Although Estonian and Lapp are not closely related genetically or geographically, being separated in both respects by northern Balto-Finnic, Lapp has developed a very similar alternation involving three lengths (cf. Estonian short, long, overlong), in response to similar diachronic processes, such as the loss of final *-n* in the genitive. As an example of the use of alternation as the sole marker of a morphological distinction, we may cite the following example from Kola Lapp (Kildin dialect): *ludd* 'bullet', nominative plural *lud*, where the nominative singular has the strong grade (cf. Finnish *luoti*) and the nominative plural the weak grade (cf. Finnish *luodit*). In discussing Estonian above, we noted that the long/overlong distinction applies to sonants, although the short/long distinction itself does not participate in alternations of sonants (cf. *ema* 'mother', nominative and genitive singular). Lapp has gone one stage further than Estonian in extending the short–long alternation to sonants too, so that we have nominative singular *nɛmm* 'name' (strong grade, cf. Finnish *nimi*), nominative plural *nɛm* (weak grade, cf. Finnish *nime-t*). Lapp thus shows an extreme form of morphologisation of the alternation: the alternation is the sole mark of certain morphological oppositions, and is extended to numerous instances where the alternation is not justified as the product of regular sound changes.

As a final example of Uralic phonology, we may expand somewhat our earlier mention of the nasalised and nonnasalised glottal stops in Nenets. The distinction among them can be seen from minimal triplets of the type *to* 'lake', genitive singular *to-ˀ*, nominative plural *to-ˀ*, although the second and third may not be distinguishable from one another phonetically in isolation. In these examples, the nasalised glottal stop derives from Proto-Uralic **n*, the nonnasalised glottal stop from Proto-Uralic **t* (cf. the genitive singular ending *-n* and the nominative plural ending *-t* in Finnish). This derivation of the glottal stops can be seen morphophonemically in the fact that the nasalised glottal stop often alternates with *n* (also with *j*), as in *weˀ* 'dog', allative *wen-dˀ*; while the nonnasalised glottal stop often alternates with *d* (and also *s*), e.g. *maˀ* 'tent', accusative *mad-mˀ*. The earlier values of these glottal stops also appear morphophonemically in certain juncture phenomena, so that if we take the words pronounced in isolation as *ti-ˀ* 'deer-GEN', *ti-ˀ* 'deer-PL', and *xoba* 'fur', plural *xoba-ˀ*, we get sequences such as *ti-ŋ goba* (for **ti-ˀ xoba*) 'the fur of the deer', *ti koba ˀ* (for **ti-ˀ xoba-ˀ*) 'the furs of the deer', giving a variety of sandhi phenomenon across word boundaries that is rare in the Uralic languages, and probably completely absent from all branches of the typologically related Altaic languages.

3.3 Morphological structure and categories

In looking at the morphological typology of the Uralic languages, it is useful to take as one's point of departure the almost canonical agglutinative, suffixing structure of the Altaic languages, especially Turkic languages, and then see how the Uralic languages depart from this type, while still being in general closer to this type than to the fusional type represented by the older Indo-European languages. The result of this inspection is that there are certain Uralic languages which are very close to the canonical agglutinative type, for instance the Ob'-Ugric languages (especially in their nominal morphology – verb morphology has more traces of fusion) and

Mari; but for most Uralic languages, even where we can posit an earlier stage closer to canonical agglutination, synchronically they depart considerably from this model. One way of carrying out this programme in a limited space is to take one branch of Uralic, and show how agglutinative structure has been destroyed in that branch, with occasional asides to other branches; from this viewpoint, Balto-Finnic is a good branch to take, since it has one of the Uralic languages with the greatest divergence from agglutination, namely Estonian. We may start by looking at Karelian, concentrating on the noun morphology.

In many respects Karelian is agglutinative, with a plural suffix *-i* (which replaces stem-final *a*), to which the same endings as in the singular are added, e.g. *hambaha-sta* 'tooth-ELAT', *hambah-i-sta* 'tooth-PL-ELAT', *hambaha-tta* 'tooth-ABESS', *hambah-i-tta* 'tooth-PL-ABESS', *hambaha-na* 'tooth-ESS', *hambah-i-na* 'tooth-PL-ESS'. However, even in a relatively straightforward area like Karelian noun morphology, there are some deviations: the plural ending *-i* is used only in the oblique cases; in the nominative the ending is *-t*, so that the nominative plural of 'tooth' is *hambaha-t*. Moreover, there are some cases where singular and plural are formed radically differently, e.g. partitive singular *hammas-ta*, plural *hambah-i-e*. In the closely related language Finnish, the complications in forming certain plural cases, namely the partitive and genitive, are widespread, and several nouns have alternative forms, even in the standard language, the results of various kinds of analogy, general and specific: thus *maa* 'land' has genitive plurals *maiden* and *maitten* (which latter violates the general rule of consonant gradation, whereby geminate consonants cannot appear in closed syllables); *kevät* 'spring' (i.e. the season) has *keväiden*, *keväitten*, and *kevätten*.

When one looks over to Estonian, the situation is even less systematisable, as can be imagined from the discussion of section 3.2. Many forms are distinguished solely by internal alternations, such as nominative singular *sõda* 'war' versus genitive singular *sõja*, or even more clearly nominative singular *jalg* 'leg', genitive singular *jala*, partitive singular *jalga*, partitive plural *jalgu* (the corresponding Finnish forms are *jalka*, *jala-n*, *jalka-a*, *jalko-j-a*). While the basic Balto-Finnic plural endings *-t* and *-i* are still often recognisable, other plural forms seem quite idiosyncratic, e.g. partitive plural *jalgu*, where the *u* was originally a morphophonemic variant of stem-final *a* (cf. Finnish *jalko-j-a*), but with the loss of the original suffixes has become the sole marker of partitive plural. Although, to a certain extent, abstract phonological analyses can bring some appearance of systematicity to Estonian inflection, a number of completely ad hoc statements still remain to be made, and it is not clear that traditional Estonian grammar is so far wrong in simply setting up different declensional classes of noun, on the Latin, Ancient Greek, or Sanskrit model. One complication which Estonian, like the other Uralic languages, does not share with Indo-European languages, however, is a gender or class distinction.

While some deviations from strict agglutination in Uralic languages represent innovations, such as those mentioned above, others seem more likely to be very archaic, such as the formation of plural demonstratives in Balto-Finnic by replacing initial *t* or *s* by *n*, e.g. Estonian *see* 'this', *nee-d* 'these'.

In terms of noun categories, most Uralic languages agree in having number, case, and possession, although possessive suffixes have been lost, clearly as a recent phenomenon, in several Balto-Finnic languages and are restricted in use in Lapp. Beyond this, the Mordva languages are unique within Uralic in having developed a postponed definite article, as in Erzya *kudo* 'house', *kudo-ś* 'the house'. The kinds of segmentation problems mentioned above for Estonian apply also to many Mordva forms, so that the article is not always so readily segmentable as in this example, e.g. Moksha *alaša* 'horse', genitive *alaša-ń*, definite genitive *alaša-ť*. With respect to number, most Uralic languages have a singular/plural opposition, but Lapp, the Ob'-Ugric and Samoyedic languages also have a separate dual.

The range of cases found in individual Uralic languages varies considerably, mainly because individual Uralic languages have innovated new cases, from postpositions for the most part. Thus the Central Ob' dialect of Khanty has only three cases in noun declension (nominative–accusative, dative–allative, locative–instrumental), while Komi-Permyak has as many as seventeen. The comitative in *-ka* or *-ke* found in the majority of Balto-Finnic languages is a recent innovation from reduction of a postposition similar to Finnish *kanssa* or *kera*, meaning 'with'. In Hungarian, almost all the local case suffixes are innovations, so that forms like *ház-ban* [haazban] 'house-INESS', *ház-ból* [haazbool] 'house-ELAT' were originally possessive constructions of the type 'at the house's inside', 'from the house's inside', where only the final parts of the suffixes (*-n*, *-l*) continue Proto-Uralic case suffixes.

The range of cases that is found in most languages includes nominative, accusative (**-m*, not however used for all direct objects, see pp. 128–9), genitive (**-n*, though accusative and genitive have been largely lost from the Ob'-Ugric languages), and three spatial cases for location at, motion towards, and motion from. The complex systems found in individual languages are all based on this system. While most of the newer cases are formed from postpositions, themselves often deriving from possessive constructions, the system in Balto-Finnic is rather more idiosyncratic. Basically, there are suffixes **-na* for location, **-ne* for direction, and **-ta* for movement away (locative, allative, ablative). Depending on whether the relevant space is inside or not (on top of, beside, etc.), a different consonant is placed before the case ending, giving complex case endings **-sna* (inessive), **-lna* (adessive), **-sne* (illative), **-lne* (allative), **-sta* (elative), **-lta* (ablative); the consonants then contract with the original case endings to give *-ssa*, *-lla*, *-sse*, *-lle*, *-sta*, *-lta*. With the exception of *-sse* (which is found in Estonian), these are the modern Finnish forms.

Further changes have again obscured the system in some languages, for instance the merger of the adessive and allative to -*lla* in Karelian.

One of the main morphological discrepancies among the Uralic languages concerns the order of possessive and case suffixes when both are present on the same stem, with the languages dividing into those (Ugric) where the case suffixes always follow the possessive suffixes, those (Balto-Finnic, Lapp, Samoyedic) where the possessive suffixes usually follow the case suffixes, and those where both orders are found, depending on individual combinations of case and number, sometimes with alternatives possible (Volgaic and Permic languages). Thus Finnish *talo-ssa-ni* 'house-INESS-1SG', i.e. 'in my house', contrasts with Mansi *kol-əm-n* 'house-1SG-LOC' (same meaning); within Komi-Zyryan, contrast *kerka-śi-nim* 'house-ELAT-1PL', i.e. 'out of our house', with *kerka-nim-lən* 'house-1PL-GEN', i.e. 'of our house'. In some Balto-Finnic languages, recently developed case endings, such as the comitative, follow the possessive ending, retaining their original order in the sequence noun–possessive followed by postposition, which suggests that this order may overall be an innovation in Uralic, with the order case–possessive as the original order, reflecting the later development of possessive suffixes relative to at least the original case suffixes; this would parallel the development in Mongolian and Tungusic languages, rather than in Turkic languages (p. 75).

Many of the verb categories that are found in individual Uralic languages or branches are innovations of the language or branch in question. For instance, some Uralic languages have a number of different tenses, but the only semantic tense distinction that can be traced back to Proto-Uralic is past versus nonpast, and it is usually this distinction which is posited as the tense distinction for Proto-Uralic. The present tense has no marker, or, in certain languages, e.g. Balto-Finnic, a final **-k*. There are at least two past tense markers that are widespread, -*i* and -*s*, both of which are found, for instance, in Estonian, although they do not contrast, each verb taking only one or the other: thus *saa-ma* 'receive-INFIN' has *sa-i-n* 'I received', while *kirjuta-ma* 'write-INFIN' has *kirjuta-si-n* 'I wrote'. The possibility that there may have been two different past tenses in Proto-Uralic cannot be excluded, especially when it is noted that Vakh Khanty actually has four different past tenses, differing in degrees of remoteness and aspect, of which one has no suffix (the present tense has -*l*) and one has the suffix -*s*. In the discussion of syntax below, we shall examine some of the other verb categories, in particular voice.

3.4 Syntax

The internal structure of noun phrases in Uralic languages is very similar to that of Turkic languages, with the exception that preposed relative clauses are not the rule in a large number of Uralic languages, as will be shown in greater detail below. The general rule that the adjunct precedes its head does, however, hold, as in the Estonian noun phrase *tugeva mehe tegu* 'strong-GEN man-GEN deed', i.e. 'a strong man's deed', where the adjective *tugeva* precedes its head *mehe*, and the whole genitive noun phrase *tugeva mehe* precedes its head *tegu*. No Uralic language has the inverse word order as its general rule, and in those languages where inversion is reasonably common, this may well be attributable to Russian influence.

Possessive constructions in Uralic languages show a range somewhat similar to that found in Turkic languages, though it is usually the case that a given Uralic language will have only one of the possible constructions, and the most widespread Turkic construction with the genitive suffix on the adjunct and possessive suffix on the head is rare in Uralic: it occurs as a less preferred alternative in Hungarian, with the dative substituting for the genitive (lost in Hungarian), as in *a szóba-nak az ajta-ja* [a sobaanak az ajtaja] 'the room-DAT the door-3SG', i.e. 'the door of the room', although the more common construction is *a szoba ajta-ja*. The most common Uralic construction is like English, just having the genitive marking on the adjunct, as in the Estonian example given above. The Ugric languages (which have no genitive case) usually express possession by having an unmarked adjunct and the head with a possessive suffix, e.g. Mansi *kol ala-te* 'house roof-3SG', i.e. 'the roof of the house'.

Although agreement of attributive adjectives with their head seems to be an innovation in those Uralic languages that have it, it is fairly widespread in Uralic, and in some languages it is quite clearly the norm: thus in Finnish, it would be a clear violation of (nonprescriptive) norms for agreement not to be made. Agreement is most widespread in Balto-Finnic, Lapp, and Samoyedic, though the amount of agreement varies from language to language. In Estonian, for instance, there is a generalised oblique (originally, genitive) form that is used instead of complete agreement in many cases, so that one has complete agreement in nominative singular *ametlik teade* 'official news item', genitive singular *ametliku teate*, partitive singular *ametlikku teadet*, ablative *ametlikult teatelt*, nominative plural *ametlikud teated*, but only partial agreement in essive *ametliku teatena*, abessive *ametliku teateta*, and comitative *ametliku teatega*. With the comitative, this could be accounted for in terms of the relatively recent development of this case from a postposition, but the essive is a case inherited from the Proto-Uralic locative.

Most Uralic languages have postpositions, and in most branches of Uralic there are no prepositions, such as Mari *ðeke* 'towards', in *pört ðeke* 'towards the house'. In Balto-Finnic languages, however, there are several prepositions, in addition to postpositions, and even some items that can be used as either. Thus Estonian has the postposition *all* 'under' (with the genitive case), as in *laua all* 'under the table', the preposition *piki* 'along' (with the partitive case), as in *piki metsa* 'along the forest', and *mööda* 'along' (with the partitive), which can be either a preposition or a postposition, e.g. *mööda maanteed* or *maanteed mööda* 'along the highway'.

When we turn to the order of major constituents within the clause, there is rather less homogeneity across Uralic languages; in particular division must be made between those languages that have subject–object–verb as their basic word order (Samoyedic languages, Ob'-Ugric languages, Mari), and those that have subject–verb–object (Permic languages, Mordva languages, Lapp, Balto-Finnic languages). Although this classification gives the basic word order for the various Uralic languages, word order in Uralic languages is in general fairly free, so that deviations from this word order are not uncommon in order to express specific pragmatic (topic–comment) functions. Moreover, Hungarian has not been included in the above classification since it is difficult to reach a definitive decision on whether Hungarian is basically subject–object–verb or subject–verb–object, the choice between these two being determined much more than in other Uralic languages by considerations of topic–comment structure; indeed, good Hungarian style lays down that, where a clause contains a number of nonsubject noun phrase arguments, these should be positioned roughly equally before and after the verb.

In the more detailed discussion of word order and related typological parameters below, we shall concentrate on a comparison between Vakh Khanty, a fairly strict subject–object–verb language, and Estonian, with its basic subject–verb–object word order. Most of the points made will apply to other Uralic languages with the same basic word order, although some specific discrepancies will be noted. The division of Uralic languages into two groups according to basic word order corresponds roughly to an east/west division, the westerly languages being those that have been most subject to influence from Germanic and Slavonic languages with their basic subject–verb–object order. The possibility that contact was influential in the distribution of word order patterns is further strengthened by the anomalous position of Mari, more westerly situated than the Permic languages, but with verb-final word order and a strong Turkic influence.

Example (18) below illustrates the basic word order of Vakh Khanty, with the subject sentence-initially, the verb sentence-finally, the direct object preceding the verb, and other constituents arranged between the subject and the object:

(18)   mä mäntim sem- yə̑l -äm -nə̑   ti̮ tə̑yi̮ ə̑jnäm
       I   myself eye   DU 1SG INSTR this   all
       wu -yal   -im
       see PAST-INDEF-REM 1SG-DEF-OBJ
       'I saw this all with my own eyes'

Variations on this word order are most likely to concern the order of noun phrase arguments, although the final position of the verb is by no means absolutely rigid. As we shall see below, the position immediately before the verb is reserved for the focus (essential new information) constituent, which has a strong tendency to be the direct object where there is no other marked topic–comment structure.

In Estonian, on the other hand, a clause usually begins with the subject immediately followed by the verb – the subject may be omitted if it is an unstressed pronoun and the verb shows agreement with this omitted pronoun, in which case the verb will be initial. This is illustrated in example (19):

(19)   *ema   saati-s   mu-!le   paki*
        mother send PAST-3SG I   ALL parcel-GEN
        'mother sent me a parcel'

It should be noted that, in general, this same word order holds in both main and subordinate clauses, as can be seen if we embed (19) under the verb *luge-si-n* 'read-PAST-1SG':

(20)   *lugesin, et ema saatis mulle paki*
        'I read that mother sent me a parcel'

While this applies to finite subordinate clauses, it is less true of nonfinite substitutes for subordinate clauses (see pp. 134–6 for a fuller discussion of these). In example (21) below, the nonfinite construction *lugedes raamatut* 'while reading the book' could equally well be phrased as *raamatut lugedes*, whereas this kind of object preposing would clearly be more marked for a finite clause:

(21)   *luge-de   -s   raamatu-t,   istu-s   ta*
        read INFIN-2 INESS book   PARTIT sit PAST-3SG he
        aia   -s
        garden INESS
        'while reading the book he sat in the garden'

With participial constructions substituting for relative clauses, the participle regularly occurs final to this construction, so that there is a clear difference in word order between finite relative clause and nonfinite participial construction, as in (22) and (23) respectively:

(22)   *vanake silmitse-s   kaua   inimes-t,*
        old-man observe PAST-3SG for-a-long-time person PARTIT
        kes sammu-s   üle   õue   elumaja
        who go   PAST-3SG across courtyard-GEN residential
        poole
        building-ILL

(23)   *vanake silmitses kaua üle õue elumaja poole sammu-vat*
                                                        go   PRES-PART
        inimes -t
        person PARTIT
        'for a long time the old man observed the person who was going across the courtyard to the residential building'

In certain more specific instances, the influence of foreign word order patterns on certain Uralic languages is more clear. For instance, in Estonian the past participle in the compound perfect is positioned at the end of its clause, away from the auxiliary verb 'to be', precisely mirroring the German word order in this construction, whereas the other Balto-Finnic languages usually have auxiliary verb and past participle adjacent in sentence-second position:

(24)   õpilane ol -i   oma vihiku   kooli
       pupil   be PAST-3SG own notebook-GEN school-ILL
       unusta-nud
       forget PAST-PART
       'the pupil had forgotten his notebook at school'

Compare German: *der Schüler hatte sein Heft in der Schule vergessen*. Even the final position of participles in sentences like (23), and corresponding sentences in other Balto-Finnic languages, corresponds to the verb-final participial constructions found in German and, under German influence, Swedish, so that they cannot without further investigation be adduced as relict evidence in favour of an earlier period where verb-final word order was the norm.

As was noted at the beginning of the discussion of word order of major clause constituents, in the verb-final Uralic languages the immediately preverbal position is reserved for the focus element. One particularly clear illustration of this is to look at special question and answer sequences, where the special question word (interrogative pronoun) and likewise the noun phrase substituting for it in the reply occur preverbally, e.g. Vakh Khanty:

(25)   lanpöŋk möɣöli-kɔ̈   wer -l   -in
       file   what   TRANSFORM make PRES 2SG-DEF-OBJ
       'what do you make the file out of?'

This preverbal focus pattern also characterises Hungarian, where it has been investigated in detail by Kiefer (1967). In the subject–verb–object languages, the usual order is that found in the majority of European languages, with the interrogative pronoun sentence-initial; moreover, although this sentence-initial position characterises the special question word, it is not used for the noun phrase substituting for it in the reply, which either takes the position in the sentence determined by its grammatical relation (e.g. subject before the verb, object after the verb), or gravitates towards sentence-final position, for new information, e.g. Estonian:

(26)   kust   sa tul -i   -d? tul -i   -n   kooli -st
       whence you come PAST 2SG come PAST 1SG school ELAT
       'where did you come from? I came from the school'

Table 3.3. *Subject-agreement in Estonian*

PRESENT		PAST	
tule-n	'I come'	tuli-n	'I came'
tule-d	'you come'	tuli-d	'you came'
tule-b	'he comes'	tuli	'he came'
tule-me	'we come'	tuli-me	'we came'
tule-te	'you come'	tuli-te	'you came'
tule-vad	'they come'	tuli-d	'they came'

In all Uralic languages, there is subject–verb agreement, and in all languages nearly all predicates agree with their subject in this way, with a distinction for three persons and two numbers (three numbers in languages with a separate dual). In the third person, there is often a zero agreement marker, especially in the singular, though in some languages this also applies to the plural, in which case third person singular and plural are identical; where third person, especially third person singular, endings do exist, they are usually of nominal, including participial, origin (e.g. Estonian third person plural -*vad* in the present tense, originally the plural of the present participle). Table 3.3 illustrates this with some present and past tense forms in Estonian; it will be noted that the subject-agreement suffixes are very similar, though not invariably identical, across different tenses. In a few instances in certain languages, there is no subject–verb agreement. In Estonian, for instance, the inferential does not change for person and number of the subject, i.e. *ma tulevat* 'I am said to come', *sa tulevat* 'you are said to come', *ta tulevat* 'he is said to come'; in origin, this verb form is the partitive of the present participle. Similarly, Estonian lacks subject–verb agreement in the negative, e.g. *ma ei tule* 'I do not come', *sa ei tule* 'you do not come', *ta ei tule* 'he does not come'.

In some Uralic languages we also find object–verb agreement, or at least encoding of certain features of the direct object in the verb. In all Uralic languages that have object-agreement, this agreement is triggered only by definite direct objects, although the precise characterisation of the set of triggering direct objects varies somewhat from language to language (for Hungarian, see Comrie (1978)). In the Samoyedic and Ob'-Ugric languages, for instance, it seems also to depend on topic–comment structure, while in the Mordva languages verbs agree with their direct objects only when the sentence has perfective aspectual value.

The simplest system of 'object–agreement' is found in Hungarian, where the so-called definite object conjugation merely encodes whether or not there is a definite direct object of the third person, without encoding any further features (e.g. number) of that direct object. Intransitive verbs, of course, have only the indefinite conjugation (e.g. *megy-ek* [meḋek] 'go-1SG', i.e. 'I go'), while transitive verbs have

Table 3.4. *Indefinite object and definite object conjugations in Hungarian*

INDEFINITE			DEFINITE		
olvas-ok	[olvašok]	'I read'	olvas-om	[olvašom]	'I read it'
olvas-ol	[olvašol]	'you read'	olvas-od	[olvašod]	'you read it'
olvas	[olvaš]	'he reads'	olvas-sa	[olvašša]	'he reads it'

Table 3.5. *Definite and indefinite conjugations of Mansi tee- 'eat'*

SU	INDEF OBJ	SG DEF OBJ	DU DEF OBJ	PL DEF OBJ
1SG	tee-γəm	tee-γ-l-əm	tee-γ-aγ-ˑm	tee-γ-an-əm
2SG	tee-γ-n(ən)	tee-γ-l-ən	tee-γ-aγ-n(ən)	tee-γ-an/tee-γ-aan-ən
3SG	tee-γ	tee-γ-t-e	tee-γ-aγ-e	tee-γ-an-e

both forms, depending on the definiteness of the direct object; the indication of the
definiteness of the direct object is fused in the verb with the subject-agreement
marker, as can be seen in Table 3.4.

A somewhat more prolific system is found in the Samoyedic and Ob'-Ugric
languages, where the verb encodes in addition the number of the direct object. Table
3.5 gives some appropriate Mansi forms, and it will be noted that here it is possible to
identify a suffix indicating the definiteness and number of the direct object (singular -
l/-t, dual *-aγ*, plural *-an*). In the Mordva languages, illustrated here by the Erzya
forms in Table 3.6, the suffix encodes the person and number of both subject and
direct object; etymologically, at least, many of these combinations are segmentable
into a subject-agreement suffix and an object-agreement suffix.

One of the most fascinating areas in the syntax of simple clauses in Uralic
languages concerns the case-marking of subjects and direct objects, since in many
languages a variety of formal cases can be used in the same function (i.e. to encode a
given grammatical relation), depending on various semantic, syntactic, and other
factors.

The most complex systems are found in Balto-Finnic languages, and we shall start
here with one distinction, that between total and partial noun phrases, that is
restricted to these languages and Lapp, though very characteristic of them. For
intransitive subjects and transitive direct objects, a semantic distinction is drawn
between an entity that is totally affected by the situation described and one that is
only partially affected by the situation described: the noun phrases referring to such
partially affected entities stand in the partitive case, while total subjects stand in the
nominative and total direct objects are assigned case according to principles to be

Table 3.6. *Erzya-Mordva verb forms (past tense of* kund- *'catch') showing subject and object agreement*

OBJ:	No object	1SG	2SG	3SG
SU: 1SG	kund-i-ń		kund-i-t́iń	kund-i-ja
2SG	kund-i-t́	kund-i-mik		kund-i-k
3SG	kund-i-ś	kund-i-mim	kund-i-ńźit́	kund-i-źe

noted below. The precise semantic differentiation of partial from total is one of the most complex areas in the description of any Balto-Finnic language, so here we shall restrict ourselves to certain salient distinctions that provide specific instances of the general difference, taking examples from Estonian. In intransitive subject position, the distinction is particularly common with the verb 'to be' and close synonyms where the intransitive subject is a plural count noun or a mass noun, in which case the total/partial distinction corresponds to that between 'the X' (i.e. all of the X) and 'some X' (i.e. some of the X):

(27)   *leib   on   kapi   -s*
         bread be-3SG cupboard INESS
         'the bread is in the cupboard'

(28)   *kapi   -s   on   leiba*
         cupboard INESS be-3SG bread-PARTIT
         'there is some bread in the cupboard'

In direct object position, the partial/total opposition can also correspond to that between definite and indefinite with plural count or mass nouns:

(29)   *õpilane võtti-s   leiva   /leiba*
         pupil   take PAST-3SG bread-GEN bread-PARTIT
         'the pupil took the/some bread'

However, the notion of partial affectedness of an entity can also have aspectual value, as in the following pair of examples:

(30)   *õpilane luge-s   raamatu*
         pupil   read PAST-3SG book-GEN
         'the pupil read the book'

(31)   *õpilane luge-s raamatu-t*
                          book   PARTIT
         'the pupil was reading the book'

In (30), with a total direct object, the sense is that the effect of the action on the entity is complete, i.e. perfective aspect; in (31), with a partial direct object, the sense is that the effect on the entity is not (yet) complete, i.e. imperfective aspect. Although in specific instances the difference between total and partial can be expressed in English by that between definite and indefinite or nonprogressive versus progressive, it is important to bear in mind that the Balto-Finnic distinction cannot be identified with either of these. In particular, in a pair like (32)–(33) where the direct object is plural, while (32) with a total direct object can be rendered unequivocally as 'the pupil read the books', (33) with a partial object ranges across all three of English 'the pupil was reading the books', 'the pupil read some books', 'the pupil was reading some books', i.e. there is no unequivocal encoding of definiteness or aspect:

(32)   *õpilane luge-s raamatu-d*
                book   PL

(33)   *õpilane luge-s raamat-id*
                book   PARTIT-PL

Turning now to Uralic languages other than Balto-Finnic, and to the case-marking of total subjects and direct objects in Balto-Finnic languages, we find that in general only certain classes of noun phrases have a strict distinction between a nominative used only for subjects and an accusative used only for direct objects, whereas in nearly all languages for many classes of noun phrases the so-called nominative is used to encode both of these grammatical relations. The least extensive use of the accusative is found in some of the Ob'-Ugric languages and dialects. In Northern Mansi, for instance, nouns show no nominative/accusative distinction, although personal pronouns do – the case distinction with personal pronouns is common to al Uralic languages:

(34)   *ruutíwan tińśaŋ saɣ   -i*
                Rodion   lasso   weave PRES-3SG
                'Rodion is weaving a lasso'

(35)   *am naŋ-ən   waaśntaal-əs   -l   -əm*
                I   you ACC see-FREQ PAST SG-DEF-OBJ 1SG
                'I often used to see you'

For Proto-Uralic, an accusative case in *-m* can be reconstructed for nouns, but this seems to have been restricted to singular nouns, perhaps even to singular definite nouns (Wickman 1954), and restrictions of this kind still apply in most Uralic languages. In Balto-Finnic, for instance, the separate accusative case (which is homophonous with the genitive, through the merger of *-m* and *-n* in word-final position) is used in the singular, but not in the plural, as in Estonian:

(36) *õpilanes võtti-s   raamatu*
      pupil   take-PAST-3SG book-GEN
      'the pupil took the book'

(37) *õpilanes võtti-s   raamatu-d*
      pupil   take PAST-3SG book   PL
      'the pupil took the books'

Only in Mari do we find widespread use of the accusative in *-m* in the plural, essentially as a general marker of accusative, e.g. *pasu* 'field', accusative *pasu-m*, plural *pasu-βlak*, accusative *pasu-m-βlak*. (As noted on p. 75, Mari has innovated a plural marker, and this new plural marker, unusually for a Uralic language, follows the case suffixes.)

   This still does not exhaust the complexity of case-marking in Balto-Finnic (or in the Samoyedic languages, which seem to share at least some of the following unusual features with Balto-Finnic), because certain noun phrases either take the separate (genitive-like) accusative or not, depending on the syntactic configuration. Basically, the nominative direct object occurs in certain constructions that are subjectless, while the accusative is used where there is an expressed subject. More exactly, the nominative direct object occurs in imperative constructions, in impersonal constructions with an infinitive dependent on an impersonal main verb, and also in the impersonal passive. Personal pronouns are not affected by this complex case-marking: they invariably stand in the accusative when functioning as direct object, even in one of the constructions just specified. Estonian examples of the nominative direct object of an imperative and of an impersonal infinitival construction are given below ((38)–(39), respectively):

(38) *too   raamat siva*
      bring-IMPER-2SG book   hither
      'bring the book here'

(39) *on   tarvis   uus raamat ost -a*
      be-3SG necessary new book   buy INFIN
      'it is necessary to buy a new book'

   This case-marking system with the impersonal passive requires a little more discussion, and can in turn lead on to a more general discussion of some properties of voice in Uralic languages. The Balto-Finnic languages have an impersonal passive, indicating that some unspecified entity or entities did something; it is not possible to specify the agent, and the impersonal form is, of course, invariable for person and number. This form can be used from intrasitive verbs, so that from Estonian *elama* 'to live' we get the present impersonal passive *elatakse*, literally 'it is lived', i.e. 'one lives'. If we start with a transitive verb, e.g. *panema* 'to put', then again we can form an impersonal passive, in which the direct object remains as direct object but appears in the nominative case. (The fact that the direct object remains as such can be seen more clearly with personal pronouns, which stand in the accusative here.) Estonian example (40) illustrates this:

(40)   *maja -le   pan-nakse   uus katus*
       house ALL put PASS-PRES new roof
       'a new roof will be put on the house'

Nominative direct objects with subjectless constructions are interesting not only in their own right within Balto-Finnic and, perhaps, some other branches of Uralic, but also in that they form an areal feature in the Baltic, having spread to the Baltic languages Latvian and (nonstandard) Lithuanian, and apparently also to North Russian dialects (Timberlake 1974); see p. 152 for a discussion of the Latvian parallels. In the Baltic languages there is, incidentally, one difference: the nominative direct object is not used with the imperative.

In the aberrant Vakh dialect of Khanty we find, unique within Uralic, an ergative-like construction as far as case-marking is concerned, alongside the regular Uralic construction with the transitive subject in the nominative and the direct object in either the accusative (for pronouns) or the nominative. Example (41) below illustrates this Vakh construction:

(41)   *tu   sart -nə   män-t   kat́   il   kəmlaytə-yal*
       this pike LOC I   ACC almost down capsize PAST-INDEF-
       REM
       'this pike almost capsized me'

The salient features of the construction are (i) that the transitive subject takes the locative suffix -*nə*, (ii) that the direct object, if a pronoun, takes the accusative case form (other nouns lack the nominative/accusative distinction), and (iii) that the verb is a transitive active form, where appropriate of the definite object conjugation, showing subject agreement with the locative subject noun phrase. This construction contrasts not only with the regular transitive construction, but also with a passive construction, in which the agent also appears in the locative, but where the patient is in the nominative (even if a personal pronoun) and subject agreement is with this patient noun phrase:

(42) män-nə̑ peçkän-nä   jöyi -γäs   -i
      I   LOC gun   INSTR shoot PAST-INDEF-REC PASS-3SG
      'he was shot by me with a gun'

The difference between the regular and the ergative constructions has been the subject of a fairly extensive literature, the consensus being that the distinction is connected with topic–comment structure, perhaps with the definiteness or thematicity of the direct object in the ergative construction, perhaps in order to focus the subject in the ergative construction. However, the precise nature of this distinction, and its interaction with that between definite object and indefinite conjugation of transitive verbs, remains to be elaborated. In particular, much of the investigation of this problem has been carried out with reference to text collections but without access to native speakers to check out possible alternative constructions, whereas for a semantic distinction of this subtlety a combination of the two methods seems required.

Although this particular construction is restricted to Vakh Khanty, there is a phenomenon in Mansi that may conceivably be related to this, namely the frequent use of the passive. In Mansi, this passive can be formed from both intransitive and transitive verbs. When formed from an intrasitive verb, it is impersonal (with the invariable passive suffix -we, and no subject agreement):

(43) woowta jaaŋk pora-t   ti kooṅki-l   taxsa-we
      thin   ice   time LOC here skate INSTR run   PASS
      'at the time of thin ice people skate here'

Where, however, the verb is transitive, the expression referring to the patient stands in the nominative (distinct from the accusative for personal pronouns), and the verb agrees with this expression, as in *taw waa-we* 'he is known', *naŋ waa-we-n* 'you are known', *am waa-we-m* 'I am known'. The agent-expression can be included, in which case the topic–comment function of the construction is to put the agent in focus position (Rombandeeva 1973: 113):

(44) śaajaani annee-n   sakwata-we -s
      teacup Anna ALL break   PASS PAST
      'the teacup was broken by Anna'

It remains, however, a task for future research to establish whether there is a common genetic origin to the Vakh Khanty ergative and Mansi agentive passive constructions.

One of the features of Uralic, and especially Finnish, syntax that has long interested general linguists is the expression of negation. In many Uralic languages, as explained in somewhat more detail below, instead of having an invariable negative particle in conjunction with a finite verb, as in Russian *ja ne idu* 'I do not go', *ty ne ideš* 'you do not go' versus *ja idu* 'I go', *ty ideš* 'you go', we find that the lexical verb remains in an invariable form while the negative element, an auxiliary verb, shows many verb categories. In Finnish, for instance, corresponding to affirmative *luen* 'I read', *luet* 'you read', *lukee* 'he reads', we have in the negative *en lue* 'I do not read', *et lue* 'you do not read', *ei lue* 'he does not read', with the variable negative auxiliary *e-* and the invariable form *lue* of the lexical verb.

With respect to the internal typology of Uralic languages, one interesting aspect of negation is the way in which verb categories (especially person and number, tense, mood) are distributed between the negative auxiliary and the lexical verb, since the usual pattern in Uralic languages is for some of these categories to be expressed in the negative auxiliary, others in the lexical verb, occasionally with duplication in both auxiliary and lexical verb, very occasionally (as in Estonian) with loss of the overt expression of some category, expressed in neither the auxiliary nor the lexical verb. Only very few Uralic languages have invariable negative particles of the Indo-European type – the Ugric languages, including Hungarian, are of this type, e.g. Mansi positive *teeyəm* 'I eat', *teeyən* 'you eat', *teeyləm* 'I eat it', *teesəm* 'I ate', negative *at teeyəm*, *at teeyən*, *at teeyləm*, *at teesəm*. Estonian also has an invariable negative particle *ei*, but this is clearly a secondary development, with generalisation of what was originally the third person (singular) present tense of the negative auxiliary, cf. Finnish *ei* with precisely this function.

The categories most frequently expressed in the auxiliary and not expressed in the lexical verb are person and number, so that in Ingrian (Soyka dialect), for instance, corresponding to positive *kuon* 'I weave', *kuod* 'you weave', *kuottoo* 'he weaves', there is negative: *en kuo*, *ed kuo*, *ei kuo*. In some languages, the distribution of person and number across auxiliary and main verb is more complex, with some subcategories here (e.g. third person plural in Karelian) being expressed in the lexical verb rather than in the auxiliary. In Komi, the negative auxiliary typically expresses person (though it may also, optionally and redundantly, specify number), while number is expressed in the lexical verb, as in the following positive/negative pairs:

giža	'I write'	*og giž*	'I do not write'
gižan	'you write'	*on giž*	'you do not write'
gižam	'we write'	*og gižəj*	'we do not write'
gižannid	'you write'	*on gižəj*	'you do not write'

In Estonian, person and number are expressed in neither the auxiliary nor the lexical verb, so that corresponding to positive *loen* 'I read', *loed* 'you read', etc., there is only the one negative form *ei loe*; person and number of the subject must be identified by the subject pronoun. The most extreme example of arbitrary distribution of person and number between auxiliary and lexical verb is found in Liv, as can be seen from the following pairs (where the apostrophe indicates broken tone on the preceding vowel):

lugub	'I read'	*äb lug*	'I do not read'
lugud	'you read'	*äd lug*	'you do not read'
lugub	'he reads'	*äb lug*	'he does not read'
lu'ggəm	'we read'	*äb lu'ggəm*	'we do not read'
lu'ggət	'you read'	*ät lu'ggət*	'you do not read'
lu'ggəbəd	'they read'	*äb lu'ggət*	'they do not read'

Tense is also frequently expressed in the negative auxiliary in Uralic languages, though less frequently than person and number. In most Balto-Finnic languages, for instance, tense is not expressed in the auxiliary, although there are exceptions (e.g. Liv, North-Eastern and Southern dialects of Estonian). In those languages where the tense distinction is not shown in the auxiliary, the lexical verb takes on the form of the past participle in the past tense, so that in Ingrian, for instance, corresponding to positive *kuojn* 'I wove', *kuojd* 'you wove' we have negative *en kuttoond* 'I did not weave', *ed kuttoond* 'you did not weave'. In Komi, on the other hand, tense is shown in the auxiliary, and the lexical verb stands in the same form as in the present negative (see above), as in the following positive/negative pairs:

giži	'I wrote'	*eg giž*	'I did not write'
gižin	'you wrote'	*en giž*	'you did not write'
gižim	'we wrote'	*eg gižəj*	'we did not write'
gižinnid	'you wrote'	*en gižəj*	'you did not write'

The Ingrian pattern here, drawing into service a participial form, seems clearly an innovation. The same is true with the treatment of mood in languages with the Ingrian pattern: mood is shown in the lexical verb for the conditional, by using the stem of the conditional (identical to the third person singular), as can be seen from the comparison of positive *kuttojzin* 'I would weave', *kuttoist* 'you would weave', with negative *en kuttojz, ed kuttojz*. In Mari, on the other hand, which tends overall to express verb categories in the auxiliary, mood is expressed on the negative auxiliary, as can be seen from the following desiderative forms (suffix *-ne*): *už-ne-m* 'I want to see', *už-ne-t* 'you want to see', *i-ne-m už* 'I do not want to see', *i-ne-t už* 'you do not want to see'. The most extreme concentration of verb categories in the auxiliary is found in Nenets, where the various nonfinite forms have corresponding forms of the

negative auxiliary, and in some dialects even aspect is sometimes expressed in the
auxiliary rather than in the lexical verb.

In the general linguistic literature, the negative auxiliary in Uralic languages has
often attracted interest as possible evidence in favour of analysing negation as a
higher predicate. The complexities of the distribution of verb categories across
auxiliary and lexical verb in most Uralic languages make them rather poor evidence
for this hypothesis, and if such evidence is sought, it should rather be from languages
like the Tungusic language Evenki, where under negation verb categories are shown
consistently only in the negative auxiliary ə-.

As the final syntactic point in this discussion of Uralic languages, we may turn to
the distribution of finite subordinate clauses and various nonfinite constructions in
the various languages. In the more easterly languages (Samoyedic, Ob'-Ugric, to a
somewhat lesser extent the Permic and Volgaic languages), the usual construction
type here is nonfinite, and finite subordinate clauses have developed only recently,
most commonly under Russian influence. In the more westerly languages, especially
Balto-Finnic and also, in this respect, Hungarian, finite subordinate clauses are
much more normal, although nonfinite constructions do survive, most frequently in
more archaic or learned styles. We may illustrate the use of nonfinite constructions in
Vakh Khanty with two examples, (45) translating a time clause and (46) translating a
relative clause:

(45)   *töyə̆ werə̆n-tä   jə̆ -m   -il -nə̆, mä lə̆y -nä*
         fire make INFIN begin PAST-PART 3PL LOC I   they COMIT
         -ti
         PTCL
         jə̆lil-yäl   -ə̆m
         go PAST-INDEF-REM 1SG
         'when they began to make the fire (literally: at their beginning to make
         the fire), I went with them'

(46)   *əpi -m kitə̆m wel-m   -äl läŋki tu -ta*
         father 1SG recently kill PAST-PART 3SG squirrel take INFIN
         mə̆n-lə̆m   -əs
         go   INTEND PAST-DEF-REC
         'my father intended going to take some squirrels he had recently killed'

To illustrate the interplay of finite and nonfinite constructions in Balto-Finnic, we
shall cite pairs of sentences, essentially synonymous, where the one has a finite
subordinate clause (the usual method of expressing subordination in these
languages), the second a nonfinite construction. The first pair from Estonian
illustrates an object clause after the verb 'say':

(47)   *mu sõber ütle-s,*   *et ta vend tule -b*   *varsti tagasi*
         my friend say PAST-3SG that his brother come   3SG soon   back

(48)   *mu sõber ütle-s oma venna*   *varsti tagasi tule -vat*
                 own brother-GEN   come PRES-PART
         'my friend said that his brother would soon come back'

The second two pairs, again from Estonian, illustrate relative clauses, the first relativising on a subject, the second on a direct object:

(49)   *vanake silmitse-s*   *kaua*   *inimes-t,*
         old-man observe PAST-3SG for-a-long-time person PARTIT
         kes sammu-s   *üle õue*   *elumaja*
         who go   PAST-3SG across courtyard-GEN residential
         poole
         building-ILL

(50)   *vanake silmitse-s kaua üle õue elumaja poole sammu-vat*
                                           go   PRES-PART
         inimes -t
         person PARTIT
         'for a long time the old man observed the person who was going across the courtyard to the residential building'

(51)   *luuletus, mille*   *poeet ise ette kandi -s,*
         poem   which-GEN poet self forth recite PAST-3SG
         meeldi-s   *kõigi-le*
         please PAST-3SG all   ALL

(52)   *poeedi*   *enese*   *ettekan -tud*   *luuletus meeldis kõigile*
         poet-GEN self-GEN recite-forth PAST-PART
         'the poem which the poet recited forth himself pleased everyone'

Note that the subject of a nonfinite clause stands in the genitive.

   One difference between the more easterly and the more westerly languages is, as already noted, the relative weight given to finite versus nonfinite subordinate constructions. Another difference is in the range of applicability of nonfinite constructions, this range being much wider in the east. In Vakh Khanty, for instance, the nonfinite relative clause construction illustrated in (46) can be used for relativising on virtually any constituent of a clause; in the Balto-Finnic languages, however, the parallel constructions as illustrated in (50) and (52) can only be used for relativising on subject and direct object. A third difference is that the possibilities for declining verbal nouns, etc., in the more easterly languages are usually fully productive, whereas in the more westerly languages it is more typical for only a few fossilised cases to survive, often with idiosyncratic meaning: in Estonian, for instance, the infinitive in *-da* survives only in the nominative and the inessive (in *-des*, cf. *lugedes* in (21)).

TEXTS IN URALIC LANGUAGES

ESTONIAN TEXT (IN CURRENT ORTHOGRAPHY)

Ukse-le   koputamine kesti   -s,   põrutuse-d läk   -si   -d
door -ALL knocking   continue PAST shaking PL become PAST 3PL

ikka   tugeva-ma   -ks.   Sillamäe-d tõu-si   -d   kõik.
always strong COMPAR TRANSL Sillamäe PL rise PAST 3PL all

Milla riietu-s   ruttu. Aadu ja   Anu aja   -si   -d
Milla dress PAST quickly Aadu and Anu throw PAST 3PL

vammuse -d selg -a. Vana- mees kiisi-s   veel, kes
top-clothes PL back ILL old   man ask PAST again who

seal on, ja   ava -s   ukse   ning kummarda-s.
there is   and open PAST door-GEN and bow   PAST

—Käe -d   üles! karju-t   -i   ta -lle   vastu. Era   -isiku -d
    hand PL up   shout PASS PAST he ALL towards private person PL

ja   politseiniku-d karga -si   -d   sisse. Vana-d tõst -si   -d
and policeman PL spring PAST 3PL in   old   PL raise PAST 3PL

käe -d. Varsti nee -d vaju -si   -d   värise -de   -s.
hand PL soon   these PL lower PAST 3PL tremble INFIN-II INESS

Ka Milla   sõrme-d ol -i   -d   püsti.
also Milla-GEN finger PL be PAST 3PL sticking-up

See sündmüs ol -i   Sillamäe Aadu-le   rabandav.
this event   be PAST Sillamäe Aadu ALL shocking

Hariliku-le   proletaarlase-le, kes jookse-b   võidu
ordinary ALL proletarian   ALL who run   3SG victory-GEN

nälja -ga   ja   kes enda-st   ei hooli, p   -ol -nud
hunger COMIT and who self   ELAT not care   NEG be PAST-PART

säärase-d tuhnimise-d ei alandava -d ega uudise -ks.
such   PL search   PL not humiliating PL nor novelty TRANSL

Kuid abi   -meistri -le   ol -i   see ränk.
but   assistant foreman ALL be PAST this hard
  '*Kulalise-d' hüppa-si   -d   Milla   ette   ja päri-si   -d:*
  guest   PL jump PAST 3PL Milla-GEN in-front and ask PAST 3PL
—*Kas ole-te   Milla Aadu   tütar   Sillamäe?*
  Q   be 2PL Milla Aadu-GEN daughter Sillamäe
—*Mis   siis?*
  what then
—*Siin on order.*
  here is   warrant
—*ma p   - ole korteri   - peremees.*
  I   NEG be apartment owner
(Adapted from a text by J. Madarik.)

Notes

The translative case ('becoming X') is used for certain predicative complements, especially after 'become'.

For the use of the genitive *ukse* 'door' as direct object, see pp. 128–9.

värise-de-s: the inessive of the so-called second infinitive indicates a subsidiary action contemporaneous with that of the main verb.

p-ol-nud, p-ole: in addition to the regular negatives *ei ole* (present), *ei olnud* (past), Estonian also has for this one verb the special forms with prefixed *p-*.

FREE TRANSLATION

The knocking continued at the door, the shakings became stronger and stronger. The Sillamäes all got up. Milla dressed quickly. Aadu and Anu threw their top clothes onto their backs. The old man asked again who was there, and opened the door and bowed.

—Hands up! someone shouted towards him. Civilians and police sprang in. The old people raised their hands. Soon they (sc. their hands) dropped, trembling. Milla's fingers were also sticking up.

This event was shocking to Aadu Sillamäe.

To an ordinary proletarian, who runs with hunger for victory and who does not care for himself, such searches were neither humiliating nor a novelty. But to the assistant foreman this was hard.

The 'guests' jumped in front of Milla and asked:

—Are you Milla, daughter of Aadu, Sillamäe?

—What if I am?

—Here is a warrant.

—I am not the apartment-owner.

KHANTY TEXT (VAKH DIALECT)

əjlänə əpi -m kitəm wel-m   -äl jöɣərki wet
once father 1SG recently kill PAST-PART 3SG teen   five

läŋki çəpas   päni kä sas   -qən oɣtəŋ uri-ja
squirrel approximately and two ermine DU Okhteuri ALL

tu -ta   mən-ləm   -əs.   mä əti   -m
take INFIN go   INTEND PAST-DEF-REC I   elder-brother 1SG

MIRON əpi -l -na   mə-tä   wəräɣt-iɣən. əpi -m -nə
Miron father 3SG COMIT go INFIN strive 3SG father 1SG LOC

əntə wə -l   -i,   məttə jok kit -a   ḷök -nə
not take PASS PRES-3SG saying home stay IMPER-2SG way LOC

läɣərt -əɣ   pit -əŋ,   kit -w   -ən. əŋki -m -pə
difficult TRANSL become COND stay NONPAST 2SG mother 1SG TOO

löɣ-ä   köç at -w   -əl: äl   jis -ä.   köç-pə
he ALL PTCL say NONPAST 3SG NEG-IMPER cry IMPER-2SG however

jis -m   -äl -ä -ti, əpi -m ätilnäm mən-əs.
cry PAST-PART 3SG ALL PTCL father 1SG alone   go   PAST-DEF-REM

löɣ mən-m   -äl -ä -ti, əti -m nemin tä
he go   PAST-PART 3SG ALL PTCL mother 1SG truly well-then

jis -əkətə -s.   koɣ   jis -m   -äl pirnə,
cry INCH PAST-DEF-REM long-time cry PAST-PART 3SG after

əjlänə löɣ -əs.
at-last stop PAST-DEF-REM

(Extracted from N. I. Tereškin, *Očerki dialektov xantyjskogo jazyka*, I, *Vaxovskij dialekt*, Moscow–Leningrad, 1961.)

Notes

For the use of the participle to translate relative and adverbial clauses, see p. 134.

wəräɣt-iɣən: although the past definite recent tense and third person singular subject are usually zero morphemes in the active indefinite-object conjugation, for the combination of these two categories the suffix -iɣən is required.

əpim-nə: the locative is used for the agent in passive constructions.

FREE TRANSLATION

One day my father intended going to take about fifteen squirrels and two ermine that he had recently killed to Okhteuri. My elder brother Miron tried to go with his father. He wasn't taken by father, saying, 'Stay home, on the way things may get difficult, stay'. My mother too told him, 'Don't cry'. While he cried, my father went alone. When he went, well, my elder brother truly began to cry. After he had cried for a long time, at last he stopped.

SELKUP TEXT

ira   -kota   -mɨqäqi ilɨ -mpå   -qi.   śitti ija - tɨ ep-pa.
old-man old-woman AND   live NARR 3DU two son 3 be NARR

ija -qi -t qən-qo   -lam   -n   -åqi.   qət   tolći-sä
son DU 3 go   INFIN INCH INDEF 3DU in-winter ski   INSTR

täpäl   -lä   qən-på   -qi.   ukkɨr kanak-tɨ ep-pa.
hunt-squirrel GER go   NARR 3DU one   dog   3 be NARR

kora -ŋpå   -qi.   śöt -qɨt   ütɨt   åmnɨ-mpå   -qi.   kanak-tɨ
travel NARR 3DU forest LOC at-evening sit   NARR 3DU dog   3

wətto-mɨn   -tɨ   moqɨnä mutɨ-qo   -lam   -na.   kanak-tɨ åk   -tɨ
way   PROL 3DU back   bark INFIN INCH INDEF dog   3 mouth 3

ńantä   temnɨ-sä   sårei-mpå   -tɨ.   tü -m   - tɨ sirɨ   -sa
together rope   INSTR bind NARR 3DU fire ACC 3   snow INSTR

tak   -pa   -tɨ,   onti   innɨ-m   -tɨ miśal-pa   -tɨ,
extinguish NARR 3DU themselves bow ACC 3   grab   NARR 3DU

tolći-m   -tɨ tokkalɨ-mpa   -tɨ, śöt   -tɨ   nösol-på   -qi.
ski   ACC 3 put-on NARR 3   forest ALL ski   NARR 3DU

mütɨ tü   -nnɨn   -tɨ.
war   come INFER 3SG

(From: E. D. Prokof'eva, Sel'kupskij jazyk, in *Jazyki narodov SSSR*, III, Moscow, 1966.)

Notes

The suffixes -*qi*, -*ti*, glossed as '3DU' on verbs, are for intransitive and transitive verbs respectively.

qənqolamnåqi, *mutɨqolamna*: these inchoative forms are contractions of the sequence infinitive followed by the finite verb *olam-* 'begin'.

There lived an old man and an old woman. They had two sons. Their sons set off. In winter they went to hunt squirrel on skis. They had a dog. They journeyed. They sat in the evening in the forest. Their dog began to bark back along the way. They bound their dog's mouth together with rope. They extinguished the fire with snow, they grabbed their bows, they put on their skis, they skied to the forest. War was apparently coming.

FURTHER READING

There are several good introductions to Uralic comparative linguistics, including discussion of the individual languages: Décsy (1965); Collinder (1960; 1965; 1969); and a recent standard Soviet work, *OFUJa* (1974–6). A more general introduction to Uralic studies, not restricted to language, is Hajdú (1962), also available in an English translation. For the sociolinguistics of the Finno-Ugric languages, Haarmann (1974) should be consulted. Grammatical sketches of the individual languages of the U.S.S.R. constitute *JaNSSSR* III (1966). Tauli (1963) deals primarily with the typology of Uralic languages, in particular morphological typology, including the range of categories expressed in various Uralic languages.

For the Samoyedic languages, there is a useful introduction, not restricted to language, by Hajdú (1963). Castrén (1854), in German, remains an important source for grammatical description, especially in so far as recent monograph descriptions are available for few of the languages in question. Tereščenko (1973) deals with the syntax of the simple sentence in Samoyedic languages; since this term includes the various nonfinite subordinate constructions, and since finite subordinate clauses are atypical of traditional Samoyedic, this is in fact a fairly comprehensive syntax. There is a monograph description of Nenets by Tereščenko incorporated in *NenRS* (1965), and a sketch description in English in Décsy (1966). Tereščenko (1979) is a detailed monograph on Nganasan. For Selkup, the only reasonably comprehensive account is Prokof'ev (1935).

Khanty is described, with emphasis on the Central Ob' dialect, by Steinitz (1950) in German. For the aberrant Vakh dialect, Tereškin (1961) should be consulted. In English, there are sketches of the Northern and Eastern dialects in the chrestomathies by Rédei (1966) and Gulya (1966) respectively. The most comprehensive description of Mansi is Rombandeeva (1973), while there is an outline grammar in English in the chrestomathy by Kálmán (1965).

Serebrennikov (1963) provides an introduction to the comparative study of the Permic languages, with detailed consideration of morphological reconstruction and development. For Old Permic, the standard work is Lytkin (1952). There are standard grammars for each of the recognised modern languages: for Komi (-Zyryan) *SKomJa* (1955–64); for Komi-Permyak Batalova et al. (1962); and for Udmurt *GSUdmJa* (1962), *GSUdmJaSPP* (1970), and *GSUdmJaSSP* (1974).

Serebrennikov (1967) provides a comparable treatment of the Mordva languages in comparative perspective, while *GMorJa* (1962) is the first volume of a standard grammar, to be complemented by Koljadenkov (1959) on syntax. In addition, there are grammatical sketches of Mordva in the works by Paasonen (1953) and Wiedemann (1865), both in German. For Mari, there are the volumes of the standard grammar: Gruzov (1960), *SMarJaM* (1961), and Timofeeva (1961), in addition to an account in English by Sebeok and Ingemann (1961).

The Kildin dialect of Kola Lapp is described by Kert (1971).

For the Balto-Finnic languages, there are numerous descriptions of Finnish and Estonian, but comprehensive grammars of the smaller languages are much less in evidence, descriptions of these languages forming rather part of the specialist literature on dialectology. Since the more northerly Balto-Finnic languages are all quite close to Finnish, reference can conveniently be made to descriptions of Finnish, such as Hakulinen (1978), also available in English and German translations. For Estonian, there is a general introduction to the field by Raun and Saareste (1965), in addition to descriptive grammars in German (Lavotha 1973) and in English (Tauli 1973), the latter being the first volume only of a multi-volume work. There is also a pedagogical grammar in English by Oinas (1967). A brief but comprehensive description of Vot is available by Ariste (1968). For Liv, reference must be made to earlier works, in German, by Sjögren (1861) and Kettunen (1938).

4

Indo-European languages

4.1 The Indo-European family in the U.S.S.R.

Over 80% of the inhabitants of the U.S.S.R. have as their native language one of the Indo-European languages. Moreover, of the nine branches into which the living Indo-European languages are divided (or eight, if one takes Balto-Slavonic as a single branch), only one branch, Celtic, is not represented in the U.S.S.R. (Table 4.1). Indo-European languages thus play a major role in the linguistic composition of the U.S.S.R. In this chapter, we shall not give a detailed account of the Indo-European languages in general, since most Indo-European languages are not languages of the U.S.S.R., but will rather concentrate on those branches and languages that are primarily or exclusively languages of the U.S.S.R.

Two of the branches of the Indo-European family which consist of a single language each, namely Greek and Albanian, are not, by definition, languages of the U.S.S.R. and have few speakers there. There are 336,869 Greeks in the U.S.S.R., of whom only 39.3% have Greek as their native language: in fact, more Greeks have Russian as their native language than have Greek. For the most part, the Greeks in the U.S.S.R. are descendants of refugees from uprisings against the Ottoman occupation of Greece; the highest concentration of Greeks in the U.S.S.R. is to the north of the Sea of Azov, in the south-east of the Ukraine. In the U.S.S.R. there are 4,402 Albanians, 56.7% of whom speak Albanian as their native language; the major concentration is near Melitopol' in the south-eastern Ukraine, where they moved from Bessarabia in 1861. The 1959 census statistics gave 5,258 Albanians, of whom 79% spoke Albanian as their native language; judging from the large difference, the 1959 figure may include a number of Albanians from Albania temporarily in the U.S.S.R., who would naturally have Albanian as their native language.

4.2 Balto-Slavonic languages

The Slavonic languages play a major role in the linguistic composition of the U.S.S.R., especially in so far as Russian is a Slavonic language, but also in that the second and fourth largest languages of the U.S.S.R., Ukrainian and Belorussian, are also Slavonic. While the two Baltic languages, Lithuanian and Latvian, have far

Table 4.1. *Branches of the
Indo-European family
(modern languages)*

Slavonic }
Baltic   }   *Balto-Slavonic*
Indo-Iranian: Indic (Indo-Aryan)
                    Iranian
Armenian
Albanian
Hellenic (Greek)
Germanic
Italic
Celtic

fewer speakers, they are both languages of Union Republics, with over $2\frac{1}{2}$ and almost $1\frac{1}{2}$ million native speakers in the U.S.S.R. respectively.

The question of whether Balto-Slavonic represents a single branch of Indo-European, or whether the undoubted similarities between Baltic and Slavonic are the result of areal diffusion, has long been a vexed problem in the study of these language groups. For present purposes, we will merely draw attention to one remarkable similarity between the Baltic and Slavonic groups, which provides one of the strongest pieces of evidence in favour of a single Balto-Slavonic branch. The majority of Slavonic languages and both Baltic languages lack a definite article – those Slavonic languages, such as Bulgarian, Macedonian, and some Russian dialects, that have developed a definite article have done so recently – but in both groups of languages it is possible to indicate the difference between definite and indefinite noun phrases that contain an adjective, by marking the adjective. Moreover, the means of marking is the same in both groups: the appropriate form of the demonstrative *j-* is suffixed to the adjective, again in the appropriate form (i.e. agreeing with the head noun in gender, number, and case), e.g. Lithuanian *baltà lémpa* 'a white lamp', *baltó-ji lémpa* 'the white lamp'. As can be seen from this pair of examples, certain morphophonemic changes take place when the demonstrative is suffixed to the article, and with the longer adjective endings of some of the oblique cases there is contraction in the definite adjective, e.g. instrumental plural *baltomis lémpomis* 'with white lamps', *baltõsiomis lémpomis* 'with the white lamps'. The distinction between indefinite and definite adjective is found in both Lithuanian and Latvian, but within Slavonic it survives with this function only in Serbo-Croat and Slovene. The other Slavonic languages have generalised either the indefinite form (Bulgarian, Macedonian) or the definite form (all the other languages, except Russian). In

Russian, only the definite adjectives survive in attributive use, but both forms are still possible in predicative position, with complex semantic, pragmatic, and stylistic differences between them.

Although some other branches of Indo-European have distinctions approximating to this distinction in Balto-Slavonic, e.g. the strong and weak adjective declensions in Germanic or the use of the relative pronoun in older Iranian languages (see p. 168), nowhere else do we find such close parallelism as between Baltic and Slavonic, which even extends to certain specific uses of the two forms. For instance, in Lithuanian the definite adjective is used, irrespective of the definiteness of the noun phrase, where the adjective is used to define a species, e.g. *juodàsis gañdras* 'black stork (Ciconia nigra)', as opposed to *júodas gañdras* 'a black stork' (i.e. a stork that happens to be black). Precisely the same distinction is found in Serbo-Croat, e.g. *bili luk* (definite adjective), literally 'white onion', meaning 'garlic', cf. *bil luk* (indefinite adjective) 'an onion that happens to be white'.

At least as problematical as the question of Balto-Slavonic unity is that of the internal unity of Baltic, which falls into two main subgroups, West and East Baltic. The surviving languages, Lithuanian and Latvian, are East Baltic, and the best attested West Baltic language is Old Prussian. One widespread current view is that Balto-Slavonic as a whole should be regarded as a unit, which falls into three, rather than two, subgroups: West Baltic, East Baltic, and Slavonic. In the remainder of this chapter, especially as we shall not be dealing with West Baltic languages, we shall retain the traditional terms Baltic and Slavonic.

4.2.1   *Slavonic languages*

The Slavonic group of languages itself falls into three main sub-divisions: South Slavonic (Bulgarian, Macedonian, Serbo-Croat, Slovene, and the earliest attested Slavonic language, Old Church Slavonic); West Slavonic (Czech, Slovak, Polish, Upper Sorbian, Lower Sorbian, and the extinct Polabian); East Slavonic (Russian, Ukrainian, Belorussian). The South and West Slavonic languages are not languages of the U.S.S.R., though some of them have quite large numbers of speakers in the U.S.S.R., e.g. Bulgarian with 256,646 speakers, and especially Polish; there are also sizable compact Slovak populations in the parts of Transcarpathia ceded to the U.S.S.R. after the Second World War. The large Polish population in the U.S.S.R. is largely a result of the frequent border changes between Poland and Russia/the U.S.S.R., and this population is concentrated in Lithuania (where ethnic Poles constitute 7.7% of the total population), Belorussia, and the Ukraine, although many ethnic Poles were repatriated from Belorussia and the Ukraine after 1945. The number of ethnic Poles in the U.S.S.R. is 1,380,282, but only

32.5% of these gave Polish as their native language in the 1970 census, a substantial drop from 45.2% in 1959.

The three East Slavonic languages are very close to one another, with very high rates of mutual intelligibility, thus creating a massive preponderance of East Slavonic within the U.S.S.R.: over 76% of the total population has an East Slavonic language as a native language. The separation of Russian, Ukrainian, and Belorussian as distinct languages is relatively recent. At the time of the earliest attested writing in East Slavonic, around the beginning of our millennium, the major dialect division within East Slavonic was between the northern part of this area and the southern part, the dividing isoglosses running roughly through present-day Moscow. However, the weakness and internal divisions of the various East Slavonic principalities led to their domination by different outside powers, with present-day Russia under Tatar suzerainty from the mid-thirteenth century, and the more westerly areas, present-day Ukraine and Belorussia, under Polish and/or Lithuanian domination. It was during this period that many of the differences among the three languages arose, especially between Russian and Ukrainian, the two most divergent languages. Since the eastern Ukraine was not reunited with Russia proper until the seventeenth century, and the western Ukraine until the partition of Poland in 1772, the period of separation spans several centuries. Thus some of the innovations of Ukrainian did not spread to Russian, such as the shift of lengthened *o* to *i*, e.g. contrast Ukrainian *viw* 'ox', Russian *vol*. Likewise, many innovations within Russian did not spread to Ukrainian, e.g. the reduction of unstressed vowels (called *akan'e*, since one of its most characteristic features is the reduction of unstressed *o* to an *a*-like vowel [ʌ], cf. the pronunciation of *voda* 'water' as [vʌdá]); *akan'e* is a typically Southern Russian feature, though now encompassing also the standard language based on the Central dialects of the Moscow region, but it is completely absent from Ukrainian, the most southerly of the East Slavonic languages.

After the reunification of the Ukraine with Russia, the Tsarist government did not encourage the development of Ukrainian as a separate language. Indeed, the authorities even played down the existence of the Ukraine as a separate cultural area by referring to it as 'Little Russia' (Malorossija), in contrast to 'Great Russia', i.e. Russia proper; during this period the language was referred to as 'Little Russian', and was deemed to be a dialect of Russian. In the nineteenth century publication in Ukrainian was forbidden, and only in 1905, as part of the reforms following the uprising of that year, was its use allowed again. Widespread use of Ukrainian as a written language and in education dates only from after the Revolution, especially with the establishment of the Ukrainian S.S.R. Ukrainian, incidentally, has always used the Cyrillic alphabet, though with certain letters absent from Russian (e.g. the dotted *i*, dropped from the Russian alphabet in 1918 – in Russian it was previously a mere orthographic variant, used before vowels), and with different phonetic values for a few letters.

In the U.S.S.R., Ukrainian has always, and perhaps inevitably, developed somewhat in the shadow of Russian: many Ukrainians in fact speak a mixture of Ukrainian and Russian, finding it difficult to keep the two languages apart, and it is interesting to note that while the language-retention rate is high for Ukrainians living in the Ukraine (91.4%), for those living elsewhere in the U.S.S.R. it is much lower (48.4%), i.e. while Ukrainians still declare their separate ethnic status, their language loyalty is much lower. A certain number of small changes have been introduced into Ukrainian in the U.S.S.R., making it slightly more similar to Russian, for instance the replacement of the earlier word for 'ninety', *devjatdesát*, by the neologism *devjanósto*, i.e. based simply on Russian *devjanosto*, originally a Northern dialect form of unclear etymology, but perhaps meaning something like 'nonal hundred'. Outside the U.S.S.R., the largest and most compact Ukrainian community is in Canada.

Belorussian has developed even more in the shadow of Russian than has Ukrainian. The term Belorussian, incidentally, means 'White Russian', but this ethnic term is not to be confused with 'White Russian' in the political sense (opponents of the Soviet government). In the Middle Ages, an early form of Belorussian enjoyed a brief period as official written language of the Lithuanian state, most of whose citizens were at that time Belorussian; this language is usually called the West Russian chancellery language. With the reincorporation of Belorussia into Russia, Belorussian continued only as an amalgam of spoken dialects, without any developed written form, until after the Revolution, when it was recognised as a separate written and spoken language. Its development continued to be hindered by uncertainties over the most appropriate dialect to choose as the basis of the standard language, and it was not until the 1950s that this question was finally decided, necessitating revision of the grammars that had appeared previously. Language retention in Belorussia itself is somewhat lower than in the Ukraine (90.1%), and the problem of people speaking a mixture of the local language and Russian is even more acute. Belorussians living elsewhere in the U.S.S.R. have a still lower rate of language retention: 40.8%.

4.2.2 Baltic languages

Only two Baltic languages survive to the present day, Lithuanian and Latvian (Lettish), each spoken by a sizable and compact population group clearly differentiated from its neighbours. Each of the modern languages, though especially Lithuanian, is characterised by a marked degree of dialect diversity, probably reflecting the fact that the population was until recently agrarian and immobile and that both languages developed as written languages very recently, for Latvian not until the nineteenth century. The present-day Baltic languages are only a small remnant of a group of languages that once covered a much larger area: for instance, the area as far south-east as Moscow was, on the basis of toponymic evidence, once inhabited by speakers of Baltic languages, and Baltic languages have also receded before the eastward expansion of the Germans: the original Prussians were a Baltic people. Only against the Balto-Finnic languages have the Baltic languages made some inroads: to a large extent, present-day Latvians can be viewed as linguistically assimilated Balto-Finnic speakers, and this process continues to this day, with the Latvianisation of the last remaining speakers of Liv.

Both Lithuanian and Latvian belong to the East Baltic branch, which also includes the extinct languages Curonian (with some West Baltic features, especially in vocabulary), Selonian, and Zemgalian (Semigallian), all three very sparsely attested. The other branch of Baltic, West Baltic, contains one language attested in some breadth, namely Old Prussian, for which we have a small number of religious texts from the fifteenth century, just before the language finally died out and was replaced by German. In view of the marked dialect diversity, this is also a convenient place at which to mention the main dialects of the surviving languages. The two main dialect areas of Lithuanian are Aukshtayt (High Lithuanian) and Zhemayt (Low Lithuanian, also called Samogitian); although the earliest Lithuanian texts are in Zhemayt, the current standard is based on an Aukshtayt dialect. Zhemayt is spoken in the west of Lithuania. The main dialects of Latvian are the Central dialects, which include the capital Riga and on which the current standard is based, and Upper (High) Latvian, spoken to the east; other dialect groups are sometimes recognised, e.g. the dialect spoken by Liv who have been assimilated to the Latvians, but whose language shows considerable Liv influence (for instance, in the loss of the gender distinction). One dialect of High Latvian, Latgal, has been used considerably as a written language, but its use is discouraged in Soviet Latvia, where only the one standard written language is used.

The development of both Lithuanian and Latvian, and also the culturally, but not genetically, related language Estonian, took place very late by European standards, starting essentially in the seventeenth century for Lithuanian and in the nineteenth century for Latvian, and reaching full development only during the inter-War years when the Baltic states were independent countries, each using its own language as official language. The western orientation of these republics is seen not only in their traditional Catholic or Lutheran religion, but also in the adoption and retention of the Latin alphabet, modified by diacritics. Both Lithuanian and Latvian show high rates of language retention in the U.S.S.R. (97.9% and 95.2% respectively); as a result of the checkered political history of the Baltic area, there are large numbers of Lithuanian and Latvian émigrés in other European countries, North America, Australia, and elsewhere, so that in addition to 2,664,944 Lithuanians and 1,429,844 Latvians in the U.S.S.R., there are probably up to half a million members of either ethnic group outside the U.S.S.R. Both are languages of Union Republics: Lithuanians are numerically predominant in their own republic (80.1% of the population), although the capital, Vilnyus (Lithuanian: Vilnius), is somewhat atypical in this respect, having a combined Russian and Polish population slightly outnumbering the Lithuanians; in Latvia, Latvians are in a small majority (56.8%), although their percentage has fallen since 1959 (62%), and the capital, Riga, actually has more Russians than Latvians in its present population.

The initial interest among linguists in the Baltic languages, and especially in Lithuanian, resulted from the realisation that Lithuanian is extremely archaic as an Indo-European language, especially in its nominal morphology, having inflections that are often as archaic or even more archaic than those found in the earliest attested Indo-European languages from two and a half millennia ago. Apart from the archaic morphological system, and some peculiarities of phonology to be discussed below, the present-day Baltic languages are very like other European languages in their syntax, and also in general style, given that the development of the literary languages took place under strong influence from other European literary languages. They are like Slavonic languages in having a basic subject–verb–object word order, though as in Slavonic languages permutations are possible to express different informational structure without changing the cognitive meaning: this is guaranteed by the well-developed case-marking system, so that Latvian *māte* (NOM) *gaida māsu* (ACC) 'mother is waiting for sister' can be expressed equally as *māsu gaida māte*, with only a slight difference in emphasis ('as for sister, it is mother who is waiting for her'), while 'sister is waiting for mother' would have to be *māsa* (NOM) *gaida māti* (ACC), or any permutation of these words. As in Slavonic languages, adjectives precede their head noun, e.g. Latvian *balts suns* 'a white dog', but the order of genitive and head noun is different between Baltic and Slavonic: both Lithuanian and Latvian place the genitive before the head noun, e.g. Lithuanian *tĕ̃vo* (GEN) *nãmas*, Latvian *tēva* (GEN) *māja* 'father's house', cf. Russian *dom otca* (GEN). However, the partitive genitive follows its head noun, thus indicating the different nature of these two constructions, and even giving rise to minimal pairs like Lithuanian *maĩšas cùkraus* (GEN) 'bag of sugar', *cùkraus* (GEN) *maĩšas* 'sugar bag'. In the following paragraphs, some of the peculiarities of Lithuanian and Latvian will be examined that set them apart from the general run of European languages, especially Slavonic languages.

In terms of phonology, the most interesting aspect of Lithuanian and Latvian is the existence of phonemic tone. In both languages, syllable nuclei consisting of two moras (i.e. a long vowel or a diphthong, which latter includes sequences of vowel plus *m*, *n*, *l*, *r* as well as diphthongs ending in *w* and *y*, orthographically *u* and *i*) may show a distinction between different distributions of pitch across the two moras; where the syllable nucleus has just a single mora, i.e. if it is a short vowel, then there can be no pitch distinction. Beyond this general characterisation, Lithuanian and Latvian differ considerably from one another in both the phonetics of tone and its function, and there are also considerable differences between individual dialects of either language. The major difference between the two languages is that in Lithuanian the tone opposition can be realised phonetically only on the stressed syllable, and is neutralised in unstressed syllables; different morphological forms of the same word can, incidentally, be stressed on different syllables. In Latvian, the stress always falls on the initial syllable (this is an innovation), and any syllable nucleus consisting of two moras will show a distinctive tone. We may now turn to the phonetics and morphophonemics of tone.

In Lithuanian, the standard language has a two-way tone opposition on stressed syllables with two moras, between rising pitch (symbolised $\tilde{V}$ or $V\tilde{V}$) and falling pitch (symbolised $\acute{V}$ or $\acute{V}V$). The rising pitch is often called circumflex, and the falling pitch acute: the dialects on which standard Lithuanian is based, and which have the system just outlined, have historically undergone a process of switching the pitch values of the two tones, which is why the so-called circumflex, symbolised $\tilde{V}$, is rising, whereas in the discussion of most Indo-European languages with tone the circumflex is a falling tone. If the stress falls on a syllable with a short vowel, this can be symbolised $\grave{V}$ (grave). There are numerous minimal pairs for the difference between acute and circumflex tones, e.g. *áušti* 'to grow cold', *aũšti* 'to dawn'. The easiest place to observe the interaction of tone and stress change is in the declension of the noun. For prosodic purposes, Lithuanian nouns are divided into four classes. Classes 1 and 2 have the stress basically on the stem, while classes 3 and 4 have stress basically on the inflectional ending, though individual case-forms may diverge, as indicated below. Classes 2 and 4 belong together in having a circumflex or grave tone on the last syllable of the stem, when the stem is stressed; all other stem types are in class 1 or 3. Certain inflectional endings tend to draw the stress onto themselves: thus the first declension locative singular - *e* draws the stress onto itself from a preceding circumflex or grave syllable, as does the second declension nominative singular ending - *a*. Conversely, certain endings tend to throw the stress back onto the stem, for instance the first declension nominative singular ending - *as*, or the second declension nominative plural ending - *os*. Yet other endings have no effect on the stress, such as first declension nominative plural - *ai*, or second declension genitive singular - *os*. These alternations are illustrated in the noun forms in Table 4.2.

Table 4.2. *Stress and tone in Lithuanian declension*

First declension:	NOM SG	LOC SG	NOM PL
class 1: 'man'	výras	výre	výrai
class 2: 'key'	rãktas	raktè	rãktai
class 3: 'mountain'	kálnas	kalnè	kalnaĩ
class 4: 'time'	laĩkas	laikè	laikaĩ
Second declension:	NOM SG	GEN SG	NOM PL
class 1: 'crow'	várna	várnos	várnos
class 2: 'hand'	rankà	rañkos	rañkos
class 3: 'head'	galvà	galvõs	gálvos
class 4: 'beard'	barzdà	barzdõs	baȓzdos

To see that the forms in Table 4.2 illustrate the generalisations above, the following points should be noted. Class 1 nouns invariably have the stress on the stem: they are basically stem-stressed, and endings that attract stress never attract stress from a stem that does not have a final circumflex or grave tone. Class 2 nouns are also basically stem-stressed, as can be seen from forms like nominative plural *rãktai*, genitive singular *rañkos*, since these are endings that do not alter the stress; however, in the locative singular of the first declension and the nominative singular of the second declension the stress is attracted from the circumflex or grave of the stem onto the ending. Classes 3 and 4 are basically stressed on the ending – note the forms with stress-neutral endings like nominative plural *kalnaĩ*, *laikaĩ*, or genitive singular *galvõs*, *barzdõs*. However, when they take an ending that rejects stress, the stress will in fact be on the stem, e.g. nominative singular *kálnas*, *laĩkas*, nominative plural *gálvos*, *baȓzdos*: the existence of such forms provides the evidence that the stems have no final circumflex (nominative singular *kálnas*, nominative plural *gálvos*) or do have a final circumflex (nominative singular *laĩkas*, nominative plural *baȓzdos*). It should be noted moreover that each inflectional ending also has an inherent tone if it consists of two or more moras: nominative plural *-aĩ* and genitive singular and nominative plural *-õs* have circumflex tone, but the dative plural ending has acute tone, as in *kalnáms* 'mountains (DAT)', *galvóms* 'heads (DAT)'. This emphasises the morphophonemic nature of Lithuanian tone: in order to establish the tone (and inherent stress, if there is more than one syllable) of a stem, one must look for an inflectional form that is stem-stressed; to ascertain the inherent tone of an ending, one must look for a noun form where the ending is stressed. Although the diphthongs of *jaunà tautà* 'young nation' are phonetically identical, their differing morphophonemic nature can be seen from the corresponding plural *jáunos taũtos* 'young nations' (*jáunas* 'young' is class 3, *tautà* 'nation' class 4).

The above characterisation of the Lithuanian tone system is essentially synchronic, and does not take account of the complex historical stress shifts that have given rise to this system, and also to some alternations not discussed in detail here, for instance different tones on the same syllable in derivationally related words, e.g. *áukštas* 'high', but *aūkštis* 'height', where the circumflex on the latter represents a later stress retraction from the ending.

Standard Latvian has a three-way tone distinction on syllables of two moras. The lengthened tone, symbolised $\tilde{V}$, is level; it usually corresponds to Lithuanian $\acute{V}$ on the first syllable (despite the different symbolisation), e.g. *mãte* 'mother', *saũle* 'sun', *tiļts* 'bridge' (cf. Lithuanian *mótè*, *sáulè*, *tiltas* – in the last of these, Lithuanian indicates the acute tone by a grave accent, because of the phonetic shortness of the vowel *i*). The broken tone, which involves creaky voice in the second mora, rather like the Danish *stød*, is symbolised $\hat{V}$; it often represents a shift of stress relative to Lithuanian (recall that Latvian always has initial stress), e.g. *siȓds* 'heart', cf. Lithuanian *širdis*. The falling tone, symbolised $\grave{V}$, corresponds to the Lithuanian circumflex. Especially since Lithuanian has stress shifts between initial and noninitial syllable (e.g. the accusative singular of *širdis* is *širdĮ*), one might expect Latvian to have corresponding alternations in tone on the initial syllable, but in fact all such alternations have been levelled out, so that synchronically the tone type on a given syllable is constant throughout the inflection of that word. The following sentence illustrates the other main difference between Latvian and Lithuanian tone, namely that in Latvian all syllables of two moras, whether stressed or not, have the tonal opposition:

(53)   *kas   ir   laĩme?*   – *kapteĩnis   Klaũs*
         what-NOM be-3SG happiness-NOM captain-NOM Klau-NOM

         atkãrtõ
         repeat-PAST-3
         'what is happiness? – Captain Klau repeated'

Some Lithuanian dialects, incidentally, also have stress shifts from final syllables, giving rise to very complex systems with up to five distinct tones, including tonal oppositions on posttonic syllables.

As was mentioned above, one of the salient characteristics of Lithuanian within Indo-European is the conservatism of its declensional system; Latvian is considerably less conservative, as in many other respects. Recently, there has been some simplification of the inflectional system of Lithuanian, however: the standard language no longer uses the distinct dual forms in declension and conjugation, although they still survive in dialects. Currently, some of the longer nominal endings are being contracted in colloquial usage, so that *lentojė* 'board (LOC)' is being replaced by *lentõj*, *staluosė* 'tables (LOC)' by *staluõs*, and *dukterimi* 'daughter (INSTR)' by *dukterim̃*. Although Latvian still has a rich declensional system, in certain respects it places more weight on prepositions than on inflections. Thus Latvian uses the instrumental only with the preposition *ar*, e.g. *ar lāpstu* 'with a spade', whereas Lithuanian uses the instrumental without any preposition in this sense, e.g. *peiliù* 'with a knife'. In Latvian, all prepositions in the plural require the dative–instrumental (these two cases are not distinguished in the plural), thus neutralising case distinctions found in the singular, e.g. *pie galda* (GEN) 'at the table', *pie galdiem* (DAT–INSTR) 'at the tables', *pa ceļu* (ACC) 'along the road', *pa ceļiem* (DAT–INSTR) 'along the roads'.

One interesting peculiarity of Latvian syntax, which is shared by some Lithuanian dialects but not standard Lithuanian, is the use of the nominative as direct object in certain constructions. In standard Latvian, the construction in question is the debitive, expressing obligation. The verb takes the prefix *jā-*, and does not change for person and number; the noun phrase referring to the person who is obliged to carry out this action is in the dative case; the noun phrase referring to the direct object of the verb, if there is one, stands in the nominative, although otherwise Latvian has distinct nominative and accusative cases. This gives, for instance, *mums* (DAT) *jāiet* 'we must go' with an intransitive verb, and *mums* (DAT) *jālasa grāmata* (NOM) 'we must read a book' with a transitive verb. An exception is made for first and second person pronoun direct objects, which remain in the accusative: *mums* (DAT) *tevi* (ACC) *jālūdz* 'we must beg you'. With more complex constructions, for instance where the direct object is dependent on an infinitive that is itself dependent on a debitive form, or where pronouns and nonpronouns are coordinated, native speakers often allow variants with nominative or accusative. The reason why this construction has been discussed at some length here is that it appears to be an areal feature, encompassing not only Latvian and, to a lesser extent, Lithuanian, but also the Balto-Finnic languages (see pp. 129–30), and perhaps also certain North Russian dialects (Timberlake 1974). The construction may have arisen in Balto-Finnic (or earlier in Proto-Uralic) and diffused into the neighbouring Indo-European languages.

Another interesting feature of Baltic syntax, differentiating these two languages in many respects from Slavonic languages, is the use to which participles and gerunds (verbal adverbs) are put. Both Baltic and Slavonic languages have such nonfinite verbal forms, which, like participles in English, can be used instead of subordinate clauses. An unusual feature of Lithuanian is the existence of two sets of verbal adverbs, one used where the subject of the subordinate nonfinite clause is the same as that of the main clause (*pusdalyvis*), the other where they are different (*padalyvis*), effectively giving a limited switch-reference system:

(54)   *išeĩdamas   mokinỹs   pamiřšo   knỹgą*
go-out-PUSDALYVIS pupil-NOM forget-PAST-3 book-ACC
'leaving, the pupil forgot his book'

(55)   *visíems tỹlint,   vẽl   prabìlo   pirminínkas*
all-DAT fall-silent-PADALYVIS again speak-PAST-3 chairman-
NOM
'everyone having fallen silent, the chairman spoke again'

With the switch-reference *padalyvis*, the subject of the nonfinite form stands in the
dative. Both Lithuanian and Latvian use their active participles to form compound
tenses, unlike most Slavonic languages (at least synchronically), e.g. Lithuanian
buvaũ bedirbąs 'I was starting to work', with the present participle, *esù dìrbęs* 'I
have worked' (literally: 'I-am having-worked') with the past participle; compare
Latvian *esmu gaidījis* 'I have waited' (literally: 'I-am having-waited').

Lithuanian can also use its participles as main verbs. This occurs in indirect speech,
where participles replace the finite verbs of the original statement, and also outside of
direct speech where the speaker wishes not to assume responsibility for the truth of
what he is saying; this latter usage is also common in fairy-tales. First, an example
with direct and indirect speech: if the teacher's actual words were:

(56)   *tù tìngi   mókytis*
you be-lazy-2SG study-INFIN
'you are lazy in studying'

with a finite form of the verb *tingéti* 'to be lazy', then we could report this by saying:

(57)   *mókytojas   sãko, kàd tù tìngįs   mókytis*
teacher-NOM say-3 that you be-lazy-PRES-PART study-INFIN
'the teacher says that you are lazy in studying'

with the present participle *tìngįs*. As an independent sentence, one could say (58),
without accepting responsibility for the punctual departure of the train, by use of the
participle *išeĩnąs:*

(58)   *traukinỹs išeĩnąs   lýgiai   septiñtą   vãlandą*
train-NOM leave-PRES-PART prompt-ADV seventh-ACC hour-
ACC
'the train will leave promptly at seven o'clock'

In Latvian, too, the active past participle can be used to describe a situation for
whose authenticity the speaker does not vouch, and as such is particularly common
in fairy-tales, as in (59), with participles *gājis* and *nonācis:*

(59) *jaunākais*   *brālis*   *gājis*   *gājis, līdz*
        young-SUPERL-NOM brother-NOM walk-PAST-PART   until
        nonācis   *pie kādas*   *pils*
        arrive-PAST-PART at   certain-GEN castle-GEN
        'the youngest brother walked and walked, until he came upon a castle'

This form does not necessarily express doubt, it simply removes responsibility for the authenticity of the statement from the speaker. A separate form, with the suffix *-ot* (etymologically a participial ending, which is why it does not change for person or number), is used to express uncertainty about the veracity of a statement, as in (60) as opposed to (61):

(60) *viņš*   *esot*   *bagāts*
        he-NOM be-PRES-INFER rich-NOM
        'he is supposed to be rich'

(61) *viņš*   *ir*   *bagāts*
        he-NOM be-PRES-3 rich-NOM
        'he is rich'

This so-called relative mood in *-ot* is also used in indirect speech, except where the person reporting the speech has no doubts about the veracity of the statement reported. The existence of special verbal forms to cast doubt on the authenticity of, or at least not take personal responsibility for the veracity of, statements links Lithuanian and Latvian typologically with Estonian and, more distantly, with several Turkic languages (see pp. 77 and 125).

Since Lithuanian and Latvian were both fully developed as standard and written languages prior to the incorporation of these areas into the U.S.S.R. in 1940, the languages have not undergone any radical changes, other than in vocabulary, as a result of their integration into the Soviet system. One difference that strikes anyone familiar with Lithuanian publications in Lithuania and abroad is that the former spell foreign place names phonetically, in Lithuanian form, e.g. *Čikagà* 'Chicago', whereas the latter use the foreign spelling; in Latvian, use of the phonetic principle is general. In the Latvian S.S.R., the digraph *ch* has been abolished from the spelling of words, being replaced by *h*: both occur only in loans from foreign languages, though some of these are no longer rare, e.g. *himna* 'hymn, national anthem', *(c)haoss* 'chaos'. In the U.S.S.R. the use of the letter *ŗ* for a palatalised *r* has also been abolished, the simple letter *r* being used instead; this reflects a variety of pronunciation where *r* and *ŗ* are not distinguished.

4.3 **Indo-Iranian languages**

The close relation between the Indic (or Indo-Aryan) languages and the Iranian languages means that there is little doubt that they together form a single branch of Indo-European, with Indic and Iranian as two sub-branches. The precise dividing line between Indic and Iranian is more problematic, since some groups of languages (Dardic and Nuristani (or Kafiri)) form a transition between clear Indic and clear Iranian, but as these transitional languages are not spoken in the U.S.S.R. (they are spoken in the area where Afghanistan, Pakistan, and India meet) they need not concern us further here. Indic languages play a small role in the linguistic composition of the U.S.S.R., but Iranian languages are much more central, in so far as one Union Republic language (Tadzhik) and a number of languages of other autonomous areas, as well as several languages of smaller population groups, belong to the Iranian subbranch; moreover, the U.S.S.R. encompasses a significant proportion of the Iranian languages spoken today.

4.3.1 *Indic (Indo-Aryan) languages*

Only two Indic languages are languages of the U.S.S.R., namely Parya and Romany, the great mass of Indic languages being spoken in northern India, Pakistan, Bangla Desh, Nepal, and Sri Lanka. In classifying the modern Indic languages it is necessary first to split off two groups of languages which, as a result of a long period of separation from the other Indic languages, have developed many peculiarities of their own, namely Sinhalese-Maldivian (including Sinhalese, the language of the majority of the population of Sri Lanka (Ceylon), and Maldivian, the language of the Maldives) and Romany (the language of the Gypsies). The other Indic languages, spoken across the north of the Indian subcontinent, do not lend themselves very readily to classification, since dialect chains rather than clear-cut language boundaries dominate the area. In the present section, we shall be concerned only with Parya, one of these other Indic languages, and Romany.

Surprisingly, the discovery of Parya as an independent language of the Indic subbranch dates only from the mid 1950s. The Parya are called *afgon* (i.e. Afghan) by their neighbours, reflecting the fact that the home of the Parya immediately prior to their move to their present area was in Afghanistan, and this misleading ethnonym served to conceal their presence. None of the general works on languages of the U.S.S.R., including *JaNSSSR* I (1966), mentions the Parya, and they are not listed separately in any nationality or language statistics. They number about 1,000, and live in the Gissar valley and adjacent areas, stretching from the suburbs of the Tadzhik capital Dushanbe westwards across the border into Uzbekistan. All adult Parya, including women, are bilingual in Parya and Tadzhik, some of the men also speak Uzbek, and all Parya children grow up speaking Parya; knowledge of Russian comes only from the educational system. Although the Parya are not distinct from their Tadzhik and Uzbek neighbours in appearance or customs, they do maintain their distinctness, often forming separate sections of settlements, and rarely marrying outside of the Parya community. This is therefore a remarkably successful instance of language retention, with complete bilingualism, despite the small size of the community.

Linguistically, Parya is closest to the Central group of Indic languages, which includes Hindi-Urdu, Gujarati, Punjabi, and Rajasthani as its best-known members, although Parya also has some features in common with the North-West group, including Sindhi and Lahnda. Its status as a language distinct from any of these is clear, although the relatively small amount of work that has been done on Indic languages of Afghanistan does not make it possible to assign a precise position to Parya within Central and North-West Indic as a whole. Some of the most distinctive linguistic features of Parya, in relation to other Indic languages, are as follows. Phonetically, Parya has lost the so-called voiced aspirate series of plosives, replacing them by unaspirated plosives, voiceless initially and finally, usually voiced intervocalically (e.g. *kas* 'grass', cf. Hindi *gʻaas*, *pabi* 'elder brother's wife', cf. Hindi *bʻaabʻii*); loss of aspiration in the voiceless aspirates seems to be an ongoing process, with doublets for many lexical items. The binary gender opposition masculine/feminine found in the closely related languages is retained, though in weakened form, in Parya, in that there are many exceptions to the traditional rules for gender agreement, preference being given to the masculine form; with predicative adjectives, non-agreeing masculine forms with feminine subjects are the rule. Parya is one of the few modern Indic languages (along with Lahnda, Sindhi, and Punjabi) to have enclitic pronouns, in Parya for the third person possessive, e.g. *beṭa-so* 'his son'. Like the other closely related Indic languages, Parya uses an ergative construction with transitive verbs in the perfective aspect only, the subject taking the postposition *na*; in Parya, however, the verb in this construction does not agree with the direct object, but remains in the unmarked, masculine singular, form, even though with intransitive verbs there is agreement in number (and rarely in gender) with the subject.

The fact that Romany, the language of the Gypsies, is an Indic language is quite clear from the morphology and basic lexicon, although the precise point or points of origin of the Gypsies within India and the time of their migration(s) from there remain unclear. Equally difficult to determine is the total number of Romany speakers in the world, with estimates varying from half a million to one million. In part this is related to the similar problem of determining the total number of ethnic Gypsies (estimated at from one to two million), in part to the difficulty in determining the borderline between a speaker of Romany and a Gypsy speaking another language (usually that of the surrounding population) with heavy lexical borrowing from Romany – Romany vocabulary has been used to create secret languages, incomprehensible to the general population, by Gypsies and also certain non-Gypsy groups. For the U.S.S.R., we have the official census statistics of 1970, according to which 70.8% of the 175,335 Gypsies speak Romany as their native language. However, the census statistics for 1959 indicated that only 59.3% of the 132,014 Gypsies registered in that census spoke Romany as their native language. Such a large increase in the percentage of Romany speakers seems unlikely, and it may be that the Soviet authorities find it no easier than authorities in other countries to establish reliable statistics concerning their Gypsy population.

Romany divides into three main dialects (or perhaps one should say three Romany languages, since they are not mutually intelligible): Syrian (or Asiatic), Armenian (boša), and European. Most of the Gypsies in the U.S.S.R. are speakers of the European dialect group, especially as the Armenian Gypsies are largely assimilated linguistically to the surrounding Armenian population. The European dialect group breaks down further into a number of subdivisions, corresponding in large measure to the traditional area of settlement of the various Gypsy groups in Europe (Table 4.3). One characteristic of all European Romany is the presence of a number of loans from Greek, since Greece was a staging-post for all the European Gypsies on their journey from India. These include lexical loans such as *drum* 'way' (Greek *dromos*), and also the numerals *eftá* 'seven', *oxtó* 'eight', *eñá* 'nine'. In addition, the nominative forms of the definite article, masculine *o*, feminine *e/i* are borrowed from Greek, though not the oblique forms. Each of the individual European dialects is further characterised by strong influence from the surrounding language, especially in the lexicon, though also in phonology, morphology, and syntax. For instance, the Carpathian dialects have such loans from Hungarian as *maa* 'already', *gondolin-* 'to think' (Hungarian *már* [maar], *gondol*). The Baltic dialects have borrowed a large number of prefixes, and have virtually lost the definite article. The Wallachian dialects form several noun plurals in *-ura* and its dialect variants, borrowed from Romanian *-uri*. The Balkan dialects have replaced the original future tense by a new form using a reduced form of the verb 'to want' preposed to the main verb, e.g. Crimean *kan-ḱeráv* 'I will do', cf. Modern Greek *θa na káno*, Bulgarian *šte pravjó*, Romanian *voi face* [voj fáče], in all of which the first word is a reduced form of the verb 'to want'.

As will be seen from Table 4.3, the dialects of Romany spoken in the U.S.S.R. do not form a homogeneous set, and are largely the chance result of migration patterns and, especially, frontier shifts. Most Romany speakers in the U.S.S.R. are also fluent in Russian or one of the other languages of the surrounding community. For these reasons, Romany is not used as a written language or in education.

Table 4.3. *European dialects of Romany*

Baltic: North Russian (rúska romá, xəladítka romá)
  Latvian (lotfitka romá): western Latvia, Estonia
  Central Polish (pólśka fəldítka romá)
  Laius (lajenge roma): formerly spoken in the village of Laius in eastern Estonia; all speakers
    of this dialect were killed by Nazi occupation forces during the Second World War
German (sintí, sasítkə romá): Germany, France, Poland, Czechoslovakia, Yugoslavia,
    northern Italy, Austria; a few families in the U.S.S.R.
Carpathian: Slovakian (sə́rvika romá): northern and eastern Slovakia
  Hungarian (úngrike romá): southern Slovakia, northern Hungary; there are some speakers
    of Carpathian Romany in the U.S.S.R. as a result of frontier shifts after the Second World
    War
Balkan: jerlídes: western Bulgaria, Macedonia, southern Serbia
  ursári: Romania, Moldavia
  Crimean (kərəmítika romá)
  drindári: central Bulgaria
Wallachian: čače (subgroups: lindurári, zlətári, kəkavjári): Romania, Moldavia
  kəldərári: to mid-nineteenth century on the Hungarian-Romanian linguistic border in the
    Austro-Hungarian Empire; now widespread throughout Europe (including U.S.S.R.) and
    also in America
  lovári: many European countries (including U.S.S.R.) and U.S.A.
  gurbéti: Yugoslavia, especially Bosna (Bosnia) and Hercegovina
Ukrainian: Left-Bank Ukrainian (sə́rvi): Ukraine east of the Dnieper, adjacent parts of the
    R.S.F.S.R.
  Right-Bank-Ukrainian (plaščúnuja, volóxuja): Ukraine west of the Dnieper
Finnish (fíntikə rómma)
Welsh (volšənə́nge kalə́)

4.3.2 *Iranian languages*

Iranian languages are at present spoken across a wide belt of territory stretching from eastern Turkey (Kurdish) to the Sinkiang province of China (Sarikoli) and the shores of the Arabian Sea in western Pakistan (Beludzh). This territory consists almost entirely of uplands, and includes the whole of the area of modern Iran, where Persian and a variety of other Iranian languages are spoken, and of modern Afghanistan, where the official languages are Pashto and Dari (a variety of Persian).

Within the U.S.S.R., Iranian languages are spoken in two main areas, the Caucasus in the west and Tadzhikistan in the east. In the Caucasus, the predominant Iranian language is Ossete, though smaller groups speak Tat, Talysh, and Kurdish. The latter two languages are also spoken, and in the case of Kurdish predominantly, outside the U.S.S.R. In Tadzhikistan, the predominant language is Tadzhik, with over 2 million speakers. The name Tadzhik is also applied, primarily by Soviet linguists, to the variety of Persian spoken by a significant number (up to $3\frac{1}{2}$ million) of Afghans. Also spoken in Tadzhikistan are Yagnob and the various languages of the Pamir group: Shugn, Rushan, Bartang, Oroshor, Yazgulyam, Ishkashim, and Vakh; of this group, Shugn, Rushan, Ishkashim, and Vakh are also spoken in neighbouring areas of Afghanistan along the banks of the river Pyandzh.

In the central areas, along the long border between Soviet Turkmenia and Iran and Afghanistan, Iranian languages only marginally encroach on Soviet territory. The exceptions are Kurdish, spoken by a small group of Kurds in the region of Ashkhabad, and Beludzh, spoken by a small group of settlers in the neighbourhood of Mary. Both these encroachments are of comparatively recent date. Additionally represented in Turkmenia and in Uzbekistan are various speakers of Persian (rather than Tadzhik) dialects, of which the most important are the so-called Irani, descendants of the population of ancient Merv who were forced to disperse after the destruction of the city by the Emir of Bukhara at the end of the eighteenth century.

From a genetic point of view, the Iranian languages are traditionally divided into a Western and an Eastern group, each of which is further subdivided on a north–south basis to give North-Western, South-Western, North-Eastern, and South-Eastern subgroups. The geographical significance of these names lies more in the distribution of forms of Old and Middle Iranian than in the actual location of the modern languages. For example Ossete, which belongs to the North-Eastern subgroup, is spoken in the Caucasus, which represents the north-west of the present Iranian language area, and Beludzh, which belongs to the North-Western subgroup from a linguistic standpoint, is in fact located in the extreme south-east.

The two attested forms of Old Iranian are Old Persian, in the inscriptions of the Achaemenian emperors of the sixth to the fourth centuries B.C., and Avestan, represented by the surviving portions of the Zoroastrian scriptures. From a dialect point of view, Old Persian is easily fixed as the dialect of Fars, a southern province of present-day Iran, and belongs to the South-Western subgroup. The linguistic position of Avestan is more complex, but it is commonly treated as transitional between the Eastern and Western groups. No pure form of East Iranian is available to us from the Old Iranian period.

The attested forms of Middle Iranian (fourth/third centuries B.C. to eighth/ninth centuries A.D.), on the other hand, are rather more diverse. To the North-Western subgroup belong languages spoken on the territory of ancient Media and Parthia to the south-east of the Caspian Sea. Parthian is known from inscriptions and ostraca found at the site of the ancient Parthian city of Nisa, in present-day Soviet Turkmenia, and from a few Manichean manuscripts. Median is known solely from loanwords and place-names. To the South-Western subgroup belongs Middle Persian (Pehlevi), a direct descendant of Old Persian and the language of the

Sassanid emperors of the third to seventh centuries A.D., again in the province of Fars. By contrast with Median and Parthian, Middle Persian is exceptionally well documented.

For the North-East subgroup there are three representatives. Sogdian, which was spoken throughout the extensive Sogdian empire centred on Samarkand, is well-known through numerous Manichean, Buddhist, and Christian texts of the seventh to the ninth centuries A.D., while Khwarezmian, located in the territory occupied by present-day Turkmenia, is attested in documents and inscriptions from the second to the eighth centuries A.D., as well as in later Islamic texts from the eleventh to the fourteenth centuries. The language of the Alan (Scythian) tribes, who once populated an area extending from northern Central Asia across the northern shores of the Black Sea as far as the Danube, is, however, only sketchily documented. Finally, to the South-Eastern subgroup belong Saka (Khotanese) and Bactrian, the former known through translations of Sanskrit Buddhist texts found in present-day Sinkiang and dated to the fifth to tenth centuries A.D., and the latter represented by an inscription of 25 lines dating from the first or second century A.D. and discovered in excavations at the site of the great temple of Surkh Kotal in northern Afghanistan.

Returning to the Modern Iranian period, which extends from the eighth/ninth centuries A.D. up to the present day, we find in certain cases a direct genetic relationship between the modern Iranian languages and the attested forms of Old and Middle Iranian. Persian and Tadzhik, for instance, are both direct descendants of Old and Middle Persian from the South-Western subgroup, whilst within the North-Eastern subgroup Ossete is the sole survival of the language of the Pontic Scythians from the Black Sea area, and Yagnob is of particular interest as a direct continuation of one of the dialects of Sogdian. The remaining two subgroups, North-Western and South-Eastern, do not provide us with such direct relationships.

In full, the modern Iranian languages group genetically as in Table 4.4; for languages of the U.S.S.R., the usual Iranianist name is given in parentheses. It will be noted that the U.S.S.R. is the only modern state in which representatives of all four subgroups may be found.

The criteria distinguishing the groups are primarily phonological. For instance, West Iranian preserves the Proto-Iranian initial voiced stops *b, *d, *g, whereas East Iranian has the corresponding fricatives, e.g. Tadzhik *barodar*, Yagnob *viroot* 'brother'. One of the characteristics of South-West Iranian is the shift of initial prevocalic z to d, e.g. Kurdish *zån*, Tadzhik *don* 'to know'. A morphological innovation characterises the North-Eastern group: the development of a regular plural marker -t, e.g. Yagnob *pooda* 'foot', plural *poodoo-t*, Ossete *sər* 'head', plural *sər-tə*.

We may now turn to a brief survey of the individual Iranian languages of the U.S.S.R., following the order of Table 4.4.

Table 4.4. *Genetic classification of modern Iranian languages*

North-West Iranian:
  Kurdish (Turkey, Iran, Iraq, Syria, U.S.S.R.)
  Talysh (tališi) (U.S.S.R., Iran)
  Beludzh (baluči, balochi) (Pakistan, Iran, Afghanistan, U.S.S.R., Persian Gulf)
  Gilaki (Iran)
  Mazandarani (Iran)
  Parači (Afghanistan)
  Ormuri (Afghanistan, Pakistan)
  some dialects of central Iran

South-West Iranian:
  Persian (Iran, Afghanistan, U.S.S.R.)
  Tadzhik (tožiki) (U.S.S.R.)
  Tat (tati) (U.S.S.R.)
  Luri (Iran)
  Baxtiari (Iran)
  dialects of Fars (Iran)

North-East Iranian:
  Ossete (U.S.S.R.)
  Yagnob (jaɣnobi) (U.S.S.R.)

South-East Iranian:
  Rushan (rošani) (U.S.S.R., Afghanistan)
  Bartang (bartangi) (U.S.S.R.)
  Oroshor (orošori) (U.S.S.R.)
  Shugn (šuɣni) (U.S.S.R., Afghanistan)
  Yazgulyam (jazgulami) (U.S.S.R.)
  Ishkashim (iškašmi) (Afghanistan, U.S.S.R.)
  Sangleči (sangliči) (Afghanistan)
  Zebaki (Afghanistan)
  Vakh (waxi) (Afghanistan, U.S.S.R., Pakistan, China)
  Sarikoli (China)
  Munži (Afghanistan)
  Pashto (Afghanistan)

The number of Kurds living in the U.S.S.R. according to the 1970 census is 88,930, of whom 87.6% consider Kurdish to be their native language. This number is, however, only a minute proportion of the world's total Kurdish population, estimated at between $7\frac{1}{2}$ and 12 million by Kurdoev (1978: 21). According to Bakaev (1966: 257), the distribution of this population outside the U.S.S.R. is as follows: Turkey (4 million), Iran ($3\frac{1}{2}$ million), Iraq (2 million), Syria (250,000). A basic dialect division exists between Kurmandzhi – northern or north-western Kurdish spoken in Turkey, north-western Iran and the Iranian province of Khorasan, northern Syria, and the Mosul district of Iraq – and Sorani – southern or central Kurdish, which itself divides into two main variants: Mukri, centred on Mahābād in Iran, and Sulaymani, centred on Sulaymānīyah in Iraq. The Kurdish spoken within the U.S.S.R. belongs to the Kurmandzhi group.

The Kurdish population of the U.S.S.R. itself falls into four main groups, settled in Armenia (and the Nakhichevan A.S.S.R.), Georgia, Azerbaydzhan, and Turkmenia respectively. The Kurds of Armenia are the strongest and largest group (37,486 according to the 1970 census), and literature based on the Armenian variant of Kurdish is published in Yerevan. The Kurds of Georgia live mostly in the environs of Tbilisi, whilst those of Azerbaydzhan occupy primarily the western area of Azerbaydzhan along the border with Armenia. Almost all Kurds in Azerbaydzhan also speak Azerbaydzhan, even within the family, and many children do not know Kurdish. The Kurds of Turkmenia, living mainly around Ashkhabad, are emigrants from Iran, probably sent in the sixteenth to eighteenth centuries to help defend the northern borders of the Persian Empire. All adults are bilingual in Turkmen, and as in Azerbaydzhan the language is not much used by children. In the 1930s, however, the Kurds of Turkmenia used their own Latin script to publish mainly textbooks.

Kurdish has a long literary history, dating back to the tenth and eleventh centuries. The original script was Arabic, which is still widely used (alongside the Latin script) by Kurds outside the U.S.S.R. Within the U.S.S.R., an Armenian-based script was introduced in 1920, to be replaced in 1927 by Latinisation and then in 1945 by a Cyrillic script.

Talysh is spoken in the south-east of the Azerbaydzhan S.S.R., as well as contiguously in the Iranian province of Gilan. According to Pirejko (1966: 302), the total number of speakers in the U.S.S.R. was estimated in 1931 at about 89,400, and in Iran in 1949 at 84,700. The majority of the Talysh population in the U.S.S.R. also speaks Azerbaydzhan, which is the language of schooling and administration, and in census statistics ethnic Talysh are not counted separately from ethnic Azerbaydzhan. In the early 1930s an attempt was made to introduce a written form of Talysh, but this attempt was soon abandoned.

Beludzh is spoken predominantly in so-called Baluchistan, which occupies the territory of present-day south-western Pakistan (Baluchistan Province) and south-eastern Iran. Outside this area, it is also spoken in Afghanistan along the southern border with Pakistan, in the Pakistan provinces of Punjab and Sind, in the north-eastern regions of Iran (Khurasan and Sīstan), as well as in parts of India and in the countries of the Persian Gulf. Approximate numbers, as estimated by Rastorgueva (1966: 323) are: Pakistan (1 million), Iran (600,000), Afghanistan (200,000), India (50,000), and Persian Gulf (10,000). Within the U.S.S.R., Beludzh is spoken by settlers in the neighbourhood of Mary in Turkmenia. These are considered to have emigrated from north-eastern Iran around the turn of the century, and number

12,582 according to the 1970 census, of whom a massive 98.1% consider Beludzh their native language. The basic dialect division in Beludzh is between an Eastern (or Northern, North-Eastern) dialect and a Western (or Southern, South-Western) dialect, the dividing line being the strip occupied by Brahui speakers in Pakistan. The more archaic Western dialect is the dialect of the Beludzh population in Iran and hence in the U.S.S.R. A modicum of Beludzh literature is published in Pakistan using the Arabic script. In the U.S.S.R., an attempt was made in the 1930s to introduce a written language, but this met with little success. The Beludzh population in the U.S.S.R. is bilingual in Turkmen, which is the language of education and administration.

In its widest sense, the term Persian can be attached to all the Iranian dialects descended from Pehlevi (Middle Persian) and currently spoken for the most part in Iran (9–10 million), Afghanistan (perhaps $3\frac{1}{2}$ million), and Tadzhikistan (over 2 million). A preliminary main dialect division can be made between a Western and an Eastern group, with a boundary near the central deserts of Iran; dialects of eastern Iran (Khurasan) are therefore to be classified together with Afghan Persian (Dari) and Tadzhik. Western Persian (as opposed to Tadzhik) dialect speakers are only sporadically represented in the U.S.S.R., mainly in Uzbekistan and Turkmenia; in 1970 they numbered 27,501, of whom only 36.9% considered Persian their native language. For the U.S.S.R., then, we may concentrate our discussion on Tadzhik.

Tadzhik is the predominant language of the Tadzhik S.S.R., and of the 2,135,883 Tadzhik in the U.S.S.R. 98.5% have Tadzhik as their native language. The Tadzhik S.S.R. also has substantial Uzbek (23%) and Russian (11.9%) minorities, and although bilingualism is not widespread outside the main towns, it is possible to find many bilingual and even trilingual Tadzhiks. The influence of Uzbek on the literary language and many dialects is fairly strong: see, for instance, the discussion of verbal forms and constructions on pp. 177–8. The Tadzhik of Tadzhikistan represent 76.3% of the total Tadzhik population of the U.S.S.R., most of the remainder living in Uzbekistan (21% of the total). Tadzhik is also the native language of certain other small ethnic groups of Central Asia, including the Central Asian Gypsies and the Jews of Samarkand and Bukhara in Uzbekistan. It is the second language of speakers of Yagnob and the various Pamir languages, as well as of many Uzbek.

The Tadzhik share with all Persian-speaking peoples the classical literature of poets such as Rudaki (tenth century), Firdousi (tenth–eleventh centuries), and Saadi (thirteenth century), as well as a host of later works. The divergence of modern dialects from this classical standard has, however, as in Iran, led to the need for a new standard more suited to the cultural and economic needs of a newly literate population. In Tadzhikistan, the outcome of long discussion was a linguistic conference held in Stalinabad (now Dushanbe), which established the new norm in

1930. An outstanding figure in this process was the author and lexicographer Sadriddin Ajni (1878–1954) from Bukhara, and it is indeed on the northern dialects of Samarkand and Bukhara – the oldest centres of Tadzhik culture, though now in Uzbekistan – that the Tadzhik standard written language is essentially based. At present there are systematic radio and television broadcasts in Tadzhik in both Tadzhikistan and Uzbekistan, as well as dozens of newspapers and journals. The publishing houses of Dushanbe produce a steady stream of technical, cultural, and educational works, and there is also a theatre which performs exclusively in Tadzhik.

The name Tat is sometimes applied generally to communities speaking an Iranian language in both Soviet and Iranian Azerbaydzhan, which are predominantly Turkic-speaking, but will here be reserved for the language of the Tat of the U.S.S.R., who are descended from the inhabitants of ancient military colonies from south-western Persia. There are two main groups, one traditionally Jewish (mainly in Dagestan and northern Azerbaydzhan), and one traditionally Muslim (in eastern Azerbaydzhan), to which may be added a small group of Christian ('Armenian') Tat, who belong linguistically to the Muslim group. According to the 1970 census, there were 17,109 Tat in the U.S.S.R., of whom 72.6% considered Tat their native language. This figure may, however, be an underestimate, as many Tat in Azerbaydzhan are bilingual and consider Azerbaydzhan to be their ethnic allegiance. Grjunberg (1963) estimates the total of Tat at the rather higher figure of 20,000 to 30,000. Tat has been a written language since the end of the 1920s, and at present literature in Tat is published in Makhachkala (Dagestan) and Moscow, primarily for the Jewish Tat.

The Ossete form the basic population of the North-Ossete A.S.S.R. within the R.S.F.S.R., and of the South-Ossete A.O. within the Georgian S.S.R.. In 1970 there were 488,038 Ossete in the U.S.S.R., of whom 88.6% considered Ossete to be their native language. Ossete divides into two main dialects, Digor(on) and Iron. Digor is spoken in the west (Digora and Iraf) and to some extent the north (Mozdok) of North Ossetia, and the total number of speakers is about 80,000, representing one sixth of the total Ossete population. The majority dialect, Iron, is spoken in the remaining areas of North Ossetia, including the capital Ordzhonikidze, as well as throughout South Ossetia. Iron forms the basis of the current standard language, and publication in Digor has been discontinued. The Ossete script was invented in the mid-nineteenth century on the basis of the Cyrillic script, and apart from a brief interlude from 1923 to 1938, when a Latin script was used, this script has been maintained. From 1938 to 1954, the South-Ossete A.O. used the Georgian script, but then reverted to Cyrillic.

The original home of the Yagnob is the isolated upper valley of the river Yagnob, which runs between the Zeravshan and Gissar ridges about sixty miles to the north of

Dushanbe; some villages in the valley, however, are Tadzhik-speaking. In this century, however, there has been a continuous movement of people from the Yagnob valley into the more amenable Varzob and Gissar valleys, and into the capital Dushanbe. According to Xromov (1972: 6), there were a total of about 1,500 Yagnob speakers in the Yagnob valley itself, and about 900 elsewhere. Due to the severity of the winter of 1971, however, all the remaining speakers of Yagnob were compelled to leave their home valley, and are only now gradually returning. Almost all Yagnob speakers are bilingual in Tadzhik, which is the language of schooling.

The Pamir languages are spoken primarily along the valley of the river Pyandzh and its tributaries in the Mountain-Badakhshan A.O. in Tadzhikistan, and also in the neighbouring Badakhshan province of Afghanistan. Only one Pamir language, Sarikoli, is not spoken within the U.S.S.R., speakers of this language having at some time traversed the Sarikol ridge into Chinese Sinkiang. Another language, Old Vandzh (Vanǯi) was formerly spoken in the Vanch valley within Tadzhikistan, but is now extinct, having been replaced almost within living memory by a dialect of Tadzhik. Outside the Pamir area itself, Munǯi, which is spoken further south in Afghanistan, is sometimes included within the group on linguistic rather than geographic grounds.

Within the Pamir group, the Shugn-Rushan subgroup comprises four languages: Rushan, Bartang, Oroshor, and Shugn. Rushan, with its related dialect Khuf (xufi), is spoken along the river Pyandzh on the Soviet side of the border, and in the neighbouring areas of Afghanistan. Estimated numbers of speakers are about 10,000 in the U.S.S.R., plus about 1,000–1,500 Khuf, and possibly about 3,000 in Afghanistan, although this latter estimate dates back to 1931 and may be unreliable. Bartang is spoken along the river Bartang, a tributary of the Pyandzh located exclusively within the U.S.S.R., and has about 2,300 speakers. Oroshor is spoken in the Roshorv valley at the source of the river Bartang and its feeders; this is one of the least accessible regions of the Pamir. The number of speakers is estimated at a little over 2,000. Shugn is spoken south of Rushan along the Pyandzh. The estimated number of speakers is about 20,000 in the U.S.S.R., and across the border in Afghanistan about 15,000–20,000.

Of the other Pamir languages, Yazgulyam is spoken in the valley of the river Yazgulem, a tributary of the Pyandzh; the number of speakers is about 1,500–2,000. Ishkashim is spoken primarily in Afghanistan, where the number of speakers is about 1,500, but has about 500 speakers in the U.S.S.R. Related to Ishkashim are Zebaki and Sangleči (Sangliči), spoken further south and exclusively in Afghanistan. Finally, Vakh is spoken east of Ishkashim along the Pyandzh. Outside the U.S.S.R., Vakh is spoken primarily in Afghanistan on the opposite bank of the Pyandzh, though there are also speakers in the border areas of all three of Afghanistan,

Pakistan, and China. Overall numbers are about 20,000, of which 6,000–7,000 are to be found within the U.S.S.R.

For speakers of Pamir languages within the U.S.S.R., Tadzhik is the language of education and administration, and the influence of Tadzhik, particularly in the more accessible regions, is very strong. Tadzhik also serves as the main language of intercommunication between speakers of distinct Pamir languages. However, the languages of the Shugn-Rushan subgroup are very closely related and speakers of these languages readily understand one another. Shugn, which is the most widely spoken of all the Pamir languages, also serves as a language of intercommunication, and an attempt was made to introduce a Latin script for Shugn in the 1930s. The use of this script has, however, since died out.

Phonologically, the most marked shift in the Iranian languages of the U.S.S.R. has been in the vowel system, where Old Iranian opposed three vowel qualities (i, u, a), long and short, and two diphthongs (ay, aw), which latter monophthongised to ee, oo in Middle Persian. Phonemic vowel length (typically with more long than short phonemes) is retained in some of the smaller Iranian languages (e.g. within the Shugn-Rushan group), but elsewhere has a strong tendency to be lost, often with qualitative redistribution, e.g. Persian neutralises ii and ee to i while lowering Middle Persian i to e, whereas many Tadzhik dialects merge long and short i. In some languages the length distinction has been replaced by one between stable vowels (articulated peripherally to the oral cavity, with little allophonic variation) and unstable vowels (articulated more centrally, subject to wide allophonic variation, and even loss in unstressed syllables); such an opposition is found in Kurdish, Talysh, Tat, Ossete, Yazgulyam, and Ishkashim. One frequent typological characteristic of Iranian languages of the U.S.S.R. is the bunching of vowel phonemes in the high back rounded area: thus Tadzhik, for instance, distinguishes u (from Middle Persian u, uu), $ŭ$ (from oo), and o (from aa). An unusual phoneme distinction is that between plain and pharyngalised $ä$ in the Kurdish of Armenia, e.g. $b\ddot{a}r$ 'sea' (cf. Sorani $bəh(i)r$) versus $b\ddot{a}r$ 'front'.

For consonants, again it is useful to discuss the main innovations relative to Old Iranian, with Persian, Tadzhik, and Tat occupying a particularly conservative position here, apart from some phonemes borrowed along with loans from Arabic: all dialects of Tadzhik, for instance, have assimilated q, e.g. aql 'intelligence'. The development of the dental affricates c, $ʒ$ is a defining characteristic of all East Iranian languages. Ishkashim and Vakh have developed a series of retroflex consonants distinct from the palato-alveolars, a frequent source being clusters with r, giving rise to oppositions like $šot$ 'supper', $ṣot$ 'avalanche'. Languages of the Shugn-Rushan group, together with Vakh, have dental fricatives, while these together with Ishkashim distinguish velar from uvular fricatives (most Iranian languages have only uvulars). More language-restricted developments are those of phonemic aspiration of plosives in Kurdish (Kurmandzhi dialects), of distinctive labialisation of velars and uvulars in Yazgulyam, and of phonemically distinctive ejective plosives in Ossete: in Ossete, many of these occur in words of Caucasian origin, e.g. *k'ere* 'flat loaf' from Georgian, *k'uməl* 'malt beer' from Chechen, but also in native Iranian words, e.g. *ənt'oxun* 'to throw', and as equivalents to the unaspirated voiceless plosives in loans from Russian, e.g. *p'ap'iros* 'cigarette'.

The categories for which nouns may inflect in the Iranian languages of the U.S.S.R. are: case, number, gender, and definiteness or indefiniteness. However, not all the languages exhibit inflection for all these categories. As in the modern Iranian languages as a whole, there is little that remains of the original full declensional system of Old Iranian, which involves eight cases (nominative, accusative, instrumental, dative, ablative, genitive, locative, and vocative), three numbers (singular, dual, and plural), and three genders (masculine, feminine, and neuter). Instead of the old declensions, we generally find more analytic forms such as postpositions or prepositions, and where nominal inflection does exist, it is as often as not an innovation, resulting from the agglutination of postpositions, prepositions, and other particles to the nouns they accompany. The extent to which this secondary agglutination has taken place varies considerably from language to language.

Within the West Iranian group, the most analytic forms are found in Persian, Tadzhik, and Tat, which have preserved none of the Old Iranian declension system – this includes loss of grammatical gender – apart from a relict plural marker used solely for a limited number of animate nouns. This marker (Persian *-ån*, Tadzhik *-on*, Tat *-un*) derives from the Old Persian genitive marker *-aanaam*, which in the early Middle Persian period, in the shape *-aan*, formed the regular plural of all nouns. In the modern languages, however, it has been ousted almost completely by a different suffix (Persian *-hå* Tadzhik *-ho*, Tat *-(h)å*), whose origin is probably the collectivising suffix *-θwa*, the same suffix which gives the characteristic *-t* plurals of North-East Iranian (see p. 160). These plural suffixes are the only true nominal inflections in the three languages, attaching as they do to the stem of the noun. Other nominal suffixes attach to the rightmost element of a nominal group, whether this element is the head noun or not, and are therefore more akin to postpositions.

One such postposition is the so-called 'ezafe', which automatically follows any nominal group which is itself modified by an adjectival or nominal group. In Persian and Tadzhik, the ezafe (*-e* and *-i* respectively) is most extensively used in the literary languages: alternative constructions exist in colloquial speech and dialects. When used, however, (with examples from literary Tadzhik), it follows a noun modified by an adjective, e.g. *xona-i surx* 'red house', or by an ordinal numeral, e.g. *xona-i panžŭm* 'fifth house', or by another noun in a possessive construction, e.g. *xona-i* *padar* 'father's house, or by another noun in an appositional construction, e.g. *šahri-dušanbe* 'the city of Dushanbe'. Further modifiers can be added to a complex formed in this way, leading to a chain of ezafes, e.g. *RESPUBLIKA-i SOVIETi-i SOCIALISTi-i tožikiston* 'Tadzhik Soviet Socialist Republic'. Etymologically, the ezafe derives from the Old Iranian relative pronoun (Old Persian *hjaa*). In Tat, it is restricted to the possessive type of construction.

Two further postpositions mark definiteness and indefiniteness. The first (Persian *-rå*, Tadzhik *-ro*, Tat *-(r)ä*) is restricted to definite direct objects, and is always the final element in any nominal group, e.g. Tadzhik *xona-i surx-ro* 'the red house (ACC)'. More accurately, this postposition marks a referentially prominent, rather than strictly definite, direct object (Comrie 1978): thus, in the Tadzhik text on page 191, the noun phrase *parda-e-ro* 'a certain curtain (ACC)' is explicitly marked as indefinite (*-e*, see below), and the suffix *-ro* implies that the referent of this noun phrase will recur subsequently in the discourse. This postposition derives from the Old Persian postposition *raadij*, indicating goal or direction, and is used in some dialects to mark indirect objects. In some dialects of Tadzhik and in Tat, it is used as a genitive marker in a possessive construction, alternative to the ezafe described above, and paralleling that of Turkic languages (p. 78), e.g. Tat *pijär-ä xunä-ji* 'father's house', literally 'father-GEN house-3SG'.

The second postposition (Tadzhik *-e*, Persian *-i*) simultaneously marks both indefiniteness and singularity, regardless of syntactic function, e.g. Tadzhik *xona-i surx-e* 'a red house'. In Tat, it is replaced by the more analytic combination of the numeral *jä* 'one' with a following invariant noun (*jä kitåb* 'a book'), an alternative that is also available in Persian and Tadzhik, e.g. Tadzhik *jak xona-i surx* 'a red house'. Etymologically, the indefinite singular marker derives from the Old Iranian numeral *ayva* 'one'.

Within the East Iranian group, the most analytic nominal forms are found in the Shugn-Rushan group. In these languages, nouns inflect for number, and in a limited way also for gender. The plural endings, *-een* in Rushan, Bartang, and Shugn, and *-iif* in Oroshor, are generalised from the genitive and dative/ablative plural endings of Old Iranian respectively, and the masculine/feminine distinction, which is manifested in a limited number of nouns of natural gender by internal vowel alternations (e.g. Rushan *kud* 'dog', *kid* 'bitch', *čux* 'cock', *čax* 'hen'), derives from the Old Iranian declension by a process of umlaut triggered by endings which are now lost. All nouns in fact belong to one gender or the other, but this may only be revealed by patterns of agreement with demonstratives, adjectives, and verbs. As far as case is concerned, nouns in all four languages are invariant apart from a special ending *-(j)aa* which occurs in a possessive construction similar to that found in Tat and Tadzhik dialects. The ending *-(j)aa* is suffixed to the possessor, and the possessed is preceded by a demonstrative pronoun in oblique case agreeing with the possessor. This pronoun replaces the clitic suffix of the Tat and Tadzhik constructions, e.g. Rushan *pid-aa waj čod* (father-GEN his house) 'father's house'. Like the ezafe construction, which is not found in the Shugn-Rushan group, this construction can be iterated, e.g. Rushan *rajiis-aa waj puc-aa waj puc* (president-GEN his son-GEN his son) 'the son of the son of the president'.

Amongst the Pamir languages, Yazgulyam and Ishkashim are also to a large extent analytic. Both languages lack gender distinctions, but Yazgulyam possesses, in addition to the usual kind of plural endings (*-aθ*, *-en*, *-ežg*, and *-an*), a special prefix *š(ə)-*/*ž(ə)-* which marks nouns preceded by the preposition *na* 'from', e.g. *na ž-web* 'from the box (of corn)'. This prefix arises out of the agglutination of a former preposition, with the same meaning as *na*, to the following noun. Yazgulyam also has two possessive constructions, one of which is the ezafe construction borrowed from Tadzhik. The second involves the optional use of a genuine case ending *-(j)i* derived from the genitive singular ending *-ahjaa* of Old Iranian, e.g. *ðod-i bi* (smoke-GEN smell) 'the smell of smoke'. The same ending survives in Ishkashim, but as an optional marker of direct objects, whether definite or indefinite. The only other nominal suffixes in Ishkashim are the plural endings *-o*, *ɨn*, and *-on*, and the indefinite singular marker *-(j)i*, this latter identical in form to the direct object suffix, but deriving as in Tadzhik from the numeral 'one'. In possessive constructions, Ishkashim uses the postposition *-noj*: *ṣtok-noj avzuk* (girl-GEN heart) 'the girl's heart'.

The remaining languages, whether from the Western or the Eastern group, all make more extensive use of case distinctions. The distinction which is most widespread and most typical of the Iranian languages is a distinction between an absolute case and an oblique case, in which the absolute case derives from the Old Iranian nominative, whilst the oblique case is generalised from the Old Iranian genitive, dative, ablative, or instrumental. In terms of function, the absolute is characteristically the case of predicate nominals, and the oblique is the case of indirect and prepositional or postpositional objects. The distribution of the two cases between the major functions of subject and direct object may, however, depend in a complex way on the type of construction (ergative or nominative–accusative) and the category of definiteness and indefiniteness, as discussed below.

From a morphological point of view, Talysh and Yagnob provide the most straightforward illustration of the absolute/oblique case distinction. In both languages, the oblique case ending is *-i*, both in singular and plural forms, although the ending is a reflex of the Old Iranian genitive singular *-ahjaa*. In Yagnob, for example, we have *kat* 'house', *kat-i* 'house-OBL', *kat-it* 'house-PL', and *kat-t-i* 'house-PL-OBL'. The absolute case is used for predicate nominals, subjects and indefinite objects in the nominative–accusative construction, and objects in the ergative construction, whereas the oblique case is used for indirect and prepositional objects, for possessors in the possessive construction (*qosim-i kat* 'Qosim's house'), for subjects in the ergative construction and for definite objects in the nominative–accusative construction.

The morphology of the absolute/oblique distinction in Kurdish is rather more fusional than this, in particular given the different forms for masculine and feminine in the singular. In the singular, the absolute case has no ending, while the oblique has *-i* (masculine) or *-ä* (feminine) (the forms cited here and below are from the dialect of Azerbaydzhan). This distinction is seen most clearly when the noun has the suffixed indefinite article *-äk*, e.g. absolute *t'ɔʒɪr-äk* 'a merchant', oblique *t'ɔʒɪr-äk-i*, absolute *käč'ɪk-äk* 'a girl', oblique *käč'ɪk-äk-ä*. These suffixes derive from the Old Iranian genitive singular inflections *-ahjaa* (masculine *a*-stem) and *-aajaa* (feminine *aa*-stem), though the possibility of separating this inflection from the stem by the indefinite article is an innovation. In the absence of the indefinite suffix, the feminine oblique has the same ending (e.g. *käč'ɪk-ä* from *käč'ɪk*), but for masculines the oblique is shown by umlauting the stem vowel, e.g. *t'eʒɪr* from *t'ɔʒɪr*; where the vowel is not amenable to umlaut, absolute and oblique cases have the same form, e.g. *sä* 'dog'. In the plural, there is no gender distinction and the absolute case has the ending *-idä*, e.g. *sev-idä* 'apples', although this is dropped where the number is expressed elsewhere, for instance in the verb, e.g. *sev k'ät-ɪn* 'the apples fell', where *-ɪn* is the third person plural ending. The oblique plural ending is *-ɔn*.

The distinction of gender is maintained in the Kurdish ezafe construction. The extent of use of the ezafe construction varies from dialect to dialect, as does the precise form itself. The dialect of Azerbaydzhan, for instance, does not use the ezafe with adjectival modifiers, which simply follow the noun or nominal group they modify, e.g. *käč'ɪk-ɔ sůlt'en bučuk* (girl-EZAFE Sultan-OBL little) 'Sultan's little girl'. In the dialect of Turkmenia, on the other hand, we find long chains of ezafes similar to those found in Persian and Tadzhik, e.g. *hävɔl-e mɪn-i ɔyɪl-i fɪnd* (friend-EZAFE my-OBL-EZAFE good) 'my good clever friend'. The ezafe itself agrees in number and gender with the preceding modified noun, a reflex of its origin as a relative pronoun. In the Kurdish of both Azerbaydzhan and Turkmenia, the ezafe *-ɔ* is used with feminine singular nouns, and the ezafes *-e* and *-i* are used with masculine singular nouns.

Although the main case distinction in Kurdish is between the absolute and the oblique cases, the language also preserves the remnants of a vocative case. The endings are *-o* (masculine singular), *-e* (feminine singular), and *-no* (plural), e.g. *lɔkk-o* 'boy!', *žɪnɪk-e* 'wife!', and *käč'ɪk-no* 'girls!'. Many Kurdish scholars also treat as secondary case endings the three postpositions *-ŕä* (in Azerbaydzhan and

Turkmenia -ɨɔ), -vå (in Azerbaydzhan -vä, in Turkmenia -vɔ), and -då (in Azerbaydzhan and Turkmenia -dɔ), which are used in conjunction with the oblique case. Their most case-like feature is the fact that they occur not only in isolation, but also in tandem with a range of prepositions. For instance, in the dialect of Turkmenia the preposition *säwɔ* 'to' combines with the postposition -ɨɔ, and the preposition *lä* 'in' with the postposition -dɔ, e.g. *säwɔ derwiš-ɨɔ* 'to the dervish', *lä t'urɨ-dɔ* 'in the bag'. However, when the noun is followed by modifiers in the ezafe construction, the postposition attaches to the final modifer, e.g. *wä mɔl-e mɨ-dɔ* (in house-EZAFE my-OBL-LOC) 'in my house'.

Similar secondary case endings have also arisen in Vakh, for example the dative ending -*ərk* and the ablative ending -*ən*. These both attach to the oblique stem, which is the same as the absolute in the singular, but distinguished by the suffix -*əv* in the plural, e.g. *kənd* 'the woman', *kənd-ərk* 'to the woman', *kənd-ən* 'from the woman', *kənd-iš(t)* 'the women', *kənd-əv-ərk* 'to the women', *kənd-əv-ən* 'from the women'. Etymologically, the oblique ending -*əv* is probably derived from the dative/ablative plural in Old Iranian, whereas the endings -*ərk* and -*ən* arise from the agglutination of postpositions to the preceding noun. Because nominal modifiers in the native Vakh construction are preposed to the nouns they modify, the endings -*ərk* and -*ən* are, unlike in Kurdish, rarely displaced from the head noun. The only exceptions to this rule occur in the ezafe construction, which is borrowed from Tadzhik and rarely used, and in coordinate nominal constructions, when the endings follow the final noun only, e.g. *cə diw-i safid-ən* (from spirit-EZAFE white-ABL) 'from the White Spirit', *dilowar-ət jaw nan-ən* (Dilowar-AND his mother-ABL) 'from Dilowar and his mother'. Vakh also possesses, in both singular and plural, the ending -*i*/-*əj* (from Old Iranian -*ahjaa*) as a definite direct object marker; e.g. *kənd-əj* (singular) and *kənd-əv-əj* (plural).

The most innovative case system is that of Ossete, which has an agglutinative system of nine cases (eight in Digor), typologically much more similar to those of the neighbouring Caucasian languages. Table 4.5 gives the appropriate forms for the Iron dialect. (The homophony of oblique and interior-locative does not, incidentally, apply to all paradigms.) The absolute case is used for subjects, predicate nominals, and indefinite direct objects, while the oblique case, apart from being used with postpositions, also marks definite direct objects and the possessor in one of the two genitive constructions, e.g. *mad-ɨ rəvdɨd* 'mother's love'. The other genitive construction uses the dative of the possessor and an oblique (i.e. possessive) pronoun, e.g. *mad-ən jə rəvdɨd*.

All the languages without exception possess independent personal pronouns, and these generally show the same case distinctions and enter into the same constructions as full nouns. Where discrepancies exist, the pronouns show more distinctions than

Table 4.5. *Declensional forms of Ossete*
(Iron) sər *'head'*

	Singular	Plural
Absolute	sər	sər-tə
Oblique	sər-ɪ	sər-t-ɪ
Dative	sər-ən	sər-t-ən
Directional	sər-mə	sər-tə-m
Ablative	sər-əj	sər-t-əj
Interior-Locative	sər-ɪ	sər-t-ɪ
Exterior-Locative	sər-ɪl	sər-t-ɪl
Comparative	sər-aj	sər-t-aj
Comitative	sər-imə	sər-t-imə

the nouns, as for example in the languages of the Shugn-Rushan subgroup, where the singular forms have an absolute/oblique case distinction absent in the nouns, e.g. Rushan *az* 'I-ABS' versus *mu/mo* 'I-OBL', *tu/to* 'you-ABS' versus *taa* 'you-OBL'.

Enclitic personal pronouns may be found in Beludzh, Tadzhik, Ossete, Yagnob, and marginally in Kurdish. In function, they are used firstly as possessive pronouns and provide an alternative construction to the one used for full nouns and independent pronouns. Compare, for example, the two Tadzhik constructions *kitob-am* and *kitob-i man* 'my book', the first with an enclitic first-person pronoun *-am* and the second with the ezafe preceding the independent first-person pronoun *man*. Secondarily, the enclitic pronouns attach to verbs as verbal arguments, and most typically as direct objects. In Tadzhik, again, we find the alternative constructions *didam-aš* and *vaj-ro didam* 'I saw him', the first with an enclitic third-person pronoun *-aš* and the second with the independent third-person pronoun *vaj*, marked as a definite direct object with the postposition *-ro* and preceding the verb. The smallest range of enclitic pronouns occurs in Kurdish, which has an isolated third-person singular form *-e* used as an indirect object, and the widest range is found in Ossete, which has enclitics for all persons and all cases except the absolute and the comparative.

The Iranian languages of the U.S.S.R. do not in general possess declined relative pronouns, using instead constructions involving invariant conjunctions. An exception is provided by Kurdish, which has the forms *je* (masculine singular), *ja* (feminine singular), and *jed* (plural).

The verb is without doubt morphologically the most complex of all lexical categories in the modern Iranian languages, including those of the U.S.S.R. Verbforms are based primarily on two stems, a present stem and a past stem. However, whereas the present stem is a more or less direct reflex of the present tense in Old Iranian, the past stem derives from a perfect participle ending in -*ta* (or augmented -*ta-ka*) rather than from any of the regular past tenses of Old Iranian. Much of the present complexity in verbal morphology can be related to the fact that for intransitive verbs, this participle had an active orientation, but for transitive verbs, the orientation was passive. In other words, the present-day active forms of transitive verbs in the tenses based on the perfect participle in -*ta* go back to passive originals. As we shall see, this leads to intriguing distinctions in the paradigms of transitive and intransitive verbs.

The most direct reflex of the original system is found in the Kurmandzhi dialects of Kurdish (and hence in the Kurdish of the U.S.S.R.). The dialect we shall illustrate here is that of Azerbaydzhan, in which there are two classes of regular verb. In the first class, consisting exclusively of transitive verbs, the present stem ends in -*in* and the past stem in -*ɔnd*, e.g. *tɨs-in* versus *tɨs-ɔnd* 'fall'; while in the second class, the present stem ends in zero and the past stem in -*i*, -*jɔ* or -*ɔ*. On the other hand, there is a sizable class of verbs for which the relation between the present and past stems is not so easily predictable, for example *kʻäv* (present) versus *kʻät* (past) 'fall' and *šin* (present) versus *šɔnd* (past) 'send'. The distribution of the two stems is seen most clearly in the indicative, where the present stem is used for the present and future, and the past stem for all past tenses – irrespective, incidentally, of aspectual distinctions, such as continuous or perfect.

Some indicative forms are tabulated, for the singular only, in Table 4.6, and it will immediately be noticed that there are two distinct forms of conjugation. In the subjective conjugation, which is used for both transitive and intransitive verbs in tenses based on the present stem, but only for intransitive verbs in tenses based on the past stem, the verb agrees in person and number with the subject. The endings -*ɪm*, -*i*, and -*ä* in the present are descendants of the regular person–number endings of Old Iranian, whereas the endings -*(ɪ)m* and -*(j)i* in the simple past are in origin clitic forms of the verb 'to be'. Simultaneously in the subjective conjugation, the subject assumes the absolute case in both transitive and intransitive sentence types, and the direct object is oblique. (The suffix -*(j)i* which we see attached to the subject in the present is nothing to do with the case-marking system, but is a kind of mood marker which helps differentiate the indicative and subjunctive moods.)

In the objective conjugation, which is used for transitive verbs in the tenses based on the past stem, the verb agrees in person and number with the direct object. Simultaneously, the direct object assumes the absolute case, and the subject assumes the oblique case, giving an ergative construction. It is this ergative construction in transitive past sentences which originates from the reanalysis of the passive perfect participle in Old Iranian as an active construction in Kurdish. The copula in the

Table 4.6. *Indicative verb forms in Kurdish of*
Azerbaydzhan

A. Subjective conjugation
1. Present tense (intransitive)

äz-i	*dä-šıyŭl-ım*	'I work'
tŭ-ji	*dä-šıyŭl-i*	'you work'
äw-i	*dä-šıyŭl-ä*	'he works'

2. Present tense (transitive)

äz-i	*dä-šin-ım*	'I send'
tŭ-ji	*dä-šin-i*	'you send'
äw-i	*dä-šin-ä*	'he sends'

3. Simple past tense (intransitive)

äz	*šıyŭli-m*	'I worked'
tŭ	*šıyŭli-ji*	'you worked'
äw	*šıyŭli*	'he worked'

B. Objective conjugation
4. Simple past tense (transitive)

	äz	*šɔnd-ım*	'he sent me'
wı	*tŭ*	*šɔnd-i*	'he sent you'
	äw	*šɔnd*	'he sent him'

original passive construction would agree with the subject of the passive verb, and when this subject was reanalysed as a direct object, the orientation of agreement was preserved. At the same time, the original case-marking was maintained, with the object in the absolute case appropriate to its former status, and the new subject in the oblique (originally genitive) case of the passive agent.

Ergative constructions in the transitive past also occur in Yagnob and Talysh. However, in these two languages the pattern of verb-agreement is not so exclusively oriented towards the direct object. In Yagnob, for instance, agreement with the direct object is still maintained in the perfect and pluperfect, which are the only forms derived from the *-ta* participle, the simple past being formed (rarely) from the present stem. This object-agreement in person and number derives as in Kurdish from forms of the copula (in the examples below, the third-person singular *-x*). The subject may, however, also be expressed in the verb by means of clitic pronouns placed between the stem and the object-marker:

(63)   *weeta   -m   -x*
         see-PERF 1SG 3SG
         'I have seen (him)'

(64)   *weeta*   *-t*   *-x*
         see-PERF 2SG 3SG
         'you have seen (him)'

(65)   *weeta*   *-š*   *-x*
         see-PERF 3SG 3SG
         'he has seen (him)'

These clitic pronouns, which might be treated as incipient subject-agreement markers on the basis of their boundedness to the verb stem, nevertheless must be omitted whenever a full lexical subject is present in the sentence. Historically, they are a direct reflex of pronominal agents in the original passive construction.

In Talysh, we pass one stage further in the shift of orientation of verb-agreement in transitive past sentences from object to subject. The copula is still present as a reflex, but in an invariant third-person singular form which serves therefore solely as a tense-marker and not as an object-agreement marker. It has the forms *-e* (simple and resultative past), *be* (remote past), and *baj* (past subjunctive). The clitic pronouns are, however, further grammaticalised as subject-agreement markers, in that they can be used when a full lexical subject is present, and even move freely about the clause, being attached to any preverbal major constituent. Sentence (66) below illustrates this first property, and sentences (67)–(68) illustrate the second:

(66)   *aj*   *ekya*   *-š*   *-e*   *čəmə pas*
         he-OBL strike-PAST 3SG SIMPLE-PAST my   sheep-ABS
         'he struck my sheep'

(67)   *av*   *vind*   *-əm* *-e*
         he-*ABS* see-PAST 1SG SIMPLE-PAST
         'I saw him'

(68)   *av*   *-əm* *vind*   *-e*
         he-ABS 1SG see-PAST SIMPLE-PAST
         'I saw him'

Such moving subject-agreement particles are also a typical feature of the Pamir group of languages, where not only the transitive forms (based originally on the clitic agent pronouns), but also the intransitive forms (based originally on clitic forms of the copula) can occur at a distance from the verb. In addition, in the languages of the Shugn-Rushan subgroup, the past stem (and the perfect stem derived from it) preserves, in the case of intransitive verbs only, a form of gender and number agreement with the subject. An example of this agreement is provided by the verb *sidoow* 'to go' in Rushan. The present stem is invariant (*saa(w)-* or *sa-*), but in the past stem we find two forms: *sut* and *sat*. The first of these is used when the subject is masculine singular, and derives from the masculine singular form of the Old Iranian participle **šu-ta* after the loss of the final vowel. The form *sat*, on the other hand, derives via a process of umlaut from the feminine form **šu-taa*. This second form is also used for all plural nouns. Turning then to the perfect stem, which has its origin in the augmented form of the Old Iranian participle (**-ta-ka*), we find three forms: *suž* (masculine singular), *siž* (feminine singular) and *saž* (plural). We conclude by noting that in a sentence like (69) below, verb-agreement with the subject occurs twice, once in the moving particle *-um* (first-person singular) and secondly in the perfect stem (masculine singular):

(69)   *az-um   pa χaraʁ   suž*
         I   1SG to Khorog go-PERF-MASC-SG
         'I (male speaking) have gone to Khorog'

Interesting as these verb-agreement patterns are, it is probably true to say that the greatest typological interest of the Pamir languages lies in their case-marking systems, which have departed from the straightforward ergative pattern for transitive past sentences. In particular, Rushan shows the rare double-oblique system, in which the direct object takes the same oblique case as the transitive subject, whilst the intransitive subject takes the absolute case:

(70)   *mu   dum   kitoob xeejt*
         I-OBL this-OBL book   read-PAST
         'I read this book'

(71)   *jaa   pa χaraʁ   sut*
         he-ABS to Khorog go-PAST-MASC-SG
         'he went to Khorog'

In Yazgulyam we find the equally rare tripartite system, in which the direct object is marked distinctly from both the oblique case of the transitive subject and the absolute case of the intransitive subject:

(72)   *mon   š   -tu wint*
         I-OBL ACC you see-PAST
         'I saw you'

(73)   *az   -əm dəri ður šod*
         I-ABS 1SG into gorge go-PAST
         'I went into the gorge'

In the remaining languages, with the loss of the oblique case-marking for transitive subjects, the distinction between transitive and intransitive sentence types is essentially lost. In the Upper dialect of Vakh, however, the oblique case has extended to intransitive past subjects, but only for the singular personal pronouns (Laškarbekov 1975):

(74)   *maẓ   taw-əj   wind(-əj)*
        I-OBL you ACC see   PAST
        'I saw you'

(75)   *maz   rəɣd(-əj)*
        I-OBL go   PAST
        'I went'

(76)   *wuz   rəç-əm*
        I-ABS go   1SG
        'I am going'

Otherwise, all subjects are in the absolute case, regardless of transitivity or tense. In Tadzhik (as in Persian), the ergative morphological system has been lost completely, but the first person singular pronoun *man* continues the old oblique case rather than the absolute case.

The most radical realignment of the tense–aspect–mood system is found in the northern dialects of Tadzhik (and, thus, in the standard language). The impetus for the semantic distinctions made, and in some instances even the forms, stems from strong Uzbek influence. These innovatory forms are not found in other dialects of Tadzhik or in Persian. Of the new nonfinite verb forms, the most interesting are the participles in *-agi*, which have an Uzbek pedigree. When used as attributes, they form part of a postposed relative clause construction in which the agent can be expressed either by means of a full noun or by a clitic pronoun:

(77)   *kitob-i   ahmad xarid-agi   dar xona ast*
        book EZAFE Ahmad buy   PAST-PART in   house be-3SG
        'the book bought by Ahmad is at home'

(78)   *maktub-i   navišt-agi   -am -ro   ba qutti-i*
        letter   EZAFE write   PAST-PART 1SG ACC in box EZAFE
        POČTA andoxt   -am
        mail   throw-PAST 1SG
        'I threw the letter I wrote into the mailbox'

When used predicatively, however, in conjunction with suffixed forms of the copula, they form part of the presuppositional mood:

(79)   *DELEGAT-ho pagoh   me   -omad-agi   -and*
         delegate   PL tomorrow CONT come PRESUP 3PL
         'the delegates must be coming tomorrow'

As can be seen from this example, the closest equivalent forms in English involve epistemic *must*.

The inferential mood is likewise a feature of the northern dialects, and is based on perfect forms of the verb, characteristically formed by suffixing the copula to the past gerund. The perfect itself (*navišt-a-am*) can belong either to the indicative or to the inferential mood. In function, the inferential mood is used when the speaker wishes to indicate that he himself has no direct evidence for the assertion about to be made: he has either heard someone else assert it or he has inferred it indirectly from the surrounding situation:

(80)   *rahim dar xona kor kard-a   istod-a   bud-a   -ast*
         Rahim in house work do   GER stand GER be   GER 3SG
         'Rahim, it seems, was working at home (at that time)'

The verb form in (80) uses the auxiliary verbs *bud-an* 'to be' and *istod-an* 'to stand', as well as a typical compound verb comprising a noun (*kor* 'work') and a semantically weak verb (*kard-an* 'to do'). Inferential forms based on the perfect may also be found in a number of Pamir languages.

With respect to voice, passive verb forms in the Iranian languages of the U.S.S.R. are usually formed analytically by means of auxiliary verbs and participles. However, several languages have an extensive system of morphological causatives, formed by suffixation or internal vowel modifications. An example of the former is the suffix *-(i)v* (present)/*-ovd* (past) in Vakh, which gives such pairs as *čǝrm-* 'enter', *čǝrm(i)v-/čǝrmovd-* 'introduce'. Internal vowel modifications relate causative and noncausative forms in the languages of the Shugn-Rushan subgroup. In Rushan, for instance, we find pairs like *θud* (masculine past stem)/*θad* (feminine past stem) 'burned (intransitive)' versus *θeewt* (invariant past stem) 'burned (transitive)'.

The basic word order of the Iranian languages of the U.S.S.R. is subject–object–verb (SOV). However, this order is rarely rigid, and it is possible to find complement clauses and definite direct and indirect objects postposed to the right of the verb. Topicalisation of definite direct and indirect objects to sentence-initial position also occurs.

Although the basic word order is SOV, the Iranian languages of the U.S.S.R. are in many respects not typical SOV languages. While it is generally true that modifying expressions precede the constituents they modify, this is not the case in those languages like Tadzhik and Kurdish which possess the ezafe construction in nominal groups. The pattern then is that only demonstratives and numerals precede the head noun, while all other adjectival and nominal modifiers follow. Simultaneously, languages like Tadzhik possess almost exclusively prepositions rather than postpositions, and postposed rather than preposed relative clauses. However, one also finds languages like Ossete, which conform more to the norm, with a highly developed system of postpositions, or languages like Vakh, which have a mixed system of postpositions and prepositions.

4.4 Armenian

Armenian (native name: *haj* '(an) Armenian') forms an independent branch of the Indo-European family. When Indo-Europeanists first approached Armenian in the nineteenth century, it was for many years considered an Iranian language, but this erroneous impression stemmed solely from the large number of Iranian loans, reflecting close contact between speakers of Armenian and various Iranian languages.

The term Armenian refers in fact to three codified languages, in addition to their numerous dialects. Classical Armenian (*grabař*) refers to the old language, for which a special script was, according to tradition, invented by Mesrop in the fifth century A.D.; this script still serves the modern languages. Modern Western Armenian developed in those parts of traditional Armenia that are now in Turkey, and refers to the language of Armenians in Turkey and of émigré communities in many Middle Eastern countries and the West. Modern Eastern Armenian is the language of Soviet Armenia, and it is primarily with this standard language that we shall be concerned here.

There are 3,559,151 ethnic Armenians in the U.S.S.R. according to the 1970 census, 91.4% of whom have Armenian as their native language, despite the fact that Armenians are scattered across several Union Republics: only 62% live in Armenia, with 13.6% in Azerbaydzhan, 12.7% in Georgia, and 8.4% in the R.S.F.S.R. The Armenian S.S.R., however, is ethnically the most homogeneous Union Republic, 88.6% of its population being ethnically Armenian (Russians make up only 2.7%). Within Armenia, 99.9% of ethnic Armenians have Armenian as their native language, making Armenia also very homogeneous linguistically, Armenian being the predominant language of education and literature as well as of daily intercourse. In addition to the Armenian S.S.R., ethnic Armenians also form a substantial majority (80.5%) of the population of the Mountain-Karabakh A.O. in Azerbaydzhan. The number of Armenians outside the U.S.S.R. is estimated at $1\frac{1}{2}$ million, though not all of these speak Armenian.

As mentioned above, the alphabet devised by Mesrop (with some modifications introduced in the twelfth century) is still used for both varieties of modern Armenian.

In the U.S.S.R., however, a slight orthographic reform was instituted in the use of the letters transliterated *e* and *ee*, *o* and *oo* for Classical Armenian: except word-initially, the members of each pair have merged phonetically, and only the *e*, *o* symbols are used in Eastern Armenian; word-initially, original *e*, *o* became *je*, *vo*, while original *ee*, *oo* became *e*, *o*, and the four orthographic symbols mentioned above now represent *je*, *e*, *vo*, and *o*, respectively, in word-initial position.

The vowel system of Eastern Armenian has *a*, *e*, *i*, *o*, *u*, and *ə*. The schwa is largely predictable, serving to break up what would otherwise be impermissible consonant clusters, although there are minimal pairs, for instance involving the suffixed definite article -*ə*, e.g. *girk* 'book', *girk-ə* 'the book'. Stress is regularly on the last vowel of the word, unless this is schwa. The main feature of the consonant system of Eastern Armenian is the three-way opposition, for plosives (including affricates) between voiced (e.g. *b*), voiceless ejective (e.g. *p'*), and voiceless aspirate (e.g. *p*). (In Western Armenian, only a two-way distinction *b–p* is made in many dialects, with *b* corresponding to Classical/Eastern *p'*, and *p* to *b* and *p*.) The presence of a distinctive series of ejectives is unusual for an Indo-European language, and it can hardly be coincidental that the Indo-European languages with ejectives (Armenian and the Iranian language Ossete) are spoken in the Caucasus, where Caucasian languages have a distinctive ejective series. Until recently, it was assumed that the ejectives in Armenian are due to the influence of Caucasian languages, but more recently it has been suggested that there is some internal evidence in favour of reconstructing a distinctive ejective series for Proto-Indo-European. Another unusual phonemic distinction is that between two rhotics, symbolised *r* (approximant) and *ṙ* (tap or trill): the latter derives in most instances from Proto-Indo-European **sr*, also from **r* before **n*. In the modern languages, the two rhotics have a tendency to merge.

One of the main typological differences observable between Classical and Modern Armenian lies in the declension of nouns: Classical Armenian was still to a large extent fusional, whereas in the modern languages the segmentability of number and case marking is transparent (though, under the influence of tradition, classical forms do sometimes find their way into the modern languages). This can be seen by comparing some case forms of *ban* 'word, thing' in Classical Armenian and Modern Eastern Armenian (Table 4.7). In Classical Armenian, only the instrumental plural could conceivably be segmented into separate markers of case and number. The modern languages, especially Eastern Armenian, still have traces of the different declensional classes that Armenian inherited from Proto-Indo-European, e.g. the genitive–dative of *ban* is *ban-i*, while that of *mard* 'man' is *mard-u*. Armenian does not, however, retain gender distinctions, nor do attributes agree with their head.

Eastern Armenian has an overt distinction between nominative and accusative for

Table 4.7. *Declensional forms of Armenian* ban *'word, thing'*

| | Classical | | Modern Eastern | |
	Singular	Plural	Singular	Plural
Nominative	ban	ban-k	ban	ban-er
Genitive- Dative	ban-i	ban-ic	ban-i	ban-er-i
Ablative	i ban-ee	i ban-ic	ban-ic	ban-er-ic
Instrumental	ban-iw	ban-iw-k	ban-ov	ban-er-ov
Locative	i ban-i	ban-s	ban-um	ban-er-um

personal pronouns only, although for definite human noun phrases the genitive–dative serves to express the direct object; otherwise, nominative and accusative are identical:

(81)   *jes   t'esa   kaγak-ə*
         I-NOM see-AOR-1SG town   DEF
         'I saw the town'

(82)   *menk   lav   dasat'u -ner unenk*
         we-NOM good teacher PL have-1PL
         'we have good teachers'

(83)   *jes   t'esa   ašak'ert'-i   -n*
         I-NOM see-AOR-1SG pupil   GEN-DAT DEF
         'I saw the pupil'

Classical Armenian has a small amount of morphological ergativity, namely the use of the genitive (rather than the nominative) for transitive subjects in the compound perfect; both modern languages simply use the nominative here (but see the discussion below for the use of the genitive as subject of a participle in the participial relative clause construction). Genitive and dative are not distinguished morphologically for nouns, although only in dative function can this form take the suffixed definite article.

A three-way deictic system has survived from Classical Armenian, as in the Eastern Armenian demonstratives *sa* 'this (near me)', *da* 'that (near you)', *na* 'that (near him)'. In Classical Armenian, the suffixed definite article showed a similar three-way distinction: *-s* 'the (near me)', *-d* 'the (near you)', *-n* 'the (near him)', but in the modern languages these have been reinterpreted as the corresponding possessive suffixes, e.g. *girk-əs* 'my book'; *-n/-ə* serves both as a third person possessive and as a general definite article.

The verbal system of Eastern Armenian shows a considerable shift towards analytic forms (using a nonfinite form of the lexical verb and the finite copula as an auxiliary) relative to Classical Armenian, and even relative to Western Armenian. The only simple indicative tense-aspect in Eastern Armenian is the aorist: *greci* 'I wrote', *grecir* 'you (SG) wrote', *grec* 'he, she, it wrote', *grecink* 'we wrote', *grecik* 'you (PL) wrote', *grecin* 'they wrote'. The present and imperfect subjunctives (continuing, formally, the Classical Armenian indicatives) are also simple: present *grem* 'I may write', *gres*, *gri*, *grenk*, *grek*, *gren*; imperfect *grei* 'I may have written', *greir*, *grer*, *greink*, *greik*, *grein*. The present and imperfect indicative, however, use a nonfinite form in *-um* (etymologically the locative of a verbal noun) and the verb 'to be' as an auxiliary: present *grum em*, *es*, *e*, *enk*, *ek*, *en*; imperfect *grum ei*, *eir*, *er*, *eink*, *eik*, *ein*. One of the ways of forming the future and future-in-the-past is similar, using the nonfinite form *grelu* (etymologically the genitive of the infinitive), e.g. *grelu em* 'I will write', *grelu ei* 'I would write', while the others simply prefix *k'ə* or *p'it'i* to the subjunctive, e.g. *k'ə/p'it'i grem* 'I will write', *k'ə/p'it'i grei* 'I would write'. The forms with *p'it'i* can also mean 'must'. (In Western Armenian, the corresponding forms with *gə* express the present and imperfect indicative respectively, while those with *bidi* function as future and future-in-the-past.)

The imperative is another simple verb form, as in second person singular *gri* 'write!'; other imperative forms are borrowed from other paradigms, e.g. the second person plural from the aorist: *grecek* 'write!'. Other nonfinite forms are the infinitive, e.g. *grel* 'to write', *k'ardal* 'to read'; the past participle in *-el*, e.g. *grel* 'having written', *k'ardacel* 'having read', the gerund *grelis*, *k'ardalis* (formed by adding *-is* to the infinitive), the present participle *groγ*, *k'ardacoγ*, and the resultative participle *grac'*, *k'ardacac'*. The perfect and pluperfect have the forms *grel em* 'I have (apparently) written', *grel ei* 'I had (apparently) written'. The resultative participle has the suffix *-ac'*, and is used to form a compound tense with strictly resultative (stative) meaning, e.g. *grac' em* 'I am in the state of having read'; in Modern Eastern Armenian, for transitive verbs this construction exists only in the passive (Kozinceva 1975), with the suffix *-v* after the root, e.g. *grvac' e* 'it has been written, it is written', *grvac' er* 'it had been written, it was written'.

The last-mentioned forms also show that Armenian has a synthetic, and productive, passive voice using the suffix *-v*, e.g. present *grvum e* 'it is being written', aorist *grvec* 'it was written'. The synthetic causative, with the suffix *-cn*, is formed particularly from intransitive verbs, e.g. *vazel* 'to run', *vazecnel* 'to cause to run', while transitive verbs prefer an analytic causative with the infinitive of the lexical verb and the conjugated auxiliary *t'al* 'to give'.

In syntax, modern Armenian has many of the properties of a subject–object–verb language, though not rigidly so. Lest this be considered a remnant of the possible SOV nature of Proto-Indo-European, it should be noted that modern Armenian is actually more SOV-like than the classical language, probably reflecting the continued symbiosis with Turkish. In finite clauses, basic word order fluctuates between subject–object–verb and subject–verb–object. The focus position (including that for interrogative pronouns, and for the negative particle *č* 'not') is immediately before the finite verb. The copular auxiliary usually follows the nonfinite verb form, as in the examples given above, but will precede it if required to follow a focused constituent immediately, e.g. *č-em grum* 'I do not write', *inč es grum* 'what do you write?'. Demonstratives, numerals, adjectives, and adnominal genitives predominantly precede their head noun. Although both prepositions and postpositions exist, the latter outnumber the former, which is a complete reversal of the situation in Classical Armenian.

Subordination can be expressed by means of both finite and nonfinite constructions, though the former predominate, and many finite constructions are not replaceable by nonfinite equivalents. There are two equivalents of the subordinating conjunction 'that', namely, *te* and *vor*, the basic difference being that *vor* is preferred for factive clauses (where the speaker presupposes the truth of the proposition expressed by the clause) (Abeghian 1936: 144). This formal distinction is found otherwise in languages of the Balkan area, cf. Serbo-Croat nonfactive *da* versus factive *što*.

The variation between finite and nonfinite means of expressing subordination can be seen particularly clearly in relative clauses (Hewitt 1978). The finite construction uses a clause-initial relative pronoun, identical in form with the interrogative pronoun, and this construction can be used for relativising on all constituents of the clause; the relative clause follows its head. The participial construction precedes its head. The participle in *-ac'* here has relative past time reference, and can be used – in its active form even with transitive verbs – for relativising on subjects, direct objects, and also certain adverbials, e.g. locatives. The following example illustrates relativisation on a direct object:

(84) *suren -i   k'ardac-ac'   girk -ə   jes vayuc   em*
      Suren GEN read   PART book DEF I   long-time be-PRES-1SG
      k'ardac-el
      read   PAST-PART
      'it's a long time since I read (literally: have read) the book that Suren read'

Note that the subject of the participle stands in the genitive.

4.5 Germanic languages

Two Germanic languages are spoken by sizable populations in the U.S.S.R., German and Yiddish. The 1970 census recorded 1,846,317 ethnic Germans (which may conceal some under-reporting), meaning that there are more Germans in the U.S.S.R. than representatives of the following Union Republic nationalities: Turkmen, Kirgiz, Latvian, Estonian. Language retention among the Soviet Germans is not particularly high, the reported figure being 66.8%, but this still leaves more native speakers of German than of Estonian. Nearly all the Germans in the U.S.S.R. are the descendants of colonists invited into the Russian Empire, first by Catherine the Great in the 1760s, to settle the vacant steppe area across the Volga from Saratov. Before the Second World War, most Soviet Germans continued to live in this area, and they had their own autonomous republic, the Volga-German A.S.S.R., with its capital at Engel's (named after Friedrich Engels). With the Nazi invasion of the U.S.S.R. in 1941 and the imminent offensive in areas near Engel's, it was decided for security reasons to dismantle the Volga-German A.S.S.R. and deport ethnic Germans to areas where they would be unlikely to have any contact with the invading armies. Ethnic Germans were moved to Kazakhstan, for the most part, where the vast majority of them remain to this day. Like the Crimean Tatars, and unlike the other ethnic groups that were deported from the Caucasus and nearby areas in the early 1940s, the Soviet Germans have not been allowed to resettle in their former home. In Kazakhstan there are many villages which are entirely or almost entirely populated by Germans, and German is used in the school system. As part of the rapprochement between the Federal Republic of Germany and eastern European countries, many Soviet Germans have taken advantage of the increased possibilities for emigration to the Federal Republic.

Yiddish is the traditional language of the Ashkenazic Jews, i.e. those Jews who inhabited German-speaking areas during the Middle Ages and their descendants, and who speak a language deriving, in its basic structure and vocabulary, from the Central dialects of Middle High German. In terms of the subsequent development of the native German component, Yiddish does not stand particularly apart from the general mass of modern German dialects, and is indeed much closer to modern standard German than are, for instance, many dialects of Switzerland. However, in terms of the influence of other languages Yiddish is markedly different from German, to the extent of being incomprehensible to speakers of German (or any of its dialects).

One of the main differences is that Yiddish has absorbed a large number of vocabulary items from Hebrew (or, more accurately, Hebrew and Aramaic, two very closely related Semitic languages), the religious language of the Jewish community. Although many of these are words dealing with aspects of Jewish religion and custom, such as *bar-mícve* 'Bar-Mitzvah' (coming-of-age ceremony for Jewish boy), a large number are ordinary words having no particular connection with the Jewish way of life, e.g. *šo* 'hour', *éjce* 'advice'. Hebrew–Aramaic words were taken into Yiddish in their Ashkenazic pronunciation: in Israel, the current pronunciation of Hebrew is basically that of the Sephardic Jews, i.e. those who inhabited Spain in the Middle Ages, so that the pronunciation of Hebrew–Aramaic words is often rather different in Yiddish and Israeli Hebrew, e.g. Yiddish *milxómes*, Israeli Hebrew *milxamót* 'wars'. When nouns were taken into Yiddish from Hebrew–Aramaic, they were usually taken along with their distinctively Hebrew plural formations, so that in modern Yiddish such words have plural formations using suffixes or vowel alternations that are not found in German, e.g. *guf* 'body', plural *gúfim*, *nes* 'miracle', plural *nísim*. Hebrew–Aramaic verb morphology has not had a similar effect on Yiddish, since Yiddish uses the borrowed noun with *hóbn* 'to have' or *zajn* 'to be', e.g. *xásene hóbn* 'to get married', literally means 'to have marriage'.

The other main foreign influence in the development of Yiddish was from Slavonic languages. Ashkenazic Jews moved eastwards as part of the general German expansion during and after the Middle Ages, while further east the liberal policy on religious toleration practised by the Polish Republic encouraged many Jews to settle there. In the areas populated primarily by speakers of Slavonic languages, Yiddish underwent a strong Slavonic influence in vocabulary, and also in phonology, morphology (especially derivational morphology) and syntax. Many everyday words are of Slavonic origin, including concrete nouns (e.g. *káčke* 'duck', cf. Polish *kaczka* [*kačka*]), kinship terms (e.g. *táte* 'father', cf. Czech *tata*), verbs (e.g. *blónžen* 'to get lost', cf. Polish *błądzić* [*błonžić*]), and other parts of speech (e.g. *xoč* 'although', cf. Polish *choć* [*xoć*]). The development of phonemically distinctive palatalisation is attributable to Slavonic influence, e.g. *ńańe* 'children's nurse' (cf. Polish *niania* [*ńańa*]), as is the existence of affricates like *ž* (cf. *blónžen* above). In morphology, the Slavonic feminine suffix *-ka* (Yiddish *-ke*) tends to replace the earlier suffix *-n* (cf. German *-in*), e.g. *šnájder* 'tailor' (of German origin, cf. German *Schneider*), feminine *snájderke* (cf. German *Schneiderin*). In Yiddish, general (yes–no) questions are formed by prefixing *ci*, cf. Polish *czy* [*či*], to the sentence, e.g. *ci hot er gegésn* 'has he eaten?' (cf. German *hat er gegessen?*, Polish *czy (on) pojadł?*). Another syntactic idiosyncrasy of Yiddish that is attributable to Slavonic influence is the use of the reflexive pronoun *zix*, originally third person (cf. German *sich*), for all persons and numbers (cf. Polish *się*, and likewise in all Slavonic languages), e.g. *ix ze zix* 'I see myself' (German *ich sehe mich;* Polish *(ja) widzę się*).

The policy of the Russian Empire was to forbid Jews to settle there, but with the partition of Poland in 1772 the Empire found itself with a Jewish population of some nine million. Anti-Jewish discrimination was practised widely (e.g. with regard to possible residence, education, employment), and pogroms were at the very least not prevented by the authorities. The Revolution promised a fairer deal for Jews, as for other ethnic groups, and many Jews took an active part in the Revolution. The readjustment of the Soviet–Polish frontier by the Treaty of Brest-Litovsk, with western Ukraine and western Belorussia being ceded to Poland, substantially reduced the number of Jews in the U.S.S.R., but the Soviet expansion following the non-aggression pact with Germany reversed this, giving a Jewish population in the U.S.S.R. of some five million. During the Nazi occupation of large parts of the western U.S.S.R., Jews in these areas suffered the same persecution as in other Nazi-occupied areas, and in the 1970 census the number of Jews in the U.S.S.R. was given as 2,150,707. Although most of these (but excluding Jews in Central Asia, for instance) are the descendants of Yiddish speakers, only 17.7% of them gave Yiddish as their native language in the 1970 census, a very small figure even if one adjusts for under-reporting: more than four times as many Jews gave Russian as their native language.

The treatment of Jews has been one of the least successful aspects of Soviet nationalities policy, by any account. Since the U.S.S.R. does not as a matter of general principle encourage emigration by any ethnic group, Zionism has always been anathema, and only in recent years has the policy on Jewish emigration softened. The Soviet attempt to set up a Jewish homeland within the U.S.S.R., the Jewish A.O. in the Far East, has met with minimal success: in 1970, only 11,452 Jews lived there, constituting just over 6% of the A.O.'s population. The tradition of anti-Semitism going well back in Russian history is often bolstered by security considerations (many Jews have relatives abroad) and by affirmative action programmes: for instance, the percentage of Jews with higher education far exceeds that for any other ethnic group (in the R.S.F.S.R., 46.8% of Jews in the working population have had higher education, compared to only 6.5% of Russians), so that it is easy to justify giving preference to other ethnic groups in order to maintain an ethnic balance. The general result of all this seems to be that those Jews who wish to insist on their Jewish identity try to emigrate to Israel, while others prefer to assimilate to the surrounding population, which probably accounts for the decline in the reported number of ethnic Jews between 1959 (2,267,814) and 1970 (2,150,707).

The Yiddish language has also suffered from this process. Soviet policy still regards Yiddish as being the language that corresponds to the ethnic group Jewish, thus causing potential terminological confusion: the official term for 'Yiddish' in Russian is not *idiš*, but rather *evrejskij jazyk*, literally 'Jewish language', even though with regard to Biblical times *drevneevrejskij jazyk*, literally 'Ancient Jewish language', refers to Ancient Hebrew; in Russian, Modern Hebrew is called *ivrit*, the Modern Hebrew name for 'Hebrew'. During the early years of Soviet power, there was a considerable volume of publishing in Yiddish, and Yiddish-medium schools functioned. An orthographic reform was even introduced: previously, and still in Yiddish published outside the U.S.S.R., words of Hebrew–Aramaic origins were spelled according to Hebrew orthographic conventions (for instance, without indication of many vowels, and with distinction of certain consonants that are pronounced alike in Yiddish). In the U.S.S.R., it was decided to spell Yiddish consistently according to its pronunciation: thus the word *milxómes* 'wars' mentioned above is spelled phonetically in Soviet Yiddish, but with the Hebrew letter sequence *mlxmwθ* elsewhere. The use of the Hebrew alphabet, written from right to left, was, however, retained. Since at least the early 1940s, however, there seem not to have been any Yiddish schools. Publication in Yiddish resumed after a long absence, but it is clear that the audience for this literature is small and diminishing. The fate of Yiddish in the U.S.S.R. has not been markedly different qualitatively from its fate elsewhere: its association with ghetto culture has appealed neither to Zionists, who prefer Hebrew, nor to those who seek a role in their native country, who have preferred to assimilate linguistically even if not in other respects.

4.6 Romance languages

The Romance languages, descendants of Latin, are the only surviving members of the Italic branch of Indo-European. The only Romance language that is a language of the U.S.S.R. is Moldavian, the language of the Moldavian S.S.R. This Union Republic corresponds closely to the area known traditionally as Bessarabia. For a long time under Ottoman rule, Bessarabia was ceded to Russia in 1812, but formed part of Romania in the inter-War period. The area was incorporated into the U.S.S.R. in 1940 as the Moldavian S.S.R., although the effect of this was not really felt until after the cessation of hostilities in the Second World War. Moldavian is the native language of 95% of the 2,697,994 ethnic Moldavians in the U.S.S.R., 85.4% of whom live in the Moldavian S.S.R., where they comprise 64.6% of the total population.

In terms of its structure and lexicon, Moldavian differs only minimally from standard Romanian. Both languages share the same history, being descendants of the Vulgar Latin spoken in or near the Balkans. The basic vocabulary and morphology are clearly Romance, although there has also been a massive influx of loans from neighbouring languages, especially Slavonic (e.g. *rəzbój* 'war'), though also from Greek (e.g. *drum* 'way'), Hungarian (e.g. *fəgəduí* 'to promise'), and Turkish (e.g. *duláp* 'cupboard'), in addition to a number of words apparently from the pre-Romance language(s) of the area (e.g. *brínzə* 'kind of cheese'). In addition, there are a number of features of the Balkan sprachbund (which includes, in addition to Romanian: Bulgarian, Macedonian, Albanian, and modern Greek), such as the postponed definite article (e.g. *óm-ul* 'the man', cf. *om* 'man'; this is found also in

Albanian, Bulgarian, and Macedonian, though not in Greek), and the tendency to replace infinitive constructions by subordinate clauses (e.g. *a inčepút sə ploáje* 'it has begun to rain', literally 'it-has begun that it-rain'; this feature is also found in Albanian, Bulgarian, and, in its most extreme form, modern Greek).

The development of Moldavian as a literary language is also inextricably bound up with that of Romanian. The earliest texts of Romanian–Moldavian were written in the Cyrillic alphabet (Orthodoxy is the traditional religion of the area), but in the nineteenth century the rise of Romanian nationalism, coupled with the strong sense of being speakers of a Romance language and distinct from the surrounding Slavs, led to the adoption of the Latin alphabet, and also the widespread replacement of non-Romance vocabulary by words calqued on Romance languages of western Europe, e.g. *nóbil* 'noble' for earlier *evgenikós* (a loan from Greek). The classics of the nineteenth century are viewed as the precursors of modern standard Moldavian and Romanian alike.

The separate development of Moldavian really dates from the end of the Second World War, with the consolidation of the national frontier between Romania and the U.S.S.R. in its present position. In the Moldavian S.S.R., the orthography reverted to a Cyrillic base. However, the current standard language is extremely close to standard Romanian, apart from the differences resulting from the different orthographic systems. In the early years of the Moldavian S.S.R., attempts were made to use spellings that captured some of the phonetic peculiarities of Moldavian dialects as opposed to standard Romanian (based primarily on dialects of Muntenia), for instance by representing orthographically the backing of vowels after sibilants, e.g. *sənín* 'clear' rather than *senín*, *zi 'day'* rather than *zi*, *pucín* 'a little' rather than *pucin*. In 1957, however, this policy was abandoned, and the spellings transliterated as *senin*, *zi*, *pucin* adopted as official, cf. Romanian *senin*, *zi*, *puţin*. Although the orthography of Moldavian is now essentially the same as that of Romanian, substituting Cyrillic for Latin, it remains unclear to what extent this affects pronunciation, since little work has been done on the question of Moldavian standard pronunciation.

The main difference between Moldavian and Romanian at present, apart from the different alphabets, lies in the fact that Moldavian uses a number of Russian loans that are not used in Romanian, including stump-compounds of the type *rajkóm* (in full in Russian: *rajonnyj komitet* 'regional committee'). The procedure of forming stump-compounds is even transferred to native morphemes, e.g. *korsát* 'village correspondent' (cf. *korespondént* 'correspondent', *sat* 'village'), although the native order with the modifier after the head is retained (cf. Russian *sel'kor*). Although Moldavian is currently little different from Romanian, it is likely that continued political separation will serve to increase these differences with time.

TEXTS IN INDO-EUROPEAN LANGUAGES OF THE U.S.S.R.

LITHUANIAN TEXT (IN CURRENT ORTHOGRAPHY, WITH TONE MARKS ADDED)

Àtmen   *-u*   *- buv-aũ*   *dár jáun* *-as*   *gimnãzij*   *-os*
remember 1SG be PAST-1SG still young NOM grammar-school GEN
mokin-ỹs.
pupil NOM
  Nórs   *jaũ*   *pavãsari-o*   *sáulė*   *linksm-aĩ*   *žiūrė́j-o*
  although already spring   GEN sun-NOM merry ADV look PAST-3
prõ   *màn-o*   *láng*   *-ą,*   *nórs*   *or -ė̃*   *spróg*   *-o*   *iř*
through I   GEN window ACC although air LOC blossom PAST-3 and
žydė́j *-o*   *mẽdži-ai,*   *tačiaũ*   *sėdė́j-au*   *sàv -o*
blossom PAST-3 tree   NOM-PL however sit   PAST-1SG self GEN
kambar-ỹ: *rengi* *-aũ*   *-s*   *egzamin*   *-áms.*   *Bùv-o*
room   LOC prepare PAST-1SG REFL examination DAT-PL be   PAST-3
rýt   *-as,*   *giẽdr-as,*   *ram -ùs*   *iř*   *malon*   *-ùs . . .*
morning NOM clear NOM quiet NOM and pleasant NOM
  Štaĩ at-si   *-dãr -o màn-o*   *kaṁbari-o*   *dùr -ys, iř*
  then   REFL open 3 I   GEN room   GEN door PL and
uždùs-ęs,   *sukaĩt-ęs,*   *linksm-omìs*   *dẽg -ančì*
pant PAST-PART sweat PAST-PART merry FEM-INSTR-PL burn PRES-
  -omis   *ak -imìs*   *į -bė́g-a Rõk* *-us,*   *màn-o*
PART FEM-INSTR-PL eye INSTR-PL in run 3 Rokus NOM I   GEN
draũg -as.
friend NOM
  —Ař žin *-aĩ*   *k*   *-ą̃?*   *- sušùk-o*   *jìs: - darbiniñk-ai*
  Q know 2SG what ACC   shout PAST-3 he   worker   PL-NOM
streikúoj-a!
strike   3
  —K *-às,*   *kuř?*   *- kláusi-u*   *àš, pašók-ęs*   *iř*   *išskė̃t-ęs*
  what NOM where ask   1SG I jump PAST-PART and open PAST-
  ak -ìs.
PART eye ACC-PL
  —Sak-aũ,   *darbiniñk-ai*   *streikúoj-a! - rė̃ki* *-a,*
  say PAST-1SG worker   NOM-PL strike   3   shout 3

mojúo-damas   *rañk -omis*   *Rõk -us.*   *- Jùk*   *šiañdien*
shake   PUSDALYVIS hand INSTR-PL Rokus NOM   you-see today
Gegužẽ-s   *Pirm -ó*   *-ji!*
May   GEN First   FEM-NOM DEF
   —Gegužẽ-s   *Pirm -ó*   *-ji?*   *streikúoj-a? - pér*   *-ein-a*
    May   GEN First   FEM-NOM DEF strike   3   through go 3
peř   *gálv -ą*   *mint*   *-is,*   *nušvieči -a prõt -ą:*   *pa-si*   *-dãr*
through head ACC thought NOM illuminate 3 mind ACC   REFL make
-o liñksm-a   *iř*   *leñgv-a;*   *iš*   *džiaŭgsm-o*   *nór -i -si*
3 merry   NEUT and light   NEUT from joy   GEN want 3 REFL
iř   *veřk-ti,*   *iř*   *juõk -ti*   *-s,*   *iř*   *šók -ti.*
and cry   INFIN and laugh INFIN REFL and dance INFIN
(Extracted from J. Biliūnas, *Pirmutinis streikas*.)

Notes

at-si-dãr-o, pa-si-dãr-o: when a verb form is prefixed, the reflexive affix occurs between prefix and root, rather than finally, as in nonprefixed verb forms.

   dùrys 'door': in Lithuanian this is a plurale tantum.

   liñksmomìs, dẽgančiomis akimìs: in Lithuanian, *akìs* 'eye' is feminine, whence the feminine adjectives.

FREE TRANSLATION

I remember – I was still a young grammar-school boy.

   Although the spring sun was already looking merrily through my window, although the trees were blossoming out and blooming in the air, yet I was sitting in my room: I was preparing for exams. It was morning, clear, quiet, and pleasant . . .

   Then the door of my room opens, and in runs Rokus, my friend, panting, sweating, and with merry, burning eyes.

   – Do you know what? he shouted, the workers are on strike!

   – What, where? I ask, jumping up and opening my eyes.

   – I said, the workers are on strike! Rokus shouts, shaking his arms, You see, today is the First of May!

   – The First of May? On strike? the thought goes through my head, illuminates my mind; things become merry and light; out of joy I want both to weep, and to laugh, and to dance.

TADZHIK TEXT

du suratkaš dar ustodi va san᾿atkori bo   ham   mudom
two artist   on skill and artistry with each-other continually
bahs   me   -kard   -and. suratkaš-i   jakům surat -i   jak
argument CONT do-PAST 3PL artist   EZAFE first   picture EZAFE one
sar   angur -ro čunon ustodona kaš -id, ki dar did-an   az
bunch grapes ACC so   skilfully paint PAST that on see INFIN of
angur -i   haqiqi he ž farq   kun -ond -an   mumkin na -bud.
grapes EZAFE real   any difference make CAUS INFIN possible NEG be-PAST
vaqt-e   ki suratkaš on surat -ro ba šox -i   daraxt-e
time REL that artist   that picture ACC on branch EZAFE tree   INDEF-SG
ovext   -a   mon -d,   baaze parranda-ho angur -i   haqiqi gumon
hang-PAST GER leave PAST some bird   PL grapes EZAFE real   thought
kard   -a,   omad   -a   ba vaj nůl me -zad   -and.
do-PAST GER come-PAST GER to it beak CONT strike-PAST 3PL
suratkaš in hol   -ro ba raqib-i   xud nišon dod   -a,
artist   this situation ACC to rival EZAFE own sign give-PAST GER
balandi -i   san᾿at-i   xud -ro isbot kard.
greatness EZAFE art   EZAFE own ACC proof do-PAST
    suratkaš-i   dujům baroi nišon dod -an   -i   san᾿at-aš
    artist   EZAFE second for   sign give INFIN EZAFE art   3SG
suratkaš-i   jakům-ro ba xona -aš burd   va parda -e
artist   EZAFE first   ACC to house 3SG take-PAST and curtain INDEF-SG
-ro nišon dod   -a   guft: san᾿at-ho -i   man dar
ACC sign   give-PAST GER say-PAST art   PL EZAFE I   in
pušt -i   hamin parda istod   -a   -and, kušo-d   -a
back EZAFE this   curtain stand-PAST GER be-3PL open PAST GER
bin,   ki me   -pisand-i jo ne.
see-IMPER that CONT like   2SG or not
    suratkaš-i   jakům dast burd   -a   me -xost   parda
    artist   EZAFE first   hand reach-PAST GER CONT want-PAST curtain
-ro bar -dor -ad, lekin don -ist, ki on parda na -bud   -a,
ACC apart hold 3SG but   realise PAST that that curtain NEG be-PAST GER
surat -i   parda -e   bud   -a   -ast, ki dar
picture EZAFE curtain INDEF-SG be-PAST GER be-3SG that on
devor-i   xona mohirona kaš -id   -a   šud   -a   -ast.
wall EZAFE house skilfully   paint PAST GER become-PAST GER be-3SG
(From A. Dehoti, *Latifahoi to ž iki* (Tadzhik anecdotes).)

Notes

Phonetic: *x* represents a voiceless uvular fricative.

parda-e-ro: for the combination of indefinite singular suffix *-e* and so-called definite direct object suffix *-ro*, see page 168.

Note the frequent use of compound verbs with a noun and auxiliary verb *kard-an* 'to do' or *dod-an* 'to give', e.g. *isbot kardan* 'to prove' (literally 'to do/make proof'), *nišon dodan* 'to show' (literally 'to give sign'); such compounds can be transitive, taking a direct object.

FREE TRANSLATION

Two artists were continually arguing with each other about skill and artistry. The first artist painted a picture of a bunch of grapes so skilfully that on seeing real grapes it was impossible to make any difference. When the artist left the picture hanging on the branch of a tree, some birds, thinking the grapes to be real, came to them and pecked them. The artist showed this to his rival and proved the greatness of his art.

The second artist, in order to show off his art, took the first artist to his house and, indicating a curtain, said, 'My art stands behind this curtain, open it and see whether you like them or not'.

The first artist reached with his hand and was intending to hold the curtain open, but realised that it was not a curtain, but a painting of a curtain that had been skilfully painted on the wall of the house.

ARMENIAN TEXT

k'arč' žamanak' naje -c   inʒ   zarmac   -ac',   het'o us   -er -ə
short period   look AOR I-ACC be-surprised RESULT then shoulder PL 3SG

totove-c   t'arak'usank-ov   jev glux -ə   noric k'axe-c   gərk -i
shrug AOR hesitation   INSTR and head 3SG again hang AOR book GEN

vra, ařanc aʒlevs voč mi xosk art'asane -l,   -u.   əst'
on without still   not a word pronounce INFIN GEN from

jerevujt -i   -n   uz -um   er   hask'a   -cne -l,
appearance GEN DEF want PRES COP-PAST-3SG understand CAUS INFIN

vor hangist' toɣne-m   iren   jev heřana-m.
that peace   let   1SG she-ACC and leave 1SG

   bajc jes hamařoren k'angn-ac'   ei   nəra   aržev
   but I stubbornly stand   RESULT COP-PAST-1SG she-GEN in-front-of

jev ak'ama hian -um   ei,   dit'e -l   -ov   nəra
and willy-nilly admire PRES COP-PAST-1SG observe INFIN INSTR she-GEN

geɣecik' glux -ə   šat' harust', papuk' jev pajlun maz -er -ov,
beautiful head 3SG very rich   delicate and shiny hair PL INSTR
voronk   nor c'ag-ac'   arev -i   tek   čaŕagajt-ner-i   t'ak'
which-PL new rise RESULT sun GEN oblique ray   PL GEN under
bazmazan erang-ner ein   əndun -um . . .
various   shade PL COP-PAST-3PL take-on PRES
— *ajst'eɣ naje -cek   – asa-c -i, t'esne-l -ov, vor*
   here look IMPER-2PL say AOR 1SG see   INFIN INSTR that
glux -ə č -i   uz -um gərk -i vraj-ic barʒra-
head 3SG NEG COP-PAST-3SG want PRES book GEN on ABL rise
cne -l.
CAUS INFIN
  naje -c.
  look AOR
č'ak'at'-s dr -i hracan-i -s poɣ -i c'ajr-i -n,
   brow 1SG move-AOR 1SG gun GEN 1SG muzzle GEN end GEN DEF
isk' vot'-s šnik'-i vra.
and foot 1SG cock GEN on
(Extracted from Nar-Dos, *Sp'anvac' aɣavnin.*)

Notes

aŕanc . . . art'asanelu: aŕanc 'without' is one of the relatively few prepositions in modern Armenian (cf. also *əst'* 'from, according to' below); it takes the genitive case, here of the infinitive *art'asanel.*

   toɣnem, heŕanam: these forms are present subjunctive.

   dit'elov, t'esnelov: note the use of the instrumental of the infinitive to indicate a subordinate action.

FREE TRANSLATION

For a short period she looked at me surprised, then she shrugged her shoulders hesitantly and again lowered her head into her book, still without saying a word. Apparently she wanted to give me to understand that I should leave her in peace and go away.

   But I stood stubbornly in front of her and willy-nilly admired her, observing her beautiful head with very rich, delicate, and shiny hair, which took on various shades under the oblique rays of the newly risen sun.

   —Look here – I said, seeing that she did not want to raise her head from the book. She looked.

   I put my brow on the end of the muzzle of my gun, and my foot on the cock.

FURTHER READING

Since this chapter is not concerned with Indo-European languages as a whole, we shall merely refer the reader to two introductory works on Indo-European by Lockwood (1969; 1972), as well as to the more formal introduction to Indo-European comparative linguistics by Szemerényi (1970). Sketch grammars of the Indo-European languages of the U.S.S.R. (other than Parya) are provided in *JaNSSSR* I (1966).

A volume on Slavonic languages is currently in preparation for the Cambridge Language Survey series, and in the meantime we may refer the reader to the brief survey by Jakobson (1955) and to the compendium of outline descriptions of Slavonic languages by De Bray (1969) – note that the account of Belorussian in the first edition of this work does not deal with the current standard language. There is a pedagogical grammar of Ukrainian in English by Luckyj and Rudnyćkyj (1958), and a more Soviet-orientated textbook by Zhlutenko et al. (1978).

For the Baltic languages, there is an introductory account by Fraenkel (1950), in addition to the standard comparative grammars by Stang (1966) and Endzelīns (1948), the latter also in an English translation. Of the numerous solid descriptions of Lithuanian, that by Senn (1957) is readily available, and there is also a pedagogical grammar in English by Dambriūnas et al. (1972). The comprehensive grammar of Latvian by Endzelīns (1922) remains unsurpassed, and is especially advantageous in that all tones are marked. Gāters (1977) provides a detailed introduction to comparative Latvian dialect studies, while the pedagogical grammar by Budiņa Lazdiņa (1966) is one of the best volumes in the *Teach Yourself* series. The standard reference grammar for Old Prussian is Endzelīns (1943), also available in German.

The most comprehensive work to date on Parya is Oranskij (1977), although the grammatical sketch is necessarily abbreviated in a work that has other primary aims. There are also some brief remarks in English in Oranskij (1963b). A general account, with bibliography, of Romany dialect studies is provided in *JaAA* I (1976), while Ventcel' (1964) concentrates on the North Russian dialect; Table 4.3 is based on these sources. For the dialects of southern Russia and the Ukraine, there is Barannikov (1933), also available in an English version.

Two comprehensive surveys of the Iranian languages are available in German, *GIP* (1895–1904) and *HdO* I, 4.1 (1958). Oranskij (1960) is an introduction to Iranian philology in general, not restricted to language, while Oranskij (1963a), also available in a French translation, is a survey of the various Iranian languages; Oranskij (1975) is a survey in German of the Iranian languages of the U.S.S.R., the second volume being an extensive bibliography. Further bibliographic guides and discussion are provided by MacKenzie (1969) on Iranian languages in general, Lazard (1970) on Persian and Tadzhik (including a detailed comparison of the two), and Redard (1970) on other Iranian languages. The two-volume *OIIIJa* (1975) discusses the typological development of the phonology and morphology of the Iranian languages. The discussion of ergativity in the present chapter is expanded in Payne (1979).

For Kurdish, there is a recent comparative grammar by Kurdoev (1978), including comparison of Kurmandzhi and Sorani, while in English there is the dialect survey by MacKenzie (1961–2). The standard description of the Kurdish of Azerbaydzhan is by Bakaev (1965), that of Turkmenia by Bakaev (1962). For Talysh, we may refer to Miller (1953). The form of Beludzh spoken in the U.S.S.R. is described by Sokolov (1956), while more general accounts are available by Frolova (1960) in Russian and Elfenbein (1966) in English.

The sketch of Tadzhik grammar by Rastorgueva (1954) is also available in an English translation. For comparison with Persian, a useful grammar of (modern literary) Persian in English is Lambton (1961). The most detailed description of Tat is Grjunberg (1963).

There are numerous descriptions of Ossete, especially the Iron dialect, including an early grammar in German by Miller (1903); a more recent account is Abaev (1959), also available in an English translation. Isaev (1966) is the current standard treatment of the Digor dialect. For

Yagnob, the only published grammar is Xromov (1972).

For the Pamir languages, there is a general guide by Paxalina (1969), as well as the following grammars of individual languages: Rushan (Fajzov 1966); Bartang (Karamxudoev 1973); Oroshor (Kurbanov 1976); Shugn (Karamšoev 1963); Yazgulyam (Èdel'man 1966); Ishkashim (Paxalina 1959); Vakh (Paxalina 1975; Grjunberg and Steblin-Kamenskij 1976). For the languages spoken outside the U.S.S.R., we have Paxalina (1966) for Sarikoli, and Grjunberg (1972) for Munǯi. In addition, there are discussions of some of the Pamir languages in English and German by travellers who approached the area from the Afghan side; among these, we may cite the comparative works of Grierson (1920) and Morgenstierne (1938), and the grammar of Vakh by Lorimer (1958), based on material gathered in the 1930s.

Standard descriptions of Classical Armenian are available in French (Meillet 1936) and German (Jensen 1959), The main features of the Armenian dialects before the diaspora are described in Adjarian (1909). For Western Armenian, there are pedagogical grammars in English (Fairbanks 1958; Bardakjian and Thomson 1977) and in French (Feydit 1948). Standard Eastern Armenian is described by Abeghian (1936), and there is also a pedagogical grammar in English (Fairbanks and Stevick 1958).

Beranek (1958) may be consulted for a description, in German, of a variety of Yiddish (Lithuanian–Belorussian) representative of the U.S.S.R; for more general background, there is the survey and grammar by Birnbaum (1979). For Moldavian, reference may be made to the authoritative two-volume *KLMLK* (1956–9).

5

Caucasian languages

5.1 The individual languages and their subgrouping

The great mountain range of the Caucasus, stretching for five hundred miles from the Black Sea to the Caspian, is the traditional frontier between Europe and Asia. Since the time of the ancient Greeks, the area has been famous for its multiplicity of languages, being described by an Arab geographer of the tenth century as the 'mountain of tongues'. Many of the languages spoken in the area are Caucasian only in a geographic sense, for they belong either to the Indo-European or Turkic families. In this chapter we shall be concerned exclusively with those languages that belong to what, for all practical purposes, may be described as the indigenous languages of the region – in other words, with those languages which, from a strictly linguistic point of view, may be styled Caucasian (or Ibero-Caucasian, where the term Iberian refers solely to the South Caucasian or Kartvelian group and does not imply any connection with any language spoken in western Europe's Iberian peninsula, specifically Basque).

One Caucasian language is no longer spoken in the Caucasus and is virtually extinct in Turkey, where the entire Ubykh people migrated following the Russian subjugation of the north-western Caucasus in 1864. The present writer, on a visit to the Ubykh village of Haci Osman Köyü in 1974, met only four elderly male speakers, one of whom, Fuat Ergün, had seven children, all of whom could speak only Circassian and Turkish. But, as Dumézil (1931: xii) observed, even before the migration, Ubykh was losing ground to Circassian. The traditional homeland of the Laz people, who speak a Kartvelian language, is the southern shore of the Black Sea in present-day Turkey, where there are some 50,000 speakers; only a very few Laz speakers are to be found within the U.S.S.R. – notably in the village of Sarpi on the Soviet–Turkish border (Asatiani 1974: 3–4). Otherwise, apart from various émigré communities predominantly in Turkey and the Middle East, all the Caucasian languages are confined within the frontiers of the U.S.S.R. The 38 languages which thus form the object of this survey are listed in Table 5.1; added in parentheses after each language are the latest available figures for the speakers of the language and the general location where each is spoken.

Table 5.1. *Genetic classification of the Caucasian languages*

South Caucasian (Kartvelian)
  Georgian (Georgian S.S.R. – 3,310,917)
  Svan (north-western Georgia – 43,000)
  Mingrelian (Megrel) (Georgia – 360,000)
  Laz (Chan) (southern coast of Black Sea – 50,000)
North-West Caucasian
  Abkhaz (Abkhaz A.S.S.R. – 79,835)
  Abaza (Karachay-Cherkes A.O. – 24,449)
  Adyge (West Circassian) (Adyge A.O. – 96,331)
  Kabard-Cherkes (East Circassian) (Kabard-Balkar A.S.S.R., Karachay-Cherkes A.O. –
    311,078)
  Ubykh (Haci Osman Köyü, Turkey – ?)
North-Central Caucasian (Nakh, Veynakh)
  Chechen (Chechen-Ingush A.S.S.R. – 604,655)
  Ingush (Chechen-Ingush A.S.S.R. – 153,483)
  Bats (northern Georgia – 3,000)
North-East Caucasian (Dagestanian)
  Avar-Andi-Dido
    Avar (north-western zone of Dagestan highlands – 385,043)
    Andi languages (to the west of the Avar region)
      Andi (9,000)
      Botlikh (3,000)
      Godoberi (2,500)
      Karata (5,000)
      Akhvakh (5,000)
      Bagval (4,000)
      Tindi (5,000)
      Chamalal (4,000)
    Dido (Tsez) languages (immediately south of Andi)
      Dido (7,000)
      Khvarsh (1,000)
      Ginukh (200)
      Bezhti (Kapuch) (2,500)
      Gunzib (600)
  Lak-Dargva (central zone of the Dagestan highlands)
    Lak (82,010)
    Dargva (east of Lak – 227,302)
  Lezgian (south-eastern zone of the Dagestan highlands)
    Archi (between Lak and Avar – 1,000)
    Tabasaran (southern Dagestan – 54,574)
    Agul (southern Dagestan – 8,782)
    Rutul (southern Dagestan – 11,933)
    Tsakhur (southern Dagestan, northern Azerbaydzhan – 10,719)
    Budukh (northern Azerbaydzhan – 1,000)
    Khinalug (northern Azerbaydzhan – 1,000)
    Udi (northern Azerbaydzhan and the eastern Georgian village of Oktomberi – 4,000)
    Lezgi (southern Dagestan, northern Azerbaydzhan – 304,087)
    Kryz (Kryts) (northern Azerbaydzhan – 6,000)

As many of these languages are spoken in only a few villages – in some cases, in one village only – it is not possible here to present a more precise demarcation of the locality of the speakers. The status of some of the languages listed is disputed – for instance, within the U.S.S.R. Laz and Mingrelian are regarded as dialects of a single language, Zan. Also now viewed as dialects of a single language are Tindi and Bagval (Gudava 1967: 351), and possibly also Botlikh and Godoberi (Čikobava 1974: 37). From a purely structural point of view one would have to treat Abaza as a (divergent) dialect of Abkhaz, a view enshrined in the very title of Lomtatidze's description of the main Abaza dialect (1977): 'The Tapanta dialect of the Abkhaz language'. Kubachi is sometimes considered a dialect of Dargva, sometimes a separate language. The precise genetic affiliations of Archi and Khinalug are also not finally settled, some commentators preferring to consider them as language-isolates.

As regards the division into four main areal groups, it may be said that, within each group, all the languages are clearly related (with the exception of the two just mentioned), but the relationships, if any, existing between the groups is far from clear. Whilst the majority of scholars insist on working with North-Central Caucasian and North-East Caucasian as separate language-families, others admit the inclusion of the Nakh family into the North-East Caucasian group, so that there would then be a Nakh subgroup of North-East Caucasian on a par with the Lak–Dargva, Avar–Andi–Dido and Lezgian subgroups, and we would then have only three Caucasian families of North-West Caucasian, North-East Caucasian, and South Caucasian. Although there is a basis for supposing a remote link between all the languages of the northern Caucasus, there is as yet no sound evidence for assuming any genetic association between South Caucasian and these northern groups. However, a number of Soviet scholars, particularly in Georgia, accept the common origin of all the Caucasian languages as an article of faith, which has thus become the working hypothesis underlying their research.

Twelve of the Caucasian languages have the status of literary languages within the U.S.S.R.: Georgian (own name *Kartveli* '(a) Georgian'), Abkhaz, Abaza, Adyge, Kabard-Cherkes, Chechen, Ingush, Avar, Lak, Dargva, Lezgi, and Tabasaran. Of these, only Georgian has its own script of 33 characters (Old Georgian had 5 extra), the invention of which is ascribed to Mesrop in the early fifth century, who, in addition to being credited with the establishment of the Armenian orthography, is also said to be the inventor of the long defunct script of the little known language of the Caucasian Albanians, who may have been the linguistic ancestors of the present-day Udi speakers. The current forms of the letters, the so-called civil (*mxedruli*), as opposed to religious (*xucuri*), alphabet, make no distinction between upper and lower case. Mesrop's considerable linguistic talents are confirmed by the fact that, among the Caucasian orthographies, only that for Georgian is fully phonemic, i.e.

for both consonants and vowels. Thus, whilst Georgian enjoys the distinction of possessing an exceedingly rich literary tradition spanning fifteen centuries, the heritage of the remaining eleven literatures really began, apart from a few earlier attempts in the nineteenth century, only in the Soviet period. Perhaps the oldest attested examples of a Caucasian language other than Georgian are the bilingual inscriptions in Avar and Georgian that have been discovered in Dagestan and dated, in some cases, to as early as the tenth–eleventh centuries (see Gambašidze 1977).

The present-day, post-Revolutionary orthographies are all based on Cyrillic. Except in Abkhaz, only one non-Cyrillic sign is employed, and this is capital I, which, depending on the language concerned, may signify a glottal stop, glottalic initiation, or either pharyngal or uvular articulation. As the Caucasian languages possess richer consonantal (and, generally, vocalic) inventories than Russian, the result is that certain phonemes have to be represented by means of digraphs, trigraphs, and, in one rare instance (the Kabard voiceless aspirated labialised uvular plosive) a tetragraph кхъу. In different languages, moreover, the same sign may have different values: for instance, the digraph кь in Abaza is [ǩ], but in Avar it is [kɬ']; and the same phone may be represented by different signs, e.g. [ç] is тш in Abaza but чъ in Adyge. But this desire to endow each literary language with its own distinctive orthographic identity has resulted in the following absurd situation obtaining in the orthographies of such closely related languages as Adyge and Kabard: the palato-alveolar voiceless fricative [š] in Adyge is щ and in Kabard ш, whilst щ in Kabard represents the alveolo-palatal voiceless fricative [ś], which in Adyge is written щъ. However, the strangest of the new orthographies incontrovertibly belongs to Abkhaz. Apart from employing 14 characters unknown in Cyrillic, it is amazingly inconsistent in its marking of aspirates and ejectives.

For a language to have literary status means that newspapers, journals, and books are published in it, and that it is the medium of instruction in the specifically non-Russian schools up to at least the age of ten, when lessons are conducted in Russian – the one exception being Georgian (as opposed to Russian) schools in Georgia, where one's entire education to the end of a university course may be exclusively in Georgian (apart from Russian language lessons). This means that children born into communities whose language is nonliterary will be bilingual (if not multilingual) by the age of ten – for example, Botlikh children are educated in Avar. The dialect selected to form the basis of the literary language is usually the one which is phonemically simplest – hence the choice of the southern Abzhuy dialect of Abkhaz, with its 58 consonants, to replace the northern, Bzyp, dialect, which was in use prior to the Revolution, with its 67. In the case of Avar, the northern dialect of Khunzakh was long established as a lingua franca in central Dagestan, so that the choice of the literary dialect was already settled.

5.2 **Phonology**

A glance at the Georgian consonant system (Table 5.2) quickly gives the lie to the popular belief that all Caucasian languages are characterised by a large stock of complex consonant phonemes: Georgian possesses 28 consonants. Apart from the two velar fricatives, which are by no means unknown in western European languages, a native speaker of English would here find only the six ejectives somewhat odd. The Old Georgian voiceless uvular plosive q, preserved in Svan, has merged with the voiceless velar fricative x. The consonant systems of the remaining South Caucasian languages differ only minimally from that of Georgian: the basic differences are that both Mingrelian and Laz have the glottal stop $ʔ$, and Laz uses f in foreign words containing this sound. Ejectives in Svan are pronounced with greater intensity than in Georgian.

What the foreigner does find unusual in South Caucasian are the massive consonant clusters. For Georgian, Vogt (1958) illustrates four 6-term clusters, twenty-one 5-term, and a hundred and forty-eight 4-term. As an example of a 6-term cluster we have *mc'vrtneli* 'trainer', and, if one cares to imagine a personified orange saying 'he peels us', we can produce an 8-term cluster: *gvprckvnis*.

Twenty-three of the North-East Caucasian languages have from 30 to 46 consonants, but three of the languages exceed this number: Akhvakh with 49, Khinalug with 76, and Archi, which, according to Kibrik et al. (1977, I: 223), has 70, though earlier Mikailov (1967: 20) had given 40, and Xajdakov (1967: 608) 49. Common to all the North-East and North-Central Caucasian languages is an opposition between nonintensive and intensive consonants, though Kibrik et al. (1977, I: 239) exclude the latter from Archi, whilst those of Ingush appear to be losing their phonological value (Črelašvili 1975: 111). Catford (1977: 289) states that the intensive consonants are realised in various ways: 'Generally in Lak, Dargva, and the Lezgian languages intensive stops . . . are tense unaspirated, and, when intervocalic, geminate. The corresponding affricates . . . are likewise tense and have a lengthened stop portion and tense unaspirated affrication. In Avar and most of the Andi languages the "intensive" stops are strongly affricated, intensive affricates have lengthened affrication and are unaspirated, and the intensive fricatives are lengthened and unaspirated.' We may, thus, examine the consonant system of Avar, where the intensives (sometimes also described as strong or geminate consonants) are marked by a superscript macron (Table 5.3). Note that the velar fricatives $γ, x, x̄$ are described as back velars, but that their point of articulation is still not identified with that of the uvular series, which most Georgian linguists confusingly term pharyngal. It is interesting to observe that the Georgian fricatives $γ, x$ are similarly described as back velars, but, whilst Šanidze (1973: 15) decides that they are basically velars, Žgenti (1956: 178 ff.) concludes that they are rather uvulars. Indeed, in such

Table 5.2. *Consonant system of Georgian*

Bilabial	b	p	p'	m								
Labio-dental										v		
Alveolar	d	t	t'	n	ʒ	c	c'		z	s	l	r
Palato-alveolar					ǯ	č	č'		ž	š		
Velar	g	k	k'							ɣ	x	
Uvular			q'									
Laryngal/Glottal										h		

Table 5.3. *Consonant system of Avar*

Bilabial	b	p										m	w
Alveolar	d	t	t'		c	c̄	c'	c̄'	z	s	s̄	n	r
Palato-alveolar					č	č̄	č'	č̄'	ž	š	š̄		j
Lateral						k̄ł		k̄ł'		ł	ł̄		l
Palatalised Velar										x̄'			
Velar	{	g	k	k̄	k'	k̄'							
								ɣ	x	x̄			
Uvular						q̄		q̄'					
Pharyngal									ʕ	ħ			
Laryngal/Glottal			ʔ							h			

cases it is perhaps truer to say that the realisation of the fricative ranges from the velar to the uvular regions according to context.

Table 5.3 also indicates another feature that is particularly characteristic of the Avar–Andi–Dido subgroup, namely the wealth of laterals. No Avar dialect contains more than five laterals, but in Andi there are six, as a result of the addition of the nonintensive ejective lateral affricate *kł'*. Akhvakh, on the other hand, attains the full set of seven by including the nonintensive nonejective affricate *kł*.

Secondary articulations (labialisation, palatalisation, and pharyngalisation) are not unknown amongst the North-East Caucasian languages. We may illustrate pharyngalisation with data from the Kubachi dialect of Dargva (A. A. Magometov– personal communication):

buxij	'to become'	*bux̣ij*	'to quilt'
biq'ij	'to ripen'	*biq'ij̣*	'to hush'

For labialisation, compare the following Tabasaran oppositions:

g°ar	'pitcher'	*gar*	'egg-shell'
naq°'	'grave'	*naq'*	'yesterday'

Table 5.4. *Consonant system of Ubykh*

Bilabial plain	b	p	p'	w			m	
Bilabial pharyngalised	ḅ	p̣	p̣'	w̦		f	ṃ	
Labio-dental plain						f		
Labio-dental pharyngalised				v̦				
Alveolar plain	d	t	t'				n	r
	ʒ	c	c'	z	s			
Alveolar labialised	d°	t°	t°'					
Alveolo-palatal plain	ʒ́	ć	ć'	ź	ś			
Alveolo-palatal labialised	ʒ́°	ć°	ć°'	ź°	ś°			
Palato-alveolar	ǯ	č	č'	ž	š			j
Palato-alveolar labialised				ž°	š°			
Retroflex	ʒ̣	ç	ç'	z̧	ş			
Lateral			ɬ'	l	ł			
Velar	(g)	(k)	(k')	ɣ	x			
Fronted velar	ǵ	ḱ	ḱ'					
Labialised velar	g°	k°	k°'					
Uvular		q	q'	ʁ	χ			
Palatalised uvular		q́	q́'	ʁ́	χ́			
Labialised uvular		q°	q°'	ʁ°	χ°			
Pharyngalised uvular		q̣	q̣'	ʁ̣	χ̣			
Labialised and pharyngalised uvular		q̣°	q̣°'	ʁ̣°	χ̣°			
Laryngal/Glottal					h			

Avar, as we have seen, uses palatalisation:

  baxin 'crossing'   *bax̄in* 'white'

Archi and Khinalug achieve their impressive inventories by extensive use of labialisation and palatalisation respectively, but it is with the North-West Caucasian languages that widespread use of secondary articulations (and, thus, complex consonantal systems) is especially associated.

Kabard-Cherkes, with 48 consonant phonemes, is the least well endowed of all the languages of its group. Ubykh (Table 5.4), with 80 phonemes (83 if one includes the velar triad found only in words of foreign origin), was for many years thought to be the world record-holder in this respect, but it now appears that it may be surpassed by some African languages, such as the Chadic language Margi.

Labialisation has at least three different realisations. The simplest type is that accompanying the velars and uvulars, which may be termed lip-rounding, by which is meant that, while the back of the tongue is forming the velar or uvular component, the lips take up the position appropriate for the pronunciation of *w*; this type also characterises the palato-alveolars. The second is rather labio-dentalisation: the accompanying lip position is that appropriate to the pronunciation of *f* or *v*; for

Ubykh, Vogt (1963) suggests rather a bilabial fricative articulation. This variety is found with the alveolo-palatals. The third kind involves complete bilabial closure and is restricted to the alveolar plosives. Labialised alveolar plosives exist only in Ubykh and Abkhaz (not in Abaza). Only Bzyp, the northern dialect of Abkhaz, shares with Ubykh all ten members of the two alveolo-palatal series (plain and labialised), literary Abkhaz (Abzhuy) retaining only the three labialised affricates. Circassian languages possess at least a triad of plain fricatives from the alveolo-palatal series *ś, ź, ś'*, whose articulation is described by Catford (1977: 290) thus: 'the tip of the tongue rests against the alveoles of the lower teeth . . . but the main articulatory channel is at the back of the alveolar ridge . . .' It seems to the present writer that the labialised members of this series that are attested in Adyge are characterised by the 'bi-labial' variety of labialisation rather than by the labio-dental variety described above – this triad has developed to *f, v, f'* in Kabard-Cherkes (and the presence of such labio-dentals is a diagnostic for the East Circassian dialects). Bzyp is also alone in sharing with Ubykh the feature pharyngalisation, but it possesses only two pharyngalised phonemes, namely χ, $\chi°$.

As regards the laterals, Circassian languages differ from Ubykh in having a voiced lateral fricative *ɮ* and no simple approximant. Abkhaz has the approximant only, whereas Abaza shows both the approximant and the voiced fricative, but employs a lateral affricate *kɬ* in place of the plain fricative *ɬ*.

The labialised voiced pharyngal fricative of Abaza *ʕ°* is not attested in standard Abkhaz, where it has the reflex [ẅ], henceforth symbolised *j°*. And it is the [ẅ]-type of labialisation we find accompanying Abkhaz *ħ°*.

A peculiarity of the Shapsug and Bzhedug dialects of Adyge is the opposition aspirated/unaspirated for the voiceless plosives (including affricates) and fricatives. The unaspirated member is styled preruptive by Soviet scholars, and this opposition is reminiscent of the intensive/nonintensive opposition discussed above for North-East Caucasian and North-Central Caucasian, except that an aspirated/unaspirated opposition obviously has no relevance for the ejectives, whereas we have already met intensive and nonintensive ejectives in Avar. Table 5.5, adapted from Colarusso (1977: 90), gives the consonant system of Bzhedug. This gives a total of 68 phonemes. Notice here the labialised glottal stop; apparently the Abdzakh dialect of Adyge also has a slightly palatalised one (Catford 1977: 289).

Vowel systems present much less homogeneity across Caucasian languages. Georgian has the 5-term system *a, e, i, o, u*. Laz and Mingrelian add to this a schwa. But the most complex system in South Caucasian is attained by the Upper Bal dialect of Svan. Not only does this dialect manifest the schwa, but the feature of length is distinctive for all of the basic six vowels. To the twelve phonemes thus established the following six must be added: *ä, ö, ü, ää, öö, üü*. The conditions motivating this

Table 5.5. *Consonant system of the Bzhedug dialect of Adyge*

Labial	p'	p	b	p'		f		w	m
Alveolar	t'	t	d	t'				n	r
	c'	c	ʒ	c'		s	z		
Alveolo-palatal						ś	ź	ś'	
„ (labialised)	c'°	c°	ʒ°			ś°	ź°	ś'°	
Lateral						ɬ	ɮ	ɬ'	
Palato-alveolar	č'	č	ǯ	č'	ǯ'	š	ž		j
Retroflex	c̣'	c̣	ʒ̣	c̣'	ṣ'	ṣ	ẓ		
Velar		k		k'	x'	x	ɣ		
Velar (labialised)	k°'	k°	g°	k'°					
Uvular	q'	q				χ	ʁ		
Uvular (labialised)	q°'	q°				χ°	ʁ°		
Pharyngal						ħ	ʕ		
Laryngal/Glottal				ʔ		h			
„ (labialised)				ʔ°					

process of umlaut are set out in Šanidze (1957: 325–6). Both *e* and *i* may cause umlaut on the vowel of the previous syllable, but their umlauting potential is by no means equal, since *e* may cause only the umlaut of *a*, and this *e* must itself be short, whilst both long and short *i* produce the same result on all three umlauting vowels. As regards the vowels *o* and *u*, these may not umlaut if they are part of a prefix. And as *o* is not found in suffixes, *ö* is only actually possible within roots; no such restriction applies to the umlaut of *a*, so that *ä* is the most widely attested umlauted vowel. As regards the phonetic realisation of *o* and *u*, Šanidze and Topuria (1939: xx) observe that they are often pronounced [we] and [wi] respectively. A further phonetic transformation now usually occurs, with the result that the bilabial continuant is shifted to stand behind the following consonant, e.g. *k'alp'et'w* 'river bed' (Georgian *k'alap'ot'i*), *č'abwig* or *č'abigw* 'lad' (Georgian *č'abuk'i*); as is clear from the absence of *-i* in these examples, syncope is also a feature of Svan vocalism.

Palatalisation is also a striking feature of the Nakh languages, where nasalised monophthongs and diphthongs also occur, although, regarding nasalisation in Ingush, Magomedov (1974: 239) has this to say: 'Nasalised vowels in Ingush are found only in the structure of monosyllabic words which historically ended in the sonant consonant *n*. At the end of the forms of the genitive case of nouns, adjectives, of the adverb and of the infinitive, nasality of the vowel does not appear as a sign of phonological significance for Ingush, and it is so weakly pronounced that, for all practical purposes, it is possible to talk of its non-existence.' Magomedov (1974: 9–11) also sets out the most complex vowel system attested in Nakh, namely that of Lowland Chechen, as in Table 5.6. It should also be remarked that the initial vowels in Nakh are preceded by what is often called a voiced pharyngal plosive – this so-

Table 5.6. *Vowel system (including diph-*
thongs) of Lowland Chechen

a	e	i	o	u
aa	ee	ii	oo	uu
ä	ö	ü		
ää	öö	üü		
ã	(å̃)	ĩ		ũ
ãã	ẽẽ	ĩĩ		ũũ
je	wo	wö		
jee	woo	wöö		
jẽ	wõ	[wõ̃]		
jẽẽ	woõ	[woõ̃]		

called strong onset is also characteristic of some of the North-East Caucasian languages, e.g. Avar and Andi. Catford (1977: 289) describes this sound as involving 'tight closure of the ventricular bands (as well as the vocal cords) and some constriction of the pharynx', which leads him to define it as 'a (pharyngalised) ventricular + glottal stop'.

Nasalised vowels are also quite common in North-East Caucasian. Botlikh, for example, has the five basic vowels *a, e, i, o, u,* plus the nasalised counterparts of these; Bagval complicates this somewhat by admitting distinctive degrees of length, most frequently for *aa* (versus *a*) and *ĩĩ* (versus *ĩ*).

Another vocalic feature found in Dagestan is that of pharyngalisation (also found in Ubykh). It is particularly associated with Dido and Khvarsh, as well as the Lezgian languages Archi, Tsakhur, Rutul, and Udi. According to Ibragimov (1968: 28, 34), there are in Tsakhur six short pharyngalised vowels *ạ, ọ, ụ, ị, ỵ, ẹ,* plus the two that are susceptible to lengthening *ạa, ọo.* Commenting on this phenomenon, Catford (1977: 294) states that 'pharyngalisation takes the form of retraction of the tongue-root, and it appears to induce, as a side-effect, a certain degree of fronting of back vowels, particularly the closer vowels *u* and *o.* The exact mechanism of this is not clear, but the fact is that in Tsakhur and Udi the pharyngalised *u* and *o* have a distinctly central quality.' Udi possesses the five pharyngalised vowels *ạ, ẹ, ọ, ụ, ị,* as well as three umlauted vowels *ä, ö, ü;* the system is then completed by the simple *a, e, i, o, u, ə,* and the two diphthongs *ow* and *ej.* For a recent discussion on pharyngalisation in the Caucasus, see Kibrik and Kodzasov (1978: 101), where it is treated as a suprasegmental category.

However, the best known, and most discussed, and the most contentious question concerning Caucasian vocalism centres around the issue of the North-West Caucasian vowel systems. For languages, like those of the North-West Caucasian family, with large consonantal inventories, it is easy to imagine how some of the subtle differences that differentiate certain of the consonantal articulations need to be buttressed by the timbre differences that they impose upon neighbouring vowels. Now, the range of allophones for each vowel phoneme will obviously be quite large in languages endowed with perhaps as many as 83 consonants – this is, of course, the reason why one perceives so many vowel phones when listening to these languages being spoken. It thus follows that, for the system to work smoothly, a relatively small number of vowels will achieve efficiency of a high order. We shall, then, expect to discover minimal vowel systems in North-West Caucasian, but just how minimal are they? Herein lies the controversy.

In 1923 the great Caucasologist Jakovlev set up the triad /ə – a – aa/ as the vocalic system for Kabard. Trubetzkoy (1925), reinterpreting this triad, proposed the linear/vertical system of /ə – e – a/, where only the differing degrees of aperture (high, mid, low, respectively) are relevant for differentiating the phonemes. However, in 1956, on the basis of his analysis of material collected from an Abaza informant, Allen tentatively suggested a monovocalic interpretation for this language, the single vowel being /a/. Genko (1955) worked with two vowel phonemes /ə – a/ in this same language, but in a subsequent paper (1957: 199; quoted by Lomtatidze 1977: 34) he maintained that there were grounds for hypothesising the same monovocalic analysis as Allen; this was a conclusion reached independently of Allen, for Genko's work was actually prepared in the 1930s.

Then in 1960 Kuipers advanced the proposition that Kabard is (phonologically) a totally vowelless language. Having rejected the idea of any distinctive difference in aperture existing between Trubetzkoy's /e/ and /a/, Kuipers is left with the opposition /ə – a/. For the elimination of schwa as a phoneme he uses the arguments that, in initial and accented syllables, absence of /a/ implies the presence of schwa. By classifying consonants and consonant clusters according to the particular system Kuipers himself prescribes, the postaccentual occurrences of schwa can be predicted by simple rules. This leaves the question of schwa in noninitial preaccentual positions. Such schwas are analysed in terms of juncture phenomena, and this, in Kuiper's view, satisfactorily disposes of 'schwa' as a phoneme. He then argues that *a* be regarded merely as a consonantal feature of openness, on a level with such familiar features as labialisation and palatalisation. This line of argument allows him to postulate the existence of Kabard as a language devoid of (phonological) vowels.

Perhaps more interest was generated in the North-West Caucasian phonological systems than would otherwise have been the case (although no one would dispute their intrinsic claim for the linguist's attention) because of their typological parallels with the proposed reconstruction of Proto-Indo-European (without positing any necessary genetic connection) (Allen 1956: 172). However that may be, it was the

Indo-Europeanist Szemerényi who responded to the views of both Kuipers and Allen with a violent critique in 1967. Allen's second paper appeared in 1965, which was followed by Kuiper's apologia, published in 1968. The generative phonologist Halle entered the lists in 1970 with an article which rejected in detail the arguments of Kuipers (1960). Parts of Halle's refutation are also applicable to Allen's analysis of Abaza, so that for both languages we are left with the two vowel phonemes /ə/ and /a/.

As regards Ubykh, Dumézil (1958) admits only the same two vowels upon which Halle insists for the two sister-languages. However, Vogt (1963) further sets up the two long vowels /oo/ and /aa/, the former because of such an opposition as *səqʷᵊmáaloo* 'I shall play' (where *oo* can be shown to derive from **aw*): *səqʷᵊmáalaw* 'my game'; the latter because not all instances of phonetic *aa* are analysable as a conjunction of two instances of short *a* (e.g. *báada* 'all').

Three scholars have more recently expressed their opinions on this matter, and the evidence they adduce leads them to conclude that the extreme positions of Kuipers and Allen are not borne out by the facts. Kumaxov (1973) reverts to the three-way contrast /ə – e – a/ for Circassian languages, whilst allowing a binary opposition /ə – a/ for Abkhaz and Ubykh. Lomtatidze (1977: 37–45), restricting herself to a consideration of Abkhaz, agrees with the conclusion of Kumaxov, though she naturally deals in much greater detail with the Abkhaz data. Finally, Colarusso (1975) addresses himself to all the languages of the group and feels justified in positing only the binary opposition /ə – a/ for them all. And so, perhaps the last word on this matter has yet to be uttered.

We may close this section on phonology with a fleeting reference to the massive work of Gamkrelidze and Mačavariani (1965). An English summary of the essential conclusions of this magnum opus was presented by Gamkrelidze (1966). The Proto-Kartvelian sound system which these scholars reconstruct incorporates a binary vowel opposition of /*e – *a/, about which we read (1966: 80): 'We may envision an earlier stage of Common Kartvelian with no phonemic contrasts between vowels, assigning the two vowels **e* and **a* as allophones to one original vowel, which later split into different phonemic units according to the character of its allophones.' And so, Proto-Kartvelian too has a strong claim to be included in any typological studies involving Proto-Indo-European and North-West Caucasian.

5.3 Morphology

Widespread among North-East Caucasian and North-Central Caucasian is the distribution of nouns into classes. The nouns themselves generally do not carry any marker to indicate their class, though there are instances of nouns possessing their appropriate class-indicator (e.g. Avar *w-ac̄* 'brother', *j-ac̄* 'sister'):

the category may thus be styled covert. But the markers do appear in those words which contract a concord relationship with that noun which stands in the absolutive case. In Avar, for example, there are the three classes (a) human male, (b) human female, (c) neither, whose concord markers are (a) *w*, (b) *j*, (c) *b*, all correlating with the marker *r* (giving *l* in word-final position) when plural. And so we have the following illustration of concord relationships:

(85) ki-w-e   hit'ina-w w-as   une-w w-uge-w
      whither little   boy-ABS going COP-PART
      'where is the little boy going?'

(86) ki-j-e hit'ina-j j-as une-j j-ige-j
      'where is the little girl going?'

(87) ki-b-e k'udija-b bac' une-b b-uge-b
      'where is the big wolf going?'

(88) ki-r-e hit'ina-l łimal une-l r-uge-l
      'where are the little children going?'

   The number of classes in any given language varies; there are no classes in Lezgi, Agul, and Udi; two in nonliterary, northern Tabasaran; three in Avar, six of the Andi languages, and Dargva; four in Dido, Ginukh, Bezhti, Lak, and six languages of the Lezgian group; five in Andi – though the dialects vary in this respect – and Chamalal; six in Khvarsh, Gunzib, Chechen, and Ingush; and eight in Bats. In the singular there is always a distinction between human and nonhuman. The added division in the three-class languages is between male and female within the human class. The four-class languages tend to make a distinction between animals and other nonhuman objects, but this characterisation is not without exceptions. Whilst of the two five-class representatives Andi restricts its class III to animals, Chamalal in an apparently arbitrary manner allocates both animals and other objects to any of classes III, IV, and V. The Nakh languages carefully distinguish human male from human female (though *nuskal* 'bride' belongs to class III in Chechen at least), but there seems to be no rationale determining distribution among the remaining classes. Some languages have classes containing only one or two nouns, e.g. 'child' in Gunzib and 'child' and 'family' in Khvarsh. Different languages also amalgamate their classes in different ways in the plural: Dido and Ginukh have male human versus all others; Bezhti, Tsakhur, and Kryz have human versus nonhuman; Lak has animate versus inanimate; Budukh has male human, female human, and nonhuman; while Rutul, Archi, and Khinalug have no class distinctions in the plural.

   The nominal category of class does not feature in the South Caucasian languages, although various attempts have been made to find traces of such a system. Of the North-West Caucasian family, only Abkhaz–Abaza make any such distinctions, and these are restricted to an opposition human/nonhuman, which is relevant to the numeral system and partially to both the pronominal system and the pronominal affixes that appear in verbal complexes, in which latter case a third person singular affix marking either a transitive subject or an indirect object further distinguishes human male and human female, a distinction which also characterises the second person singular affixes. The independent pronouns, however, whilst preserving this distinction in the second person singular, have only two third person singular forms, namely *lará*, human female, and *jará*, human male and nonhuman.

Any survey of nominal characteristics will clearly have to include reference to the category of case. It is often stated that cases do not exist in Abkhaz–Abaza. Such a statement is too strong, for it neglects the predicative (adverbial) case in *-s*, e.g.

(89) *ħ°əzba-k°á-s   jə   -rə   -pχaʒó -jt'*
      knife   PL ADV 3PL-ABS 3PL-ERG regard FIN
      'they regard them as knives'

The postposition *-da* 'without', in association with singular nouns, may also appear to be interpretable as a case, but its true status as a postposition is revealed when construed with plural nouns, cf. singular *ħ°əzbá-da* 'without a knife' but plural *á-ħ°əzba-k°a rə́-da*, literally 'DEF-knife-PL they-WITHOUT', i.e. 'without the knives', where the suffix does not attach to the noun. The Circassian languages distinguish four cases: nominative, oblique (whose functions include those of ergative, dative, etc.), instrumental, and transformative (adverbial, which is the equivalent of the Abkhaz predicative or adverbial). On the other hand, there is a rich profusion of cases in North-Central Caucasian and North-East Caucasian (the maximum being 53 in one dialect of Tabasaran) resulting from the large numbers of locative cases, which no doubt derive from the coalescence of what were once nouns with postpositions (Mačavariani 1970: 167). It is customary to differentiate between basic or grammatical and local cases, and we shall return to the latter later.

As regards the grammatical cases, all our languages, except Abkhaz–Abaza (where the distinction is purely syntactic), distinguish an ergative and an absolutive. However, some languages use their ergative exclusively to represent the subject of transitive verbs, whereas in others some additional function is fulfilled by this same case: in Avar and the Andi group ergative and instrumental functions combine, in Lak ergative and genitive, in Svan ergative and adverbial, in some ergative and locative. Other grammatical cases also attested are the comparative case of Nakh, and the affective case (pp. 223–4) in six of the Andi languages and Tsakhur.

Table 5.7. *Locative cases in the Kubachi dialect of Dargva*

		Allative	Essive	Ablative
I	'on'	-že	-ži-w/j/b	-ži-l
II	'under'	-gu	-gu-w/j/b	-gu-l
III	'in front of'	-ta	-ta-w/j/b	-ta-l
IV	'in'	-če	-či-w/j/b	-či-l
V	'by, alongside'	-šu	-šu-w/j/b	-šu-l
VI	'inside, completely enveloped by'	-n(a)	-na-w/j/b	-na-l

A feature of the inflection of Avar, which is also found elsewhere in Dagestan, in North-Central Caucasian, and, to a limited extent, in Svan, is the so-called double-rooted declension, by which is meant that one oblique case-form acts as the base for the other oblique cases. This may be illustrated by the following Avar pattern: from the absolutive singular *wač* 'brother' one can form the ergative *wač-aš*, from which in turn one can form other cases, e.g. genitive *wač-aš-ul*, dative *wač-aš-e*; compare *jač* 'sister', ergative *jač-aɬ*, genitive *jač-aɬ-ul*, dative *jač-aɬ-e*.

As a typical example of how most of the North-East Caucasian and North-Central Caucasian languages create their impressive array of locatives, let us examine those of the Dargva dialect Kubachi. There are six series of locatives. Each series specifies a particular location ('in', 'under', etc.), and within each series there are three cases, the first expressing motion towards the location concerned (allative), the second simple stationary position (essive), the third movement away from the location (ablative). There is one basic exponent associated with each series and this acts as the allative component. From this allative the essive is produced by adding the class-marker appropriate to the concord-determining absolutive noun, whilst the ablative is derived from the allative by the addition of *-l*. This gives the pattern of Table 5.7 – the endings sometimes attach to the absolutive form, sometimes to the ergative. This gives examples like *kisa-n(a)* 'into the pocket', *bik'li-če* 'into the head', *laq'ujli-ta* '(to) in front of the cradle', *laq'ujli-ta-b* 'in front of the cradle', *laq'ujli-ta-l* 'from in front of the cradle'. Not all North-East Caucasian languages have such a wealth of locatives: Udi has only an ablative in *-(ax)-o*, an inessive/adessive in *-(as)-t'a*, an allative in *-(a)-č'*, and a superessive in *-(a)-l*; its other 'postpositional' cases are a comitative in *-(ax)-ol-(an)*, and a causative (benefactive) in *-(en)-k'ena/-en-k'*.

Udi, thus, bears a greater resemblance to South Caucasian, where Georgian, for instance, has six basic cases (nominative–absolutive, vocative, genitive, dative–accusative, instrumental, adverbial), plus eleven secondary cases which are based on the genitive, dative, and, in two instances, nominative, though the instrumental and adverbial each also serve as the base for a single postpositional case. The cases are: superessive (dative + *-ze*), inessive (dative + *-ši*), adessive dative + *-tan*), equative I (dative/nominative + *-vit*), benefactive (genitive + *-tvis*), directive (genitive + *-k'en*), ablative (genitive + *-gan*), temporal ('as soon as') (genitive + *-tanave*), equative II (genitive/nominative + *-(m)ebr*), elative (instrumental + *-dan*), terminative (adverbial + *-mde*).

Common to all Caucasian languages are personal, demonstrative, possessive, reflexive, interrogative, definite (e.g. 'each one', 'everyone'), and indefinite pronouns. Demonstratives fulfil the role of the personal pronouns of the third person where these latter are absent. For the personal pronouns of the first and second person no distinction is made between the absolutive and ergative in North-West Caucasian, South Caucasian, and ten North-East Caucasian languages. Svan, Avar, North-Central Caucasian, the Andi group, and about half the Lezgian languages have the opposition inclusive/exclusive in the first person plural; in Abkhaz, this also applies to the second person plural, though the distinction is not always observed for either first or second person. There is a general three-way deictic opposition 'this (near me)' 'that (near you, or visible to or quite close to us both, depending on language)', 'that (near him, or invisible or more remote from us both)'. But further degrees of deixis may be introduced, as in Lak, where, in addition to the above, *k'a* signifies 'that (up above)' and *ga* 'that (down below)'. Apart from *čaač'u* 'no-one' and *seeč'u* 'nothing' in the Kubachi dialect of Dargva, only in South Caucasian and in Bats (which has been heavily influenced by South Caucasian) do we find negative pronouns, the North Caucasian equivalent expressions being a combination of indefinite pronoun and negated verb.

Only in South Caucasian do we find relative pronouns – see pp. 228–30 for the syntax of North Caucasian relative clauses – which differ only minimally from the interrogatives. In Old Georgian three varieties of relative pronoun are attested: (a) pure equivalence with the interrogatives (e.g. *romeli* 'which one'); (b) interrogative + particle, which latter may be (i) a demonstrative (e.g. *romeli-igi*, where the demonstrative is invariable) or (ii) the coordinating clitic 'and' (e.g. *romeli-c(a)*); (c) interrogative + both these particles (e.g. *romeli-ca-igi*). In modern Georgian only type (bii) occurs (though the particle *-c* is sometimes absent, as in the genitive). In Mingrelian types (a) and (bi) are found (the Mingrelian demonstrative particle being *-ti*), whilst in Svan, though types (bi) and (bii) are not unknown, the most frequent variety is (c) with the suffixes in reverse, e.g. Upper Bal *jär* 'who?' and *jer-vää-j* 'who (relative)', where *-j* is the coordinating particle and *-va-* a pronominal root.

Attributive adjectives sometimes do not alter at all when their head noun declines (North-West Caucasian, Mingrelian, Svan, Udi), sometimes they agree with the noun in number (Kubachi), sometimes they manifest an absolutive and an oblique form (Nakh), whilst consonant-stem adjectives in Georgian (these being the majority) have one form for nominative, genitive, and instrumental, another for dative and adverbial, and one each for vocative and ergative. Vowel-stem adjectives do not change at all. Substantivised adjectives usually simply behave as nouns, but in Nakh the absolutive singular carries an extra marker (e.g. Chechen *leqa-nig* 'the high one', cf. *leqa kert* 'high fence'); substantivised participles in Nakh also have their own markers for the absolutive singular.

The comparative grade may be formed analytically (e.g. with Georgian *upro*, Abkhaz *jaħá* 'more'), synthetically (e.g. Chechen *dika* 'good', *dika-x* 'better' – note that intensification of the medial consonant, *dik̄a-x*, intensifies the meaning to 'even better'), or it may not be expressed by any morphological exponent, being rather a function of the syntax: compare Andi *čonči wošo* 'good boy' and

(90)   *joši   wošu-č'u čonči (i)*
        girl-ABS boy   ON good is
        'the girl is better than the boy'

This construction exactly parallels the alternative Georgian formation:

(91)   *ama   -ze grʒeli c'erili*
        this-one ON long letter
        'a letter longer than this one'

Superlatives are usually formed periphrastically, as in Chechen, where *uggar* 'most' precedes the positive form, or in Georgian, where *q'vela-ze* 'on (i.e. than) all' precedes either the positive or analytic comparative, though Georgian also has the circumfix *u-...-esi*, which may have comparative or superlative force as in *u-lamaz-esi* 'more/most beautiful' from *lamazi* 'beautiful'.

Adverbs may coincide with adjectives (Avar, Chechen, etc.), or derive from adjectives by the addition of an adverbial ending (South Caucasian, North-West Caucasian).

The cardinal system is vigesimally based, except in Lak, Dargva, and Archi, though in some subdialects of Avar, particularly Durangi, a system based on units of ten is also recorded (Čikobava and Cercvadze 1962: 203), as also in the Lashkh and Upper Bal dialects of Svan.

The languages are almost exclusively postpositional.

Negation is by no means treated uniformly. Adyge suffixes *-(r)ăp* to the positive of its finite verbal forms, whilst *m(ə)-* is placed before the root of nonfinite (including imperative) forms. In Abkhaz *m(ə)-* is similarly the only possibility for nonfinite forms, whereas finite forms, although they use only this same exponent, place it preradically or word-finally (or there will be a final sequence *-m-z-t'*) depending on the tense. Kubachi similarly employs prefixed, infixed, or suffixed negative particles depending on the tense of the verb (Magometov 1954: 208). Avar has only suffixes and apportions them as follows: *-ro* (present and future), *-č'o* (aorist), *-ge* (imperative). It is usual for there to be at least a special particle for prohibitions, as in Chechen, where *ma* is used for prohibitions, as against *ca* elsewhere. Georgian has developed the three-fold opposition, *ar* for simple negation, *nu* for prohibitions, *ver* for negative capability ('cannot'); this three-fold distinction is also applicable to the negative pronouns, adjectives, and adverbs.

As finite subordinate clauses are virtually restricted to South Caucasian, only in this group do we find subordinating conjunctions.

If the North-East Caucasian and North-Central Caucasian languages are generally endowed with rich noun declensions, their verbal complexes are correspondingly rather simple. It is possible to classify the languages into four groups depending upon their type of conjugation: (a) conjugation by noun class only (Chechen, Ingush, Avar–Andi–Dido group, the majority of the Lezgian group); (b) conjugation by class and person (Bats, Lak, Dargva, Tabasaran); (c) conjugation by person only (Udi); (d) conjugation by neither class nor person (Agul, Lezgi itself). And so, the only type of exponent appearing within the verbal complexes and common to all these languages will be the varying sets of suffixes each individual language employs to build its own system of tenses, moods, participles, gerunds, verbal nouns, and infinitives. Thus, while the overall system may be quite extensive, the structure of any given complex will be relatively simple.

Given the impressive arrays of locative cases we have seen to be characteristic of North-Central Caucasian and North-East Caucasian as a whole, it will come as no surprise to learn that there are languages in this area (such as Avar, Lak, etc.) which make no accommodation in their verbal complexes for either directional or orientational preverbs. However, it certainly is surprising not merely to find such preverbs attested in these languages at all, but to see their extent and the systems associated with them. In Tabasaran, directional preverbs recapitulate not only the meaning of the locative cases but also their forms (e.g. *k̄-* 'under', *q-* 'behind', *ɣ-* 'between', *k-* 'against', *ʔ-* 'in', *x̌-* 'around', *il-* 'on'). Dargva has a system of the four orientational preverbs as follows: *ka-batij* 'to give (downwards)', *ha-batij* 'to give (upwards)', *sa-batij* 'to give (hither)', *bid-batij* 'to give (thither)'. This is in addition to a full set of directional preverbs.

As stated earlier in the discussion on noun classes, where examples will be found, the class marker in verbs taking class markers (and in those languages where class is a feature of the conjugation by no means all verbs accommodate them) always agrees in class with the absolutive noun phrase. Where a verb does contain a slot for a class marker, such a slot will almost without exception be prefixal. If, on the other hand, the language has developed a personal conjugation, then the personal endings will agree with the verb's subject, which may be in a variety of cases (ergative for transitive verbs, absolutive for intransitive, dative for verbs of feeling or perception). Note, however, that there are examples from Tabasaran of verbs agreeing by person with both subject and direct object together (Magometov 1965: 202 ff.). The personal endings of Bats, Udi, and Tabasaran are quite clearly derived from the appropriate case form of the relevant personal pronoun, as is seen in these examples from Tabasaran:

(92)   *uzu   aldakura-zu*
        I-ABS fall   1SG
        'I fall'

(93)   *uwu   aldakura-wu*
        you-SG-ABS fall   2SG
        'you fall'

(94)   *uzuz   uwu   ƙunǯa(-zuz)*
        I-DAT you-ABS love   1SG
        'I love you'

In Kubachi, though not in Dargva proper or Lak, the personal endings are identical to the corresponding forms of the copula.

Causatives are formed in some instances morphologically, in others analytically; indeed both synthetic and analytic causatives may exist in the same language, for example in Lezgi, where the morphological type is chiefly used to produce causatives from basically intransitive roots, whereas the analytic variety is the more usual means if the embedded verb is transitive (Topuria 1959: 83–5). Examples of matrix verbs used are 'to do/make' (Avar, Nakh), 'to allow' (Lezgi), and 'to overcome' (Kubachi).

In comparison with the relatively uncomplicated structures of North-Central Caucasian and North-East Caucasian, the picture in South Caucasian is somewhat more complex. Deeters (1930: 6) lists twelve meaning-bearing elements that may appear in a Kartvelian verb complex, although they may not all appear at one and the same time:

1. Preverb(s)
2. Personal prefix(es) (subjective or objective)
3. Character- or version-vowel
4. Root
5. Passive suffix *-en/-d*
6. Causative suffix(es)

7. Plural suffix (for nominative–absolutive noun)
8. Present stem-formant
9. Imperfect suffix
10. Mood-vowel
11. Personal ending
12. Subjective plural suffix

We notice immediately that South Caucasian has a synthetic causative; while double causatives are feasible, in practice they are extremely rare. With reference to the passive, of all Caucasian languages only South Caucasian possesses a fully developed passive morphology. For reasons of space, consideration of the South Caucasian verb must be restricted to items 1, 2, 3, and 7 above.

The preverbs may be divided into those that signify direction and those that indicate orientation. Of the former there are seven in Georgian (more in Laz and Mingrelian, fewer in Svan), of the latter Georgian has two: *mo-* 'hither', *mi-* 'thither' (where 'hither' is defined as motion towards first or second person). In Georgian, only *mo-* combines as second member with the directional preverbs, for lack of *mo-* implies 'thither'-deixis. But this original state of affairs is preserved only for verbs of motion, as exemplified by the verb 'to carry':

a-a-kv-s	'he carries it up (*a-*) thither'
a-mo-a-kv-s	'he carries it up (*a-*) hither (*mo-*)'
še-a-kv-s	'he carries it in (*še-*) thither'
še-mo-a-kv-s	'he carries it in (*še-*) hither (*mo-*)'

However, the most common function of the preverbs in modern South Caucasian is to mark perfective aspect, so that the present and imperfect tenses of most verbs (other than those indicating motion) will be without preverbs, whereas the preverb appropriate to the root in question will appear in the aorist and future (perfective future in Svan, while Laz regularly has a different future formation altogether), e.g. Svan (Lentekh dialect) *a-mar-e* 'he prepares it', *an-a-mar-i* 'he will prepare it', as against the imperfective future *a-mar-wn-i* 'he will be preparing it' (Topuria 1967: 245a). Another function of the preverbs is to form new verbs, so that from the Georgian root *š(a)l*, we can produce *a-šla* 'to loosen', *ga-šla* 'to spread', *da-šla* 'to dissolve', *mo-šla* 'to break up', *še-šla* 'to derange', *c'a-šla* 'to erase'. As the preverbs are excluded from the imperfective, the context alone must determine which meaning is appropriate in such cases.

By means of their personal prefixes the South Caucasian languages mark subject, direct objects, and indirect objects, but this does not mean that, if all these three arguments stand together in a sentence, each will correlate with its own affix within the verbal complex. Only one pronominal affix is permitted preradically in the modern languages, so that rules are required stating which affix will appear from any particular sequence: for instance, for the combination 'first person singular subject + second person direct object', the first person affix disappears, as in Georgian *g-abruneb* (for **v-g-abruneb*) 'I turn you', Svan *žə-t'xə* (for **xw-žə-t'xə*) 'I turn you'. As the third person direct object affix is zero, it will be obvious that the question of affix-reduction is somewhat simplified. Should both direct and indirect objects be first or second person, then Georgian solves this difficulty by turning the problematic direct object into a third person form, as follows: 'he gives you to me' is rephrased as 'he gives your head to me':

(95)   *igi   šens tav -s   m   -aʒlev-s*
         he-NOM your head ACC 1SG-OBJ give   3SG-SU

Pronominal affixes are only found in finite verbal forms, and herein lies an important difference in comparison with North-West Caucasian.

There are four types of 'version' in South Caucasian, and they are represented by their appropriate vowel(s), placed immediately before the root. The four types are: (a) subjective, (b) objective, (c) superessive/locative, and (d) neutral. Type (a), whose vowel is *i-*, is used in transitive verbs to show that the subject is acting upon his own person, upon an article he happens to be wearing, or, generally, in his own interest, as in (96) from Mingrelian, (97) from Georgian, (98) from Svan, and (99) from Georgian again:

(96)   *p'is   i-bon -s*

(97)   *p'irs   i-ban -s*
         face-ACC   wash 3SG
         'he washes his face'

(98)   *xw -i-qni*

(99)   *v   -i-xnav*
         1SG plough
         'I plough it (for myself)'

Type (b) indicates a special relationship between subject and indirect object for intransitive verbs, and between direct and indirect objects of transitives; the relationship may be one of possession or it may be that the action is done in the interest of the indirect object or in his vicinity; example (100) is from Svan, (101) from Georgian:

(100)   x   -o-rdi   -(∅)

(101)   (∅)   -u-zrdi   -s
             FOR-HIM   raises 3SG
             'he raises him for him'

(In these last examples, three different participants are involved.)

The superessive/locative version serves to show that the action is such as to place the direct object upon the indirect, or, in the case of intransitive verbs, the subject will be shown to be upon the indirect object; the vowel is a-, as in Georgian:

(102)   mč'ad -s   niaxur-i   da   -v   -a-č'eri
             shashlik DAT celery   ABS PREV 1SG   cut-AOR
             'I cut the celery over the shashlik'

The vowel for the neutral version is also a-, but there is no special function that can be ascribed to it; it is merely a necessary (and, therefore, meaningless) element in the structure of some verbs – as a general rule, all denominals will have it – as in Georgian:

(103)   v   -a-tetreb
             1SG   whiten
             'I whiten it'

Cf. *tetri* 'white'. The subjective version also has a role to play in the formation of one type of passive, whilst the objective version is also crucial to the formation of the third (perfect) tense-group, but these are secondary developments that cannot be examined here.

In Old Georgian, the plurality of a third person absolutive noun (either intransitive subject or transitive direct object) was indicated by means of a postradical plural marker in verbs in the aorist tense. Modern Svan still has the facility of indicating such plurality. The absolutive plural nominal marker is -al, and it is this element which is used (just as Old Georgian used -(e)n, its nominal plural marker being -n(i)). This gives, in the Upper Bal dialect, a-maar-e 'he prepares it', but a-maar-ääl-i 'he prepares them'. As Svan is like Georgian in having a dative–accusative direct object in the present series of tenses, we may assume that this use of the suffix -al in verbs has been extended to other tenses from being limited originally to the aorist (where the verbal affix and the pluraliser on this affix's coreferential noun would have been formally identical), as was the corresponding suffix in Old Georgian. Modern Georgian still contrives to observe this distinction in a number of marginal instances, though the means are different: apart from the few verbal roots which have suppletive forms to mark plurality of their direct objects (if transitive) or subjects (if intransitive), several verbs, in their perfective tenses, use the preverb *da-* to indicate such plurality in place of the preverb normally associated with them.

Any complexity that might strike the reader as being characteristic of the verb complexes of South Caucasian to judge by the evidence of the presentation just offered pales into insignificance when we turn to the complexes of North-West Caucasian, where the extreme polypersonalism is such that virtually the entire syntactic structure of the sentence is recapitulated in the verb. Verbs are divided into stative and dynamic. Although the former manifest a number of differences in comparison with the latter, we shall concentrate rather on the dynamic verbs in attempting to convey as clear an idea as possible in the space available of the variety of exponents that may appear in the verb complex. Since the complexes of all North-West Caucasian languages conform to virtually the same structural pattern, we shall concentrate on Abkhaz below.

There exist three sets or columns of pronominal affixes, of which column I correlates with intransitive subjects and transitive direct objects (i.e. absolutive), column II with indirect objects, column III with transitive subjects (i.e. ergative); in Abkhaz, in the absence of case-marking for the major verbal arguments, only by reference to these affixes can we determine the precise role a noun phrase is playing in the sentence. In North-West Caucasian as a whole, these affixes indicate person and number only, but, as remarked upon earlier, Abkhaz distinguishes humans from nonhumans in column I for the third person singular, and male humans from female humans in both the second person singular and columns II and III of the third person singular; for details of the actual forms in North-West Caucasian languages, see Paris (1969). Each series of affixes is ordered crucially with respect not only to the other series but also to the other exponents that enter into the complex. Preceding the root, which usually consists, like most North-West Caucasian roots, of a single consonant or consonant + vowel, there are ten essential elements, ordered thus:

1	2	3	4
Column I –	Adverbial –	Conjunction/Question –	Relation –

5	6	7	8	9
Orientation –	Column II –	Direction –	Column III –	Negation –

10	
Causative –	Root

This notation requires some elucidation. What we have already said about the pronominal affixes means that, regarding slots 1, 6, and 8, we need only elaborate on the column I position by noting that the reflexive affix ç(ə)- will occupy this position if it is functioning as direct object (if the reflexive is indirect object, there will be no reflexive affix in the complex); in this case it will be preceded by the appropriate possessive marker, and possessive affixes are identical to column II affixes. In Abaza this possessive affix is absent as a result of Circassian influence, where the reflexive affix takes the form z(ə)-. Lacking any possessive prefix but also possible in place of a column I affix are ak'ər-/ak'rə- 'something' and eǵ- (with negation) 'nothing'. A column II affix will also always precede what we have styled above 'relation(al) particles)', of which there are four main ones: a- 'addressing oneself to', z(ə)- 'for' (benefactive), ć°(ə)- 'to the detriment of', c(ə)- 'with'. Also possible here is the marker of unwillingness amxa-. The column III affix and all column II affixes (except that accompanying the reflexive ç(ə)-) may be replaced, under appropriate conditions, by reciprocal markers (Hewitt: 1979b). All pronominal affixes, once again under appropriate conditions, may be replaced by a relative affix; see pp. 229–30.

Two adverbial elements, ajta- and aǵ-, both meaning 'again', may occupy slot 2.

Slot 3 is taken by four elements that function as conjunctional particles, and their presence requires the verb to be nonfinite; they are an(ə)- 'when', ş(ə)- 'how', ax(ə)- 'where', z(ə)- 'why'. By adding the particle ba-, we obtain the corresponding interrogative forms, hence the notation Conjunction/Question.

The fifth slot belongs to four orientational preverbs: aa- 'hither', na- 'thither', la- 'downwards', j°a- 'upwards', this being the same orientational system as earlier described for Dargva (p. 213). By far the most common of these is aa-, which can convey a variety of other nuances depending upon the root with which it is associated. Note that if the verb complex contains a directional preverb at slot 7, then any orientational preverb will stand after term 3, i.e. before the sequence: column II affix + relational particle. These preverbs may even occupy this slot in the absence of a directional preverb:

(104)   j   -aa   -sə   -zə́ -m   -k'ə -jt'
           3SG-INAN HITHER 1SG-COL-II POT NEG seize FIN
           'I couldn't get hold of it'

Term 7 is represented by the directional preverbs and also by the so-called determiners, which are nouns functioning as preverbs; if determiner and directional preverb co-occur, the determiner stands first. Both may govern an indirect object, column II affix, so that in such circumstances one might almost describe them as intraverbal postpositions. An interesting feature of both types of element is that many of them have two forms, one with a and one without (sometimes with ə).

Presence versus absence of *a* corresponds to the meaning difference illative/ablative, as in the following examples:

(105) *də*   *-c'a*   *-lá -zaap'*
       3SG-HUM-COL-I (TO)-UNDER go INFER
       'he apparently crawled under it'

(106) *w*   *-á*   *-c'ə*   *-m   -c'ə*
       2SG-MALE-COL-I 3SG-COL-II (FROM)-UNDER NEG come
       -n
       PROHIB
       'don't come out from under it'

   The negative particle *m(ə)-* occupies slot 9 in all nonfinite forms, including the imperative (and a subsidiary word-final *-n* also appears in such prohibitive forms), as well as in certain finite complexes.

   The causative formative immediately precedes the root. Double morphological causatives are not permitted in Abkhaz, although Abaza, under Circassian influence, does allow them.

   In practice the postradical structure of the complex is usually relatively straightforward in comparison with the preradical structure. However, the number of elements which in theory may occur here is extremely large (Šaduri: 1974). Let us address ourselves first to the question of finite versus nonfinite forms. All North-West Caucasian languages allow only one finite verb to appear in each sentence, and so they possess a variety of nonfinite forms. All North-West Caucasian languages concur in requiring the negative particle of their nonfinite forms to be prefixed before the root no matter what its place in the corresponding finite form. With the exception of this fundamental change, and a few minor alterations, virtually all finite forms in Ubykh and Circassian may function as nonfinites – and this means, among other things, that they may take case-endings and act as nouns. However, Abkhaz diverges from its sister-languages in this respect. Each tense has its own finite ending, which disappears when the nonfinite form is required, so that each tense has its own special finite and nonfinite correlates. We shall say no more about tense suffixes (be they finite or nonfinite) or mood suffixes, apart from underlining that they stand after the root, as in all other Caucasian languages.

   Immediately after the root we may find one of two suffixes, *-aa* or *-la*, which are obviously related to two of the orientational preverbs seen above; these suffixes require a directional preverb to stand preradically, and *-la* will be used if the preverb is in its *a*-grade, *-aa* with the zero-grade. Various adverbials also occupy this position, such as *-x* 'again' and some intensifiers like *-ć°q̇'a* 'indeed', *-la*, which stresses the repeated nature of the action, and *-ʒa*, the (generally negative) intensifier. The nominal plural marker for nonhuman nouns, *-k°a*, is also found here emphasising the plurality of any of the preradical affixes (Hewitt: 1979c), although one wonders if originally it might not have been limited to stressing the plurality of intransitive subjects or transitive direct objects, as was *-(e)n* in Old Georgian, and, indeed, as is the corresponding pluraliser *-x* for the third person in the modern Circassian languages. At any rate, this suffix *-k°a* may also indicate the manifold nature of the verbal action, just as may the corresponding pluraliser *-al* in Svan, so that it almost parallels the meaning of the repetitive suffix *-la* in this function:

(107) jə   -q'a   -l   -c'a-ló-n
       3SG-INAN-COL-I PREVERB 3SG-FEM-COL-III do
       (*-la   -wa   -n)
            ITER DYN IMPERF
       'She used to do it regularly'

(108) *jə-q'a-l-c'a-k°ó-n (*-k°a-wa-n)*
                            PL
       'she used to do it several times'

This conveniently introduces the element *-wa*, which appears in the present and imperfect tenses. It is interpreted as the characteristic marker of dynamic verbs. Kabard also preserves such a dynamic marker, but in this language the relevant affix appears preradically.

Following *-wa* may stand the special question particles *-da* 'who(m)?', *-zəj/-zej/-j* 'what?'. After the nonfinite marker *-z* come the conjunctional, or perhaps rather postpositional, elements *-cəpχaʒa* 'every time that', *-aanʒa* 'until', *-nac'ə* 'as long as', and *-jžtej* 'since'. Mention should also be made of the conditional particle *-r*, to which may be added *-c*, thereby producing a purposive or purpose clause equivalent.

Various other postradical components could be introduced into this discussion, but we may close by observing that, where the finite markers *-(j)t'*, *-w-p'* occur, the only element that may follow them is the clitic *-ej*, used to indicate a strong contrast or contradiction, or strong assertion.

To summarise, then, one of the most significant features of the North-West Caucasian languages is the extraordinary polypersonalism of their verb complexes. Since there exists a high degree of uniformity in the structure of these complexes between all the languages of this group, although no-one would pretend that anything like a one-to-one correspondence obtains (and even where the morphemes do closely correspond, there may be no similarity of actual morphs), it was deemed advantageous to present a fairly detailed, though by no means complete, description of the verb complex in just one member of this language family, Abkhaz. It is hoped that the reader will now at least have an accurate appreciation of just what is meant by the term polypersonalism as it is applied to these languages. Since it should now be clear what a vast amount of information these languages can convey in so small an amount of phonic material (given the monoconsonantal nature of many of their morphemes), it would be difficult to imagine how languages could differ more sharply in respect of the structure of their verb complexes than those of North-West Caucasian, on the one hand, and Lezgi and Agul on the other.

5.4 Syntax

As a general rule preferred sentence word order is subject–object–verb, although subject–verb–object is by no means uncommon, especially in South Caucasian. As already observed, the languages are predominantly postpositional. Adjectives in South Caucasian, North-Central Caucasian, and North-East Caucasian normally precede their nouns, but in North-West Caucasian only those signifying nationality, indefinite adjectives, and ordinals may do so, adjective + noun or noun + adjective in North-West Caucasian often forming a single compound word. Adnominal genitives also generally precede their nouns, and indeed they must do so in North-West Caucasian. The North-West Caucasian possessive construction differs from that of the other Caucasian languages and resembles that of Turkish: not only does the possessor stand in the genitive, which is identical to the dative and ergative (and we are here talking specifically of Circassian and Ubykh, for these case endings do not exist in Abkhaz–Abaza), but the possessed noun also carries the appropriate pronominal possessive prefix. A unique feature of Adyge (together with the Besleney dialect of Kabard-Cherkes) is the distinction between alienable and inalienable possession. The inalienable set, which includes blood relatives (except for *ană* 'mother' and *ată* 'father') (Rogava 1974), is marked by attachment of the simple personal prefix to the head noun:

(109)   ł'ə -m   ə   -nă
         man GEN 3SG eye
         'the man's eye'

For alienable objects, a compound prefix is used, which consists of the personal prefix plus *j-* as the marker of alienability:

(110)   sə   -j-wəna
         1SG   house
         'my house'

Since, in a work of this nature, a detailed study of the syntax of some 38 languages is out of the question, we shall now concentrate on two main topics: ergativity and relative clause formation.

It is well-known that the Caucasus is the only region in Europe where large numbers of ergative languages are located. And it was the discovery of ergativity in the Caucasus that first aroused the interest of western scholars in these languages. With the sole exception of Mingrelian, ergativity is a phenomenon which is relevant to all Caucasian languages. The typical ergative language will have a special case (ergative) to mark the subject of transitive verbs, whilst direct objects and subjects of intransitive verbs will stand in the same case (absolutive). We can illustrate this with an Avar example:

(111)   *wač   -aš   šiša   b   -ekana*
           brother ERG bottle-ABS CLASS-III broke
           'the brother broke the bottle'

(112)   *šiša b-ekana*
           'the bottle broke'

Incidentally, we meet here in passing another regular feature of North-East Caucasian, namely that verb roots may be either transitive or intransitive depending upon the syntax of the sentence: in the presence of an ergative subject they are transitive, otherwise intransitive; these are the so-called labile verbs.

However, there is more to the question of Caucasian ergativity than the simple presentation of such a canonical ergative structure. First, we must mention that verbs of feeling or perception in North-Central Caucasian and North-East Caucasian are frequently treated completely differently. Some nine North-East Caucasian languages have a special affective case, whose function is to represent the subject of such verbs, as in Andi:

(113)   *imuwo   woči   w   -uson*
           father-AFF brother-ABS CLASS-I found
           'father found (his) brother'

Languages not possessing a special affective case may use the dative (Chechen, Lezgi, etc.), or, as happens in Avar, the dative for verbs of feeling but one of the locative cases for those of perception. South Caucasian has a number of so-called inverted verbs requiring a dative subject, but the verbs of this type are not in one-to-one correspondence with the North-Central and North-East Caucasian verbs of feeling and perception; the typical construction for the perfect series of tenses in South

Caucasian is also inverted, in as much as the subject stands in the dative with transitive verbs, the direct object in the nominative–absolutive.

The situation in South Caucasian is somewhat anomalous. Georgian and Svan restrict their ergative construction to the aorist series (indicative, subjunctive, and imperative). We have just observed what happens in the perfect series, and yet another construction applies to the present series: subject in the nominative–absolutive, direct object in the dative–accusative. There are two verbs in modern Georgian, both meaning 'to know', which have an ergative subject (and nominative–absolutive direct object) in the present tense, but these are fossilised so-called permansives, which in Old Georgian (and some modern mountain dialects) form an aspectual (habitual) derivative of the aorist stem; hence they require the typically aorist construction. The probable primary state of affairs prevailing in Svan and Georgian has been developed by Laz and Mingrelian, each in its own way: Mingrelian has extended the range of the ergative case so that it now designates all subjects of aorist verbs, transitive or intransitive, and the result is that the Mingrelian so-called ergative case has become a redundant aorist marker, and the language no longer exhibits any true ergative construction. Laz, on the other hand, has extended the range of the ergative so that it marks all transitive subjects regardless of tense (present, aorist, and noninverted perfect). Wherever the ergative is used, the direct object stands in the absolutive. (It may be observed at this point that in Udi the direct object is found not only in the absolutive but also in both of Udi's dative cases, a fact which has stimulated a debate about the possibility of there being an accusative case in Udi.) Finally, in connection with South Caucasian, we should note that, even outside Mingrelian, cases of the ergative accompanying intransitive verbs are not rare. This has in turn given rise to a recently expressed view (Klimov 1976; Harris 1976) that South Caucasian should not be regarded as representative of ergative languages, but rather of active languages. However, it must be said that, as the traditionally interpreted ergative case is not found with anything like all active (agentive) verbs, little seems to be gained by this departure.

An interesting, but severely limited feature of Bats, is that a small number of intransitive verbs take an ergative first or second (but not third) person subject, where the subject deliberately effects the action, but an absolutive subject if the subject is unintentionally affected by the action: Dešeriev (1953: 226) lists six such verbs (e.g. 'to be anxious/worry').

Despite its lack of case endings, we know that Abkhaz–Abaza is ergative because of the concord relationships established between the verb arguments and the series of pronominal affixes in the verb complex, the column I affix correlating with transitive direct objects and intransitive subjects, the column III affix only with transitive subjects. We thus see that the verb 'to hit' is intransitive (taking an indirect object):

(114)   s   -bɔ́   -s -we -jt'
         1SG-COL-I 2SG-FEM-COL-II hit DYN FIN
         'I hit you'

This may be compared with a regular transitive structure:

(115)   sə   -b   -bó-jt' (*-ba -wa -jt')
         1SG-COL-I 2SG-FEM-COL-III   see DYN FIN
         'you see me'

Certain verbs in Circassian languages permit both the regular ergative construction and the, as it were, reversed or so-called antipassive configuration exemplified in Abkhaz sentence (114), as in the following two Bzhedug sentences:

(116)   č'aɮ̆ă-m   ç'əg°ə-r   (∅)   -j   -ă -ź°ă
         boy OBL field   ABS 3SG-COL-I 3SG-COL-III DYN plough
         'the boy is ploughing the field'

(117)   č'aɮ̆ă-r   ç'əg°ə-m   (∅)   -j   -ă -ź°ă
         boy ABS field   OBL 3SG-COL-I 3SG-COL-II DYN plough
         'the boy is ploughing away at the field'

Sentences of type (117) are rarer, and more marked, than those of type (116). There is also a significant difference in meaning between the two: (116) means 'the boy is ploughing/ploughs the field', while (117) means rather 'the boy is ploughing away at the field'. Type (116) sentences may be described as effect-orientated, in that they indicate a bond between verb and object, whereas type (117) expressions focus our attention on the subject (Catford 1977: 306; Colarusso 1977: 132); alternatively, the ergative construction may be described as 'aim-ful', implying the actor's intention to carry the action to completion, whereas the second construction is 'aim-less', in that the action is not necessarily completed, for we are merely interested in the subject's activity at the time of discourse. If this description of the ergative construction as effect-orientated and, conversely, the interpretation of the antipassive construction as subject-orientated is correct, then we are approaching an explanation of why the ergative is often confined to past, perfective tense–aspects (as in the case of Georgian and Svan among the Caucasian languages); by definition, the action of a past perfective verb is completed and its effect has been achieved, whereas the action of a nonpast imperfective verb is, equally by definition, incomplete, telling us more about the relationship between subject and verb than between direct object and verb.

Abkhaz does not admit any choice between ergative and antipassive constructions of the sort we have just described for Circassian, and no data are available for Ubykh. However, similar choices do occur in Dagestan languages, for instance in Dargva:

(118)   *nu-ni   žuz   b   -uč'ul-ra*
         I   ERG book-ABS CLASS-III read 1SG
         'I read the book'

(119)   *nu   žuz -li   (Ø)   -uč'ul-ra*
         I-ABS book ERG CLASS-I read 1SG
         'I am reading the book'

The semantic distinction nondurative versus durative is suggested by Byxovskaja (1938).

The situation in Avar is somewhat different, although the double absolutive sentence-type to be examined in Avar is also found in the majority of the Dagestan languages (Kibrik 1979). One may choose the ergative or nonergative construction only for the compound tenses consisting of present participle and copula, tenses which are inherently durative, e.g. (S. Crisp – personal communication):

(120)   *hez   nux   ha-b-ule-b   b   -ugo*
         they-ERG road-ABS making-CLASS-III CLASS-III COP
         'they are building the road'

(121)   *hel   nux   ha-b   -ule-l   r-ugo*
         they-ABS road-ABS   CLASS-III   CLASS-I-PL COP
         'they are engaged on building the road'

It stands out immediately that the configuration present in (121) is not exactly the reverse of that in (120), for, although the subject is indeed absolutive, the object is also absolutive and not ergative.

The Nakh languages are in fairly close agreement with Avar. We shall illustrate with Chechen examples. The basic transitive structure (with a noncompound verb) may be exemplified by the simple sentence:

(122)   *as   bolx   b   -o*
         I-ERG work-ABS CLASS-V do
         'I do work'

A parallel for the Avar sentence (121) will be:

(123)   *so   bolx   b   -eš   w   -u*
         I-ABS work-ABS CLASS-V doing-GER CLASS-I COP

Jakovlev (1940) styles this type of structure the generalising construction since 'it expresses the action . . . as the usual occupation of the subject, as his professional occupation'. The example may be glossed 'I am in the habit of working' or 'I usually work'. Note that the gerund appears where Avar employs the present participle, but that it still agrees with its own direct object by virtue of its class prefix, whilst the class-marker on the copula is in concord with the sentential subject.

The Chechen construction parallel to Avar (120) would be:

(124)   *bolx   as   b   -eš   b   -u*
          work-ABS I-ERG CLASS-V doing CLASS-V COP

This structure is designated the processual construction and is described as expressing 'the subject's being in the process of acting upon a definite individual object, in such a way that the process of action occupies not only the given, concrete moment, but also a span of time up to and beyond the present moment'. We may thus translate: 'I am involved in (a particular) piece of work'. Observe the peculiar word order associated with this latter type of structure. While Avar and Chechen manifest quite close formal parallelisms, from a semantic viewpoint there are considerable differences, in particular the Avar double-absolutive construction with compound verb seems to correlate with the Chechen ergative construction with compound verb, rather than with its formal near-equivalent. These variations on the ergative theme serve to demonstrate that ergativity is by no means a unified phenomenon in Caucasian languages.

Relative clause formation in South Caucasian is straightforward, as it basically follows the normal Indo-European pattern of relative pronoun plus finite verb, together with variants involving participial phrases, which, as with adjectives generally, will precede their head nouns. The following is an example of a participial relative from Georgian:

(125)   *ʒlivsʒlivobit   daašora   mat   tavisi*
          with-great-difficulty he-separated from-them his-own
          siʒe   mis - gan dat'anʒulma p'lat'on-ma
          brother-in-law-ABS him by   tormented Plato   ERG
          'with great difficulty did Plato, who had himself been tormented by him
          (sc. his brother-in-law), separate his brother-in-law from them'

The last three words may be expressed, more expansively, by a full relative clause:

(126)   *. . . p'lat'onma, vin-c   misgan dat'anʒuliq'o*
                        who REL   he-had-been-tormented

Mingrelian, however, exhibits some interesting features, as in the following example (Hewitt 1977):

(127)   *so   re ti boši namusu -tu c'igni   mepči*
           where is that boy to-whom REL book-ABS I-gave-it-to-him
           'where is the boy to whom I gave the book?'

In this simple relative clause we have an ordinary finite verb in the aorist, and the only mark of subordination is the relative pronoun. However, we may add to the verb a subordinating enclitic particle -*n*(*i*). We may now do away with the relative pronoun and move what remains of the subordinate clause into the position preceding the head noun. The result is the most acceptable and natural Mingrelian equivalent of the English sentence above:

(128)   *c'igni mepči-ni ti boši so re*

Once the subordinate clause is in this preposed position and virtually functioning as a participial expression, the subordinating enclitic may be omitted, so that the only sign of the subordinate status of *c'igni mepči* is its position in front of the head noun.

    The participial construction is the only possible means of producing relative clauses in all the North Caucasian languages, but there are many differences which force us to treat North-West Caucasian separately. In North-East Caucasian and North Central Caucasian the participial expression must precede the head noun. All arguments of the verb remain in the same cases as they would have shown in the full clause to which the relative participial construction corresponds; in this respect the participial constructions of North Caucasian differ sharply from participial relatives in South Caucasian, the peculiar Mingrelian construction illustrated above crucially retaining its finite verb, which correlates with the absence of change to the cases of the verbal arguments in such relative expressions in that language. In Avar, all participials end in a class marker, and this marker is always determined by the class of the head noun. However, it will be recalled that verbs containing class markers as a rule accommodate them prefixally, so that many participles will contain two class markers. In such circumstances, the first class-marker will agree with any absolutive noun that may appear within the actual relative clause. The following examples clarify this:

(129)   *ebelaⱦ   ha   -w   -ura-w   was*
           mother-ERG having-made CLASS-I   CLASS-I boy-ABS
           'the boy whom the mother bore'

(130)   *was ha-w   -ura-j   ebel*
              CLASS-I   CLASS-II mother-ABS
           'the mother who bore the boy'

(131)   ebelaɬ jas   ha-j   ura-b   ruq̄'
           girl-ABS   CLASS-II   CLASS-III   house-ABS
           'the house where the mother bore the girl'

In these examples, was is class I, ebel and jas class II, and ruq̄' class III.

In Chechen, the participles do not end in a class-marker, but agree with their head nouns, at least to the extent of distinguishing an absolutive from an oblique. Otherwise the construction for relatives follows the Avar pattern:

(132)   ʔürre   bolx   b   -wolina   -ču
           early-in-the-morning work-ABS CLASS-V having-begun OBL
           KOLXOZxo   -čo
           collective-farmer ERG
           'the collective-farmer who began work early in the morning'

In Lezgi, of course, the participle neither agrees with any argument within the relative construction (as a result of the absence of any sort of verbal concord) nor can it agree with the following head noun, even to the limited extent that such agreement is possible in Nakh, since Lezgi adnominal adjectives do not undergo any changes. And so, a Lezgi relative expression is extremely simple:

(133)   stχa   q'eji   ruš   eq̄eč'na
           brother-ABS having-died girl-ABS went-out
           'the girl whose brother had died went out'

Compare this with the following:

(134)   vaχ   q'eji stχa   eq̄eč'na
           sister-ABS   boy-ABS
           'the boy whose sister had died went out'

As regards the formation of relative clauses in North-West Caucasian, detailed studies for Abkhaz and Adyge are already available (Hewitt, 1979c; 1979d); so we shall illustrate with examples from Adyge (Temirgoy dialect). It will be obvious from what has already been said that nonfinite verb forms are used; they precede their head noun. If the relative clause is in construction with that noun whose pronominal affix in the relative verb complex belongs to column I, then no change takes place to the affixal structure of that complex in both Circassian and Ubykh (Abkhaz–Abaza here deviates from the sister-languages in replacing the appropriate nonrelative column I affix by the special relative form jə-); note that in the present tense of nonstative (dynamic) verbs in Circassian the relative participle is produced by suffixing -ră, otherwise the nonfinite form differs only slightly from the finite:

(135)   *qǎ   -k°'ǎ -ʁ*
PREV come PAST
'he came'

(136)   *qǎ-k°'a-ʁǎ-r*
'the one who came'

In (136), *-r* is the definite absolutive marker. However, if the relative is in construction with a noun represented by a column II or column III affix within the relative complex, then a special relative affix replaces the non-relative affix; in Circassian and Abzhaz–Abaza this is *z(ə)-*, in Ubykh *d(ə)-*:

(137)   *ś°əzə -r   zə -wəč'ə-ʁǎ   ɬ'ə -r*
woman DEF-ABS REL kill   PAST man DEF-ABS
'the man who killed the woman'

Compare this with the finite clause:

(138)   *ɬ'ə -m   ś°əzə -r   ə - wəč'ə-ʁ*
man ERG woman DEF-ABS he kill   PAST
'the man killed the woman'

A very common variant of this basic pattern in both Circassian and Ubykh (but not in Abkhaz) is for the head noun to appear at the beginning of the relative construction and to stand in the adverbial case, leaving the relative participle to carry the relevant case suffix conveying the function of the head noun within the main clause:

(139)   *ɬ'-ǎw ś°əzə-r zə-wəč'ə-ʁǎ-r*
'the man who killed the woman'

In this example, *-ǎw* is the adverbial case ending, and *-r* the suffix for definite absolutive. There seems to be no semantic difference associated with the choice between these two constructions.

This short survey of North Caucasian relative constructions quite clearly demonstrates the fundamental role played by the participle in just this one type of subordinate clause. It was mentioned earlier that subordinating conjunctions are virtually confined to South Caucasian. The North Caucasian languages make extensive use of participles and other nonfinite verbal forms to express subordination. The role played by such nonfinite verb forms is one of the most striking features of North Caucasian syntax.

TEXTS IN CAUCASIAN LANGUAGES

GEORGIAN TEXT

p'lat'on-i   k'idev did -xan -s   i   -q'o
Plato   NOM again long time DAT SU-VERS be-AOR-3SG-NOM

u   -guneb -o   -d   mart'o-d   m   -ǯd -om   -i
NEG temper NEG ADV alone   ADV ACT-PART sit THEM NOM

zal   -is   k'utxe   -ši p'at'ara rgval magida-s   -tan, čai-t
guest-room GEN corner-DAT IN small   round table   DAT AT tea INSTR

c'in   da ǯer k'idev ver   da   -e   -c'q'nar-eb
in-front and as-yet   not-POT PREV PLUP-3-ERG calm   THEM

-in   -a   tav-is   -i   gul -i.   ra   -rig -ad   ar
CAUS 3SG-ABS self GEN ABS heart ABS what way ADV not

lanзy-av   -d   -a   da a   -gin   -eb   -d
abuse THEM IMPERF 3SG-NOM and VERS swear-at THEM IMPERF

-a   tav-is   tav-s, rom gada -r   -e   -ul
3SG-NOM self GEN self ACC that PREV mad THEM PAST-PART-PASS

k'ac   -tan   mgzavr-ob-a   ar da   -i   -šal
man-DAT WITH journey ABSTRACT-ABS not PREV SU-VERS forbid

-a   da am -den -i   u   -siamovn-eb-a   da
AOR-3SG-NOM and thus much ABS NEG pleasure ABSTRACT-ABS and

ga   -c'val -eb-a   ga   -mo   -i   -ar -a . . .
PREV torment ABSTRACT-ABS PREV PREV SU-VERS pass AOR-

*   ga   -c'val -eb-a   ga   -c'val -eb-a*
3SG-NOM PREV torment ABSTRACT-ABS PREV torment ABSTRACT-ABS

i   -q'o,   magram mas   upro si   -rcxv
SU-VERS be-AOR-3SG-NOM but   he-ACC more ABSTRACT shame

-il   -i   h   -k'l -av   -d   -a,   am
ABSTRACT NOM 3-DO kill THEM IMPERF 3SG-NOM this-OBL

c'q' -e   -ul   -ma rom mtel sa -zog -ad   -o
damn THEM PAST-PART-PASS ERG that whole ADJ some ADV ADJ

-eb-a   -ši c'a -mo -i   -зax -a
ABSTRACT-DAT IN PREV PREV SU-VERS shout AOR-3SG-NOM

da mis   -i   sa-iduml -o   ga   -a
and he-GEN NOM N secretly N-ABS PREV NEUTRAL-VERS

-mžyavn -a.   ra   -sa   -k'virv -el
disclose AOR-3SG-NOM what FUT-PART surprise FUT-PART

-i   -a,   axla sa-masxr-o -d   i   -kn-eb   -od
NOM be-3SG but N jest   N ADV SU-VERS be THEM COND

-a   a   -gd -eb   -ul   -i   am
3SG-NOM PREV throw THEM PAST-PART-PASS NOM these-OBL

q'mac'vil-eb -isa   -gan, romel-ni   -c   dil   -i   -dan
youth   PL GEN BY who NOM-PL REL morning INSTR FROM

sa-ɣam -o -mdis   mxolod im-it   a   -r -i
N night N UNTIL only   it INSTR NEUTRAL-VERS be THEM

-an   ga -rt -ul   -ni,   rom sa- oxunž-o,
3PL-NOM PREV occupy PAST-PART-PASS NOM-PL that N joke   N

sa-sacil-o da sa-masxr-o sagan -i   ram an   mo
N fun N and N jest   N subject ABS any either PREV

-i   -gon   -o   -n   an še   -a
SU-VERS think-up AOR-SUBJ 3PL-NOM or PREV LOC-VERS

-mčn -i   -o   -n   vis   -me.
notice THEM AOR-SUBJ 3PL-NOM anyone-DAT INDEF

ama   -ze i   -k'l -av -d   -a   tav-s   p'lat'on
this-DAT ON SU-VERS kill THEM IMPERF 3SG-NOM self ACC Plato

-i   da im   -nair   guneba -ze da -dg -a,
NOM and that-OBL KIND-OF mood-DAT ON PREV stand AOR-3SG-NOM

rom mza -d   i   -q'o   xel -i a   -e
that ready ADV SU-VERS be-AOR-3SG-NOM hand ABS PREV PLUP-3-

     -ɣ   -o   tav -is   gan -zrax -v   -a   -ze,
ERG raise 3SG-ABS self GEN PREV intend THEM INFIN-DAT ON

mi -e   -t'ov -eb -in -a   tav -is -i
PREV PLUP-3-ERG abandon THEM CAUS 3SG-ABS self GEN ABS

sakme,   am   -c'am -s -ve   uk'an ga -brun -eb
business-ABS this-OBL second DAT EMPH back PREV return THEM

-ul   -i   -q'o   saxl   -ši, tav -i
PAST-PART-PASS SU-VERS be-AOR-3SG house-DAT IN self ABS

mi -e   -neb -eb -in -a   q'ovel -i
PREV PLUP-3-ERG leave THEM CAUS 3SG-ABS everyone NOM

-ve   -sa   -tvis da dae,   ra -c u-nd-a is
EMPH GEN FOR and OPT-PTCL which REL must it-NOM

mo -m   -xd   -ar   -i
PREV PAST-PART-ACT happen PAST-PART-ACT SU-VERS

q'o.
be-AOR-3SG-NOM

(From D. K'ldiašvili, *Samanišvilis dedinacvali*, Tbilisi, 1962.)

Notes

Nouns in the nominative–absolutive and dative–accusative cases are glossed NOM or ABS, DAT or ACC, according to their syntactic function in the sentence in question. Likewise, verb agreement markers are often glossed NOM, ABS, ERG according to the system by which they show agreement.

Where a noun is followed by a postpositional suffix, the case indication for the noun gives the case that the postposition governs.

In transitive pluperfect forms, the prefix after the preverb may show the person and, in the first person, number of the transitive subject; in the examples in the text (*daec'q'narebina*, *aeyo*, *miet'ovebina*, *mienebebina*), this is always third person singular. The formation of the intransitive pluperfect *momxdariq'o* is different, consisting of a reduced form of the aorist of the copula with the past participle.

šeamčnion: the locative version prefix *a-* here correlates with the third person indirect object.

tav-: the literal meaning is 'head', but this form is also used as a reflexive and emphatic pronoun.

Note the meanings of the following polymorphemic words, which are given morph-by-morph glosses in the text: *sazogadoeba* 'company', *sayamo* 'evening', *rasak'virvelia* 'of course'.

FREE TRANSLATION

Plato was out of sorts for a good while yet, sitting alone by a small round table in a corner of the guest-room with his tea before him; he had not yet been able to calm himself down. In what way did he not abuse and swear at himself for not having refused to travel with a mad man and for having gone through so much unpleasantness and harassment ... Harassment was harassment, but he was rather overcome with shame that this damned man before the entire company had shouted out and disclosed his secret. Of course, he would now be made an object of fun by these youths who, from morning to evening, are consumed only with trying either to think up or to discern in anyone you like any old subject for joking, for fun, for jest. This was the matter over which Plato was tormenting himself: his mood was such that he was ready to give up what he intended, to abandon his business, to return back home at once, to leave them all to themselves, and – to hell with the consequences!

ABKHAZ TEXT

aps-nə́	*a*	*-ps*	*-a*	*-bá*
Abkhazia	3SG-NONHUM-COL-II	soul	3SG-NONHUM-COL-II	see

-ra	*(∅)*	*-ssə́jrə*	*-w-p'*, *wə*	*-g°ə́*
ABSTRACT	3SG-NONHUM-COL-I	wonderful	STAT 2SG-MALE	heart

-wə   -psə́ jə   -wə   -z
2SG-MALE soul 3SG-NONHUM-COL-I 2SG-MALE-COL-II POT
-á   -l   -x   -wa -m.   á   -mra (Ø)
3SG-NONHUM-COL-II FROM take-out DYN NEG DEF sun 3SG-
                    -xáa -w-p'. aps-nə́ es -pxən-rá a   -wáa
NONHUM-COL-I sweet STAT Abkhazia every summer DEF folk
sas -rá   j   -a   -z   -aa -wé -jt'.
guest ABSTRACT 3PL-COL-I 3SG-NONHUM-COL-II FOR come DYN FIN
áps-w   -aa -gə   wə-rt g° -á   -x°a -rə
Abkhazian PL AND these heart 3SG-NONHUM-COL-II please ABSTRACT
-la   jə   -r   -pə́lo   -jt'. aps-nə́ z-nə́
INSTR 3PL-COL-I 3PL-COL-III welcome-DYN FIN Abkhazia once
jə   -z   -bá -z   es-nág (Ø) -aa
3SG-NONHUM-COL-I WHO see NONFIN-PAST-INDEF always DEF come
-rá   (Ø)   -r   -g°a -pxó   -jt'.
MASDAR 3SG-NONHUM-COL-I 3PL-COL-II heart warm-DYN FIN
aps-nə́ jə́   -na   -l   -s -áa
Abkhazia 3PL-COL-I THITHER PREVERB pass HITHER
-l   -s -nə jə   -g°á   -r
PREVERB pass GER 3SG-NONHUM-COL-I PREVERB 3PL-COL-III
-ta -lo   -jt', áps-wa   TEATR (Ø)   -áx́-gə
view ITER-DYN FIN Abkhazian theatre 3SG-NONHUM-COL-II to TOO
jə   -né-j-lo   -jt'.
3PL-COL-I go ITER-DYN FIN

Notes

Phonetic: The definite article prefix *a-* is omitted before the vowel of the same quality in *aa-rá*, for *a-aa-ra*; likewise the third person singular nonhuman column II prefix *a-* in *áx́-gə*, for *a-ax́-gə*. In *áps-w-aa-gə*, the addition of the collective plural suffix *-aa* to the stem *aps-wa* leads to omission of the stem-final *a*.

a-ps-a-bá-ra 'its nature', *g°-á-x°a-rə-la* 'with pleasure': note the compound nouns, with the internal structure 'soul's sight' (literally: 'soul its-sight'), 'heart's pleasure' (literally: 'heart its-pleasure'), where the genitives are *objective*.

FREE TRANSLATION

The natural beauty of Abkhazia is superb, you can't get it out of your being. The sun is sweet. People come to Abkhazia every summer as visitors. And the Abkhazians welcome them with open arms. Those who have once seen Abkhazia always enjoy coming back. They view Abkhazia by travelling all around it, and they regularly visit the Abkhazian theatre too.

AVAR TEXT

ɣadi -da   co   ħani -l   kesek   b -atu -n
crow LOC one cheese GEN piece-ABS-III III find PAST-GER
b -uk'a -na.   ħan   -gi   k'aldi -b   ƙu -n,
III COP PAST cheese-ABS AND mouth INSIDE seize PAST-GER
he   -b co ɣot'o-de b -axa   -na.   cara-da he   -b
it-ABS III one tree   ALL III ascend PAST fox   LOC it-ABS III
b -iх̃a-na   wa he-ɬ   he   -b guƙi -ze   q̄'asd
III see PAST and it   ERG it-ABS III cheat INFIN decision-ABS
ha   -bu-na.   cer   ɣot'o-de   ʕagar-ɬa   -na   wa rač̃ -gi
make III PAST fox-ABS tree   ALL near   BECOME PAST and tail-ABS AND
х̃waʕu-la   -go he-ɬ   k'aɬa -ze   b -aj -b -iх̃a -na:
shake PRES GER it   ERG speak INFIN-III III begin III begin PAST
—dir   х̃irij-a -b ɣedo!   dur
I-GEN dear ADJ III crow-ABS-III you-SG-GEN
bercin -ɬi   š̃i -b! mun -go -gi   bercin -a -b,
beautiful ABSTRACT-ABS-III what III you-SG SELF AND beautiful ADJ III
haraƙ̄ɬ'-gi   bercin -a -b žo   b -ugo   mun.
voice   AND beautiful ADJ III thing-ABS III COP-PRES you-SG
co keč̃'   aħ -e!   neče -č̃'o   -go aħ -e!
one song-ABS cry IMPER ashamed NEG-PAST GER cry IMPER
he-ɬ   aħi-ze   b -aj -b -iх̃a -na.   ɣadi -l
it   ERG cry INFIN-III III begin III begin PAST crow GEN
k'aldi -ša(n)   haraƙ̄ɬ'   b -aq̄i -ne -ʕan   čebe
mouth INSIDE-ABL voice-ABS-III III emerge INFIN BEFORE before
ħan   cara-l   k'aldi -be   ƙa -na.
cheese-ABS fox   GEN mouth INSIDE-ALL fall PAST

Notes
Noun class affixes have been indicated by Roman numerals giving the class number: in the text, only class III (*b-*) occurs. To clarify which noun phrase triggers the agreement in question, Roman numerals have, where appropriate, been added to the glosses of nouns to indicate their class membership; note, in this connection, that the infinitive in *-ze* is of class III.

For the spatial cases Avar has, in addition to the three-way opposition locative/allative/ablative, a further five-way opposition relating to the specific spatial orientation (e.g. 'inside' versus 'under'). In the text, the most general spatial case (traditionally numbered 'one') has been indicated as LOC/ALL/ABL; for the other cases, the gloss is the appropriate English preposition in upper case letters, accompanied by ALL or ABL where motion is involved.

Link vowels and thematic vowels have been assigned to the preceding morpheme.

FREE TRANSLATION

A crow had found a piece of cheese. And, having snatched up the cheese in its mouth, it went up into a tree. A fox saw it and determined to cheat the crow. The fox approached the tree and, shaking its tail, it began to speak:

—My dear crow! How beautiful you are! You are both beautiful yourself and a creature with a beautiful voice. Sing a song – don't be ashamed, sing!

The crow began to sing. Even before a sound came forth from the crow's mouth, the cheese fell into the mouth of the fox.

FURTHER READING

A useful introduction to the peoples of the Caucasus as a whole, including those speaking languages other than Caucasian languages, is Geiger et al. (1959). Good introductions to the general field of Caucasian languages are Catford (1977) and Klimov (1965); the latter is also available in a German translation. *JaNSSSR* IV (1966) provides grammatical sketches of all the Caucasian languages, and is considerably more up-to-date than Dirr (1928). A further general survey is *HdO* I, 7 (1963). The fullest treatment of ergativity in Caucasian languages is Catford (1976), although many problems still remain to be investigated, in particular the extent to which the 'agent' or the 'patient' in the transitive construction (two-place predicate construction) shares syntactic properties in common with the intransitive subject.

Within the South Caucasian family, material on Georgian is plentiful, while material on the other languages is either very specialised or inaccessible. For the comparative study of the South Caucasian languages, reference may be made to Klimov (1962) on the noun and Deeters (1930) on the verb. For Old Georgian, there is a grammar in French by Marr and Brière (1931). For the modern languages, there are grammars in French by Vogt (1971) and in German by Tschenkéli (1958). Harris (1976), though largely an exposition and exemplification of the theory of Relational Grammar, also contains a good exposition of Georgian syntax in so far as it relates to arguments of the verb. For a discussion of version, see Boeder (1968).

Dumézil (1933) provides an introduction to comparative North Caucasian studies. For the North-West Caucasian languages, there is a general survey by Colarusso (1977), in addition to a partial comparative morphology by Dumézil (1932). A comprehensive description of Abkhaz is now available in English (Hewitt 1979a). For Abaza, there is the standard account by Genko (1955), and also a detailed account in English of the crucial verb complex by Allen (1956). The standard grammar of Adyge is Rogava and Keraševa (1966), that of Kabard-Cherkes *GKČLJa* (1957). For Ubykh, reference should be made to Dumézil (1931; 1975). Al-Mufti (1978) has so far been unavailable to me.

Of the current Chechen standard grammar, only one volume (phonetics) has appeared to date (Dešeriev 1960); in addition, there is a classic description of Chechen syntax by Jakovlev (1940). The standard grammar of Ingush is Mal'sagov (1963). The fullest description of Bats is Dešeriev (1953).

Bokarev (1961) provides a general introduction to the Dagestanian languages. In addition, monograph descriptions are available for many of the individual languages, though not all; many of these descriptions are available only in Georgian. Thus the most comprehensive grammar of Avar, Čikobava and Cercvadze (1962), is in Georgian, though there is also a classic description of Avar syntax by Bokarev (1949b). For the Andi languages we have Cercvadze (1965) on Andi (in Georgian); Gudava (1963) on Botlikh (in Georgian); Magomedbetkova (1971) on Karata (in Russian); Magomedbetkova (1967) on Akhvakh (in Russian); Gudava (1967) on Bagval (in Georgian); and Bokarev (1949a) on Chamalal (in Russian). The Tsez (Dido) languages are surveyed over all by Bokarev (1959) (in Russian), while there are monograph descriptions in Russian for Ginukh (Lomtadze 1963) and Bezhti (Madieva 1965).

The standard account of Lak is Žirkov (1955). For Dargva, reference should be made to Abdullaev (1954) for phonetics and morphology, and Abdullaev (1971) for syntax; for the aberrant Kubachi dialect, see Magometov (1963).

Most material on the Lezgian languages is in Russian. The four-volume description of Archi by Kibrik et al. (1977) makes Archi perhaps the best described of all the Dagestanian languages; an earlier description is by Mikailov (1967). For Tabasaran, the standard account is by Magometov (1965); for Agul, Magometov (1970); for Rutul, Ibragimov (1978). The standard account of Khinalug is Dešeriev (1959), though many new data and insights are provided by Kibrik et al. (1972). Two descriptions of Udi are available in Georgian: Džeiranišvili (1971) and Pančvidze (1974). For Lezgi, the most recent comprehensive grammar is Žirkov (1941); for syntax, see Gadžiev (1954–63).

Paleosiberian and other languages

In this chapter we shall be concerned with the remaining languages of the U.S.S.R., those which do not fit into any of the major genetic families that we have discussed in previous chapters. Some of these are languages whose status as languages of the U.S.S.R. is even more accidental than usual, and results from the interaction of population migration with the way in which the borders of the Russian Empire, and subsequently the U.S.S.R., became fixed. The two languages in this group are Aramaic, a Semitic language, and Dungan, a Sino-Tibetan language, indeed structurally a dialect of Mandarin Chinese. The others are the so-called Paleosiberian (Paleoasiatic) languages, especially if this term is taken to include Eskimo-Aleut.

Although we have used the term Paleosiberian (for which Soviet scholars usually prefer Paleoasiatic) in the title of this chapter, this does not imply that Paleosiberian is a genetic family in the sense of Uralic, or even a possible genetic family in the sense of Altaic or Caucasian. The Paleosiberian languages are defined in essentially negative terms: they are those languages of Siberia that do not belong to any of the major language families of Siberia, all of which have moved into most of Siberia relatively recently – these major families are Altaic (Turkic, Mongolian, Tungusic, whether or not genetically related), Uralic, and, last of all, Indo-European. The so-called Paleosiberian languages cannot be shown to be genetically related; they are not particularly similar to one another typologically, indeed one of them, Ket, differs radically in many other respects from all other languages of Siberia (see section 6.4); moreover, they are spoken in widely different geographical locations, the only common feature of these locations being their isolation.

The peoples speaking these languages (with the exception of Eskimo and Aleut, relatively recent immigrants from North America) are probably the remnants of once much larger populations speaking a wider range of languages related to the surviving Paleosiberian languages. For instance, although Ket is now a language-isolate, we know that in the eighteenth century there were related languages spoken in Siberia, namely Arin, Assan, and Kott; these died out in the early nineteenth century. Since Altaic, Uralic, and Indo-European languages are relatively recent newcomers to Siberia, there must have been population groups there before, who were either assimilated or driven out by the newcomers. Thus the present-day Paleosiberian languages are almost certainly just a remnant of an earlier much richer linguistic picture in Siberia, and thus occupy a position somewhat analogous to that of Basque in western Europe.

Since the term Paleosiberian has never been intended as either a genetic or a typological grouping, we may stop briefly to consider the languages and language-groups that fall within it, before proceeding to the more detailed discussion in individual sections below. The term covers two small genetic families: Chukotko-Kamchatkan, i.e. the languages spoken in the peninsulas of Chukotka and Kamchatka in eastern Siberia; and Eskimo-Aleut, consisting of Eskimo and Aleut, although, as we shall see in section 6.2, it is misleading to think of Eskimo as a single language. Since the centre of gravity and of dispersion of Eskimo-Aleut is on the North American continent, Eskimo-Aleut is often not considered as part of Paleosiberian, although it does have some typological features in common with Chukotko-Kamchatkan languages in particular (in addition to marked differences). The other members of Paleosiberian are all, at present, language-isolates, namely: Yukagir, Ket, and Nivkh (Gilyak).

A further addition is sometimes made to the Paleosiberian group, namely Ainu, although an Asiatic mainland home for the Ainu is controversial. Since there were once Ainu in the Russian Empire, we may briefly consider their present status here. The home of the Ainu was on Sakhalin island, the Kuriles, and Hokkaido, the most northerly of the large Japanese islands. The area has long been in dispute between Russia/the U.S.S.R. and Japan: after the Russian defeat in the Russo-Japanese War of 1905, Russia ceded southern Sakhalin to Japan, with the result that all Ainu were then in Japan; in 1945, southern Sakhalin, and also the Kuriles, were ceded by Japan to the U.S.S.R. The published account of a Soviet linguistic expedition to Sakhalin in 1949 notes explicitly that the members came across a few Ainu, including some who could speak Ainu (Novikova and Savel'eva 1953: 128–33). However, recent works on the languages of the U.S.S.R. make no mention of Ainu, and we must conclude that, even if there are still ethnic Ainu on Sakhalin, they have not retained their language. In Japan (Hokkaido), the process of assimilation ot Ainu speakers linguistically to Japanese has also been very intense, and the language is on the verge of extinction.

As a final point in this introduction to Paleosiberian, we may note that a further synonym that is sometimes found in the earlier literature is Hyperborean, reflecting the fact that the languages in question are spoken in the Far North.

6.1 Chukotko-Kamchatkan languages

Chukotko-Kamchatkan is a small group of genetically related languages, spoken in the peninsulas of Chukotka and Kamchatka in the far east of Siberia. The name for the family which we are using here, following the usual Soviet term *čukotkso-kamčatskie jazyki*, simply reflects the geographical location of the languages within the group, much as does Indo-European. Since the term is not particular euphonious in English, other terms have been used in the literature, such as Chukchi-Kamchatkan, Luoravetlan, Chukotian, but these are potentially misleading, since the term Luoravetlan has never been used as a self-designation by the Itelmen, and the other two terms suggest a unique position for Chukchi within the family.

The three major languages within the family are Chukchi, Koryak, and Itelmen, and these are the three ethnic groups which are listed separately in Soviet census statistics. Of the three languages, Chukchi and Koryak are very close to one another, indeed were it not for the clear ethnic distinction between the Chukchi and Koryak they might well have been regarded as dialects of one and the same language. Itelmen is very different from the other languages, both in typology and in basic vocabulary, but attempts to argue against their genetic relationship on these grounds are unconvincing, in view of the large number of correspondences among bound morphemes, including bound morphemes that participate in relatively abstract patterns. For instance, all Chukotko-Kamchatkan languages have subject prefixes for both transitive and intransitive verbs, except that in the second person plural there is a suffix (Chukchi *-tək*, Itelmen *-sx*).

Although these are the three major members of the family, it is probable that further languages might have to be recognised. For instance, Alyutor and Kerek have traditionally been considered dialects, Alyutor of Koryak and Kerek of Chukchi, which reflects in large measure the present greater ethnic similarity between Alyutor and Koryak, between Kerek and Chukchi. However, in terms of linguistic structure Alyutor and Kerek are not noticeably more similar to either Chukchi or Koryak, though each is very similar to both of these languages, so that, as suggested above, all four of Chukchi, Koryak, Alyutor, and Kerek could be regarded, in terms of structural similarity, as dialects of a single language. In recent Soviet linguistic work, Alyutor and Kerek have been treated increasingly as separate languages (for instance, in *JaNSSSR* V (1968)).

What remains at present of Itelmen is but a small fragment of the related languages or dialects that were spoken during the eighteenth century when early Russian explorers, in particular Krašeninnikov, first noted down vocabulary lists of the languages of this most easterly part of Siberia. From these vocabulary lists it seems that, although the speech varieties called Kamchadal (i.e. Itelmen) by Krašeninnikov were genetically related, they were remarkably divergent from one another. At that time there were probably at least three Itelmen languages, rather than dialects, at least in terms of lexical divergence: Northern, Southern, and Western Itelmen. At present, only Western Itelmen survives, the other two forms of Itelmen having died out finally in the late nineteenth or early twentieth century – before, unfortunately, any significant volume of linguistic work was done on them, which means that to a large extent we must still rely on vocabulary lists noted down by untrained observers in the eighteenth century.

The problem of ethnonyms for the speakers of Chukotko-Kamchatkan languages (with the exception of Alyutor and Kerek) has been acute, and the current names Chukchi (Russian uses *čukči*, singular *čukča*, as the ethnonym, and *čukotskij* as the adjective), and Koryak are not the names by which these people call themselves (indeed, the dialect of Koryak on which the standard language is based lacks a rhotic phoneme), this being an exception to the general rule in the U.S.S.R. whereby native ethnonyms are used. However, there is no native ethnonym which refers exclusively and comprehensively to either the Chukchi or the Koryak. The current standard Chukchi name for themselves is *ləʔoravetlʔen*, which means literally 'proper person', but unfortunately this same term is used by the Koryak in reference to themselves, with the result that the attempt in the inter-War years to adopt Luoravetlan as the ethnonym of the Chukchi has been discontinued. Apart from this term which does not distinguish between the Chukchi and Koryak, other terms refer to only part of the Chukchi or part of the Koryak (or even part of both together). Thus *čavčəv* is the name by which the Chukchi refer to reindeer-breeding Chukchi (it is also a common noun meaning 'reindeer-breeder'), but it does not include the Chukchi of the coast who do not breed reindeer, and is also used to refer to reindeer-breeding Koryak; it is, however, probably the native name from which the terms Chukchi and Chukotka derive in European languages. In the 1930s and 1940s Koryak was often referred to as Nymylyan, from Koryak *nəməlʕən* 'village-ADJ'. However, this is the term by which nomadic (reindeer-breeding) Koryak refer to their settled compatriots, and has never been used as a general ethnonym for all the Koryak. Thus the terms Chukchi and Koryak are retained here, in the absence of any preferable alternative and in accordance with current Soviet usage.

The term Itelmen is somewhat less complicated, since it is clear that this term was used by all the Itelmen to refer to themselves at the time Krašeninnikov visited them. Subsequently, however, this term fell out of use, and was replaced by the term Kamchadal, which could, however, also refer to people of Russian origin who lived among the Itelmen – contact between the two ethnic groups was very close in Kamchatka, giving rise both to Russianisation of Itelmen and Itelmenisation of Russians, until the current preponderance of Russians in the population led to the virtual extinction of Itelmen as a language. Kamchadal is also the term most frequently used outside the U.S.S.R., but here we have, in accord with our general policy, preferred to use the current official term Itelmen, which was revived after the Revolution.

Chukchi is the largest of the Chukotko-Kamchatkan languages, being spoken by 82.6% of the 13,597 ethnic Chukchi according to the 1970 census returns. Although this percentage is high by Siberian standards, it represents a marked decrease from 93.9% in 1959. The territory inhabited by the Chukchi, the Chukotka peninsula, is one of the most isolated parts of Siberia – especially its tundra portion away from the sea – which has kept the Chukchi relatively isolated hitherto, although influx of Russian population could affect this balance rapidly. 80.9% of the Chukchi live in the Chukchi N.O., where they form, however, only 10.9% of the population, the overwhelming majority being Russian.

Prior to European settlement in Chukotka, Chukchi was the dominant language of this part of eastern Siberia, used as a lingua franca by other small peoples, including in particular the Eskimo, so that Siberian Yupik Eskimo contains a large fund of loans from Chukchi, including many particles and conjunctions which have brought about major changes in Eskimo syntax, as will be shown in section 6.2. The Chukchi fall into two main groups, the Tundra Chukchi, the majority, whose traditional occupation is reindeer-breeding, and the Maritime Chukchi who live along the shores of the Bering Strait and adjacent areas and engage primarily in fishing and hunting of sea mammals. Despite the huge area over which Chukchi is spoken, dialect differentiation is slight: one reason may be the traditional nomadic existence, which brought different groups of Chukchi into frequent contact with one another, but more important is probably the fact that the Chukchi have only relatively recently expanded to occupy much of their present territory, assimilating large numbers of Eskimo in the process. Chukchi was developed as a written language during the 1930s, and is currently used in publishing and also in education, in the first grades of primary school.

Koryak is spoken by 81.1% of 7,487 ethnic Koryak, again representing a substantial fall from 90.5% in 1959. The Koryak live in the northern part of Kamchatka, though in recent times they have also been pushing further southwards, assimilating certain Itelmen groups. In contrast to Chukchi, Koryak is characterised by marked dialect diversity, probably reflecting their generally more established, sedentary existence. Koryak was, like Chukchi, developed as a written language in the 1930s, but now has a very limited use. In particular, Koryak was discontinued as a medium of instruction in schools in the 1950s (Žukova 1972: 3), so that all Koryak-speaking children now have their education in Russian from the first grade.

Since they were not counted separately in recent census statistics, reliable figures

Table 6.1. *Consonant system of Chukchi*

p	t		k	q	ʔ
		ć			
	l				
m	n		ŋ		
v	r	j	ɣ		

are not available for the number of Alyutor, who live on the north-eastern coast of Kamchatka, or the Kerek, who live together with Chukchi on Cape Navarin. In the 1926 census, about 2,000 Alyutor were listed, but the number of people speaking Alyutor is now certainly much smaller, as the result of linguistic assimilation. Kerek is now spoken by only a few families, with perhaps around 100 speakers.

Itelmen, or more accurately Western Itelmen, was claimed as a native language in 1970 by 35.7% of 1,301 ethnic Itelmen, almost exactly the same percentage as in 1959 (36%). However, this must reflect some misinterpretation of the language question, since recent observers, in particular Volodin (1976), have observed that the number of fluent Itelmen speakers is much lower, with the youngest being aged around forty. The language is thus on the point of extinction. In the early 1930s a written form of Itelmen was devised, and a primer and basic arithmetic textbook published, but they were apparently never used in practice. The marked tendency for Itelmen to be replaced by Russian meant that there was little demand for a separate Itelmen written language, and no further attempts have been made to create one.

The consonant system of Chukchi (Table 6.1) is among the simplest of any language of the U.S.S.R., with only 14 distinct consonant phonemes. Although the number of phonemes is small, the phonetic value of some of them is rather unusual, in particular the only lateral, here symbolised in broad transcription as *l*, is phonetically a voiceless lateral fricative. In the Chavchuven dialect of Koryak, on which the standard language is based, *r* and *j* have merged to *j*, but in general Koryak has more phonemic distinctions than Chukchi, although some of these are of low functional yield. Thus, where Chukchi has *v* (phonetically usually a bilabial fricative), Koryak distinguishes labio-dental *v* from bilabial *w* (although the opposition is neutralised to *w* in syllable-final position). Koryak also distinguishes between *t*, *l*, *n* and palatalised *t́*, *ĺ*, *ń*, as in *wanaw* 'pitch' versus *wańaw* 'word', although strict minimal pairs of this type are very rare, and palatalisation plays primarily an affective role, being used in the formation of diminutives, e.g. *lewət* 'head', *ĺawtəpíĺ* 'little head'. The phonetic values of some of the corresponding phonemes are also different as between Chukchi and Koryak: for instance, Koryak *l* is a voiced frictionless continuant, and Koryak has pharyngal ʕ corresponding to Chukchi ʔ (although Chukchi ʔ also has pharyngal constriction).

The consonant system of Itelmen stands in marked contrast to these simple systems, since Itelmen distinguishes plain and ejective plosives (bilabial, dental, palatal, velar, and uvular), has voiced and voiceless fricatives (bilabial, alveolar, velar, and a voiceless fricative only in the uvular region), in addition to having three lateral phonemes, voiced *l* and *ĺ* (though the functional yield of the opposition between these two is low) and voiceless *ł*.

In traditional Chukchi society, the pronunciation of consonants among women differed slightly from that of men, in the replacement of *r* and *č* by *c*, with further assimilation of a following *k*, giving some words a very different appearance, e.g. *cəccə* 'walrus' for *rərkə*. The standard language is based on the male pronunciation, and the separate women's pronunciation is now discouraged.

Of more structural interest is the vowel system of Chukchi and the closely related languages, especially in view of the vowel harmony system that pervades the language. The system contains a schwa, which is largely predictable, especially in Koryak, although even here there are some instances where this is not so, e.g. in the opposition between the second person plural suffixes *-tək* (for intransitive subject or direct object) and *-tkə* (for transitive subject). In Chukchi, as a result of diachronic processes of vowel reduction (reconstructable in part on the basis of synchronic alternations between *e/a* and schwa), there are far more instances of nonpredictable schwa, e.g. in word-final position (cf. Chukchi *kukeŋə* 'pot', Koryak *kukeŋe*). The simplest vowel system is found in Alyutor, which has only the three phonemes *i, u, a* (apart from the schwa), and this triadic system is a useful starting point in considering vowel harmony in Chukchi and Koryak. Itelmen, incidentally, has the 5-vowel system *i, e, a, o, u*, and although there are vowel alternations in Itelmen, it is not clear that these can be related to the vowel harmony alternations of Chukchi and Koryak.

We shall illustrate vowel harmony by means of examples from Chukchi, although the system is virtually identical in Koryak. Each of the three vowels found in Alyutor has two correspondents in Chukchi, giving in effect two triadic systems, one dominant (*e, o, a*), one recessive (*i, u, e*), i.e. overall the system can be represented as *i/e, u/o, e/a*, where in each pair the first vowel is the recessive vowel corresponding to the dominant vowel after the oblique stroke. It will be noted that the vowel *e* has a double function, being either the dominant counterpart of recessive *i* or the recessive counterpart of dominant *a*; the question of whether these morphophonemically distinguishable vowels are also phonetically distinct, at least for some speakers, remains open. The vowel schwa is neutral with respect to vowel harmony, but otherwise a given Chukchi word must contain either all dominant vowels or all recessive vowels. In native words, there are no exceptions to this rule, since even compounds, including incorporative complexes (see pp. 250–1) are subject to vowel harmony; more recent loans from Russian, which are taken over in their Russian form, may combine dominant and recessive vowels.

A given morpheme in Chukchi is either dominant or recessive, i.e. in particular will contain either all dominant or all recessive vowels (in addition to the possibility of the neutral vowel schwa). Thus the lexical morpheme *milɣ-* 'match' is recessive, while *kojŋ-* 'cup' is dominant; the grammatical morpheme *-u* marking the essive case ('as X') is recessive, while the comitative suffix *-ma* is dominant. (This comitative suffix requires the obligatory presence of the recessive prefix *ɣe-*, which will thus, for reasons now to be discussed, appear in this environment as *ɣa-*, giving the appearance of a circumfix *ɣa-* . . . *-ma*.) When morphemes are combined together into words, if the word as a whole contains at least one dominant morpheme, then the vowels of all recessive morphemes are changed to the corresponding dominant vowel. One effect of this is that recessive vowels will appear in a word only if all morphemes are recessive, e.g. *milɣ-u* 'as a match'. Contrast *kojŋ-o* 'as a cup', where the dominant vowel of the first morpheme affects the vowel of the second, and *ɣa-melɣ-əma* 'with a match', where the dominant vowel of the suffix affects the vowels of root and prefix. In *ɣa-kojŋ-əma* 'with a cup', both root and suffix are lexically dominant. One interesting aspect of this kind of vowel harmony, distinguishing it sharply from that found in Altaic or Uralic languages, is that the direction of the harmony is determined solely by the distinction between dominant and recessive, the trigger always being the dominant morpheme(s) of a word, irrespective of whether or not these are in the root; in Altaic and Uralic languages, the trigger is always a vowel of the root.

As indicated above, vowel harmony applies equally when several lexical morphemes are combined together, most typically by incorporation, so that the appearance of a root can be rather different when it appears in isolation and when it appears in an incorporative complex, e.g. *kupre-* (absolutive singular *kupre-n*) 'net', but *pəlvəntə-kopra-* (absolutive singular *pəlvəntə-kopra-n*) 'metal net', where the first morpheme is dominant. This example also introduces another feature of Chukchi vowel harmony, namely that a given morpheme is necessarily either dominant or recessive, even if contains only the vowel schwa, indeed even if it contains no vowel at all. Thus the morpheme *pəlvənt-* 'metal' is dominant, whereas *ənpə-* 'old' is recessive, e.g. *ənpə-riquke-t* 'old polar foxes' (*riquke-* 'polar fox'; *-t* is the absolutive plural suffix). The suffix *-n* (stem *-nv-*), which forms locative derivatives, is dominant despite the absence of vowels, e.g. *təle-* 'to go', *təla-n* (stem *təla-nv-*) 'road, way'.

In Koryak, to a different extent in different dialects, the vowel harmony system is partially disrupted in that, in many forms, for the pair *e/a* one finds *a* rather than *e* in words with overall recessive vocalism, e.g. *maniɣətʕul* 'material, cloth' (cf. Chukchi *meniɣ*); this is probably to be viewed as an intermediate stage between the strict Chukchi vowel harmony system and the Alyutor system with only three vowels, i.e. with no distinction at all between dominant and recessive, *a* being retained of the *e/a* pair.

In addition to vowel alternations conditioned by vowel harmony, and alternation between schwa and zero conditioned by general (though, in part, morphologised) phonological rules, Chukchi and the closely related languages have also a number of consonant alternations, the sum total of which can lead to quite striking deformations in the shape of a morpheme. Thus 'kill' appears as *təm-* in *təm-nen* 'he killed him', but as *-nm-* in *tə-nm-ətək* 'I killed you' (where *tə-* is the first person prefix, *-(ə)tək* the second person plural suffix).

The morphology of Chukchi is largely agglutinative, although there is some fusion, especially in the verb, as in the opposition between *tə-viri-y²ek* 'I descended' and *mə-viri-y²ek* 'may I descend', where the prefix *tə-* combines the semantic units of first person singular and indicative, while *mə-* is first person singular and imperative. In noun morphology, Chukchi distinguishes singular from plural (as does Itelmen), while the other languages have a separate dual, as elsewhere in their morphology. As in most other languages of Siberia, a small number of cases is distinguished, including some basic spatial cases. Beyond this, there are several unusual features in the noun morphology of Chukchi and the closely related languages. There are various possibilities for the formation of the absolutive singular of nouns, and in general one simply has to learn the appropriate form for each individual noun: use of the stem alone (e.g. *mićyir* 'work'); the stem alone with vowel reduction (e.g. *valə*, stem *vala-* 'knife'); partial reduplication (e.g. *nutenut*, stem *nute-* 'tundra'; *tumɣətum*, stem *tumɣ(ə)-* 'friend'); suffixation (e.g. *kupren*, stem *kupre-* 'net'; *ləlalyən*, stem *ləla-* 'eye'; *jaraŋa*, stem *jara-* 'house'). Especially with reduplication and the longer suffixes, the result is often that the absolutive singular is one of the longest forms in the noun paradigm: contrast absolutive singular *tumɣətum* with absolutive plural *tumɣə-t* and instrumental singular *tumɣ-e*.

For purposes of declension, Chukchi nouns divide into two main natural classes, which differ on a number of parameters. The distinction between the two classes is not, however, rigid, in that certain nouns can be declined according to either pattern. The first pattern is obligatory for proper names and certain kin terms, and optional for other human nouns. The second pattern, in addition to being usual for human common nouns, is also obligatory for all nonhuman nouns (other than proper names of domestic animals, which are assimilated to the first class). For certain cases, the two classes have different suffixes, e.g. the first class has *-ne* (recessive) in the locative while the second class has *-k*. A more basic distinction, however, is that, whereas both classes distinguish singular from plural in the absolutive, in other cases the number distinction is neutralised in the second class, but retained in the first. A further distinction concerns the expression of the ergative relation (i.e. the case-marking of transitive subjects): neither class has a separate ergative case, nouns of the first class using the locative, while nouns of the second class use the instrumental; only personal pronouns (of all three persons) have an ergative case separate from both locative and instrumental.

Verbs in Chukchi and related languages agree with their subject (whether transitive or intransitive) and with their direct object (if transitive). Only one verb, 'give', shows agreement with the indirect object (although this stands in the allative case, not in the absolutive), and then only when the indirect object is first or second person (V. P. Nedjalkov – personal communication). The morphology of subject and object agreement is complex, with idiosyncratic formations for certain combinations (e.g. the suffix *-nin* for third person singular acting on third person singular), and forms borrowed from other paradigms (e.g. derived intransitives) for certain other combinations. Nonetheless, the following general system can be discerned behind these various complications. Most verb forms have both a prefix and a suffix (although the prefix is often zero, except in the first person). With intransitive verbs, both prefix and suffix encode the intransitive subject, as in the imperative forms *mə-viri-ɣʔek* 'may I descend' and *qə-viri-ɣe* 'may you descend (SG)'. With transitive verbs, the prefix encodes the subject, the suffix the object, as in the following imperative forms: *m-imti-ɣət* 'may I carry you (SG)', *m-imti-tək* 'may I carry you (PL)', *mən-imti-ɣət* 'may we carry you (SG)', *mən-imti-tək* 'may we carry you (PL)'. The prefixes are thus on a nominative–accusative pattern (encoding transitive and intransitive subject), while the suffixes work on an ergative–absolutive pattern (encoding intransitive subjects and transitive direct objects).

Although a number of Chukchi verbs are labile, i.e. can be used without modification either transitively or intransitively, in general the distinction between transitive and intransitive in Chukchi and related languages, especially the closely related languages, is well marked, for instance by the ergative construction for transitive verbs discussed below. Another reflection of the basic transitive/intransitive distinction is the existence of a number of constructions utilising auxiliary verbs, where the verb *it-* 'be' is used as the auxiliary for intransitive verbs and the verb *rət-* 'have' with transitive verbs. In the text on p. 274, the first sentence illustrates the use of *qol it-* (transitive: *qol rət-*) together with another finite verb as the equivalent of 'once (upon a time) . . .' Another frequent use of these auxiliaries is in one of the commonest negative constructions, where the lexical verb stands in a nonfinite form with the circumfix *e-* . . . *-ke* (recessive) and the auxiliary shows tense, person and number, etc., categories. Thus we have, citing infinitives with the suffix *-(ə)k*: *tejkev-ək* 'to fight', *e-tejkev-ke it-ək* 'not to fight'; *ketʔo-k* 'to remember', *a-ketʔo-ka rət-ək* 'not to remember'.

In the following discussion of syntax of Chukotko-Kamchatkan languages, we shall concentrate on Chukchi, which differs little if at all from the closely related languages on the parameters discussed. Itelmen material will be cited only in order to draw specific comparisons. Our knowledge of Itelmen syntax is much more restricted than that of the other languages, and in large measure this ignorance is now irremediable, given that the language is virtually extinct. Thus Volodin (1976: 326–7) notes that we may never know how comparatives were constructed in Itelmen, because there are no clear textual attestations, the only native construction, known only to the oldest speakers, has a different range of meaning (including diminutive, i.e. 'rather wide', in addition to 'wider'), and the only construction that corresponds exactly to a comparative uses the comparative suffix *-čeje* derived from Russian, and even this construction is normally only given in response to direct elicitation.

Case-marking of subjects and direct objects in Chukchi and the closely related languages is on an ergative–absolutive basis, with a different case for transitive subject (instrumental, locative, or ergative, depending on the class of noun phrase) from that for intransitive subject and direct object:

(140) *rultəŋe -ne rəvenŋ-ənin penvel*
   Rultinge LOC skin 3SG→3SG buck
   'Rultinge skinned the buck'

(141) *qupute-t riŋemjet-ərkət*
   petrel ABS-PL fly PRES-3PL
   'petrels fly'

Indeed, in Chukchi the ergativity of this case-marking is one of the most consistent found in any language of the world: virtually every noun phrase participates in this ergative/absolutive opposition, the only exceptions being the emphatic pronouns, where the ergative form together with *ćinit* 'self', e.g. *yəm-nan ćinit* 'I myself', can be used for transitive and intransitive subject and for direct object.

In addition to the ergative construction illustrated in (140), Chukchi also has an antipassive construction, in which the verb is detransitivised by the prefix *ine-* or the suffix *-tku*, the subject (now intransitive) stands in the absolutive, and the patient is either omitted or (very rarely) put in the instrumental or locative, as can be seen from comparing the following two sentences:

(142) *tumy -e kupre-n na-ntəvat-yʔan*
   friend INSTR net ABS-SG put 3PL→3SG
   'the friends put the net'

(143) *tumy -ət kupre-te ena-ntəvat- yʔat*
   friend ABS-PL net INSTR put 3PL

As indicated, the antipassive with an expressed object is very rare in Chukchi, and the functional difference between sentences like (142) and (143) has not yet been made explicit in the literature. There is, however, one area where the function of the antipassive is clear, and this is one of the few areas where Chukchi evinces ergative syntax, namely in the construction with participles in *-lˀ-*. These participles can be used for forming a relative clause on either an intransitive subject, as in (144), or on a direct object, as in (145):

(144)   *e -tipˀejŋe-kə -lˀ -in   ŋevəćqet raytə -yˀe*
          NEG sing   NEG PART ABS-SG woman go-home 3SG
          'the woman who did not sing went home'

(145)   *iyər a   -joˀ -kə -lˀ -etə enm-etə mən*
          now NEG reach NEG PART ALL hill ALL IMPER-1PL
          -əlqən-mək
           go   1PL
          'let us now go to the hill that [we] did not reach'

If it is necessary to form a relative clause on a transitive subject, then the verb must be used in its antipassive form, i.e. the relative clause is effectively formed on an intransitive subject:

(146)   *en-aγtat-kə -lˀ -a   qaa -k   ˀaaćek-a*
           chase NEG PART INSTR reindeer LOC youth INSTR
          n   -ine-vinret-qinet   ŋevəćqet-ti
          IMPERF   help 3SG→3PL woman ABS-PL
          'the youth who did not chase the reindeer helped the women'

(In (146), the prefix *en-* is a vowel harmony variant of *ine-*, with loss of the final vowel before another vowel; the negative prefix *e-/a-* also loses its vowel, i.e. becomes zero, before the following vowel of *en-*.)

    Ergativity is one parameter where Itelmen differs from the other Chukotko-Kamchatkan languages, since in Itelmen both transitive subject and direct object stand in the citation form:

(147)   *ɸitβit šnkčiŋ-nen   əńč*
          seal   catch 3SG→3SG fish
          'the seal caught the fish'

Examples like (148) below were sometimes cited in the earlier literature to suggest that Itelmen has an optional ergative construction, but Volodin (1974) demonstrates that such constructions are more akin to a passive than to an active ergative construction:

(148)   *mińĺ n-ə̆nk   - kičen χiŋ -enk*
          hare catch-PASS 3SG wolf LOC
          'the hare was caught by the wolf.'

In (148), omission of the instrumental noun phrase gives a sentence meaning 'the hare was caught'.

One of the aspects of Chukchi syntax that has aroused much interest in the literature is incorporation, whereby a number of root morphemes can be combined together productively to produce a single word with complex meaning. The unity of the word is demonstrated, for instance, by the spread of vowel harmony right through it, in addition to other word-internal phonological alternations. Thus another way of saying 'the friends put the net' would be by incorporating the direct object into the verb, to produce a new verb *kopra-ntəvat-* 'to net-put'; this new verb is intransitive, giving the sentence:

(149)   *tumɣ -ət   kopra- ntəvat-ɣʔat*
          friend ABS-PL net   put   3PL

With respect to incorporation in Chukchi, it should be noted that while this syntactic device is very common in traditional tales, it is much less frequent in current writing, and virtually absent in translations from Russian, i.e. incorporation seems to be on the wane in the modern language. (In Itelmen, incidentally, there are no clear attestations of incorporation as a productive process; if it ever existed, it must have disappeared very early on, possibly under Russian influence.) In addition to incorporation of direct objects, various other verb arguments and adverbials can be incorporated into verbs, as in the following examples:

(150)   *tə -majŋə- vetɣav- ərkən*
          1SG loud   speak PRES
          'I am speaking loudly'

(151)   *tə - ɣətɣ- əlqət-ərkən*
          1SG lake go   PRES
          'I am going to the lake'

(151) can also be expressed as (152), without incorporation:

(152)   *ɣətɣ-etə   tə -lqət-ərkən*
          lake ALL 1SG go PRES

Incorporation is also possible within the noun phrase, with incorporation of attributes (adjectives, genitives) into the head noun, cf. the following pair:

(153)   *teŋ -tur -meniɣ*
          'good new cloth'

(154)   *nə-teŋ-qin nə-tur-qin meniɣ*
          'good new cloth'

(Note that unincorporated adjectives take the prefix *nə-* and the suffix *-qin*.) Traditionally, the distribution of incorporated and nonincorporated attributes seems to have been that incorporation did not usually take place in the absolutive, but was obligatory in the oblique cases. In present-day Chukchi this rule is not observed rigidly, and it is possible to find oblique case noun phrases where the adjective agrees in case with its head rather than being incorporated. In the comitative with the circumfix *ɣa-. . . -ma*, however, incorporation is still apparently obligatory, as in the following:

(155)   *ɣa-taŋ -tor - maneɣ-ma*
              good new cloth   COMIT
          'with good new cloth'

(156)   *ɣa- mor-ək -tor -orv   -əma*
              we   OBL new dogsledge COMIT
          'with our new dogsledge'

The choice between agreement or incorporation here is reminiscent of the behaviour of direct objects: if they are not incorporated, the verb will agree with them, if they are incorporated, it will not.

Within the incorporative complex, Chukchi has rigid morpheme order of adjunct before head, i.e. in an incorporative verb complex the verb stands last, in an incorporative noun complex the head noun stands last. Where separate words rather than incorporation are used, Chukchi word order is very free: while subjects usually precede their verb, the predominance of object–verb over verb–object is slight, and attributes occur freely before and after their head. One area where Chukchi does, however, conform to the subject–object–verb word order type is in having postpositions rather than prepositions, e.g. *ətləy-ək reen* 'with father', literally 'father-LOC with', *jara-k ɣəryoća* 'above the house', literally 'house-LOC above'.

Unlike nearly all other languages of Siberia, Chukchi makes frequent and regular use of finite subordinate clauses, and has a wide range of native subordinating conjunctions, e.g. *miŋqəri qun* 'because', *iŋqun* 'in order that', *evər* 'if', *ŋe(v)eq* 'although', *ećɣi* 'as soon as', and even *enmen* 'that', used for instance to introduce indirect speech. This seems to be a long-established traditional means of expressing subordination, free from foreign influence, and indeed Chukchi has even been influential in introducing this pattern into Siberian Yupik Eskimo (see p. 257). However, Chukchi does also have a number of nonfinite forms, in particular of gerunds which can substitute for various adverbial clauses. In Chukchi, these gerunds are invariable, in particular showing no subject or object agreement. The subject of a gerund is either taken to be the same as that of the main verb, or interpreted according to what makes sense in the context, or expressed overtly. In (157) below, with the gerund in *-ma*, the two clauses have the same subject:

(157)   *ŋevǝćqet-ti,   meyćeran-ma tamennǝra-k,   amqǝnˀǝćo*
           woman ABS-PL work   GER workshop LOC always
           nǝ   - tipˀejŋe- qinet
           IMPERF sing   3PL
           'the women, while working in the workshop, always sing'

In (158) and (159), with the gerund in *ɣa-... -ma* (like the comitative of nouns), the subjects of the two clauses are different, and that of the gerund is expressed overtly; note that the subject stands in the same case as if with a finite verb, i.e. absolutive for intransitive verbs, ergative (in form, ergative, locative, or instrumental) for transitive verbs:

(158)   *ɣa - raćqev-ma ǝnpǝnaćɣ-ǝt,   ˀaaćek-ǝt   qut-ɣˀet*
           GER enter GER old-man ABS-PL youth ABS-PL rise 3PL
           'when the old men entered, the youths rose'

(159)   *ɣǝm-nan ɣa - lqaɣnav-ma, aćˀeq ćǝpet-ɣˀi*
           I   ERG GER shoot   GER duck dive 3SG
           'when I shot [it], the duck dived'

6.2 Eskimo-Aleut languages

The Eskimo-Aleut family has two branches, Eskimo and Aleut. The relationship of Aleut to Eskimo, though distant, is now generally recognised and well established. Aleut, most of whose speakers live in the Aleutian Islands, which form part of the state of Alaska in the U.S.A., is a relatively homogeneous language, with mutual intelligibility among all dialects, although the Western dialect (Attu Island) is the most divergent. In the U.S.S.R., Aleut live on Bering Island (Ostrov Beringa) and Copper Island (Mednyy Ostrov). They are not native to these islands, but were moved there by the Russian authorities in the early nineteenth century, from Atka to Bering Island and from Attu to Copper Island. According to the 1970 census, Aleut was spoken by 21.8% of the 441 Aleut in the U.S.S.R., i.e. by 96 people all told. Since

Table 6.2. *Verb forms in Aleut dialects of the U.S.S.R.*

Bering Island	Copper Island	
awa-ku-q	aba-ju	'I work'
awa-ku-χt	aba-iš	'you (SG) work'
awa-ku-χ	aba-it	'he works'
awa-ku-s	aba-im	'we work'
awa-ku-χt-xičix	aba-iti	'you (PL) work'
awa-na-χ	aba-l	'(he) worked'
awa-ŋan ana-χ	bud-et aba-í	'he will work'
ajγaγ-laka-s	ni-aγjaγa-im	'we don't go'
awa-ǯa	aba-j	'work (SG)!'

Aleut is only rather marginally a language of the U.S.S.R., we shall not discuss it in detail here, except to note one interesting instance of language contact that has affected the Copper Island variety of Aleut under strong Russian influence (Menovščikov 1968: 405).

On Bering Island, those Aleut who still retain their native language also retain the basic morphological traits of Aleut. On Copper Island, however, the original conjugational suffixes of the Aleut verb have been replaced by Russian suffixes, and other ways of constructing verb forms (such as the negative prefix *ne*, the compound future with the auxiliary *bud-* and the infinitive in *-t́*); there has been no similar influence on noun morphology. Table 6.2 gives some parallel forms from Bering Island and Copper Island. This borrowing is all the more surprising given that the verb inflections of Russian, a fusional language, are not always immediately and obviously segmentable.

Although the layman often thinks of the Eskimo as a single ethnic group, speaking dialects of a single language, in fact the divergences among different forms of Eskimo are sufficient to impede mutual intelligibility, and moreover the Eskimo have never developed a common ethnonym for all Eskimo. In particular, there is a major linguistic barrier which divides the Eskimo into two major groups, the Yupik and the Inuit (Iñupiaq). This boundary runs across Alaska from west to east, and is sufficient to impede communication across it; there are no transitional forms from Yupik (to the south of this line) to Inuit (to the north). Inuit is a dialect chain stretching from the northern part of Alaska across Canada to Greenland: although the extreme ends of the chain are not mutually intelligible, there are no sharp breaks in the chain. Of the Eskimo in the U.S.S.R., only those who originally lived on Ratmanov Island (Ostrov Ratmanova, Big Diomede), the larger of the two Diomede Islands (Ostrova Diomida), spoke Inuit; the smaller Diomede Island, Little Diomede (Ostrov

Kruzenshterna) is already part of Alaska, and represents the closest contiguity between land territories of the U.S.S.R. and the U.S.A.

Yupik is much less homogeneous, with at least four mutually unintelligible varieties (and, in some instances, transitions). Two of these are restricted to Alaska: Central Alaskan Yupik and Southern Alaskan Yupik (Sugpiaq, also sometimes misleadingly called Aleut). Of the other two forms, the highly divergent Sireniki Eskimo is (or was) spoken only in the village of this name in Siberia; the other, Siberian Eskimo (in Russian usually called the language of the Asiatic Eskimo) is spoken both on the Siberian mainland and on St. Lawrence Island, part of Alaska. In the present section, we shall be concentrating on Siberian Yupik, in particular on some of the typological parameters along which Siberian Yupik (and Eskimo more generally) differs from Chukchi, the closest neighbour of Yupik in Siberia, and on some of the ways in which Siberian Yupik has been influenced by Chukchi, once the dominant language of the area.

In 1970, Eskimo was spoken by 60% of the 1,308 ethnic Eskimo in the U.S.S.R., a large drop from 84% in 1959. Since the Ratmanov Island and Sireniki forms of Eskimo are extinct or virtually so, most of these can be taken to be speakers of Siberian Yupik. Eskimo has most of its speakers outside the U.S.S.R.: about 1,000 other speakers of Siberian Yupik on St. Lawrence Island, 200 speakers of Southern Alaskan Yupik in Alaska, 14,500 speakers of Central Alaskan Yupik in Alaska, and 65,000 speakers of Inuit (6,000 in Alaska, 16,000 in Canada, and 43,000 in Greenland).

Although the Eskimo, like all other native peoples of the Americas, are thought to have migrated originally from Siberia, the present-day Siberian Eskimo are not descendants of groups who failed to cross the Bering Strait, but rather of groups who migrated back across this strait, also further populating St. Lawrence Island (from the Siberian mainland). In Siberia, Eskimo has been receding for some time before Chukchi. The number of Eskimo speakers is likely to drop rapidly as a result of recent population movements by the Soviet authorities. Although in the period up to the end of the Second World War the Soviet Eskimo remained in their original home areas, and were even allowed considerable contact with Eskimo on the American side of the Bering Strait and on American islands, this policy was discontinued when the Cold War was at its height, and Eskimo from Ratmanov Island and the settlement of Naukan on Cape Dezhnev (Mys Dezhneva, East Cape) were removed further westwards, to settlements where they are now always only one population group in a multiethnic whole, usually outnumbered by either Russians or Chukchi. Moreover, although Eskimo was developed as a written language in the U.S.S.R. during the 1930s, and still exists officially as a written language, there is scarcely any production in Eskimo at present, and Eskimo is not used as a medium of instruction. The curtailment of the functions of Eskimo in the U.S.S.R. contrasts with the opposite reversal of policy in the U.S.A. and Canada, where literacy programmes in Eskimo are currently in the process of being developed. In Greenland, under Danish administration, Eskimo (usually called Greenlandic) has been a written language since the eighteenth century; it is the language of the overwhelming majority of the population, and is now also the official language.

Phonetically, Siberian Yupik differs from Chukchi in having a rather simpler vowel system, at least in terms of qualitative oppositions, but a much more complex consonant system; indeed the consonant system of Siberian Yupik is complex even by Eskimo standards. The vowel system distinguishes *i*, *u*, *a*, also *ə* (in large measure predictable, as in Chukotko-Kamchatkan languages), but also has a phonemic length distinction. From a more westerly areal typological perspective, one of the unusual features of Chukchi is the distinction between velar *k* and uvular *q* (alongside the velar fricative *ɣ*), but this pales into insignificance in comparison with the range of distinctions made by Siberian Yupik, which has in addition to the plosives *k* and *q* a full set of voiced and voiceless velar and uvular fricatives: *x*, *ɣ*, *χ*, *ʁ*; these also occur labialised. Siberian Yupik is unusual even among Eskimo languages in having a phonemic opposition between voiced and voiceless *l* and *r*.

In nominal morphology, Eskimo has a case system similar to that of the Chukotko-Kamchatkan languages, but differs from them in also having possessive suffixes on nouns. Since a three-way number distinction (singular, dual, plural) is made for both possessor and possessed, this leads to a prolific system that has no counterpart in Chukchi. Examples are, using *aŋjaq* 'boat': *aŋja-qa* 'my boat', *aŋja-n* 'your boat', *anja-a* 'his boat', *anja-ak* 'the boat of those two', *anja-at* 'their boat', *aŋja-kək* 'his two boats', *aŋji-i* 'his boats'. The possessive suffix also plays an obligatory role in the possessive construction, e.g. *aʁna-m atku-ɣa* 'mother-GEN parka-3SG', i.e. 'mother's parka'; the case glossed here as genitive is called the relative case in traditional Eskimo grammar.

The basic structure of the simple sentence is very similar to that of Chukchi, with intransitive subject and transitive direct object in the absolutive, and transitive subject in a different case: for this different case, Siberian Yupik invariably uses the genitive (relative) in *-m*, except that for first and second person pronouns there is no distinction made between absolutive and relative (these pronouns are in any event rarely used, since verb agreement indicates the person and number of subject and direct object):

(160)   *aʁnaq   qavaʁ-tuq*
          woman-ABS sleep   3SG
          'the woman sleeps'

(161)   *aʁna -m   nəʁa-qaa   kaju*
               woman ERG eat   3SG→3SG bullhead-ABS
               'the woman eats the bullhead (fish)'

As in Chukchi, there is an intransitive correspondent to the transitive construction of (161), in which the subject stands in the absolutive, and the object is either omitted or stands in the instrumental:

(162)   *aʁnaq   nəʁa-quq*
               woman-ABS eat   3SG
               'the woman eats'

(163)   *aʁnaq   nəʁa-quq kaju   -məŋ*
               woman-ABS eat   3SG bullhead INSTR
               'the woman eats a bullhead'

There are, however, some specific differences between Chukchi and Siberian Yupik here. In Siberian Yupik, no derivational affix is required to detransitivise the verb, the transitive suffixes are simply replaced by their intransitive counterpart. While constructions of type (163) are extremely rare in Chukchi, they are very common in Siberian Yupik, the semantic difference between (161) and (163) being, as indicated in the glosses, the definiteness versus indefiniteness of the object.

As has been shown in the above examples, both Chukchi and Siberian Yupik have subject agreement with intransitive verbs and both subject and object agreement with transitive verbs, although in Siberian Yupik the marking of subject and object is exclusively suffixal and is much more fusional than in Chukchi. Overall, though, the verb morphology of Siberian Yupik is considerably more prolific than that of the Chukotko-Kamchatkan languages. To a small extent this is due to the existence of additional forms in simple sentences, e.g. the special interrogative form as in Siberian Yupik *nəʁsin* 'did you eat?'. The major difference, however, is that whereas nonfinite verb forms play a relatively small role in the construction of complex sentences in Chukchi, where these nonfinite forms are invariable for person and number, Siberian Yupik on the other hand makes widespread use of such forms, including specification of the person and number of the subject and/or direct object. In Siberian Yupik, as in Eskimo generally, it is usual to have only one finite verb per sentence, the others being various nonfinite forms. Of these nonfinite forms, we shall give a brief discussion here of the so-called connective, which illustrates the system in its full complexity.

The connective indicates, by means of person and number suffixes, not only the person and number of its own subject and direct object, but also whether or not its own subject and/or direct object are coreferential with the subject of the main clause.

This is thus a switch-reference system, though a rather well-developed one in that it can indicate not only coreferentiality of subjects across clauses, but also coreferentiality between subordinate clause direct object and main clause subject. The following examples illustrate this, where subscript *i* indicates coreference with the main clause subject:

(164)   əsʁaʁja-ɣu   quja   -aq
          see   3SG→3SG be-happy 3SG
          'when he$_j$ saw him$_k$, he$_i$ was happy'

(165)   əsʁaʁja-miɣu   quja   -aq
          see   3SG$_i$→3SG be-happy 3SG
          'when he$_i$ saw him$_j$, he$_i$ was happy'

(166)   əsʁaʁja-tni   quja   -aq
          see   3SG→3SG$_i$ be-happy 3SG
          'when he$_j$ saw him$_i$, he$_i$ was happy'

Most varieties of Eskimo lack conjunctions and other separate word particles altogether, but Siberian Yupik has borrowed a large number of these from Chukchi, such as *ama* 'and', *inqun* 'in order to', giving rise to a considerable shift in syntactic typology from nonfinite to finite constructions.

   Although both Chukchi and Eskimo share the facility for forming long words incorporating a wide range of semantic categories (polysynthesis), the typical mechanisms in the two languages are distinct. Chukchi uses primarily incorporation, whereby two or more root morphemes are combined into a single word. Eskimo never uses this device, but rather attaches affixes, in Eskimo always suffixes, to a single root. Thus we can say that Eskimo, including Siberian Yupik, is polysynthetic, but not incorporating. An example analysed by Jacobson (1977: 2–3) will serve to illustrate this:

(167)   aŋja-ʁḷa -ŋ   -juɣ -tuq
          boat AUG ACQUIRE want 3SG
          'he wants to acquire a big boat'

Although the ideas expressed by the separate English words *he, want, acquire, big, boat* are all contained in this Siberian Yupik word, the word in fact contains only one root morpheme, *aŋja-* 'boat', all the others are derivational or inflectional suffixes. These suffixes are not relatable formally to root morphemes in the language, so that even if they derive etymologically from separate words it now seems impossible to trace this development.

   As a final comment on Eskimo in the U.S.S.R., we may note the early pattern of contact with Europeans was for Siberian Eskimo to come first into contact with English-speaking Americans, while speakers of Central Alaskan Yupik came first into contact with Russians. This has given rise to the strange situation, from the contemporary political viewpoint, that Siberian Yupik has some loans from English (e.g. *kaaʁˬa* 'cow') where Central Alaskan Yupik has loans from Russian (e.g. *kuluvak* 'cow', from Russian *korova*).

6.3 Yukagir

The Yukagir live in the north-east of the Yakut A.S.S.R. There are two main groups of Yukagir, Tundra Yukagir and Kolyma Yukagir, this being also the main dialect division. The Tundra Yukagir were traditionally nomadic, wandering in the region of the rivers Alazeya and Chukoch'ya, while the Kolyma Yukagir, hunters and fishermen, live further south, along the rivers Yasachnaya and Korkodon. The Yukagir language is spoken by only 46.8% of 615 ethnic Yukagir – one of the smallest peoples in Siberia, though one whose overall number is increasing, after almost disappearing entirely in the pre-Soviet period as a result of poor economic circumstances. Although Yukagir cannot be said to have established genetic links with any other language or language family, in recent years the possibility of a genetic link between Yukagir and Uralic has been proposed energetically. Yukagir has never been given a writing system. The name Yukagir is not the native ethnonym, which is either *wadul* (stem *wadu-*, plural suffix *-l*) in Tundra Yukagir or *odul* (stem *odu-*) in Kolyma Yukagir. In the inter-War years, Yukagir as a whole was often referred to as Odul, though now the more traditional nonnative term Yukagir (of uncertain etymology) is once more official. In the discussion of Yukagir structure below, examples are taken from Tundra Yukagir.

In terms of its typology, Yukagir differs much less from the general type represented by the Altaic and easterly Uralic languages than do most of the other so-called Paleosiberian languages. For instance, its phonemic system is very straightforward, apart perhaps from the existence of the uvular phonemes *q* and *ʁ*; its syllable structure is (C)V(C)(C). In noun morphology, two numbers (singular and plural) and a small number of cases, primarily spatial, are distinguished, although there is no nominative/accusative distinction – we return to the morphology of subject and direct object below. Possessive suffixes are restricted to the third person, e.g. *ködeŋ* 'husband', *köde-gi* 'her husband'. (A number of Yukagir nouns, like *ködeŋ*, end in *-ŋ* in the citation form, this *-ŋ* being dropped before other suffixes and in certain other environments.) Verbs agree with their subject in person and number (three persons, two numbers); there is no object agreement. The morphological structure is basically agglutinative, though with a certain amount of fusion in the verb (see Table 6.3 for some examples); suffixes predominate, though there are some

Table 6.3. *Verb agreement and focus in Yukagir*
(past tense forms)

		Verb focus	Subject focus
Intransitive (*uu(l)* 'to go')			
SG1	met	mer-uu-jeŋ	met-ek uu-l
2	tet	mer-uu-jek	tet-ek uu-l
3	tudel	mer-uu-j	tudel uu-l
PL1	mit	mer-uu-jeli	mit-ek uu-l
2	tit	mer-uu-jemut	tit-ek uu-l
3	tittel	mer-uu-ŋi	tittel uu-ŋu-l
Transitive (*ai* 'to shoot')			
		Verb focus	Subject focus
SG1	met	mer-ai-ŋ	met ai
2	tet	mer-ai-mek	tet ai
3	tudel	mer-ai-m	tud ai
PL1	mit	mer-ai-j	mit ai
2	tit	mer-ai-mk	tit ai
3	tittel	mer-ai-ŋa	titt ai-ŋu
		Object focus	
SG1	met	ileleŋ ai-meŋ	
2	tet	ileleŋ ai-meŋ	
3	tudel	ileleŋ ai-mele	
PL1	mit	ileleŋ ai-l	
2	tit	ileleŋ ai-mk	
3	tittel	ileleŋ ai-ŋumle	

prefixes, as will be seen from the examples below. Attributes precede their head, e.g. *kötine-j gödeŋ* 'fat man', cf. *tudel me-kötine-j* 'he is fat'; the suffix *-j* here is a tense marker, as in Yukagir adjectives behave very much as a subclass of verbs. For the possessive construction, compare *ile-n jawul* 'the deer's track', where *-n* is the genitive suffix. Yukagir has a number of postpositions and no prepositions, e.g. *nime jeklie* 'behind the house', cf. *nimeŋ* 'house'. The usual word order within the clause is subject–object–verb, as can be seen in the following example, where neither subject nor direct object has any case-marking:

(168)   *met nimeŋ me -wie -ŋ*
           I   house FOC build 1SG
           'I built the house'

The basic means of combining clauses into complex sentences is by use of nonfinite forms; this is illustrated, specifically for gerunds, in the text on pp. 275–6. These nonfinite forms are invariable for person and number, their subject usually being the same as that of the main clause or expressed overtly.

On one parameter, however, Yukagir does differ significantly from the other languages of Siberia, and this is in its special system for indicating focus (i.e. essential new information); it is on this system that we shall concentrate in our discussion of Yukagir. For subjects and direct objects, Yukagir has special morphological marking on the noun phrase and/or verb in order to indicate whether the subject, the direct object, or the verb is in focus. Examples (169)–(176), in which the focused constituent is in italics in the English translation, will be used to illustrate the distinctions here. One easy way to appreciate the pragmatic distinctions between different focuses is to consider question and answer sequences: thus (169) would be the answer to the question 'what did the deer do?' (new information: *ran away*), while (170) would be the answer to the question 'what ran away?' (new information: *the deer*).

(169)   *ileŋ me -kötege -j*
               deer FOC run-away 3SG
               'the deer *ran away*'

(170)   *ile -leŋ kötege -l*
               deer FOC run-away 3SG
               '*the deer* ran away'

(171)   *met mer - uu-jeŋ*
               I   FOC go 1SG
               'I *went*'

(172)   *met-ek uu-l*
               I   FOC go 1SG
               '*I* went'

(173)   *met mer -ai -ŋ*
               I   FOC shoot 1SG
               'I *shot*'

(174)   *met ile mer -ai -ŋ*
               I   deer FOC shoot 1SG
               'I *shot* the deer'

(175)   *met ai*
               I   shoot(-1SG)
               '*I* shot'

(176)   *met ile -leŋ   ai   -meŋ*
          I   deer FOC shoot 1SG
          'I shot *the deer*'

(The above examples are all in the past tense, the tense marker being usually fused with that for person and number of the subject. For more details on the range of subject agreement distinctions, see Table 6.3.)

When the verb is focused, it takes the prefix *me(r)-*, and both subject and direct object are without any suffix; this is independent of the transitivity of the verb, and with transitive verbs of whether or not there is an expressed direct object. This is illustrated in examples (169), (171), (173), and (174). Whenever either the subject or the direct object is focused, the prefix *me(r)-* is omitted. In order to focus on an intransitive subject or on a direct object, the focused noun phrase takes the suffix *-leŋ*; this suffix takes the form *-k* if the noun phrase contains an attribute, as can be seen by replacing *ile-leŋ* in (170) by *amat'ed ile-k* 'good deer', and *-ek* is also used for first and second person pronouns, as in (172). Note that this gives an ergative–absolutive pattern for the distribution of *-leŋ* (like treatment of intransitive subject and transitive direct object), although otherwise Yukagir evinces little or no ergativity; see examples (170), (172), and (176). It will be noted that the verb suffixes, indicating person and number agreement, also vary according to which constituent is focused; see further Table 6.3.

Finally, in order to focus on the subject of a transitive verb (example (175)), the noun phrase takes no suffix, but the verb stands in a different form, with syncretism of subject agreement, cf. *met ai* '*I* shot', *tet ai* '*you* shot', etc.; only in the third person plural is there a separate verb form, e.g. *titt ai-ŋu* '*they* shot'. This same atrophy of subject agreement is found when focusing on an intransitive subject, e.g. *met-ek uu-l* '*I* went', *tet-ek uu-l* '*you* went', *tittel uu-ŋu-l* '*they* went'; on this parameter, the system is nominative–accusative. The relation between focus and its formal expression is thus rather complex, the relevant factors being: presence versus absence of *me(r)-* on the verb (focus on verb); presence or absence of *-leŋ* or *-(e)k* on the noun phrase (focus on intransitive subject or transitive direct object); atrophy or not of verb agreement (focus on subject, transitive or intransitive).

6.4   Ket

While the existence of any language-isolate, such as Yukagir or Nivkh, is disturbing to the general linguistic map of an area, the existence of the language isolate Ket is more disturbing than most, because not only is there no demonstrable relationship to any other language of the area (or outside it), but even from a typological perspective Ket differs radically from all the other languages of Siberia, whether or not they belong to the major families of the area or are themselves isolates. In particular, Ket is the only language of the area known to have phonemic tone oppositions, although this is a recent discovery, and the precise number of phonemic tones in the various dialects remains to be worked out, although it seems to be three or four (Dul'zon 1969; Feer 1976). Ket is the only language in the area to have a consistent gender/class system. The morphology of Ket is quite unlike anything found elsewhere in Siberia, which has a strong tendency to be an area of agglutinative languages: Ket has widespread internal flection, discontinuous roots as well as prefixing and suffixing, giving overall a picture much more similar to some of the Caucasian languages than to a Uralic or Altaic language.

Attempts to link Ket genetically with any of the major language groups remain very speculative, although one view that has gained some popularity recently is that Ket may be distantly related to Tibeto-Burman, the unity of this family having been split by the expansion of the Chinese (Dul'zon 1968; though Dul'zon is sceptical of a genetic link, as opposed to contact, and himself advocates a genetic link with North Caucasian). Although we may speak of Ket as a language-isolate at the present time, there were some closely related languages spoken into the eighteenth century, such as Arin, Assan, and Kott. Indeed, speakers of Kott were still to be found at the beginning of the nineteenth century, when M. A. Castrén noted down some Kott in addition to his more extensive Ket materials. The family as a whole to which these languages belong may be called Yeniseyan.

At present Ket is spoken by 74.9% of 1,182 ethnic Ket, the percentage for 1970 having remained remarkably constant from 77.1% in 1959. The Ket live along the river Yenisey and its tributaries, and are divided into two main dialects, Imbat and Sym, the latter having only a few score speakers at the most. The structural differences between the two would be sufficient to consider them distinct languages. In earlier literature, the Ket are often referred to as Yenisey Ostyak, correctly giving their geographical location, but misleadingly suggesting an ethnic or linguistic affiliation with the Khanty (formerly called Ostyak), a Finno-Ugric people who live to the west of the Ket. In fact, although the Ket have been in close contact with the Khanty, to the extent of adopting the ethnonym Ostyak, they are linguistically quite distinct. Although a Ket primer was in preparation in the 1930s (*KS* 1968: 13–14), Ket has never actually been used as a written language, and its speakers use Russian as their basic medium of literature and education.

The present writer has not had the opportunity of working with native speakers of Ket or of hearing Ket spoken, so the discussion below is based exclusively on the published sources listed in the Further Reading section. On several points there is lack of consistency among these sources, for instance concerning quite basic questions of phonetics, so that the actual transcriptions given below, basically following Krejnovič, are to be treated as provisional. To some extent these discrepancies may relate to dialect differences.

Although the morphology of Ket, including the complex morphology of the verb, is basically agglutinative, there are many instances where this is not the case. For instance, although most nouns form their plural by means of a suffix, e.g. *am* 'mother', *am-aŋ* 'mothers', several nouns form their plural by internal vowel or other internal change, e.g. *tiṕ* 'dog', *taṕ* 'dogs', *qɔj* 'bear', *qun* 'bears', and even by prosodic alternations, e.g. *tújas* 'receptacle made of birch-bark', plural *tujás*. In addition to suffixing, prefixing is widespread in Ket, e.g. in the possessive prefixes, cf. *am* 'mother', *(a)b-am* 'my mother', *(u)k-am* 'your mother'. In the verb morphology, as we shall see, in addition to prefixing and suffixing there is also a variety of infixing, for verbs with discontinuous roots.

Like most languages of Siberia, Ket has a small number of noun cases, including three basic spatial cases for locative, allative, and ablative; there is, however, no nominative/accusative distinction for any kind of noun phrase, the distinction between subject and direct object of transitive verbs being carried primarily by the complex verb agreement system. The most interesting feature of Ket nouns, however, is the existence of a well-defined class system, unique among Siberian languages. Ket distinguishes three classes, masculine, feminine, and neuter. To a large extent, these correlate with, respectively, male animate, female animate, and inanimate, but there are some exceptions: thus some animal names (e.g. 'fox', 'hare') are feminine irrespective of the sex of the referent: most fish names are masculine; large wooden objects are masculine, whereas small counterparts are neuter. In the plural, masculine and feminine fall together, while for certain purposes feminine and neuter fall together in the singular. Class is covert in Ket, in that the noun itself does not show any overt marker of the class to which it belongs, this class revealing itself primarily in agreement, especially predicate agreement. In addition, the spatial cases have slightly different suffixes (etymologically, apparently, suffixed pronouns) for the different classes, e.g. allative *ob-daŋa* 'father', but *am-diŋa* 'mother'. The realisation of the distinction with agreement can be seen by contrasting *bu qa-ŕu* 'he is big' with *bu qa-ŕa* 'she is big' – note that the pronoun *bu* does not itself show the class distinction. Apart from predicate agreement and the forms of spatial cases, the main realisation of class is in the possessive prefixes: contrast *da-am* or *bura-am* 'his mother' with *d-am* or *bur-am* 'her mother'.

As already indicated, the most complex area of Ket morphology is the verb, in particular the way in which verbs agree in person, class (for third person), and number with their subject (for all verbs) and direct object (for all transitive verbs) (excepting only a very few verbs which do not show agreement or fail to take certain agreement affixes). There are two main sources of complication. One is the formal structure of the verb as a lexical item, since one has to distinguish verbs with a nondiscontinuous root in final position (and thus a number of prefixes) from verbs with a discontinuous root, the latter consisting either of two root morphemes or of a root followed by a derivational suffix or a root preceded by a derivational prefix; with discontinuous roots, many affixes stand between the two parts of the root, thus giving a form of infixation (although the 'infix' stands between the two morphemes that constitute the root, rather than actually being inserted into a morpheme, as is required by the strict sense of infixation). In addition to this general division of verbs according to the structure of their roots, the application of further criteria would lead to even more and smaller subclasses. The second source of complication is the range of person/class/number affixes, which fall into two main sets, called D and B from the different initial consonants of some of the affixes, e.g. first person singular $d(i)$-/-r- versus (-)ba-/(-)$bɔ$-; only certain affixes have distinct D and B forms. The difference between these two sets does not, however, correlate at all directly with that between subject and direct object, and in many instances it seems quite idiosyncratic which set a particular verb takes, e.g. *ba-γissal* 'I spend the night', but *di-jit* 'I sneeze'. The overall complexity and idiosyncrasy of the system is such that Dul'zon (1968), the most comprehensive grammar of Ket to date, effectively takes the line that every verb is irregular, and proceeds to list a wide range of forms for each verb discussed.

Nonetheless, some systematisation can be brought to the choice and position of these affixes, which turn out to operate essentially on an ergative basis (even though Ket seems not to have any other signs of ergativity). For transitive subjects (ergative relation), only the D series is used, and prefixes encoding transitive subjects always occur initially, preceding both parts of a discontinuous root. For intransitive subjects and for direct objects (absolutive relation), either the B or the D series is used, the choice being determined lexically (apparently arbitrarily); in this function, the affixes occur before a nondiscontinuous root, but between the two parts of a discontinuous root. The ergative column always precedes the absolutive column, the two columns being adjacent in transitive verbs with a nondiscontinuous root, e.g. *d-i-tuŋ* 'he sees her', where *d-* indicates third person singular masculine subject and *-i-* third person singular feminine direct object; contrast *da-a-tuŋ* 'she sees him', where *da-* indicates third person singular feminine subject and *-a-* third person singular masculine direct object.

Some further examples will illustrate the application of these general principles. In *ba-γissal* 'I spend the night', the root is nondiscontinuous; the absolutive affix therefore precedes the root, and for this verb is of the B series. In *śug-ba-tn* 'I return', the root is discontinuous, and the affix, again of the B series, separates the two parts of the root. Comparable examples with D series absolutive marking are *di-jit* 'I sneeze' (nondiscontinuous root) and *lɔŋda-d-daŋ* 'I exercise' (discontinuous root). For transitive verbs with the D series absolutive, we have nondiscontinuous *du-ri-ś* 'he dresses me' (*du-* third person singular masculine ergative; *-ri-* first person singular absolutive), and discontinuous *d-usqi-r-it* 'he warms me'. The B series indicating a direct object is found in *ba-tuŋ* '(he) sees me', where *ba-* is the first person singular affix; in this particular form, it is apparently impossible to include an overt subject marker.

Some of the affixes, most noticeably prefixes in the D series, do not distinguish singular from plural, and many verbs indicate the plurality of their subject (transitive or intransitive) by means of a suffix, or suppletion. The usual plural suffix is *-n*, which in some verbs contrasts with singular *-p*. This gives such examples as *di-jit* 'I sneeze' versus *di-jit-n* 'we sneeze', *d-avro-p* 'I drink up' versus *d-avro-ń* 'we drink up', *ba-yistu-ṕ* '(he) covers me' versus *ba-yistu-n* '(they) cover me', *d-ɔĺ-daq* 'he lived' versus *d-ɔĺ-in* 'they lived'. In the last (suppletive) pair, *-ɔĺ-* is the past tense marker: Ket distinguishes past from nonpast, the latter often (though not for all verbs) having a zero morph. The tense affix precedes a nondiscontinuous root but occurs internal to a discontinuous root, following a B series absolutive marker but preceding a D series absolutive marker (except with transitive verbs having a third person direct object, in which case the tense marker follows the D series absolutive affix).

In terms of word order typology, Ket has many of the characteristics of the subject–object–verb type, although the order of major constituents within the clause varies between subject–verb–object and subject–object–verb; given the prolific system of subject and object agreement, many transitive sentences do not have their full complement of noun phrase arguments. Adjectives always precede their head noun, e.g. *aqta doń* 'large knife'; in general, there is no agreement between adjective and noun for any category, although some adjectives do agree in number only, thus *aqta doń-iŋ* is 'big knives', but the adjective *qa* 'large' has a plural *qa-ŋ*: *qa quś* 'large tent', *qa-ŋ qu-ŋ* 'large tents'. The genitive also precedes its head noun, and requires a possessive prefix on the head noun recapitulating the person, number, and (for third person) class of the possessor, e.g. *ob da-quś* 'father's tent', literally 'father HIS-tent', *am d-ʁuś* 'mother's tent', literally 'mother HER-tent'; the whole possessive complex is pronounced as a single word. Ket has a number of postpositions and no prepositions. The postpositions, etymologically deriving from nouns, enter into the possessive construction with the other noun, e.g. *aq na-baĺga* 'between the trees', literally 'tree-PL THEIR-between'.

Unlike many of the other languages of the area, Ket does not have a well-developed system of nonfinite forms, whereas it does have a number of conjunctions, including many native conjunctions in addition to a current tendency to borrow conjunctions from Russian. Indeed, Ket has only one nonfinite form, the so-called infinitive, which can serve both as an attribute, e.g. *śuj ḱet* 'swimming person', and as complement to the verb, e.g. *śuj di-jaq* 'I am going to swim' (where *di-jaq* has the first person prefix *di-*); the form *śuj* here is infinitive of the verb 'to swim'. A Ket text, thus, unlike texts in nearly all of the neighbouring languages, is essentially a sequence of finite clauses.

6.5   Nivkh

Nivkh is currently spoken by slightly less than half (49.5%) of 4,420 ethnic Nivkh; in 1959 the figure was 76.3%, once again demonstrating how rapidly language assimilation of a small group can take place in contact with a much more populous group. Of the 2,199 Nivkh who gave their native language as not Russian, 1,936 claimed also to be fluent in Russian. In non-Soviet literature, the Nivkh are usually referred to as Gilyak, although Nivkh (*ńivx*) is the native ethnonym, besides simply meaning 'person'. The Nivkh live on the lower reaches of the Amur river, and on Sakhalin island. There is a major dialect split between the Amur dialect and the Eastern Sakhalin dialect, such that mutual intelligibility is virtually excluded, and the question certainly arises whether or not these should be considered, from a structural viewpoint, two separate but closely related languages. The Northern Sakhalin dialect occupies an intermediate position. In many respects, the Eastern Sakhalin dialect is more archaic than the Amur dialect, which has, for instance, lost certain final consonants (especially many instances of final *-n*), and otherwise simplified consonant clusters. For instance, the Eastern Sakhalin equivalent of the Amur dialect ethnonym *ńivx* is *ńivyŋ* or *ńiɣvŋ*.

The relationship of Nivkh to any other language is very questionable, although Nivkh does show marked typological similarities in several respects to various neighbouring languages: for instance, the system of classifiers with numerals (see p. 269) is very reminiscent of Japanese. However, for any typological similarity one can find between Nivkh and any other language, one can also find typological discrepancies between Nivkh and that language: thus, Nivkh phonology is not remotely like that of Japanese. Mainly as a result of the Japanese ownership of southern Sakhalin between 1905 and 1945, most of the Soviet work on Nivkh has concentrated on the Amur dialect, while much work on the Eastern Sakhalin dialect has been done by Japanese linguists, and also other non-Soviet linguists working from the Japanese side, nowadays often with Nivkh who moved to Japan. The Amur dialect of Nivkh was developed as a written language in the early 1930s, and was transferred to a Cyrillic based writing system in 1953. However, since then scarcely anything has appeared in Nivkh, with the exception of the primer published shortly after the change-over to the Cyrillic alphabet. Recent linguistic works use different versions of the Cyrillic writing system, and in addition to this confusion the alphabet also uses some unusual symbols for consonants in the velar and uvular regions, in

Table 6.4. *Obstruent system of Nivkh (Amur dialect)*

	I	II	III	IV	V
Labial	p	pʻ	b	f	v
Dental	t	tʻ	d	ř	r
Palatal	tʹ	tʹʻ	dʹ	s	z
Velar	k	kʻ	g	x	ɣ
Uvular	q	qʻ	G	χ	ʁ

particular symbols which are not to be found in regular Cyrillic type fonts (such as loops added to Latin *h*). Given these practical complications, and the fact that virtually all Nivkh speak fluent Russian as their first or second language, it is unlikely that the written language would be revived.

While the vowel system of Nivkh is relatively simple, with only the six phonemes *i*, *e*, *a*, *ə*, *o*, *u*, the consonant system is, at least at first sight, much more complex, especially in the Amur dialect, and especially with regard to the plosives and fricatives, which are represented diagrammatically in Table 6.4. In addition, Nivkh allows quite formidable consonant clusters, especially when monoconsonantal prefixes and suffixes are added, e.g. *ń-rəf* 'my house' (where *ń-* is the first person singular possessive prefix), *fəvrk-tʹ* 'pluck' (where *-tʹ*, a phonetic variant of *-dʹ*, indicates finiteness of the verb).

The rationale of the obstruent system becomes much clearer, however, once one looks at it in terms of the initial consonant alternations that characterise Nivkh, in particular when it is realised that one of the five series in Table 6.4, namely III (voiced plosives), does not occur word-initially in the citation forms of native words, but only as a result of morphophonemic alternation. The various series of obstruents alternate with one another in context, the alternation being determined primarily by the final segment of the preceding word. Thus, column I alternates with column V after a plosive, vowel, or *j*, e.g. *təf* 'house', but *ətək rəf* 'father's house', while column II alternates with column IV in this environment, e.g. *tʹu* 'dogsledge', *ətək řu* 'father's dogsledge'. Column I alternates with column III after a nasal or *l*, e.g. *ki* 'shoe', but *tʹʻəŋ gi* 'your shoe'. The remaining alternations apply to initial consonants of verbs, but not of nouns. After a fricative, column IV alternates with column II, e.g. *řa-dʹ* 'to cook' *tʹus tʹa-dʹ* 'to cook meat', while column V alternates with column I, e.g. *vəkz-dʹ* 'to lose', *nux pəkz-dʹ* 'to lose a needle'. Column IV alternates with column II after a nasal or *l*, e.g. *seu-dʹ* 'to dry', *kelm tʹʻeu-dʹ* 'to dry raspberries', while column V alternates with column III in this environment, e.g. *vəkz-dʹ* 'to lose', *ŋirŋ bəkz-dʹ* 'to lose a cup'.

Although the alternations were originally conditioned by the phonetic nature of the final segment of the preceding word, some alternations can now be explained only historically in this way: for instance, the first person singular possessive prefix *ń-* triggers alternation of the stem-initial consonant as if this prefix ended in a vowel, e.g. *ń-rəf* 'my house' (not *ń-dəf*); etymologically, this prefix derives from the independent first person pronoun *ńi* 'I'.

In addition to the phonological conditioning, however, syntax is also crucial to an understanding of initial consonant alternation in Nivkh, because only in certain syntactic constructions does the final consonant of one word trigger alternation in the initial consonant of the next word. An attribute triggers alternation in the following head noun, as in *ətək rəf* 'father's house', and a direct object triggers the alternation in a following verb, as in *vəkz-d´* 'to lose', but *nux pəkz-d´* 'to lose a needle' and *ŋirŋ bəkz-d´* 'to lose a cup'. Especially in view of the absence of case-marking for subjects, direct and indirect objects, and genitives, initial consonant alternation is often the only outward sign of a given syntactic construction. With the verb *ẓa-* 'cook', for instance, we can see that *t´us* 'meat' is direct object in (177), but subject (or at least, not direct object) of the resultative construction in (178), even though the same semantic role is represented in both sentences:

(177) umgu t´us t´a -d´
       woman meat cook FIN
       'the woman cooked the meat'

(178) t´us ẓa -yəta   -d´
       meat cook RESULT FIN
       'the meat has been cooked'

Nivkh noun morphology distinguishes two numbers (singular, plural) and a small number of cases, including basic spatial cases. This is rather like the case system of most other languages of Siberia, although Nivkh is somewhat unusual in not distinguishing between nominative, accusative, dative (for indirect object) and genitive, all of which stand in the citation form. Given the virtual absence of verb agreement (see below), word order and the alternations triggered in noun phrases by genitives and in verb phrases by direct objects are crucial to the retrieval of grammatical relations from the surface form of sentences. In its case system Nivkh does have one rather unusual case, called dative–accusative by Panfilov (1962), though perhaps 'causee' would be a better term, since this case is used only to express the causee in a morphological causative construction, as in:

(179) ńi xevgun -ax   er -χ   qala-gu   -d´
       I Xevgun CAUSEE he ALL hate CAUS FIN
       'I will make Xevgun hate him'

In the pronoun system, a distinction is made between dual and plural in the first person only, with dual *megi* or *mege*; in the first person plural (but not dual), there is a distinction between inclusive *mer* and exclusive *ńəŋ*.

One parameter which sets Nivkh off markedly from other languages of Siberia, but relates it to other languages further south, e.g. Japanese, is the existence of a developed system of numeral classifiers. These function most clearly with the numerals 'one' to 'five', for which Nivkh nouns are divided into 26 classes, with different numeral forms for each class. In most instances, the numeral forms can readily be segmented, synchronically or at least diachronically, into a numeral element and a classifier, which latter is often relatable to a separate noun in the language. For instance, in counting boats, the forms are: *ńim* 'one boat', *mim* 'two boats', *t'em* 'three boats', *nəm* 'four boats', *t'om* 'five boats', where the final *-m* is relatable to *mu* 'boat'. Likewise, for counting dogsledges the forms are: *ńiř*, *miř*, *t'eř*, *nəř*, *t'oř*, where the final *-ř* is relatable to *t'u* 'dogsledge' (bearing in mind the alternation of initial *t'* with *ř*).

Many of the noun classes that are defined in this way by separate numeral forms are very specific, e.g. separate sets for different items of fishing tackle. Others are very general classifications, for instance people, animals, places, or relate to spatial characteristics of objects, e.g. long objects, flat thin objects, small round objects, cf. also paired objects. In addition, there is a remainder class containing all nouns that do not fit into any of the specific classes. In some few instances, the assignment of a given noun to a given class seems arbitrary, e.g. of *ku* 'day' (i.e. period of 24 hours, and not, incidentally, 'sun') to the class of small round objects, although most time units belong to the remainder class. For numerals up to five, where the classifiers are used, the usual traditional order is for the numeral-classifier complex to follow the noun, e.g. *qan mor* 'two dogs', literally 'dog two-animal'; with higher numerals, used without classifiers, the numeral precedes, e.g. *ŋamg ńivx* 'seven people'. The latter reflects the typical Nivkh order with the attribute preceding the head. The classifier construction also, in a sense, reflects this word order internally to the numeral-classifier complex, and was probably originally an appositive construction with the noun and the numeral-classifier complex in apposition. Currently in Nivkh, there is a tendency for the numeral-classifier complex to be preposed (Panfilov 1962: 191), presumably reflecting reanalysis as an attribute–head construction.

Several properties of Nivkh word order typology have already been introduced, such as the fixed attribute–head word order. Within the clause, word order is fairly rigidly subject–object–verb, with the direct object forming a particularly close unit with the verb phonologically as well as syntactically, in terms of alternation of the initial segment of verbs. Nivkh has several postpositions and no prepositions, e.g. *paχ vəj* 'under the stone', with the postposition *vəj* 'under'.

The formal structure of the verb in Nivkh is very straightforward, especially in comparison with the more prolific verb morphologies of many of the other languages of Siberia. However, one complication is the wide range of nonfinite gerunds that the language possesses, and which will be outlined below. The semantic distinctions between these various gerunds have not been fully described in the literature, and the glosses below and in the Nivkh text on pp. 276–7 are necessarily provisional and incomplete. In common with many languages of the area, Nivkh uses these gerunds to the virtual exclusion of finite subordinate clauses. Many of the points discussed below are illustrated in the Nivkh text, to which further reference should be made.

In a Nivkh simple sentence, the verb almost invariably occurs sentence-finally, and takes a closing finite suffix, the most common being -*d'*. This suffix serves essentially only to indicate finiteness, as it does not have any tense value (future tense, also with modal values, can be indicated by suffixing -*nə* before -*d'*), and does not serve any subject and/or object agreement function. Basically, in Nivkh, finite verbs do not agree with any of their arguments in person, but the suffix -*ku* and its phonetic variants, identical to the noun plural suffix, indicate a plural subject, e.g. *iṅ-d'-yu* 'they ate', at the end of the first paragraph of the text. Only in the imperative do we find full differentiation of person and number of the subject, e.g. *vi-ja* 'go!' (to one person), *vi-ve* or *vi-be* 'go!' (to more than one person), *vi-nəte* 'let's go!' (speaker addressing one other person, cf. the distinction between dual and plural in the first person), *vi-da* 'let's go!' (speaker addressing more than one other person).

One way of combining clauses together is by means of coordination, in which case in Nivkh all the verbs participating in the coordination take the same set of suffixes, namely -*ta* (phonetic variant -*da*) and -*ra*. The difference between -*ta* and -*ra* (and, more generally, between *t* and *r* forms) involves a limited range of subject agreement of verbs in Nivkh which we will encounter again in the discussion of certain gerunds. The suffix -*ta* is used if the subject is first person singular, or any person in the plural. The suffix -*ra* is used if the subject is second or third person singular. Whatever the historical origin of this unusual partition of subject agreement – it seems to have no natural semantic or pragmatic characterisation – it is characteristic of a wide range of verb forms in Nivkh. The second paragraph of the text is a long sentence containing several verbs in -*ra*, with third person singular subject. The following sentence illustrates the use of both suffixes, since the subjects are of different persons:

(180)   *t'i   tol -ux   nəŋ -ra,   ṅi miv -uin   pan   -ta*
          you water ABL walk AND   I land LOC be-born AND
          'you walk on water, and I was born on dry land'

Turning now to gerunds, there are two formal parameters according to which one can classify gerunds in Nivkh. First, there is a distinction between those gerunds which can take a specified subject of their own, and those that cannot: with the latter, the subject of the gerund is coreferential with that of the finite verb (or of the gerund that this gerund qualifies, where a chain of gerunds is formed; see example (182) below). In the text, the gerunds in *-t/-r* and in *-tot/-ror* illustrate necessary coreference, while that in *-ŋan* illustrates the possibility of noncoreference. The second parameter is whether or not the gerund agrees with its subject, according to the opposition second/third person singular versus all other person and number combinations. In the text, the gerunds in *-t/-r* and *-tot/-ror* show this distinction (the second form in each case being used for second and third person singular), while that in *-ŋan* does not. The two parameters are, incidentally, independent of one another, although there is some statistical validity to the rather unusual impression that may have been gleaned from the examples cited, namely that the gerunds requiring coreference (and where verb agreement might seem less necessary) usually have verb agreement, while those not requiring coreference tend not to have agreement.

With the gerunds that do not require coreference, it is possible to specify the subject explicitly, though not necessary to do so, and often surprisingly elliptical constructions are attested where the context makes clear which participants are involved. In the last sentence of the text, for instance, all that is made explicit is that someone is going towards the house while someone is singing inside the house; clearly the reference cannot be to the same person, and from the context the only reasonable interpretation is that the younger brother is going towards the house while someone else – from the wider context, clearly his sister – is singing inside the house:

(181) *p' -řəf erq -tox vi -ŋan təv mi -rx lu -d'*
       REFL house side ALL go GER house inside ALL sing FIN
       'when [he] went towards his house, [someone] was singing inside the house'

One final point concerning Nivkh gerunds that is revealed by a careful examination of the text relates to sentences with several gerunds, one dependent on the other, as in the following example from the text:

(182) *iɣ -ror   řək -ŋan nanak   t'evrq tupř̥ fəvrk -t'*
       kill GER-3SG bring GER elder-sister bird   feather pluck FIN
       'when he killed them, he brought them, and the elder sister plucked the birds' feathers'

The subject of the finite verb *fəvrk-t'* is *nanak* 'elder sister'. The gerund immediately dependent on this, *rək-ŋan*, does not require coreferential subjects, and it is clear from the context that the subject of this gerund is the younger brother. The gerund in

-*ror* is dependent in turn on the gerund ɣ̌ək-ŋan, not directly on the main verb; this gerund requires subject coreference, and the coreference is crucially with the subject of the verb on which the gerund in -*ror* is most immediately dependent, i.e. in this example with the subject of the gerund ɣ̌ək-ŋan, and not with the subject of the main verb. Thus the interpretation is that the younger brother killed the birds and the younger brother brought them home, while his sister plucked them.

6.6 Aramaic (Assyrian)

Semitic languages play scarcely any role in the linguistic composition of the U.S.S.R., but one Semitic language does qualify officially as a language of the U.S.S.R. The people who speak it are usually called Assyrians, or Aysor, in the U.S.S.R., and their language is a form of Aramaic, a North-West Semitic language very closely related genetically to Hebrew; their language should not be confused with Akkadian (Assyro-Babylonian), the language of the ancient Babylonian and Assyrian empires, which is in fact a much more distantly related Semitic language that has been extinct from around the middle of the first millennium B.C. Most members of the Assyrian ethnic group with which we are concerned here live in northern Iraq and adjacent parts of Iran and Syria. Accurate figures for the total number of speakers of modern Aramaic are not available, and estimates vary widely, although 100,000 is probably generous. Assyrians entered the Russian Empire as a result of the Treaty of Turkmanchai (Torkamān) (1828), by which Iran ceded eastern Armenia to Russia. They number 24,294 in the U.S.S.R., and of these 64.5% have Assyrian as their native language (the percentage was virtually the same in the 1959 census).

At the beginning of our era Aramaic was the dominant language from Mesopotamia to Palestine, having replaced Akkadian and severely restricted the area covered by several other languages, including Hebrew. However, the rapid expansion of Arabic throughout this area has led to the almost complete replacement of Aramaic. The internal classification of Aramaic is complicated by the fact that this classification must be not only geographical, but also historical, since Aramaic has been recorded for well over two thousand years, and even cultural, since different forms of Aramaic have been used by different religious traditions (Jewish, Jacobite Christian, Nestorian Christian). However, one major geographical division has been clear since the beginning of our era, between Western Aramaic and Eastern Aramaic. At present, Western Aramaic survives only in a few villages to the north of Damascus; all other Aramaic speakers, including Soviet Assyrians, speak Eastern Aramaic. One form of Eastern Aramaic, called Syriac, became the liturgical language of the Jacobite and Nestorian Christians, and in its Nestorian form still survives as the liturgical language of most Eastern Aramaic speakers; it is written in an original alphabet derived from Western Semitic, called Estrangelo.

In the nineteenth century, a written form of modern Eastern Aramaic was devised, based on the dialect of Rezā'īyeh (Urmia) in northern Iran, and using the Estrangelo alphabet. Within the U.S.S.R., where most Assyrians live in the Transcaucasian republics, though also scattered across urban centres throughout the U.S.S.R., a writing system based on the Latin alphabet was devised, and was used in the Aramaic-medium schools that existed from 1926 to 1938. At present, Aramaic is not used as a written language in the U.S.S.R.; most Aramaic speakers are also fluent in the dominant language of the area in which they live, and use this language as their written language and their medium of education.

The only other Semitic language spoken by a population group native to the U.S.S.R. is Arabic, spoken by the Arabs of Uzbekistan (in the Bukhara and Kashka-Dar'ya oblasts).

6.7 Dungan

In terms of its structure and basic vocabulary, Dungan is a form of Mandarin (Northern) Chinese, not standing out particularly from other North-Western dialects of Mandarin. However, the Dungan are an ethnic group distinct from the Chinese (Han), perhaps in large measure the descendants of prisoners-of-war brought into China first in the fourteenth century. The traditional religion of the Dungan is Islam. Most Dungan still live in China, where they number over three million; in China, they are usually referred to as Hwei. Groups of Dungan migrated westwards from China proper into Central Asia, and with the establishment of the present frontier between Russia and China in Central Asia, some of them ended up on the Russian side of the frontier. At present the main concentrations of Dungan in the U.S.S.R. are in Kirgizia and Kazakhstan, especially the former. The majority of Dungan speakers in the U.S.S.R. speak the Kansu dialect, some speak the Shensi dialect, which differ, for instance, in the number of phonemically distinct tones (three in the Kansu dialect, four in the Shensi dialect). The rate of language retention is very high: 94.3% of 38,644 ethnic Dungan have Dungan as their native language.

Perhaps the main difference between Dungan and Mandarin in the narrower sense is the presence of several Arabic and Persian loans in Dungan, in addition to a smaller number of loans from Turkic (with which the Dungan came into contact in Central Asia). Dungan as spoken in the U.S.S.R. also contains a number of loans from Russian (including international words borrowed in their Russian form), although Dungan, more than most languages of the U.S.S.R., still forms new words from its own resources (e.g. *fənč°'an* 'aeroplane'), perhaps reflecting in part the same difficulty that all other forms of Chinese have in adapting loans from European languages to the very different phonetic systems of Chinese. In the U.S.S.R., Dungan has been used in the school system since 1929, and there is a certain amount of publication in Dungan, including a newspaper. The orthography was originally on a Latin base, but was transferred to Cyrillic in the early 1950s, making Dungan one of the last languages of the U.S.S.R. to effect this change. The orthography does not, incidentally, mark tone.

In the general linguistic literature, Dungan is perhaps best known because of the claim by Trubetzkoy (1939) that it has a four-way contrast in the consonant system between plain, palatalised, labialised, and palatalised-labialised. Dungan orthography treats these as sequences of consonant followed by a semivowel, i.e. plain (e.g. *s*), palatalised (e.g. *sj*), labialised (e.g. *sw*), palatalised-labialised (e.g. *sẅ*).

TEXTS IN PALEOSIBERIAN LANGUAGES

CHUKCHI TEXT

qor   -en   ʔaqa- γərγ-ət   ənkʔam korγə- γərγ-ət
reindeer POSS bad N   PL and   joyful N   PL

  qol it -γʔi qora -ŋə ejmek -vʔi vaam-etə ekveće-nvə.
  one be 3SG reindeer ABS approach 3SG river ALL drink PURP

  ekveće-ŋŋo -γʔe ənkʔam lʔu-nin   miml -ək ćinit-kin   viilviil.
  drink INCH 3SG and   see 3SG→3SG water LOC self POSS reflection

γeta -ŋŋo -nenat   ćinit-kine -t majŋə-rənn -ət. kaćʔaravə-ŋŋo -γʔe
look-at INCH 3SG→3PL self POSS PL big   antler PL rejoice   INCH 3SG

ćenet-rənn -etə, inqun ətri nə - mejŋə-qine -t ənkʔam vərəmkə-lʔ   -ət.
self   antler ALL since they ADJ big   ADJ PL and   branch PART PL

ənqor-əm γite -ninet   ćinit-kine -t γətka-t ənkʔam ik -vʔi:
then well look-at 3SG→3PL self POSS PL leg   PL and   say 3SG

  γətka-t -əm γəm-nine -t ʔetkiŋ-ət ćama nə -rul -qine -t.
  -leg   PL well I   POSS PL awful PL also ADJ weak ADJ PL

  luur ʔey -əć -a   penr -ənen   qora -ŋə. qora
  suddenly wolf AUG ERG = INSTR attack 3SG→3SG reindeer ABS reindeer

-ŋə rʔile-γʔi nota -jekve. rʔile-pkir -γʔi omk -etə. umkə-ćəku
ABS run 3SG tundra ALONG run arrive 3SG forest ALL forest INSIDE

γəva -γʔe ənək-rənn -a   koryo-k ənkʔam ʔiγ -e
get-stuck 3SG he   antler INSTR cedar LOC and   wolf ERG = INSTR

piri -nin   ətlon.
take 3SG→3SG he-ABS

(Extracted from I. S. Vdovin and P. I. Inènlikèj, *Ləγʔoravetlʔen jiləjil*, Leningrad, 1972.)

Notes

Phonetic: *l* represents [ɬ]; *ć* varies between [ć] and [ś]; *v* is bilabial. The text illustrates several morphophonemic alternations due to vowel harmony (e.g. *-ɣʔi*, *-ɣʔe* '3SG'), schwa insertion (e.g. *-t*, *-ət* 'PL'), and adjacent vowel loss (e.g. *qora-*, *qor-* 'reindeer').

The unmarked tense is past, so none of the verbs in this text has a tense marker.

qolityʔi. . . ejmekvʔi: the combination of *qol* 'one (of several)' with the intransitive auxiliary *it-* in the same form as the intransitive main verb translates 'once. . .'

ejmekvʔi, ikvʔi: here *kv* is for **vɣ*, by regular rule.

FREE TRANSLATION

The misfortunes and joys of a reindeer

Once upon a time a reindeer approached a river in order to drink.

He began to drink and saw his reflection in the water. He began to look at his large antlers. He began to rejoice at his antlers, since they were big and branching. Then he looked at his feet and said:

—My feet are awful and weak.

Suddenly a big wolf attacked the reindeer. The reindeer ran across the tundra. Running, he arrived at a forest. Inside the forest he got stuck by his antlers and the wolf seized him.

YUKAGIR TEXT

jaŋre mer -uoŋ -ej. uodaʁawiŋ me - pun-na   -ŋ   KAPKAN-ek.
goose POSS young 3SG gosling   FOC kill INCH 1SG trap   INSTR

  maarqa-́deŋ ibal   -ʁan   mer - ewrienu-jeŋ. uodaʁawiŋ waŋt'i-r,
  one ~ ASV mountain PROL FOC walk   1SG gosling   seek   GER

qolʁo   -d   -enmur-ek   nuu-me -ŋ.   nime -ʁa   mer - uu-jeŋ. met
mammoth GEN horn   FOC find FOC 1SG house LOC FOC go 1SG I

me - pundu-ŋ:
FOC tell   1SG

  —qolʁo   -d   -enmur-ek   nuu-me -ŋ.
  mammoth GEN horn   FOC find FOC 1SG

  met ama -ńeŋ   me -kewe-́teli, nimudiŋ erimedawje weĺi -re,   me
  I   father COMIT FOC leave 1PL axe   shovel   carry GER FOC

-kewe-́teli. tu -ʁolʁo   -d   -enmur-ʁa me -kötke -t'eli. me
leave 1PL this mammoth GEN horn   LOC FOC approach 1PL FOC

-waare -t′ lukul -ʁat kin -qolʁo -d - enmur-ek. nime -ʁa mer
pull-out 1PL ground ABL two mammoth GEN horn FOC house LOC FOC
-uu-jeli. maarqan-göde mon-ni:
go 1PL one person say 3SG
  —qolʁo -d -enmur maarqa-le met-iŋ kii -ŋik. met
    mammoth GEN horn one FOC I ALL give IMPER-2PL I
t′urʁa -le giite-meŋ.
young-doe FOC give 1SG-FOC
(Extracted from E. A. Krejnovič, *Jukagirskij jazyk*, Moscow-Leningrad, 1958.)

Notes
For the morphemes glossed FOC (focus), see pp. 260–1.

FREE TRANSLATION

The geese had young. I began to kill goslings with traps.
    Once I was walking along the mountain. While seeking goslings, I found a
mammoth tusk. I went home. I told (my father):
    —I found a mammoth tusk.
    My father and I set out, carrying an axe and a spade we set out. We approached this
mammoth tusk. We pulled two mammoth tusks out of the ground. We went home.
One person said:
    —Give me one tusk. I will give you a young doe.

NIVKH TEXT

p′ -at′ik -xe p′ -nanak -xe pań -d′. atik
REFL younger-brother AND REFL elder-sister AND grow-up FIN younger-
    matka -d′. k′u -ye puńd-ye bo -ror p′u -r
brother be-small FIN arrow AND bow AND take GER-3SG go-out GER-3SG
tevrq χa -d′. iɣ -ror řǝk -ŋan nanak tevrq tupř
bird shoot FIN kill GER-3SG bring GER elder-sister bird feather
fǝvrk -t′. t′uur-tox řa -tot iń -d′ -yu.
pluck FIN fire ALL cook GER-3PL eat FIN PL
    hoŋgut′um-ke atik ǝrk pil -ra pal -rox mǝr
live-thus GER younger-brother already be-big AND forest ALL go-up
-ra t′′olŋaj xu -ra t′oχ k′u-ra q′otr k′u-ra.
AND deer kill AND elk kill AND bear kill AND

hoŋgutʿum-ke   muuv ńaqr pal -rox mər -ra qʿotr kʿu -ra   hoʁorot
live-thus   GER day one forest ALL go-up and bear kill AND then

lər   -γət   -ra.   tʿu   -in   ʁońɗi-ror   vəγi -ř̥
cut-up COMPLETE AND sledge LOC load GER-3SG drag GER-3SG

məγ   -dʹ. təf kʿikr   -tox məγ -ŋan pʿ -ř̥əf ajma
go-down FIN house upper-part ALL go-down GER REFL house look-at

-dʹ. tʿuf poj ha-dox qʿau -dʹ. hoʁor eʁ   -gur   məγ
FIN smoke billow be-INFIN NEG FIN then be-quick GER-3SG go-down

-dʹ. məγ -ra pʿ -zus -ku ńo -rx xiti -γət   -ra.
FIN go-down AND REFL meat PL barn ALL lift-up COMPLETE AND

hoʁorot pʿ   -xuku   -dʹ. pʿ -ř̥əf erq -tox vi -ŋan təv
then   REFL shake-down FIN REFL house side ALL go GER house

mi -rx lu -dʹ.
inside ALL sing FIN

(Extracted from V. Z. Panfilov, *Grammatika nivxskogo jazyka*, vol. 2. Moscow–Leningrad, 1965.)

Notes

For the syntax of sentences consisting of more than one clause, in particular for the function of verb forms glossed 'GER' and 'AND', see the discussion on pp. 270–2.

hadox qʿaudʹ: the combination of the negative auxiliary *qʿau-* with the infinitive of the main verb is one common way of expressing negation.

eʁgur: the gerund of the verb *eʁ-* 'be quick' serves as an adverbial, meaning 'quickly'.

FREE TRANSLATION

A younger brother and an elder sister grew up. The brother was small. He took his arrows and bow, went out, and shot birds. When he killed them, he brought them and the elder sister plucked the birds' feathers. When they had cooked them on the fire, they ate them.

Living thus, the younger brother was already big and went up into the forest and killed deer, killed elk, and killed bear.

Living thus, one day he went up to the forest and killed bear and then cut them up. He loaded them onto the sledge and, dragging it, came down. When he came down to above the house, he looked at his house. There was no smoke billowing. Then he came down quickly. He came down and lifted his meats into the barn. Then he shook himself down. When he went towards his house, someone was singing inside the house.

FURTHER READING

Several collections of articles have appeared in recent years in the U.S.S.R. covering the full range of Paleosiberian languages, usually also incorporating articles on Samoyedic or other languages of Siberia. In this list of references we shall concentrate on monograph studies of individual languages and, where applicable, language families. Brief sketches of all the languages discussed in this chapter are available in *JaNSSSR* V (1968).

For the languages of the Chukotko-Kamchatkan family, the standard grammar of Chukchi is Skorik (1961–77); for Chukchi syntax, there is an excellent introduction in German through the study of verb valency by Nedjalkov (1976). Bogoras (1922), though mentioning only Chukchi in the title, also covers Koryak and Itelmen, and appeared in English; while Bogoras's phonetics is impressionistic, and the attempt to describe Itelmen simultaneously with Chukchi and Koryak hardly successful, this account contains much important data and insightful syntactic observations. The standard grammar of Koryak is Žukova (1972). For the smaller languages, there are detailed accounts of Alyutor conjugation by Mel'čuk (1973), and of basic sentence structure by Mel'čuk and Savvina (1974), the latter also available in English. For (Western) Itelmen, the standard work is now Volodin (1976).

An excellent survey of Eskimo-Aleut linguistic scholarship is provided by Krauss (1973). For Siberian Yupik Eskimo, the standard Soviet works are Menovščikov (1962–7) on the Chaplino dialect (and, thus, on the written language), Menovščikov (1975) on the Naukan dialect, and also Menovščikov (1964) on the aberrant Sireniki dialect/language. Since Siberian Yupik is also spoken on St. Lawrence Island, Alaska, one can profitably refer to the accounts in English of St. Lawrence Island phonology (Krauss 1975) and morphology and syntax (Jacobson 1977).

For Yukagir, Krejnovič (1958) is the classic description. There is much less definitive material available on Ket, though Dul'zon (1968) is the most comprehensive grammar. Verb morphology is described in great detail by Krejnovič (1968), while *KS* (1968) contains many solid descriptive articles. The phonetics of Nivkh is described in detail by Krejnovič (1937), while Panfilov (1962–5) is the standard overall description.

Appendix 1

Ethnic and linguistic composition of the U.S.S.R. according to the 1970 census

Note. The language name is given first, followed by the name of the ethnic group if this is very different from the language name. The first figure in the third column gives the number of members of the ethnic group that have the corresponding language as their native language. For languages of Union Republics, the total number of speakers in the U.S.S.R. (i.e. including members of other ethnic groups who speak that language) is given in parentheses.

Language/Ethnic group	Number in ethnic group	Number of native speakers	
Russian	129,015,140	128,811,371	(141,830,564)
Ukrainian	40,753,246	34,906,299	(35,400,944)
Uzbek	9,195,093	9,070,748	(9,154,704)
Belorussian	9,051,755	7,291,277	(7,630,007)
Tatar	5,930,670	5,289,435	
Kazakh	5,298,818	5,194,996	(5,213,694)
Azerbaydzhan	4,379,937	4,301,299	(4,347,089)
Armenian	3,559,151	3,254,132	(3,261,053)
Georgian	3,245,300	3,193,491	(3,310,917)
Lithuanian	2,664,944	2,608,223	(2,625,608)
Moldavian	2,697,994	2,563,005	(2,607,367)
Tadzhik	2,135,883	2,104,023	(2,202,671)
Turkmen	1,525,284	1,508,478	(1,514,980)
Chuvash	1,694,351	1,472,156	
Kirgiz	1,452,222	1,434,434	(1,445,213)
Latvian	1,429,844	1,361,414	(1,390,162)
German	1,846,317	1,233,317	
Mordva	1,262,670	982,963	
Estonian	1,007,356	962,084	(974,649)
Bashkir	1,239,681	820,390	
Chechen	612,674	604,655	
Udmurt	704,328	581,877	
Mari	598,628	545,803	
Ossete	488,039	432,589	
Avar	396,297	385,043	
Yiddish/Jew	2,150,707	381,078	
Polish	1,167,523	379,470	

Kabard-Cherkes	319,713 (total)	311,078 (total)
Kabard	279,928	274,460
Cherkes	39,785	36,618
Lezgi	323,829	304,087
Buryat	314,671	291,432
Yakut (including Dolgan)	301,121 (total)	289,528 (total)
Yakut	296,244	285,147
Dolgan	4,877	4,381
Komi	321,894	266,335
Bulgarian	351,168	256,646
Korean	357,507	245,076
Karakalpak	236,009	228,002
Dargva	230,932	227,302
Kumyk	188,792	185,804
Karachay-Balkar	172,242 (total)	168,435 (total)
Karachay	112,741	110,616
Balkar	59,501	57,819
Hungarian	166,451	160,781
Ingush	157,605	153,483
Uygur	173,276	153,313
Gagauz	156,606	146,575
Tuva	139,388	137,607
Greek	336,869	132,303
Komi-Permyak	153,451	131,677
Kalmyk	137,194	125,781
Romany/Gypsy	175,335	124,165
Adyge	99,855	96,331
Karelian	146,081	92,019
Lak	85,822	82,010
Abkhaz	83,240	79,835
Kurdish	88,930	77,879
Romanian	119,292	76,263
Khakas	66,725	55,834
Tabasaran	55,188	54,574
Altay	55,812	48,660
Nogay	51,784	46,493
Finnish	84,750	43,208
Dungan	38,644	36,445
Abaza	25,488	24,449
Nenets	28,705	23,952
Aramaic/Assyrian	24,294	15,662
Khanty	21,138	14,562
Evenki	25,149	12,899
Tat	17,109	12,427
Beludzh	12,582	12,339
Shor	16,494	12,130
Rutul	12,071	11,933
Chukchi	13,597	11,231
Tsakhur	11,103	10,719
Persian	27,501	10,160

Czech	20,981	8,998
Agul	8,831	8,782
Nanay	10,005	6,911
Even	12,029	6,736
Koryak	7,487	6,075
Slovak	11,658	6,060
Udi	5,919	5,537
Mongolian (Khalkha)	5,170	4,803
Mansi	7,710	4,037
Pashto/Afghan	4,184	2,956
Veps	8,281	2,837
Albanian	4,402	2,496
Nivkh	4,420	2,188
Selkup	4,282	2,186
French	2,470	1,854
Ulcha	2,448	1,489
Lapp	1,884	1,058
Ket	1,182	885
Udege	1,469	809
Eskimo	1,308	785
Nganasan	953	719
Karaim	4,571	585
Oroch	1,089	529
Itelmen	1,301	464
Tofa	620	349
Yukagir	615	288
Negidal	537	286
Ingrian	781	208
Aleut	441	96
Peoples of India and Pakistan	1,945 (total)	1,706 (total)
Population of U.S.S.R.	241,720,134	226,881,774

Appendix 2

Ethnic administrative areas of the U.S.S.R.

Note. Where the name of the area, as given here, differs markedly from the Russian name, the latter is given in parentheses, as transliterated in the *Times Atlas of the World.* Included are ethnic groups constituting 5% or more of the population of the area, and also, in the case of the Khanty and Mansi, the ethnic groups after which the area is named, even though these constitute less than 5% of the population.

Area	Population	Main ethnic groups (%)	
1. S.S.R.s (Soviet Socialist Republics)			
Russian S.F.S.R.	130,079,210	Russian	82.8
Armenian (Armyanskaya) S.S.R.	2,491,873	Armenian	88.6
		Azerbaydzhan	5.9
Azerbaydzhan S.S.R.	5,117,081	Azerbaydzhan	73.8
		Russian	10.0
		Armenian	9.5
Belorussian S.S.R.	9,002,338	Belorussian	81.0
		Russian	10.4
Estonian S.S.R.	1,356,079	Estonian	68.2
		Russian	24.7
Georgian (Gruzinskaya) S.S.R.	4,686,358	Georgian	66.8
		Armenian	9.7
		Russian	8.5
Kazakh S.S.R.	13,008,726	Russian	42.5
		Kazakh	32.6
		Ukrainian	7.2
		German	6.6
Kirgiz S.S.R.	2,932,805	Kirgiz	43.8
		Russian	29.2
		Uzbek	11.3
Latvian S.S.R.	2,364,127	Latvian	56.8
		Russian	29.8
Lithuanian (Litovskaya) S.S.R.	3,128,236	Lithuanian	80.1
		Russian	8.6
		Polish	7.7
Moldavian S.S.R.	3,568,873	Moldavian	64.6
		Ukrainian	14.2
		Russian	11.6

Tadzhik S.S.R.	2,899,602	Tadzhik	56.2
		Uzbek	23.0
		Russian	11.9
Turkmen S.S.R.	2,158,880	Turkmen	65.6
		Russian	14.5
		Uzbek	8.3
Ukrainian S.S.R.	47,126,517	Ukrainian	74.9
		Russian	19.4
Uzbek S.S.R.	11,799,429	Uzbek	65.5
		Russian	12.5

2. A.S.S.R.s (Autonomous Soviet Socialist Republics)
(in R.S.F.S.R.)

Bashkir A.S.S.R.	3,818,075	Russian	40.5
		Tatar	24.7
		Bashkir	23.4
Buryat A.S.S.R.	812,251	Russian	73.5
		Buryat	22.0
Chechen-Ingush A.S.S.R.	1,064,471	Chechen	47.8
		Russian	34.5
		Ingush	10.7
Chuvash A.S.S.R.	1,223,675	Chuvash	70.0
		Russian	24.5
Dagestan A.S.S.R.	1,428,540	Avar	24.5
		Russian	14.7
		Dargva	14.5
		Kumyk	11.8
		Lezgi	11.4
		Lak	5.1
Kabard-Balkar A.S.S.R.	588,203	Kabard	45.0
		Russian	37.2
		Balkar	8.7
Kalmyk A.S.S.R.	267,993	Russian	45.8
		Kalmyk	41.1
Karelian A.S.S.R.	713,451	Russian	68.1
		Karelian	11.8
		Belorussian	9.3
Komi A.S.S.R.	964,802	Russian	53.1
		Komi	28.6
		Ukrainian	8.6
Mari A.S.S.R.	684,748	Russian	46.9
		Mari	43.7
		Tatar	5.9
Mordva (Mordovskaya) A.S.S.R.	1,029,562	Russian	58.9
		Mordva	35.4
North-Ossete (Severo-Osetinskaya) A.S.S.R.	552,581	Ossete	48.7
		Russian	36.6
Tatar A.S.S.R.	3,131,238	Tatar	49.1
		Russian	42.4
Tuva A.S.S.R.	230,864	Tuva	58.6
		Russian	38.3

Udmurt A.S.S.R.	1,417,675	Russian	57.1
		Udmurt	34.2
		Tatar	6.2
Yakut A.S.S.R.	664,123	Russian	47.3
		Yakut	43.0
(in Azerbaydzhan)			
Nakhichevan A.S.S.R.	202,187	Azerbaydzhan	93.8
(in Georgia)			
Abkhaz A.S.S.R.	486,959	Georgian	24.6
		Russian	19.1
		Abkhaz	15.9
		Armenian	15.4
Adzhar A.S.S.R.	309,768	Georgian	76.5
		Russian	11.6
		Armenian	5.0
(in Uzbekistan)			
Karakalpak A.S.S.R.	702,264	Karakalpak	31.0
		Uzbek	30.3
		Kazakh	26.5
		Turkmen	5.6

3. A.O.s (Autonomous Regions/Oblasts)
(in R.S.F.S.R.)

Adyge A.O.	385,644	Russian	71.7
		Adyge	21.1
Jewish (Yevreyskaya) A.O.	172,449	Russian	83.7
		Jew	6.6
Karachay-Cherkes A.O.	344,651	Russian	47.1
		Karachay	28.2
		Cherkes	9.1
Khakas A.O.	445,824	Russian	78.4
		Khakas	12.3
Mountain-Altay (Gorno-Altayskaya) A.O.	168,261	Russian	65.6
		Altay	27.8
(in Azerbaydzhan)			
Mountain-Karabakh (Nagorno-Karabakhskaya) A.O.	150,313	Armenian	80.5
		Azerbaydzhan	18.1
(in Georgia)			
South-Ossete (Yugo-Osetinskaya) A.O.	99,421	Ossete	66.5
		Georgian	28.3
(in Tadzhikistan)			
Mountain-Badakhshan (Gorno-Badakhshanskaya) A.O.	97,796	Tadzhik	91.9
		Kirgiz	7.1

4. N.O.s (National Areas/Okrugs)
(in R.S.F.S.R.)

Aginskiy-Buryat N.O.	65,768	Buryat	50.4
		Russian	44.0
Chukchi (Chukotskiy) N.O.	101,184	Russian	69.7
		Chukchi	10.9

Evenki N.O.	12,658	Russian	61.1
		Evenki	25.3
Khanty-Mansi N.O.	271,157	Russian	76.9
		Tatar	5.2
		Khanty	4.5
		Mansi	2.5
Komi-Permyak N.O.	212,141	Komi-Permyak	58.2
		Russian	36.0
Koryak N.O.	30,917	Russian	63.0
		Koryak	19.1
Nenets N.O.	39,119	Russian	64.5
		Nenets	15.0
Taymyr (Dolgan-Nenets) N.O.	38,060	Russian	66.9
		Dolgan	11.4
		Nenets	5.9
Ust'-Ordynskiy-Buryat N.O.	146,412	Russian	58.8
		Buryat	33.0
Yamal-Nenets N.O.	79,977	Russian	46.9
		Nenets	21.9

Appendix 3

Alphabets of the languages of the U.S.S.R.

Figure A.1. *Russian (Cyrillic) alphabet*

Cyrillic		Transliteration	Cyrillic		Transliteration
А	а	a	Р	р	r
Б	б	b	С	с	s
В	в	v	Т	т	t
Г	г	g	У	у	u
Д	д	d	Ф	ф	f
Е	е	e	Х	х	x
Ё	ё	ë	Ц	ц	c
Ж	ж	ž	Ч	ч	č
З	з	z	Ш	ш	š
И	и	i	Щ	щ	šč
Й	й	j		ъ	''
К	к	k		ы	y
Л	л	l		ь	'
М	м	m	Э	э	ė
Н	н	n	Ю	ю	ju
О	о	o	Я	я	ja
П	п	p			

The symbols transliterated *e, ë, ju, ja* are pronounced [je], [jo], [ju], [ja] word-initially, after a vowel, and after ' and ''; otherwise as [e], [o], [u], [a] with palatalisation of the preceding consonant. The diaeresis on *ë* is usually omitted in Russian orthography (and hence in the transliteration). The symbol ' indicates palatalisation, '' nonpalatalisation of the preceding consonant. The symbol transliterated *y* is pronounced [i], and *ė* as [e].

Figure A.2. *Chukchi test (page 274) in current (Cyrillic) orthography*

Ӄорэн а'ӄагыргыт ынкъам коргыгыргыт.

Ӄол итгъи ӄораӈы эйимэквъи ва-амэты эквэченвы.

Эквэченӈогъэ ынкъам льунин мим-лык чиниткин виилвиил. Гэтаӈӈонэнат чиниткинэт майӈырынныт. Качъара-выӈӈогъэ ченэтрыннэты, иӈӄун ытри нымэйыӈӄинэт ынкъам вырымкыльыт. Ынӄоры-ым гитэнинэт чиниткинэт гыткат ынкъам иквъи:

— Гыткат-ым гымнинэт э'ткиӈыт чама нырулӄинэт.

Люур э'гычга пэнрынэн ӄораӈы. Ӄораӈы ръилегъи нотаеквэ. Ръилеп-киргъи омкэты. Умкычыку гывагъэ ыныкрынна кыргок ынкъам и'гэ пири-нин ытлён.

Figure A.3. *Modern Armenian alphabet*

Capital	Small	Transliteration
Ա	ա	a
Բ	բ	b
Գ	գ	g
Դ	դ	d
Ե	ե	e, je
Զ	զ	z
Է	է	e
Ը	ը	ə
Թ	թ	t
Ժ	ժ	ž
Ի	ի	i
Լ	լ	l
Խ	խ	x
Ծ	ծ	c'
Կ	կ	k'
Հ	հ	h
Ձ	ձ	3
Ղ	ղ	γ
Ճ	ճ	č'
Մ	մ	m
Յ	յ	j
Ն	ն	n
Շ	շ	š
Ո	ո	o, vo
Չ	չ	č
Պ	պ	p'
Ջ	ջ	ǰ
Ռ	ռ	ṙ
Ս	ս	s
Վ	վ	v
Տ	տ	t'
Ր	ր	r
Ց	ց	c
Ւ	ւ	-
Փ	փ	p
Ք	ք	k
	և	ev, jev
Օ	o	o
Ֆ	ֆ	f

Based on G. H. Fairbanks and E. W. Stevick, *Spoken East Armenian*, New York, 1958, p. 74.
The sixth last letter of this figure is not used as a separate letter in Modern Eastern Armenian, but is used together with preceding (*v*)*o* to give a digraph with the phonetic value *u*.

Figure A.4. *Armenian text (pages 192–3) in current orthography*

Կարճ ժամանակ նայից իշ դարմացած, հետո ուսերը թոթվից տարակուսանքով և գլուխը նոբից կախից գրեի վրա, առանց այլևս ոչ մի խոսք արտասանելու. բառ երևայթին, ուզում էր հասկացնել, որ հասկում թույնեմ իբեն և հետանում.

Բայց ես համառորեն կանգնած էի նրա առջև և ակամա շրանում էի, գլխովով նրա գեղեցիկ գլուխը շատ հարիստա, փափուկ և փայլուն մազերով, որոնք նիր ճաքած արեի թեք հատագայթերի տակ բազմացան երանգնքեր էին ընդունում...

— Այստեղ նայեցեք, — ասացե, տեսնելով, որ գլուխը չի ուզում գրեի վրայից բարձրացնել.

Նայեք.

Ճակատս գրի նրացանիս փողե ձայրին, իսկ ոտս շիրկի վրա.

Figure A.5. *Modern Georgian alphabet (mxedruli)*

ა	ბ	გ	დ	ე	ვ	ზ	თ	ი	კ	ლ	მ	ნ	ო	პ	ჟ	რ	ს	ტ
a	b	g	d	e	v	z	t	i	k'	l	m	n	o	p'	ž	r	s	t'

უ		ფ	ქ	ღ	ყ	შ	ჩ	ც	ძ	წ	ჭ	ხ		ჯ	ჰ
u		p	k	γ	q'	š	č·	c	z	c'	č'x			ž	h

Based on H. Vogt, *Grammaire de la langue géorgienne*, Oslo, 1971, p. 6.

Figure A.6. *Georgian text (page 231) in current orthography*

პლატონი კიდევ დიღხანს იყო უგუნებოდ, მარტოდ მჯდომი ხა-
ლის კუთხეში პატარა რგვალ მაგიდასთან, ჩაით წინ და ჯერ კიდევ
ვერ დაეწყნარებინა თავისი გული. რარიგად არ ლანძღავდა და აგინებ-
და თავისთავს, რომ გადარეულ კაცთან მგზავრობა არ დაიშალა და ამ-
დენი უსიამოვნება და გაწვალება გამოიარა... გაწვალება გაწვალება
იყო, მაგრამ მას უფრო სირცხვილი ჰკლავდა, იმ წყეულმა რომ მთელ
საზოგადოებაში წამოიძახა და მისი საიდუმლო გაამჟღავნა. რასაკვირ-
ველია, ახლა სამასხროდ იქნებოდა აგდებული ამ ყმაწვილებისაგან.
რომელნიც დილიდან სარამომდის მხოლოდ იმით არიან გართულნი,
რომ საოხუნჯო, სასაცილო და სამასხრო საგანი რამ ან მოიგონონ, ან
შეამჩნიონ ვისმე. ამაზე იკლავდა თავს პლატონი და იმნაირ გუნებაზე
დადგა, რომ მზად იყო ხელი აელო თავის განზრახვაზე, მიეტოვებინა
თავისი საქმე, ამწამსვე უკან გაბრუნებულიყო სახლში, თავი მიენებე-
ბინა ყოველივესთვის და დაე, რაც უნდა ის მომხდარიყო.

References

Abaev, V. I. 1959. *Osetinskij jazyk*. Ordzhonikidze. (English translation: A grammatical sketch of Ossetic. Bloomington, Indiana, 1964.)

Abdullaev, S. N. 1954. *Grammatika darginskogo jazyka: fonetika i morfologija*. Makhachkala.

Abdullaev, Z. G. 1971. *Očerki po sintaksisu darginskogo jazyka*. Moscow.

Abeghian, A. 1936. *Neuarmenische Grammatik*. Berlin–Leipzig.

Adjarian, H. 1909. *Classification des dialectes arméniens*. Paris.

Aliev, U. B. 1972. *Sintaksis karačaevo-balkarskogo jazyka*. Moscow.

Allen, W. S. 1956. Structure and system in the Abaza verbal complex. *Transactions of the Philological Society* 1956: 127–76.

Allen, W. S. 1965. On one-vowel systems. *Lingua* 13: 111–24

Al-Mufti, S. 1978. *Die Sprachwissenschaft der Tscherkessischen: Einleitung und Lautlehre*. Heidelberg.

Ard, J. 1980. A sketch of vowel harmony in the Tungus languages. In *SLUSSR*.

Ariste, P. 1968. *A grammar of the Votic language*. Bloomington, Indiana.

Asatiani, I. 1974. *Č'anuri (lazuri) t'ekst'ebi*. Tbilisi.

Avrorin, V. A. 1959–61. *Grammatika nanajskogo jazyka*. 2 vols. Moscow–Leningrad.

Bakaev, Č. X. 1962. *Govor kurdov Turkmenii*. Moscow.

Bakaev, Č. X. 1965. *Jazyk azerbajdžanskix kurdov*. Moscow.

Bakaev, Č. X. 1966. Kurdskij jazyk. In *JaNSSSR* I.

Balakaev, M. B. 1959. *Sovremennyj kazaxskij jazyk: sintaksis*. Alma-Ata.

Barannikov, O. 1933. *Ukrajins'ki ta pivdenno-rosijski cigans'ki dijalekti*. Leningrad. (English translation: A. Barannikov, *The Ukrainian and South-Russian gypsy dialects*. Leningrad, 1934.)

Bardakjian, K. B. and Thomson, R. W. 1977. *A textbook of Modern Western Armenian*. Delmar, New York.

Baskakov, N. A. 1940. *Nogajskij jazyk i ego dialekty: grammatika, teksty i slovar'*. Moscow–Leningrad.

Baskakov, N. A. 1951–2. *Karakalpakskij jazyk*. 2 vols. Moscow–Leningrad.

Baskakov, N. A. 1958. *Altajskij jazyk: vvedenie v izučenie altajskogo jazyka i ego dialektov*. Moscow.

Baskakov, N. A. 1969. *Vvedenie v izučenie tjurkskix jazykov*. 2nd. edn. Moscow.

Baskakov, N. A. 1970. *Grammatika turkmenskogo jazyka*. Ashkhabad.

Batalova, R. M. et al. 1962. *Komi-permjackij jazyk*. Kudymkar.

Batmanov, I. A. 1939–40. *Grammatika kirgizskogo jazyka*. 3 vols. Frunze–Kazan'.

Batmanov, I. A. 1963. *Sovremennyj kirgizskij jazyk*, I. Frunze.

Benzing, J. 1953. *Einführung in das Studium der altaischen Philologie und der Turkologie*. Wiesbaden.

Benzing, J. 1955. *Lamutische Grammatik mit Bibliographie, Sprachproben und Glossar*. Wiesbaden.

Benzing, J. 1956. *Die tungusischen Sprachen: Versuch einer vergleichenden Grammatik*. Wiesbaden.

Beranek, F. 1958. *Das Pinsker Jiddisch*. Berlin.

Bertagaev, T. A. 1964. *Sintaksis sovremennogo mongol'skogo jazyka v sravnitel'nom osveščenii: prostoe predloženie*. Moscow.

Bertagaev, T. A. and Cydendambaev, C. B. 1962. *Grammatika burjatskogo jazyka: sintaksis*. Moscow.

Binnick, R. I. 1979. *Modern Mongolian: a transformational syntax*. Toronto.

Birnbaum, S. A. 1979. *Yiddish: a survey and a grammar*. Toronto.

Boeder, W. 1968. Über die Versionen des georgischen Verbs. *Folia Linguistica* 2: 82–152.

Bogoras, W. 1922. Chukchee. In *Handbook of American Indian languages* II, ed. F. Boas. Washington, D.C.

Böhtlingk, O. 1851. *Über die Sprache der Jakuten*. St. Petersburg. (Reprinted: Bloomington, Indiana, 1963.)

Bokarev, A. A. 1949a. *Očerk grammatiki čamalinskogo jazyka*. Moscow–Leningrad.

Bokarev, A. A. 1949b. *Sintaksis avarskogo jazyka*. Moscow–Leningrad.

Bokarev, E. A. 1959. *Ceskie (didojskie) jazyki Dagestana*. Moscow.

Bokarev, E. A. 1961. *Vvedenie v sravnitel'no-istoričeskoe izučenie dagestanskix jazykov*. Makhachkala.

Boldyrev, B. V. 1976. *Kategorija kosvennoj prinadležnosti v tunguso-man'čžurskix jazykax*. Moscow.

BSÈ. 1950–8; 1970–. *Bol'šaja sovetskaja ènciklopedija*. 2nd. edn, 51 vols. and 2 index vols., Moscow, 1950–8. 3rd edn, Moscow, 1970–. (English translation: *The great Soviet encyclopedia*, 3rd. edn. New York. 1973–.)

Budiņa Lazdiņa, T. 1966. *Teach yourself Latvian*. London.

Byxovskaja, S. L. 1938. Osobennosti upotreblenija perexodnogo glagola v darginskom jazyke. In *Pamjati N. Ja. Marra*.

Castrén, M. A. 1854. *Grammatik der samojedischen Sprachen*. St. Petersburg. (Reprinted: Bloomington, Indiana, 1966.)

Catford, J. C. 1976. Ergativity in Caucasian languages. *Papers from the Sixth Meeting of the North-East Linguistic Society of America*. Montreal.

Catford, J. C. 1977. Mountain of tongues: the languages of the Caucasus. *Annual Review of Anthropology* 6: 283–314.

Cercvadze [Cercvaʒe], I. 1965. *Andiuri ena*. Tbilisi.

Čikobava, A. 1974. 'The Annual', its aims and linguistic principles. *Annual of Ibero-Caucasian Linguistics* 1: 33–44.

Čikobava, A. and Cercvadze [Cercvaʒe], I. 1962. *Xunʒuri ena*. Tbilisi.

Cincius, V. I. 1947. *Očerk grammatiki èvenskogo (lamutskogo) jazyka*. Leningrad.

Cincius, V. I. 1949. *Sravnitel'naja fonetika tunguso-man'čžurskix jazykov*. Leningrad.

Colarusso, J. 1975. *The Northwest Caucasian languages: a phonological survey*. Ph.D. dissertation, Harvard University, Cambridge, Mass.

Colarusso, J. 1977. The languages of the northwest Caucasus. In *LLNRPSU*.

Collinder, B. 1960. *Comparative grammar of the Uralic languages*. Stockholm.

Collinder, B. 1965. *An introduction to the Uralic languages*. Berkeley, California.

Collinder, B. 1969. *Survey of the Uralic languages*. 2nd. edn. Stockholm.

Comrie, B. 1978. Definite direct objects and referent identification. *Pragmatics Microfiche* 3.1.

Comrie, B. and Stone, G. 1978. *The Russian language since the Revolution*. Oxford.

Creissels, D. 1977. *Les langues d'U.R.S.S., aspects linguistiques et sociolinguistiques*. Paris.

Črelašvili, K. [Č'relašvili, K'.], 1975. *Naxuri enebis tanxmovanta sist'ema*. Tbilisi.

CTL 1. 1968. *Current trends in linguistics*, ed. T. A. Sebeok. Vol. 1: *Soviet and east European linguistics*. The Hague.

Dambriūnas, L., Klimas, A., and Schmalstieg, W. R. 1972. *Introduction to modern Lithuanian*. Rev. edn. Brooklyn, New York.

De Bray, R. G. A. 1969. *Guide to the Slavonic languages*. Rev. edn. London.

Décsy, Gy. 1965. *Einführung in die finnisch-ugrische Sprachwissenschaft*. Wiesbaden.

Décsy, Gy. 1966. *Yurak chrestomathy*. Bloomington, Indiana.

Deeters, G. 1930. *Das kharthwelische Verbum*. Leipzig.

Dešeriev, Ju. D. 1953. *Bacbijskij jazyk*. Moscow.

Dešeriev, Ju. D. 1959. *Grammatika xinalugskogo jazyka*. Moscow.

Dešeriev, Ju. D. 1960. *Sovremennyj čečenskij literaturnyj jazyk*, 1: *fonetika*. Groznyy.

Dirr, A. 1928. *Einführung in das Studium der kaukasischen Sprachen*. Leipzig.

Dmitriev, N. K. 1940. *Grammatika kumykskogo jazyka*. Moscow–Leningrad.

Dmitriev, N. K. 1948. *Grammatika baškirskogo jazyka*. Moscow–Leningrad.

Dulling, G. K. 1960. *An introduction to the Turkmen language*. London.

Dul'zon, A. P. 1968. *Ketskij jazyk*. Tomsk.

Dul'zon, A. P. 1969. O tonax odnosložnyx slov ketskogo jazyka i ix zvukovyx otraženijax. In *Proisxoždenie aborigenov Sibiri i ix jazykov, materialy mežvuzovskoj konferencii 11–13 maja 1969 g*. Tomsk.

Dumézil, G. 1931. *La langue des Oubykhs*. Paris.

Dumézil, G. 1932. *Études comparatives sur les langues caucasiennes du nord-ouest (morphologie)*. Paris.

Dumézil, G. 1933. *Introduction à l'étude comparative des langues caucasiennes du nord*. Paris.

Dumézil, G. 1958. Le vocalisme de l'oubykh. *Bulletin de la Société Linguistique de Paris* 53: 198–203.

Dumézil, G. 1975. *Le verbe oubykh*. Paris.

Dyrenkova, N. P. 1941. *Grammatika šorskogo jazyka*. Moscow–Leningrad.

Džeiranišvili [ʒeiranišvili], E. 1971. *Udiuri ena*. Tbilisi.

EBM. 1974–. *Encyclopaedia Britannica: macropaedia*. 15th. edn. Chicago.

Èdel'man, D. I. 1966. *Jazguljamskij jazyk*. Moscow.

Elfenbein, J. 1966. *The Baluchi language: a dialectology with texts*. London.

Endzelīns [Endzelin], J. 1922. *Lettische Grammatik*. Riga. (Also: Heidelberg, 1923.) (Latvian translation: *Latviešu valodas gramatika*. Riga, 1951.)

Endzelīns, J. 1943. *Senprūsu valoda*. Riga. (German translation: J. Endzelin, *Altpreussische Grammatik*. Riga, 1944.)

Endzelīns, J. 1948. *Baltu valoda skaņas un formas*. Riga. (English translation: *Comparative phonology and morphology of the Baltic languages*. The Hague, 1971.)

Fairbanks, G. H. 1958. *Spoken West Armenian*. New York.

Fairbanks, G. H. and Stevick, E. W. 1958. *Spoken East Armenian*. New York.

Fajzov, M. 1966. *Jazyk rušancev sovetskogo Pamira*. Dushanbe.

Feer, B. B. 1976. Tony v ketskom jazyke: istorija voprosa. In *Jazyki i toponimija*, ed. E. G. Bekker et al. Tomsk.

Feydit, F. 1948. *Manuel de langue arménienne (arménien occidental moderne)*. Paris.

Fokos-Fuchs, D. R. 1962. *Rolle der Syntax in der Frage nach Sprachverwandtschaft (mit besonderer Rücksicht auf das Problem der ural-altaischen Sprachverwandtschaft)*. Wiesbaden.

Fraenkel, E. 1950. *Die baltischen Sprachen*. Heidelberg.

Friedrich, P. 1975. *Proto-Indo-European syntax: the order of meaningful elements*. *Journal of Indo-European Studies* Monograph No. 1.

Frolova, V. A. 1960. *Beludžskij jazyk*. Moscow.

Gadžiev, M. M. 1954–63. *Sintaksis lezginskogo jazyka*. 2 vols. Makhachkala.

Gadžieva, N. Z. 1973. *Osnovnye puti razvitija sintaksičeskoj struktury tjurkskix jazykov*. Moscow.

Gambašidze [ɣambašiʒe], G. 1977. *Kartuli k'ult'uris ʒeglebi daɣest'anši. Samšoblo* 1366: 8.

Gamkrelidze, T. V. 1966. A typology of Common Kartvelian. *Language* 42: 69–83.

Gamkrelidze [Gamq'reliʒe], T. and Mačavariani [Mač'avariani], G. 1965. *Sonant'ta sist'ema da ablaut'i kartvelur enebši*. Tbilisi.

Gāters, A. 1977. *Die lettische Sprache und ihre Dialekte*. The Hague.

GAzJa. 1971. *Grammatika azerbajdžanskovo jazyka*. Baku.

GBurJa. 1962. *Grammatika burjatskogo jazyka: fonetika i morfologija*. Ed. G. D. Sanžeev et al. Moscow.

Geiger, B., Halasi-Kun, T., Kuipers, A. H., and Menges, K. H. 1959. *Peoples and languages of the Caucasus*. The Hague.

Genko, A. N. 1955. *Abazinskij jazyk*. Moscow.

Genko, A. N. 1957. Fonetičeskie vzaimootnošenija abxazskogo i abazinskogo jazykov. *Sakartvelos SSR Mecnierebata Ak'ademiis Apxazetis Enis, Lit'erat'urisa da Ist'oriis Inst'it'ut'is Šromebi*, 28.

GIP. 1895–1904. *Grundriss der iranischen Philologie*, ed. W. Geiger and E. Kuhn. 2 vols. Strasbourg.

GKČLJa. 1957. *Grammatika kabardino-čerkesskogo literaturnogo jazyka*. Moscow.

GMorJa. 1962. *Grammatika mordovskix (mokšanskogo i ėrzjanskogo) jazykov*, I, ed. R. A. Zavodova and M. N. Koljadenkov. Saransk.

Grierson, G. A. 1920. *Ishkashmi, Zebaki and Yazghulami, an account of three Eranian dialects*. London.

Grjunberg, A. L. 1963. *Jazyk severoazerbajdžanskix tatov*. Leningrad.

Grjunberg, A. L. 1972. *Jazyki vostočnogo Gindukuša: mundžanskij jazyk*. Leningrad.

Grjunberg, A. L. and Steblin-Kamenskij, I. M. 1976. *Jazyki vostočnogo Gindukuša: vaxanskij jazyk*. Leningrad.

Gruzov, L. P. 1960. *Sovremennyj marijskij jazyk: fonetika*. Yoshkar-Ola.

GSUdmJa. 1962. *Grammatika sovremennogo udmurtskogo jazyka*. Iževsk.

GSUdmJaSPP. 1970. *Grammatika sovremennogo udmurtskogo jazyka: sintaksis prostogo predloženija*. Iževsk.

GSUdmJaSSP. 1974. *Grammatika sovremennogo udmurtskogo jazyka: sintaksis složnogo predloženija*. Iževsk.

Gudava, T. [T'.] 1963. *Botlixuri ena*. Tbilisi.

Gudava, T. [T'.] 1967. *Bagvaluri ena*. Tbilisi.

Gulya, G. 1966. *Eastern Ostyak chrestomathy*. Bloomington, Indiana.

GXakJa. 1975. *Grammatika xakasskogo jazyka*, ed. N. A. Baskakov. Moscow.

Haarmann, H. 1974. *Die finnisch-ugrischen Sprachen: soziologische und politische Aspekte ihrer Entwicklung*. Hamburg.

Hajdú, P. 1962. *Finnugor népek es nyelvek*. Budapest. (English translation: *Finno-Ugric languages and peoples*. London, 1976.)

Hajdú, P. 1963. *The Samoyed peoples and languages*. Bloomington, Indiana.

Hakulinen, L. 1978. *Suomen kielen rakenne ja kehitys*. 4th edn. Helsinki. (English translation of 1st edn.: *The structure and development of the Finnish language*. Bloomington, Indiana, 1961.) (German translation and 2nd edn.: *Handbuch der finnischen Sprache*. 2 vols. Wiesbaden, 1957–69.)

Halle, M. 1970. Is Kabardian a vowel-less language? *Foundations of Language*, 6, 95–103.

Harris, A. C. 1976. *Georgian syntax: a study in relational grammar*. Ph.D. dissertation,

Harvard University, Cambridge, Mass. Revised version to be published by Cambridge University Press.

HdO. I. *Handbuch der Orientalistik*, I: *Der nahe und der mittlere Osten*, ed. B. Spuler and H. Kees. Leiden–Köln.

HdO I, 4.1. 1958. *Iranistik: Linguistik*.

HdO I, 5.1. 1963. *Altaistik: Turkologie*.

HdO I, 5.2. 1964. *Altaistik: Mongolistik*.

HdO I, 5.3. 1968. *Altaistik: Tungusologie*.

HdO I, 7. 1963. *Armenisch and Kaukasisch*.

Herbert, R. J. and Poppe, N. 1963. *Kirghiz manual*. Bloomington, Indiana.

Hewitt, B. G. 1977. Notes on the Mingrelian relative clause. To appear in Georgian in *Tbilisis Universit'et'is Axalgazrda Mecnierta K'rebuli*.

Hewitt, B. G. 1978. The Armenian relative clause. *International Review of Slavic Linguistics* 3: 99–138.

Hewitt, B. G. 1979a. *Abkhaz. Lingua Descriptive Studies*, vol. 2.

Hewitt, B. G. 1979b. Aspects of verbal affixation in Abkhaz (Abžui dialect). *Transactions of the Philological Society*, 1979: 211–38.

Hewitt, B. G. 1979c. The relative clause in Abkhaz (Abžui dialect). *Lingua*.

Hewitt, B. G. 1979d. The relative clause in Adyghe (Temirgoi dialect). *Annual of Ibero-Caucasian Linguistics*.

Householder, F. W. and Lofti, M. 1965. *Basic course in Azerbaijani*. Bloomington, Indiana.

Ibragimov, G. X. 1968. *Fonetika caxurskogo jazyka*. Makhachkala.

Ibragimov, G. X. 1978. *Rutul'skij jazyk*. Moscow.

Isaev, M. I. 1966. *Digorskij dialekt osetinskogo jazyka*. Moscow.

Isaev, M. I. 1970. *Sto tridcat' ravnopravnyx (o jazykax narodov SSSR)*. Moscow.

Isaev [Isayev], M. I. 1977. *National languages in the U.S.S.R.: problems and solutions*. Moscow.

Isaev, M. I. 1978. *O jazykax narodov SSSR*. Moscow.

Isxakov, F. G. and Pal'mbax, A. A. 1961. *Grammatika tuvinskogo jazyka*. Moscow.

IVPN IV. 1973. *Itogi vsesojuznoj perepisi naselenija 1970 goda*, IV: *nacional'nyj sostav naselenija SSSR*. Moscow.

JaAA I. 1976. *Jazyki Azii i Afriki*, ed. N. I. Konrad et al., I: *Indo-evropejskie jazyki*, ed. M. S. Andronov et al. Moscow.

Jacobson, S. A. 1977. *A grammatical sketch of Siberian Yupik Eskimo*. Fairbanks, Alaska.

Jakobson, R. 1955. *Slavic languages: a condensed survey*. 2nd. edn. New York.

Jakovlev, N. F. 1923. *Tablicy fonetiki kabardinskogo jazyka. Travaux de la Section des Langues du Caucase Septentrional de l'Institut Oriental à Moscou*.

Jakovlev, N. F. 1940. *Sintaksis čečenskogo literaturnogo jazyka*. Moscow–Leningrad.

JaNSSSR. 1966–8. *Jazyki narodov SSSR*, ed. V. V. Vinogradov et al. 5 vols. Moscow–Leningrad.

JaNSSSR I. 1966. *Indo-evropejskie jazyki*, ed. V. V. Vinogradov et al. Moscow.

JaNSSSR II. 1966. *Tjurkskie jazyki*, ed. N. A. Baskakov et al. Moscow.

JaNSSSR III. 1966. *Finno-ugorskie jazyki i samodijskie jazyki*, ed. V. I. Lytkin et al. Moscow.

JaNSSSR IV. 1966. *Iberijsko-kavkazskie jazyki*, ed. E. A. Bokarev et al. Moscow.

JaNSSSR V. 1968. *Mongol'skie, tunguso-man'čžurskie i paleoaziatskie jazyki*, ed. P. Ja. Skorik et al. Leningrad.

Jensen, M. 1959. *Altarmenische Grammatik*. Heidelberg.

Kálmán, B. 1965. *Vogul chrestomathy*. Bloomington, Indiana.

Karamšoev, D. 1963. *Badžuvskij dialekt šugnanskogo jazyka*. Dushanbe.

Karamxudoev, N. 1973. *Bartangskij jazyk*. Dushanbe.

Kert, G. M. 1967. Saamskaja pis'mennost'. In *PFJa*.

Kert, G. M. 1971. *Saamskij jazyk (kil'dinskij dialekt)*. Leningrad.

Kettunen, L. 1938. Grammatische Einleitung. In L. Kettunen, *Livisches Wörterbuch*. Helsinki.

Kibrik, A. E. 1979. Canonical ergativity and Daghestani languages. In *Ergativity*, ed. F. Plank. London.

Kibrik, A. E. and Kodzasov, S. V. 1978. Fonetičeskie osobennosti. In *Strukturnye obščnosti kavkazskix jazykov*, ed. G. A. Klimov. Moscow.

Kibrik, A. E. et al. 1972. *Fragmenty grammatiki xinalugskogo jazyka*. Moscow.

Kibrik, A. E. et al. 1977. *Opyt strukturnogo opisanija arčinskogo jazyka*. 4 vols. Moscow.

Kibrik, A. [E.], Kodzasov, S., and Starostin, S. 1978. Word prosody in Dagestan languages. *Estonian Papers in Phonetics* 1978: 44–6.

Kiefer, F. 1967. *On emphasis and word order in Hungarian*. Bloomington, Indiana.

Klimov, G. A. 1962. *Sklonenie v kartvel'skix jazykax v sravnitel'no-istoričeskom aspekte*. Moscow.

Klimov, G. A. 1965. *Kavkazskie jazyki*. Moscow. (German translation: *Die kaukasischen Sprachen*. Hamburg. 1969.)

Klimov, G. A. 1976. Anomalii ègativnosti v lazskom (čanskom) jazyke. *Aymosavluri pilologia* 4: 150–9.

KLMLK. 1956–9. *Kurs de limbə moldoveñaskə literarə kontemporanə*. 2 vols. Kishinev.

Kolesnikova, V. D. 1966. *Sintaksis èvenkijskogo jazyka*. Moscow–Leningrad.

Koljadenkov, M. N. 1959. *Struktura prostogo predloženija v mordovskix jazykax*. Saransk.

Kononov, A. N. 1960. *Grammatika sovremennogo uzbekskogo literaturnogo jazyka*. Moscow–Leningrad.

Konstantinova, O. A. 1964. *Èvenkijskij jazyk: fonetika, morfologija*. Moscow–Leningrad.

Kozinceva, N. A. 1975. Zalogi v armjanskom jazyke. In *Tipologija passivnyx konstrukcij*, ed. A. A. Xolodovič. Leningrad.

Krauss, M. E. 1973. Eskimo–Aleut. In *Current trends in linguistics*, ed. T. A. Sebeok, vol. 10. The Hague.

Krauss, M. E. 1975. St. Lawrence Island Eskimo phonology and orthography. *Linguistics* 125.

Krejnovič, E. A. 1937. *Fonetika nivxskogo jazyka*. Moscow–Leningrad.

Krejnovič, E. A. 1958. *Jukagirskij jazyk*. Moscow–Leningrad.

Krejnovič, E. A. 1968. *Glagol ketskogo jazyka*. Leningrad.

Krueger, J. R. 1961. *Chuvash manual: introduction, grammar, reader and vocabulary*. Bloomington, Indiana.

Krueger, J. R. 1963. *Yakut manual*. Bloomington, Indiana.

KS. 1968. *Ketskij sbornik: lingvistika*, ed. V. V. Ivanov et al. Moscow.

Kuipers, A. H. 1960. *Phoneme and morpheme in Kabardian*. The Hague.

Kuipers, A. H. 1968. Unique types and typological universals. In *Pratidānam*, ed. J. C. Hoestermann et al. The Hague.

Kumaxov, M. A. 1973. Teorija monovokalizma i zapadnokavkazskie jazyki. *Voprosy jazykoznanija* 6: 54–67.

Kurbanov, X. 1976. *Rošorvskij jazyk*. Dushanbe.

Kurdoev, K. K. 1978. *Grammatika kurdskogo jazyka*. Moscow.

Lambton, A. K. S. 1961. *Persian grammar*. Rev. edn. Cambridge.

Laškarbekov, B. 1975. O govornyx različijax vaxanskogo jazyka. In *Issledovanija po grammatike jazykov SSSR, Lingvističeskie issledovanija 1975*. Moscow.

Lavotha, Ö. 1973. *Kurzgefasste estnische Grammatik*. Wiesbaden.

Lazard, G. 1970. Persian and Tajik. In *Current trends in linguistics*, ed. T. A. Sebeok, vol. 6. The Hague.

Lehmann, W. P. 1974. *Proto-Indo-European syntax*. Austin, Texas.

Lewis, E. G. 1972. *Multilingualism in the Soviet Union: aspects of language policy and its implementation*. The Hague.

Lewis, G. L. 1967. *Turkish grammar*. Oxford.

LLNRPSU. 1977. *The languages and literatures of the non-Russian peoples of the Soviet Union*, ed. G. Thomas. Hamilton, Ontario.

Lockwood, W. B. 1969. *Indo-European philology: historical and comparative*. London.

Lockwood, W. B. 1972. *A panorama of the Indo-European languages*. London.

Lomtadze, E. A. 1963. *Ginuxskij dialekt didojskogo jazyka*. Tbilisi.

Lomtatidze [Lomtatiʒe], K. 1977. *Apxazuri da abazuri enebis ist'oriul-šedarebiti analizi*, 1. Tbilisi.

Lorimer, D. L. R. 1958. *The Wakhi language*. 2 vols. London.

Luckyj, G. and Rudnyćkyj, J. B. 1958. *A modern Ukrainian grammar*. Winnipeg.

Lytkin, V. I. 1952. *Drevnepermskij jazyk*. Moscow.

Mačavariani [Mač'avariani], G. I. 1970. The system of the ancient Kartvelian nominal flection as compared to those of the mountain Caucasian and Indo-European languages. In *Theoretical problems of typology and the northern Eurasian languages*, ed. L. Dezső and P. Hajdú. Budapest–Amsterdam.

MacKenzie, D. N. 1961–2. *Kurdish dialect studies*. 2 vols. London.

MacKenzie, D. N. 1969. Iranian languages. In *Current trends in linguistics*, ed. T. A. Sebeok, vol. 5. The Hague.

Madieva, G. I. 1965. *Grammatičeskij očerk bežtinskogo jazyka*. Makhachkala.

Magomedbetkova, Z. M. 1967. *Axvaxskij jazyk*. Tbilisi.

Magomedbetkova, Z. M. 1971. *Karatinskij jazyk*. Tbilisi.

Magomedov, A. G. 1974. *Sistema glasnyx čečeno-ingušskogo jazyka*. Makhachkala.

Magometov, A. A. 1954. Otricanie v kubačinskom dialekte darginskogo jazyka. In *Jazyki Dagestana* 2: 169–208. Makhachkala.

Magometov, A. A. 1963. *Kubačinskij jazyk*. Tbilisi.

Magometov, A. A. 1965. *Tabasaranskij jazyk*. Tbilisi.

Magometov, A. A. 1970. *Agul'skij jazyk*. Tbilisi.

Mal'sagov, Z. K. 1963. *Grammatika ingušskogo jazyka*. 2nd. edn. Groznyy.

Marr, N. and Brière, M. 1931. *La langue géorgienne*. Paris.

Matthews, W. K. 1951. *Languages of the U.S.S.R.* Cambridge.

Meillet, A. 1936. *Esquisse d'une grammaire comparée de l'arménien classique*. Wien.

Mel'čuk, I. A. 1973. *Model' sprjaženija v aljutorskom jazyke*. 2 vols. *Institut Russkogo jazyka AN SSSR, Problemnaja gruppa po èksperimental'noj i prikladnoj lingvistike, Predvaritel'nye publikacii*, 45–6. Moscow.

Mel'čuk, I. A. and Savvina, E. N. 1974. O formal'noj modeli sintaksisa aljutorskogo jazyka. In *Institut Russkogo jazyka AN SSSR, Problemnaja gruppa po èksperimental'noj i prikladnoj lingvistike, Predvaritel'nye publikacii*, 55. Moscow. (English translation: Towards a formal model of Alutor surface structure: predicative and completive constructions. *Linguistics*, Special Issue 1978: 5–39.)

Menges, K. H. 1947. *Qaraqalpaq grammar*, 1: *phonology*. Morningside Heights, New York.

Menges, K. H. 1968. *The Turkic languages and peoples: an introduction to Turkic studies*. Wiesbaden.

Menovščikov, G. A. 1962–7. *Grammatika jazyka aziatskix èskimosov*. 2 vols. Moscow–Leningrad.

Menovščikov, G. A. 1964. *Jazyk sirenikskix èskimosov*. Moscow–Leningrad.

Menovščikov, G. A. 1968. Aleutskij jazyk. In *JaNSSSR* V.

Menovščikov, G. A. 1975. *Jazyk naukanskix èskimosov*. Leningrad.

Mikailov, K. S. 1967. *Arčinskij jazyk*. Makhachkala.

Miller, B. V. 1953. *Talyšskij jazyk*. Moscow.
Miller, V. F. [W.] 1903. *Die Sprache der Osseten*. Strasbourg. (Russian translation: *Jazyk osetin*. Moscow, 1962.)
Monguš, D. N. and Sat, Š. Č. 1969. Tuvinskij jazyk. In *ZRLJaTFUMJa*.
Morgenstierne, G. 1938. *Indo-Iranian frontier languages, 2: Iranian Pamir languages (Yidgha-Munji, Sanglechi-Ishkashmi and Wakhi)*. Oslo.
Mullonen, M. 1967. Vepsskaja pis'mennost'. In *PFJa*.
Musaev, K. M. 1964. *Grammatika karaimskogo jazyka: fonetika i morfologija*. Moscow.
Nadžip, E. N. 1960. *Sovremennyj ujgurskij jazyk*. Moscow. (English translation: E. N. Nadzhip, *Modern Uigur*. Moscow, 1971.)
Nedjalkov, V. P. 1976. Diathesen und Satzstruktur im Tschuktschischen. In *Studia Grammatica* 13. Berlin (G.D.R.).
NenRS. 1965. *Nenecko-russkij slovar'*, ed. N. M. Tereščenko. Moscow.
NogRS. 1962. *Nogajsko-russkij slovar'*, ed. N. A. Baskakov. Moscow.
Novikova, K. A. and Savel'eva, V. N. 1953. K voprosu o jazykax korennyx narodnostej Saxalina. In *Jazyki i istorija narodnostej Krajnego Severa SSSR*, ed. N. M. Kovjazin. (= *Učenye zapiski Leningradskogo gosudarstvennogo universiteta* 157.) Leningrad.
OFUJa. 1974–6. *Osnovy finno-ugorskogo jazykoznanija*. 3 vols. Moscow.
Oinas, F. 1967. *Basic course in Estonian*. Rev. edn. Bloomington, Indiana.
OITIIJa. 1975. *Opyt istoriko-tipologičeskogo issledovanija iranskix jazykov*, ed. V. S. Rastorgueva. 2 vols. Moscow.
Oranskij, I. M. 1960. *Vvedenie v iranskuju filologiju*. Moscow.
Oranskij, I. M. 1963a. *Iranskie jazyki*. Moscow. (French translation: *Les langues iraniennes*. Paris, 1977.)
Oranskij, I. M. 1963b. On an Indian dialect discovered in Central Asia. In *Trudy XXV Meždunarodnogo Kongressa Vostokovedov*, vol. 4. Moscow.
Oranskij, I. M. 1975. *Die neuiranischen Sprachen der Sowjetunion*. 2 vols. The Hague.
Oranskij, I. M. 1977. *Fol'klor i jazyk gissarskix par'ja (Srednjaja Azija): vvedenie, teksty, slovar'*. Moscow.
Paasonen, H. 1953. *Mordwinische Chrestomathie mit Glossar und grammatikalischem Abriss*. 2nd. edn. Helsinki.
Pančvidze [Pančviʒe], V. 1974. *Uduris gramat'ik'uli analizi*. Tbilisi.
Panfilov, V. Z. 1962–5. *Grammatika nivxskogo jazyka*. 2 vols. Moscow–Leningrad.
Paris, C. 1969. Indices personnels intraverbaux et syntaxe de la phrase minimale dans les langues du Caucase du nord-ouest. *Bulletin de la Société Linguistique de Paris* 64, 1: 104–83.
Paxalina, T. N. 1959. *Iškašimskij jazyk*. Moscow.
Paxalina, T. N. 1966. *Sarykol'skij jazyk*. Moscow.
Paxalina, T. N. 1969. *Pamirskie jazyki*. Moscow.
Paxalina, T. N. 1975. *Vaxanskij jazyk*. Moscow.
Payne, J. R. 1979. Transitivity and intransitivity in the Iranian languages of the U.S.S.R. In *The Elements: a parasession on linguistic units and levels, including papers from the Conference on Non-Slavic Languages of the USSR*, ed. P. R. Clyne et al. Chicago.
PCNSLUSSR. 1979. Papers from the Conference on Non-Slavic Languages of the USSR. In *The Elements: a parasession on linguistic units and levels*, ed. P. R. Clyne et al. Chicago.
Petrova, T. I. 1935. *Ul'čskij dialekt nanajskogo jazyka*. Moscow–Leningrad.
Petrova, T. I. 1967. *Jazyk orokov (ul'ta)*. Leningrad.
PFJa. 1967. *Pribaltijsko-finskoe jazykoznanie: voprosy fonetiki, grammatiki i leksikologii*, ed. M. Mullonen and B. Ollykajnen. Leningrad.
PhTF I. 1959. *Philologiae turcicae fundamenta*, vol. I, ed. J. Deny. Wiesbaden.
Pirejko, L. A. 1966. Talyšskij jazyk. In *JaNSSR* I.
Pokrovskaja, L. A. 1964. *Grammatika gagauzskogo jazyka: fonetika i morfologija*. Moscow.

Pokrovskaja, L. A. 1978. *Sintaksis gagauzskogo jazyka v sravnitel'nom otnošenii*. Moscow.

Poppe, N. 1954. *Grammar of written Mongolian*. Wiesbaden.

Poppe, N. 1955. *Introduction to Mongolian comparative studies*. Helsinki.

Poppe, N. 1960. *Buriat grammar*. Bloomington, Indiana.

Poppe, N. 1963. *Tatar manual*. Bloomington, Indiana.

Poppe, N. 1964. *Bashkir manual*. Bloomington, Indiana.

Poppe, N. 1965. *Introduction to Altaic linguistics*, 1. Wiesbaden.

Poppe, N. 1970. *Mongolian language handbook*. Washington, D.C.

Prokof'ev, G. N. 1935. *Sel'kupskaja (ostjako-samoedskaja) grammatika*. Leningrad.

Ramstedt, G. J. 1957–52. *Einführung in die altaische Sprachwissenschaft*. Helsinki.

Rassadin, V. I. 1978. *Morfologija tofalarskogo jazyka v sravnitel'nom osveščenii*. Moscow.

Rastorgueva, V. S. 1954. Kratkij očerk grammatiki tadžikskogo jazyka. In *Tadžiksko-russkij slovar'*, ed. M. V. Raximi and L. V. Uspenskaja. Moscow. (English translation: *A short sketch of Tajik grammar. International Journal of American Linguistics* 29, no. 4. 1963.)

Rastorgueva, V. S. 1966. Iranskie jazyki. In *JaNSSSR* I.

Raun, A. 1969. *Basic course in Uzbek*. Bloomington, Indiana.

Raun, A. and Saareste, S. 1965. *Introduction to Estonian linguistics*. Wiesbaden.

Redard, G. 1970. Other Iranian languages. In *Current trends in linguistics*, ed. T. A. Sebeok, vol. 6. The Hague.

Rédei, K. 1966. *Northern Ostyak chrestomathy*. Bloomington, Indiana.

Remmel, M. 1975. The phonetic scope of Estonian: some specifications. *Eesti NSV Teaduste Akadeemia Keele ja Kirjanduse Instituut*, preprint 5.

Rogava, G. 1974. Dedisa da mamis aɣmnišvnel saxelta p'osesivis k'at'egorisatvis adiɣur enebši. *Iberiul-K'avk'asiuri Enatmecniereba* 19: 87–92.

Rogava, G. V. and Keraševa, Z. I. 1966. *Grammatika adygejskogo jazyka*. Maykop.

Rombandeeva, E. I. 1973. *Mansijskij (vogul'skij) jazyk*. Moscow.

Šaduri, I. 1974. Apxazuri dinamik'uri zmnebis supiksur morpemata rangobrivi st'rukt'ura. In *Macne: Enisa da Lit'erat'uris Seria* 2: 125–36. Tbilisi.

Šanidze [Šaniʒe], A. 1957. Umlaut'i svanurši. *Txzulebani* 1: 323–72. Tbilisi. (Reprinted from *Arili*, 1925.)

Šanidze [Šaniʒe], A. 1973. *Kartuli enis gramat'ik'is sapuʒvlebi*, 1. Tbilisi.

Šanidze [Šaniʒe], A. and Topuria, V. 1939. *Svanuri p'rozauli t'ekst'ebi*, 1: *Balszemouri k'ilo*. Tbilisi.

Sanžeev, G. D. 1940. *Grammatika kalmyckogo jazyka*. Moscow–Leningrad.

Sanžeev, G. D. 1953. *Sravnitel'naja grammatika mongol'skix jazykov*, 1. Moscow.

Sanžeev, G. D. 1963. *Sravnitel'naja grammatika mongol'skix jazykov: glagol*. Moscow.

Ščerbak, A. M. 1970. *Sravnitel'naja fonetika tjurkskix jazykov*. Leningrad.

Ščerbak, A. M. 1977. *Očerki po sravnitel'noj morfologii tjurkskix jazykov: imja*. Leningrad.

Sebeok, T. A. and Ingemann, F. J. 1961. *An Eastern Cheremis manual*. Bloomington, Indiana.

Selickaja, A. B. 1969. Ižorskaja pis'mennost'. In *VVJaNSSSR*.

Senn, A. 1957. *Handbuch der litauischen Sprache*, 1: *Grammatik*. Heidelberg.

Serebrennikov, B. A. 1963. *Istoričeskaja morfologija permskix jazykov*. Moscow.

Serebrennikov, B. A. 1967. *Istoričeskaja morfologija mordovskix jazykov*. Moscow.

Simpson, C. G. 1957. *The Turkish language of Soviet Azerbaijan*. London.

Sjoberg, A. F. 1963. *Uzbek structural grammar*. Bloomington, Indiana.

Sjögren, A. I. 1861. *Livische Grammatik nebst Sprachproben*, ed. F. J. Wiedemann. St. Petersburg.

SKazJa. 1962. *Sovremennyj kazaxskij jazyk: fonetika i morfologija*, ed. M. B. Balakaev et al. Alma-Ata.

SKomJa. 1955–64. *Sovremennyj komi jazyk*, ed. V. I. Lytkin. 2 vols. Syktyvkar.

Skorik, P. Ja. 1961–77. *Grammatika čukotskogo jazyka*. 2 vols. Moscow–Leningrad.

SLUSSR. 1980. *Studies in the languages of the USSR*, ed. B. Comrie. Edmonton, Alberta.

SMarJaM. 1961. *Sovremennyj marijskij jazyk: morfologija*. Yoshkar-Ola.

Sokolov, S. N. 1956. Grammatičeskij očerk jazyka beludžej Sovetskogo Sojuza. *Trudy Instituta Jazykoznanija AN SSSR* 6: 57–91. Moscow.

Stang, C. S. 1966. *Vergleichende Grammatik der baltischen Sprachen*. Oslo.

Steinitz, W. 1950. *Ostjakische Grammatik und Chrestomathie*. Leipzig.

STLJa. 1969–71. *Sovremennyj tatarskij literaturnyj jazyk*, ed. X. R. Kurbatov et al. 2 vols. Moscow.

Street, J. C. 1963. *Khalkha structure*. Bloomington, Indiana.

Sunik, O. P. 1947. *Očerki po sintaksisu tunguso-man'čžurskix jazykov*. Moscow.

Sunik, O. P. 1962. *Glagol v tunguso-man'čžurskix jazykax*. Moscow–Leningrad.

Szemerényi, O. 1967. The new look of Indo-European: reconstruction and typology. *Phonetica* 17: 65–99.

Szemerényi, O. 1970. *Einführung in die vergleichende Sprachwissenschaft*. Darmstadt.

Tauli, V. 1963. *Structural tendencies in Uralic languages*. Bloomington, Indiana.

Tauli, V. 1973. *Standard Estonian grammar*, 1. Stockholm.

Tereščenko, N. M. 1973. *Sintaksis samodijskix jazykov: prostoe predloženie*. Leningrad.

Tereščenko, N. M. 1979. *Nganasanskij jazyk*. Leningrad.

Tereškin, N. I. 1961. *Očerki dialektov xantyjskogo jazyka, 1: vaxovskij dialekt*. Moscow–Leningrad.

Thomson, R. W. 1975. *An introduction to Classical Armenian*. New York.

Timberlake, A. 1974. *The nominative object in Slavic, Baltic, and West Finnic*. München.

Timofeeva, V. T. 1961. *Sovremennyj marijskij jazyk: sintaksis složnogo predloženija*. Yoshkar-Ola.

Topuria, G. 1959. *Lezgiuri zmnis ʒiritadi morpologiuri k'at'egoriebi*. Tbilisi.

Topuria, V. 1967. *Šromebi, 1: Svanuri ena: zmna*. Tbilisi.

Trubetzkoy, N. S. 1925. Review of Jakovlev (1923). *Bulletin de la Société Linguistique* 25: 277–81.

Trubetzkoy, N. S. 1939. Zum unbeendeten Artikel Trubetzkoys 'Aus meiner phonologischen Kartothek'. In *Études dédiées à la mémoire de M. le Prince N. S. Trubetzkoy*. (= *Travaux du Cercle Linguistique de Prague*, 8.)

Tschenkéli, K. 1958. *Einführung in die georgische Sprache*. 2 vols. Zürich.

Tumaševa, D. G. 1977. *Dialekty sibirskix tatar: opyt sravnitel'nogo issledovanija*. Kazan'.

Ubrjatova, E. I. 1950–76. *Issledovanija po sintaksisu jakutskogo jazyka. 1: prostoe predloženie*. Moscow–Leningrad. *2: složnoe predloženie*. 2 vols. Novosibirsk.

Underhill, R. 1972. Turkish participles. *Linguistic Inquiry* 3: 87–99.

Ventcel', T. V. 1964. *Cyganskij jazyk (severorusskij dialekt)*. Moscow.

Vogt, H. 1958. Structure phonémique du géorgien. *Norsk Tidsskrift for Sprogvidenskap* 18: 5–90.

Vogt, H. 1963. *Dictionnaire de la langue Oubykh*. Oslo.

Vogt, H. 1971. *Grammaire de la langue géorgienne*. Oslo.

Volodin, A. N. 1974. K voprosu èrgativnoj konstrukcii predloženija (na materiale itel'menskogo jazyka). *Voprosy jazykoznanija* 1: 14–22.

Volodin, A. P. 1976. *Itel'menskij jazyk*. Leningrad.

Von Gabain, A. 1945. *Özbekische Grammatik*. Leipzig–Wien.

VPNVD. 1969. *Vsesojuznaja perepis' naselenija – vsenarodnoe delo*. Moscow.

VVJaNSSSR. 1969. *Vzaimodejstvie i vzaimoobogaščenie jazykov narodov SSSR*, ed. N. A. Baskakov. Moscow.

Watkins, C. 1976. Towards Proto-Indo-European syntax: problems and pseudo-problems. In *Papers from the parasession on diachronic syntax*, ed. S. B. Steever et al. Chicago.

Wickman, B. 1954. *The direct object in Uralic*. Stockholm.

Wiedemann, F. J. 1865. *Grammatik der Erza-mordwinischen Sprache nebst einem kleinen mordwinisch-deutschen und deutsch-mordwinischen Wörterbuch*. St. Petersburg.

Wurm, S. 1954. *Turkic peoples of the U.S.S.R.: their historical background, their languages and the development of Soviet linguistic policy*. London.

Xajdakov, S. M. 1967. Arčinskij jazyk. In *JaNSSSR* IV.

Xaritonov, L. N. 1947. *Sovremennyj jakutskij jazyk*, 1: *fonetika i morfologija*. Yakutsk.

Xromov, A. L. 1972. *Jagnobskij jazyk*. Moscow.

Žgenti [Žyent'i], S. 1956. *Kartuli enis ponet'ik'a*. Tbilisi.

Zhlutenko, Yu. O., Totska, N. I. and Molodid, T. K. 1978. *Ukrainian: a textbook for beginners*. Kiyev.

Žirkov, L. I. 1941. *Grammatika lezginskogo jazyka*. Makhachkala.

Žirkov, L. I. 1955. *Lakskij jazyk: fonetika i morfologija*. Moscow.

ZRLJa. 1969–76. *Zakonomernosti razvitija literaturnyx jazykov narodov SSSR v sovetskuju èpoxu*, ed. Ju. D. Dešeriev. 4 vols. Moscow.

ZRLJaIKJa. 1969. *Iranskie i kavkazskie jazyki*, ed. N. A. Baskakov.

ZRLJaTFUMJa. 1969. *Tjurkskie, finno-ugorskie i mongol'skie jazyki*, ed. N. A. Baskakov.

ZRLJaVRSJa. 1973. *Vnutrennee razvitie staropis'mennyx jazykov*, ed. Ju. D. Dešeriev.

ZRLJaROFLJa. 1976. Ju. D. Dešeriev, *Razvitie obščestvennyx funkcij literaturnyx jazykov*.

Žukova, A. N. 1972. *Grammatika korjakskogo jazyka: fonetika, morfologija*. Leningrad.

ADDENDUM

Recent statistics and literature

As indicated in the Preface, the most recent census of the U.S.S.R. is that of 17 January 1979. Full details of ethnic and language statistics were not available as this book went to press, but some preliminary statistics are available for the ethnic distribution of population (*The USSR in figures for 1979*, Moscow, 1980, pages 15–16), and these statistics are reproduced in the table below. In addition, this same source indicates that, while ethnic Russians comprise 52.4% of the total population of 262.1 million, Russian is the native language of 153.5 million people (58.6% of the total population), of whom 16.3 million are not ethnic Russians. In addition, 61.3 million non-Russians claimed fluent command of Russian as a second language; of the non-Russian population, therefore, 13.1% have Russian as a native language, 49.2% have Russian as a second language, while 37.7% claim not to speak fluent Russian. The spread of Russian is thus noticeable relative to the position in 1970 (equivalent figures: 11.6%, 37%, 51.4%).

The figures for ethnic distribution of population in 1979 confirm the general demographic trends already visible in 1970, such as the high birth rate among the native peoples of Central Asia (for instance, the Tadzhik show a 35.7% increase over their 1970 population, and are now more numerous than the Lithuanians), and low birth rates in the Baltic (e.g. 1.3% for Estonians over their 1970 population). For those ethnic groups with very high rates of language retention (over 90% in 1970), one may assume persistence of this high rate, the increase in numbers of speakers being thus commensurate with the increase in ethnic population. For languages with lower rates of language retention, only the publication of language statistics will indicate current trends.

Table A. *Ethnic distribution of population of the U.S.S.R., January 1979*

Ethnic group	Population (in thousands)	Ethnic group	Population (in thousands)
Russian	137,397	Karachay	131
Ukrainian	42,347	Romanian	129
Uzbek	12,456	Kurd	116
Belorussian	9,463	Adyge	109
Kazakh	6,556	Lak	100
Tatar	6,317	Turk	93
Azerbaydzhan	5,477	Abkhaz	91
Armenian	4,151	Finn	77
Georgian	3,571	Tabasaran	75
Moldavian	2,968	Khakas	71
Tadzhik	2,898	Balkar	66
Lithuanian	2,851	Altay	60
Turkmen	2,028	Nogay	60
German	1,936	Dungan	52
Kirgiz	1,906	Cherkes	46
Jew	1,811	Persian	31
Chuvash	1,751	Nenets	30
Latvian	1,439	Abaza	29
Bashkir	1,371	Evenki	28
Mordva	1,192	Assyrian	25
Pole	1,151	Tat	22
Estonian	1,020	Khanty	21
Chechen	756	Shor	16
Udmurt	714	Rutul	15
Mari	622	Chukchi	14
Ossete	542	Tsakhur	14
Avar	483	Agul	12
Komi (total)	478	Even	12
Komi-Zyryan	327	Nanay	10.5
Komi-Permyak	151	Koryak	7.9
Korean	389	Mansi	7.6
Lezgi	383	Dolgan	5.1
Bulgarian	361	Nivkh	4.4
Buryat	353	Selkup	3.6
Greek	344	Ulcha	2.6
Yakut	328	Lapp	1.9
Kabard	322	Udegey	1.6
Karakalpak	303	Eskimo	1.5
Dargva	287	Itelmen	1.4
Kumyk	228	Oroch	1.2
Uygur	211	Ket	1.1
Gypsy	209	Nganasan	0.9
Ingush	186	Yukagir	0.8
Gagauz	173	Aleut	0.5
Hungarian	171	Negidal	0.5
Tuva	166	Other ethnic groups	136
Kalmyk	147		
Karelian	138	Total population	262,085

The following publications became available to me too late for inclusion in the text or general bibliography.

V. M. Solncev et al., eds, *Jazyki Azii i Afriki*, vol. III (ed. G. D. Sanžeev et al.): *Jazyki drevnej Perednej Azii (nesemitskie), iberijsko-kavkazskie jazyki, paleoaziatskie jazyki*, Moscow, 1979, contains sketches of the main language groups subsumed under Caucasian (Kartvelian, Abkhaz-Adyge, Dagestan, Nakh languages) and Paleoasiatic (Chukotko-Kamchatkan, Eskimo-Aleut languages, Nivkh, Ket, Yukagir); the sketches of Nivkh and Yukagir, both by E. A. Krejnovič, concentrate on the Sakhalin and Kolyma dialects respectively, thus complementing the contributions to *JaNSSSR* v (V. Z. Panfilov on the Amur dialect of Nivkh, E. A. Krejnovič on the Tundra dialect of Yukagir).

Harald Haarmann has published a number of books dealing with detailed statistical analysis of language and other demographic parameters, both for the U.S.S.R. as a whole and for individual ethnic groups (Romance, Gypsy): *Quantitative Aspekte des Multilingualismus: Studien zur Gruppenmehrsprachigkeit ethnischer Minderheiten in der Sowjetunion*, Hamburg, 1979; *Multilinguale Kommunikationsstrukturen: Spracherhaltung und Sprachwechsel bei den romanischen Siedlungsgruppen in der Ukrainischen SSR und anderen Sowjetrepubliken*, Tübingen, 1979; *Spracherhaltung und Sprachwechsel als Probleme der interlingualen Soziolinguistik: Studien zur Mehrsprachigkeit der Zigeuner in der Sowjetunion*, Hamburg, 1979.

For individual languages, Rombandeeva (1973), on Mansi phonetics and morphology, is now supplemented by the same author's Mansi syntax: *Sintaksis mansijskogo (vogul'skogo) jazyka*, Moscow, 1979. The publication of a new three-volume Latvian grammar in English is announced, though copies have not yet been available to me: T. G. Fennell and H. Gelsen, *A grammar of modern Latvian*, The Hague.

LANGUAGE INDEX

This index contains languages, language-groups, dialects and ethnic groups referred to in the text. It is not a mechanical listing of occurrences of language names, but rather refers the reader to those parts of the text where information is presented on the language (-group) in question. For further ease of reference, the major topics discussed for each language(-group) are also indexed. To avoid unnecessary repetition, this index does not include references to the map, to the sections on Further Reading or to the statistical appendices, nor references already covered by language(-group)s higher or lower in the family-tree. For policy on language and ethnic names, refer to page xiii; official Russian forms of names of languages in the U.S.S.R. are given in parentheses. All references are to pages.

SUBJECT INDEX

Authors listed in the References are not further indexed here. For topics relating to individual languages, the Language Index should also be consulted, especially for more sociological topics. Semicolons separate references in different chapters. All references are to pages.

A.O., 29; 284
A.S.S.R., 27, 29f.; 283f.
active (aktivnyj) construction, 224
Ajni, Sadriddin, 164
antipassive, 225–7; 248f., 256
aspect, 76, 86; 125, 127f., 133f.; 156, 182; 215, 217, 221, 224, 225–7; 268
aspiration, 52; 156, 167, 180; 203, 267
attribute agreement, 77f.; 121; 180; 211f.; 251, 256
autonomy, local, 21, 29–31; 282–5

bilingualism, 9, 25f., 28, 32, 35–7; 301
birth-rate, 16; 301
biuniqueness, 66
Buddhism, 18; 47, 56; 160

case, 74f.; 119f., 128f.; 167, 169–72; 209–11; 246f., 251, 255, 258, 263, 268; see also ergativity
case, locative, 74; 119f.; 210, 235f.
census, 2, 28, 36
census (1970), xiii; 1, 2–9 passim, 28; 279–85
census (1979), xiii; 301–3
Christianity, 47, 49; 160, 164; 272f.
clitics, 156, 172–7 passim, 193
Codex Cumanicus, 45
consonant harmony, 49, 63f., 70
consonant systems, complex, 14; 200–3; 244, 255
coreference across clauses, 82f., 84; 152f.; 252, 256f., 260, 271f.
Crisp, S., 226
culture, traditional, 17f., 33f.
Cyrillic alphabet, 23, 32f.; 55, 56; 145f., 162, 164, 188; 199; 266f.; 274; 286f.

definite adjectives, 143f.
definite article, suffixed, 119; 181, 187f.
deportation, 27, 30; 50, 56; 184
dialect and language, 6–8, 8f., 24f.
direct object, 73, 80f.; 125f.; 126–30 passim; 152, 168, 170, 171, 181; 226; 251, 256f., 258–61 passim, 268; see also ergativity
directional prefixes, 213, 215, 218f.
doubt on veracity of statement, 154

education, language of, 22, 26, 27–9 passim, 36
ejectives, 167, 180; 199, 200; 244
ergativity, 14; 130f.; 156, 169, 173–7, 181; 209, 213f., 216f., 217f., 218, 221, 223–7, 228; 247, 248–50, 255f., 261, 264
ethnic group, 2f.
ethnic group and language, 2, 4–6
expansion, Russian, 19f.

Firdousi, 163
focus, 77, 79f.; 122, 124, 131; 260f.

gender, see noun class
genetic classification, 9–11
glottal stop, 109, 110, 117; 199, 200, 203; 243
gradation, consonant/vowel, 113–17, 118
Gyarmathi, Sámuel, 94f.

Halotti Beszéd, 107

Illič-Svitič, V. M., 11
inclusive/exclusive pronouns, 75; 211; 269
incorporation, 244, 245, 250f., 257
indirect speech, 153f.